Working Models of the Capitalist Economic System

Volume I

Working Models of the Capitalist Economic System

Vol I

Derek O'Neill

Busy Pen

Published in 2001 by
Busy Pen
Leicestershire
England

Distributed in UK by
Gazelle Book Services Ltd
Falcon House
Queen Square
Lancashire LA1 1RN

A catalogue record for this book is available from the British Library

(Set) ISBN 0 - 9539911 - 0 - 5
(Vol I) ISBN 0 - 9539911 - 1 - 3

Typesetting and design by Busy Pen

Book production managed by
Amolibros
Watchet
Somerset

Printed and bound by
T J International Ltd
Padstow
Cornwall

Contents

Mathematical skills

If you can add, subtract, divide and multiply you have sufficient mathematical ability to handle ratios and simple percentages. Nothing more than this is needed to understand all the diagrams and calculations in this book.

The formulae used are as follows:

$$\text{outlay} = \text{wages} + \text{costs}$$

$$\text{profit} = \text{gross selling price} - \text{outlay}$$

$$\text{rate of profit} = \frac{\text{amount of profit} \times 100}{\text{outlay}}$$

$$\text{rate of interest} = \frac{\text{amount of interest} \times 100}{\text{loan}}$$

$$\text{percentage increase} = \frac{\text{gain} \times 100}{\text{original number}}$$

Errata

Page 55, the tenth line of text should read
"... the new float will need to be 100 × £7.70 × 90 = £69,300."

Page 113. the thirteenth line from the bottom should read
"... to prevent unit prices from falling."

Page 212, the eleventh line of text should read
"Hence we may say this."

Page 257, the name Veblen is misspelt as "Weblen".

The error on Page 278 is corrected with a pasted overlay.

Some page references to certain diagrams are inaccurate but close enough to enable the diagram to be found on a page nearby.

This book is not now distributed by Gazelle Book Services Ltd. Further copies are obtainable from the author at
Busy Pen, 1650 Melton Road, East Goscote, Leicestershire
LE7 4YQ. Tel: 0116 2607018.

Introduction: the neo-classical fraud

In the ancient and medieval worlds, when Religion was the main enemy of human intelligence, the exercise of logical reasoning was confined within limits that suited the ruling authority. Within those limits the faculty of reason continued to function, even inside the religious domain, because logical reasoning is innate in all humans and cannot be erased from the mind by decree. Instead it was harnessed to provide legitimation for state power. Thus alongside an unquestioning obedience to an overlord there existed an elaborate tapestry of catechisms and rituals, prayers and sacrifices, holy books and sanctified artefacts, woven round the concept of divine authority, all of which served to ensnare the thinking mind in bogus forms of reason and proof.

But as we approach the last two or three centuries of modern times, rule by divine authority was successfully challenged in the more advanced nations, and Religion ceased to be a source of legitimation. The state turned to a more sophisticated enemy of human intelligence, one that could fabricate new forms of reason and proof to support the existing order, but without recourse to divine will. This new enemy was Philosophy.

The self-declared role of Philosophy was to set out the rules of logic and to combine all branches of knowledge in one coherent system. Logical reasoning, a faculty possessed and exercised by everybody, was generally assumed to be the province of a superior group of people, highly gifted thinkers dedicated to the goal of Ultimate Truth. At first, these scholars opposed religious bigotry as far as they dared, and supported the new enlightenment, at great personal danger. But as the hold of religion weakened, the conflict gradually gave way to a subtle compromise with the ruling powers. The state appeared to retreat before the champions of logical truth. A new form of legitimation gradually gained ground, based on reasoned argument. In a long series of historical struggles, absolute rule by divine dispensation was replaced by a consensus allegedly drawn from all ranks of society. The familiar organs of modern democracy appeared, alongside the universal right to think and speak freely on all topics. The discipline of Philosophy, whose domain was the logical process itself and its coherent application at the most refined levels of abstraction, acquired exalted importance, becoming a kind of supervisor or guardian at the summit of knowledge, with the blessing of the state, whose legitimacy on the grounds of reason alone was steadily consolidated by these developments.

But even as its stature grew, Philosophy was under attack from another quarter. The waning of religious superstition enabled all genuine branches of learning to make spectacular progress, and to develop a methodology for problem-solving based not on the laws of logic, but on the testing of observation and theory jointly applied in controlled situations. Over the course of some three hundred years, this methodology, called Science, steadily undermined the status of Philosophy as chief consultant in the field of human understanding. While the philosophers struggled to achieve logical integrity, the real work of advancing the frontiers of knowledge was undertaken by able people who simply applied the faculties of reason that all humans possess to the solution of practical problems. Such people came from any walk of life and had no philosophical pretensions. The sterility of conceptual introspection became increasingly obvious as science advanced on all fronts. As a result, the very notion of logical integrity was subjected to intense scrutiny by the philosophers themselves, and in the event largely discredited, effectively destroying the foundations of Philosophy itself. Thus two opposed notions confronted each other at the end of the nineteenth century. The freedom to argue in open debate was the foundation which gave democratic government its legitimacy as the voice of the people. But logical consistency as a route to knowledge had proved fruitless in the hands of its greatest exponents, the philosophers, whose grand schemes had collapsed because a process of reasoning that merely follows its own definitions and procedures achieves internal consistency but loses contact with reality. If, on the other hand, internal consistency is combined with realistic data, logic is subordinated to empirical verification, and such an approach is indistinguishable from science.

Thus, as the twentieth century opened, Philosophy had lost its way, and could no longer pretend to exercise any authority over the Natural Sciences. But it kept a tight grip on the Social Sciences, in a new guise. A school of deep thinkers made their home there and have managed to survive for over a century as the last great enemy of human intelligence, installed in colleges and universities, rewarded with professorships and Nobel prizes. Their field of investigation is the network of relationships that arise from the interdependence of humans as a species, and in particular, the part played by money as an agent promoting the growth of this interdependence. Money lies at the heart of state power, and these new thinkers offered a service to the state not by virtue of their investigations, which are largely worthless, but by providing legitimation, like the priests and philosophers of old, weaving a tapestry of definitions and interconnections that are theoretically self-supporting, but empty of real knowledge, thus ensnaring the thinking mind in bogus forms of reason and proof that merely justify the existing order.

This school of deep thinkers brought to an end the so-called Classical period in economics, during which the line of enquiry had been a struggle to understand the role of money as an integral part of social organisation. All such genuine investigation of money was discontinued and replaced by an entirely new approach, in which a concept called *utility* was identified and examined as a thing-in-itself, and incorporated into a conceptual economic framework answerable to its own standards of proof. This self-contained logical system, known as Neo-Classical Economics, proclaimed itself to be value-free, and therefore truly scientific. The new approach with its appearance of scientific rigour was welcomed with enthusiasm in official circles. The state could now rely on a bogus science called Economics, which could pose as the field of scientific research into money, while its hidden purpose was in fact to prevent any such investigation. From the end of the nineteenth century, orthodox economics became a state hireling, with false academic credentials, under a bounden duty at all times to be incapable of explaining anything.

The fact that Orthodox Economics cannot explain anything is no news to anybody nowadays. The evidence is well documented in the literature. Leading economists acknowledge that the foundations of the discipline are unsatisfactory, or even indefensible. The earlier notions of conceptual consistency have steadily degenerated, lingering for a while under the heading of "philosophy of science" in the work of such writers as Popper, Kuhn and their descendants, or in recycled platitudes about "positive" economics, or the "is/ought distinction". These fool nobody. The discipline of Economics has been steadily stripped of its credibility. Nevertheless, the discipline still continues to pose as a field of scientific enquiry, and still earns state patronage by pursuing its hidden duty. It allows no intelligent understanding of the subject it presides over. This double identity of ignorance wrapped in a scientific mantle is one of the greatest intellectual frauds in the history of human learning.

How can such a subterfuge manage to maintain itself for over a century? How can a bogus science continue to masquerade as a field of scientific investigation? The answer to this puzzle can be found in the elementary economics textbooks that every newcomer to the subject is required to study. In their opening pages the unsuspecting student is led by the nose into a land of moonshine. We must examine how this trick is accomplished.

If we take a general view of the buying and selling relationship in an ordinary market, we could describe it along these lines.

The process that fixes the price of a commodity is easy to observe and describe. On the side of demand there are buyers who possess money. On the side of supply there are sellers who provide a regular quantity of the commodity. These two sides negotiate, the sellers trying to obtain as much money as they can, and the buyers trying to pay as little as they can, in the continuous exchange of money and goods. With the agreement of both sides, the exchange takes place at a bulk price which can also be expressed in the form of a unit price ratio. Thus, 80 barrels of oil bought for 2640 dollars is a price ratio of 33 dollars per barrel. Figure 1 is a simple graph that illustrates this example.

The graph itself is quite straightforward. There is only one price, the bulk price, for the market as a whole, given open competition. There is also a price ratio, 33 dollars per barrel. The broken line shows how the smaller transactions of individual traders conform to this price ratio. For instance a purchase of 20 barrels would cost 660 dollars, as shown. It is quite clear that if the quantity sold rose to 800 barrels in exchange for a total money sum of 26400 dollars, there

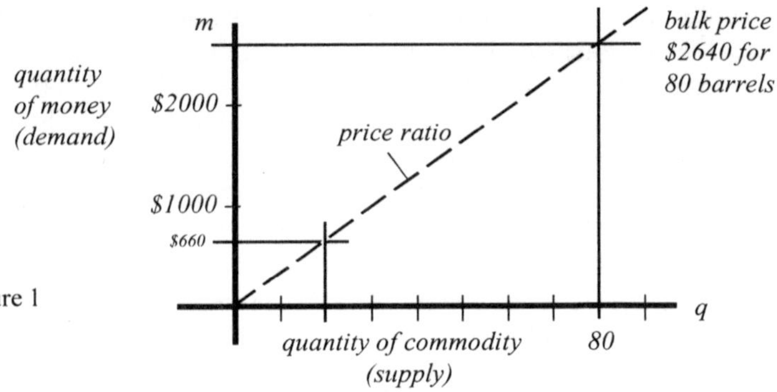

Figure 1

would be no change in the price ratio, which remains at 33 dollars per barrel. The price ratio gives no clue concerning bulk price or bulk quantity. It is also quite clear that the bulk price is free to move to any position on the working surface of the graph. The bulk price simply records, in aggregate, the joint decisions of the buyers and the sellers, whatever those decisions may be. All possible pairings in quantity of money as a demand variable, (which we may call ***m****), and quantity of commodity as a supply variable, (which we may call* ***q****) can be illustrated in Figure 1, by drawing the appropriate coordinates. The bulk price comes into existence when the bulk sum of money* ***m*** *and the bulk quantity of commodity* ***q*** *acquire their particular magnitudes in the act of exchange, and the unit price is a mathematical ratio calculated from these magnitudes, when the bulk price is divided by the bulk quantity.*

The above passage is a straightforward description of how bulk price and unit price are correlated with demand and supply. (Note that only *correlations* are explained, not actual magnitudes. The prices shown on the graph are arbitrary examples). But nothing like this can be found in any orthodox textbook. This passage represents a level of understanding that must not be allowed to reach the student. In all textbooks a graph that looks plausible but is quite nonsensical is substituted for Figure 1, and the accompanying text follows an entirely different line. In this spurious graph, the scale on the vertical axis no longer represents the bulk price for this commodity in the market. The unit price ratio is shown instead. This means that unit price, which is a mathematical ratio derived from the bulk price and the bulk quantity, is treated as a pre-existent variable in its own right and plotted against one of its own constituent parts. Every mathematician will confirm that this is a perverted procedure. The result is the bogus graph shown in Figure 2.

Unaware that his intelligence is being tricked, the student takes Figure 2 at face value and innocently awaits whatever arguments and conclusions are about to be presented. He may think his wits are intact but he has already been hoodwinked in a very significant way. The variable *m,* which stands for *quantity of money offered in the market as a whole,* (in other words, possible bulk price), has been replaced by *unit price.* This is a mathematical corruption. Variation in bulk price is explained by the movement of the intersection point

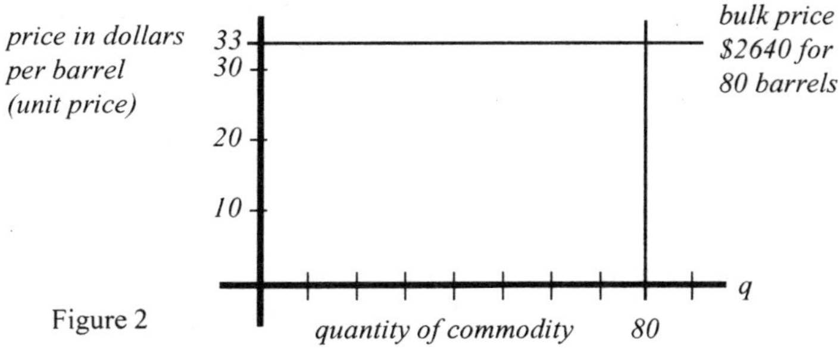

Figure 2

of two coordinates. One of these coordinates is a quantity of money and the other is a quantity of commodity, and the intersection point, on the working surface of the graph, denotes the ratio from which the unit price (quantity of money per barrel) can be calculated. This ratio has no independent existence. This price per barrel cannot be plotted on the vertical axis as if it had a prior identity. Such a procedure is nonsense. In precise mathematical terms, a ratio cannot be plotted against one of its own determinants.

But now that the unit price p has been accorded the status of an independent variable it is possible to posit an inverse relation between p and q, namely that when p rises the quantity "demanded" falls. This implies that unit price can be separated from the demand/supply relationship and allowed to move freely as an agent on its own. No such possibility exists in Figure 1. The demand by the buyers is expressed by the variable m, and if m rises or falls while q is constant then the *bulk* price is rising or falling. But the variable m is nowhere in sight. The price shown on the graph is the *unit* price, and we are presented with an alleged inverse correlation called a demand curve, shown as D in Figure 3.

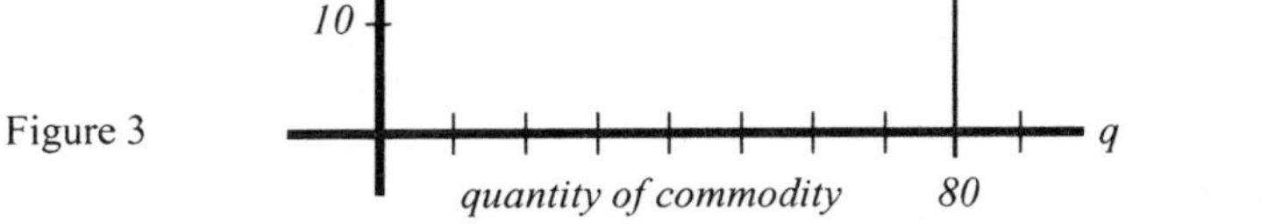

Figure 3

According to this demand curve D, buyers will buy more if the price falls and less if the price rises, caeteris paribus, and this seems plausible because a high price is a deterrent to prospective buyers and a low price attracts them. But let us put this reasoning to practical test. Imagine that 1000 pies per day are selling in the market for £2 each. Now, keeping the supply constant, raise the price to £3 per pie and consider the consequences. Will fewer pies be sold, leaving unsold pies accumulating on the shelves? And if the price is reduced to £1 will more than 1000 pies be sold even though only 1000 have been supplied? In the first case the unsold pies are bound to bring the price down, assuming competition between several pie firms. In the second case the price will be pushed up by competition between the buyers. This is how the price is established in the first place. A price change can be imposed where monopoly power exists, and demand will alter accordingly. But in an openly competitive market the only way the price of pies will change is by a change in demand or a change in supply. The price cannot wander off on its own. The price is an *outcome.* It cannot take precedence and operate as a causal agent in the process that brings it into being. Such circular logic is plainly corrupt, yet this is the "law of demand" according to orthodox theory.

The so-called supply curve is equally dubious, as presented in the text-books. When the price rises (following an increase in demand) the sellers will increase the quantity supplied. This is generally true. But a supply curve S plotted as shown on the bogus graph of Figure 3 is a false correlation between price and quantity. When price rises, quantity supplied increases. But, as everyone knows, when quantity supplied increases, price falls. Such correlations are correctly plotted in Figure 1. The curve S in Figure 3 is impossible to interpret sensibly.

Figure 1 does not explain how price is determined. It shows only how price is *correlated* with supply and demand. *If the demand rises against a constant supply the price rises. If the supply rises against a constant demand the price falls.* These are the true correlations. Price always *follows,* it never *leads.* Price depends on the bargaining process between sellers and buyers, and this is where the analysis begins. But not so in the textbooks. The student is presented with the bogus correlations described in the previous two paragraphs, (bogus because the price is treated as an independent leader), and is then told that a positive correlation can be represented by a rising curve and an inverse correlation by a falling curve. This is perfectly correct in mathematical theory, and it is quite true that the crossing point of such curves indicates an equilibrium, but this equilibrium denotes *constancy* not magnitude. The superimposition of a rising correlation on a falling correlation gives a crossing point which must occur somewhere, but no particular position or numerical value is thereby defined. The constancy can be present for any position of price on the graph. In other words, there are intersection points everywhere on the graph surface, brought into being not by the curves but by the appropriate coordinates, and then the two curves, inverse and positive, can always be drawn through any of these points, wherever they happen to be. Hence the curves determine nothing. They are always present.

The student is led through a supposedly logical train of thought but he has simply been persuaded to follow three corrupt practices: (1) to substitute unit price, which is just a subordinate ratio, for bulk price which is the operational variable in the market, (2) to regard unit price as a causal agent capable of influencing demand and supply when it is merely a mathematical expression dependent on their relationship, (3) to suppose that magnitudes are specified by mere correlations, when (as every mathematician knows) correlations can never indicate more than a condition of rising or falling or constancy in respect of those magnitudes. These three errors establish a level of ignorance that now poses as knowledge and all intelligent inquiry comes to a halt.

To summarise, a graph showing bulk price and quantity supplied simply demonstrates a relation between two coordinates that are determined by mutual agreement. Oil is sold for money in the proportions of 80 barrels for 2640 dollars, and once these *bulk* magnitudes are specified, the *unit price ratio* is also specified. Demand and supply correlations are present at the point where the coordinates meet because they are present at every point on the graph surface, and hence they cannot determine any specific price. In place of this straightforward understanding, the student is prescribed three doses of nonsense. Unit price is substituted for bulk price. Unit price is treated as an independent variable. And the equilibrium established by mere correlations is taken to define a specific magnitude when it only denotes constancy. Figure 1 displays these matters correctly, showing how bulk price and unit price alter in relation to each other when demand or supply rise and fall, without any false conclusions about the determination of actual prices. But Figure 1 is never reproduced in any standard textbook.

The consistent aim of the textbooks is to substitute a plausible rigmarole in place of real knowledge. Consider the textbook treatment of *scarcity*. If scarcity is defined in absolute terms then it may well be a permanent condition in the sense that humans are always short of something, and probably always will be. Such absolute scarcity has nothing to do with economics. The subject matter of economics is *relative* scarcity, and as everybody knows, a scale of relative scarcity is exactly the same as a scale of relative abundance. This polar unity is very clearly illustrated by the simplest of economic relations, namely a single barter transaction between two people. A man who is short of turnips but has more potatoes than he needs meets a man who is short of potatoes, but who has plenty of turnips. They can exchange to mutual advantage. Only two goods are involved in the exchange and only two people. But the exchange is polarised in four directions. Each man is in a condition of relative plenty and a condition of relative scarcity. The first man's shortage matches the second man's abundance, and the second man's shortage matches the first man's abundance. Hence the common description of simple barter as a "double coincidence of wants" is only half the story. A double coincidence of surpluses is also present. Mutually beneficial exchange is impossible if either scarcity or plenty, in relative terms, is absent. Nevertheless, the textbooks adopt the absolute version of scarcity, directing the student's attention point by point from the notion of scarce resources, to the notion of alternative choices, to the notion that all societies need an allocation system of some kind, and then to a typology of economic systems based on central planning, or on a free market, or a mixture of both.

This chain of reasoning is false. The economic concept of scarcity is wholly misrepresented when it is conceived as a universal condition. The two men who exchange their potatoes and turnips are not forced to consider alternative choices as a result of any scarcity. They both gain, and it is easy to see why. This simple barter transaction is where the study of economics begins, and the way forward lies in analysing the relation itself as a working model with real magnitudes (a procedure which is rigidly followed in this book).

The two economic concepts that we have just briefly considered, namely, the relation of price to supply and demand, and the concept of scarcity, are generally regarded as suitable entry-points for students new to the subject. But, as we have shown, these entry-points are used to ensnare the student in plausible double-talk that looks like knowledge but has no explanatory content. The result is that the basic micro elements of the subject are buried in ignorance and cannot be used as a bridge to its wider macro aspects. Such broad features of the economy as national income, savings, investment, employment, inflation, and so on, are all interpreted and modelled not, as in other fields of learning, by progressively raising the level of understanding from simple to more intricate aspects, moving continuously from micro to macro in a steady progression, but by introducing the techniques of regression analysis and advanced maths to study a macro field that is supposedly quite separate, full of correlations that are alleged to be dauntingly complex, beyond the reach of ordinary minds and properly the domain of the expert mathematician.

This is how the bogus discipline of orthodox economics is able to pose as a field of scientific learning. The profession sustains itself by an examination system based on concepts and principles that are intertwined in theoretical complexity but are empty of real knowledge. Graphical techniques are manipulated to disguise mathematical corruptions. Circular logic, which by its very nature is self-validating, is extolled as scientific on the grounds that it dispenses with the need for value-judgements. A steady stream of research papers, filled with abstruse mathematics, appears in the learned journals. In this way, an aura of impartial rigour and scholarly dedication is built round an entirely useless collection of axioms and procedures. Other approaches are condemned as "political" or "based on sentiment", and in any case students realise that they must accept and conform like the generations before them if they hope to pass exams and build a career. The profession steadily recruits students with mathematical aptitude who have no urge to challenge anything, and who become experts in highly refined correlation studies, while students who feel uneasy with the cut-and-dried logic, the convoluted mathematics and the cosy partnership with officialdom have no affinity with the subject and tend to avoid it. On this basis the profession can defend its esoteric domain very effectively, making its critics look like ignorant outsiders, lacking in expertise and driven by pet notions of their own. But this superior pose contrasts sharply with the actual competence of the profession. Economists are not regarded as experts on the economy, and wisely do not claim to be, and are in fact not intended to be. It is sufficient that they are unassailable within their own discipline, where they can produce smooth answers for everything. Thus they fulfill their hidden role, which is to obstruct understanding.

During the Classical period, the ferment of genuine debate produced many important thinkers who studied economics with detached scholarship, conducting their research with no special regard for officialdom or academic approval.

Writers like Adam Smith, David Ricardo, John Stuart Mill, Karl Marx and others sought to explain the tensions and upheavals of society in terms of conflicting economic interests, under the general heading of Political Economy, in contrast to the modern stance of academic neutrality supposedly poised above the fray in a region of mathematical purity. We have just briefly examined this mathematical purity, and we can summarise the present state of economic theory, both as a discipline and in terms of its public standing. There is an immense body of orthodox literature, posing as scientific learning, taught in colleges and universities, but which is widely recognised as a pretentious failure, defective in its theoretical foundations and lost in mathematical abstractions that have no contact with reality. There is also a tradition of genuine research from the classical period, mainly represented by the writers just mentioned. This is the background to our investigations.

It might be thought that a beginner in economics is in no position to take sides about these matters. The time for critical judgement will come later when he or she has acquired some knowledge, and is then able to join the debate, and support or oppose the many critics who accuse contemporary economics of irrelevance or mathematical obscurity, or who offer a Keynesian or monetarist or other modification, or who adopt a supposedly Marxist line, or adhere to the widely held viewpoint that the social sciences are bound to be inexact because human behaviour is always unpredictable, or give voice to some other grievance against the discipline of economics as popularly understood. Such debates give an appearance of intellectual vitality but any beginner who suspends his critical faculties in expectation of future wisdom along these lines has fallen into a well laid trap. Neo-classical economics is designed to prevent the exercise of intelligence from the very outset. The aim is to lead the beginner into a labyrinth of ignorance which is dressed up to look like knowledge. The ordinary student who keeps his wits about him can verify this for himself simply by following the elementary exercise set out below:

If a thousand pies sell per day for a bulk price of £1000, what is the price per pie?	*£1 each*
What is the total income of the pie-sellers?	*£1000 per day*
If pies sell at £3 each and the bulk supply is five hundred pies per week, what is the total income of the pie-sellers?	*£1500 per week*
What is the bulk price of the pies?	*£1500 per week*
If pies are £4 each, and the total income of the pie-sellers is £2000 per month, how many pies are being sold?	*500 per month*
What is the bulk price of the pies?	*£2000 per month*

Now examine the basic principles listed below and check that they are true in respect of four distinct variables, namely, **bulk price, bulk quantity, unit price** and **sellers' incomes**. Note particularly the connection with time.

1 bulk price is a matching of two rates, namely
(a) the quantity of money spent on a commodity per stated time period
(b) the quantity of commodity bought during that stated time period
2 unit price is (a) divided by (b)
3 bulk price expresses magnitudes linked by equal time periods
4 unit price is simply a ratio, not a magnitude, and has no time period
5 (a) can be plotted against (b), because these items are commensurable
6 unit price cannot be plotted against (b), because unit price is (a) divided by (b)
7 bulk price is identical with sellers' incomes
8 when bulk price changes, incomes change
9 when bulk price is specified, all four variables are specified
10 when unit price alone is specified, nothing can be deduced about the other variables

These summary statements are not profound or complicated. They all fit together and are illustrated by the statistics about pies on the previous page. They serve to clarify very simple concepts and linkages which must be thoroughly understood before the study of economics can begin. The student will find these principles violated as soon as he or she opens an orthodox economics textbook.

The nineteenth century classical economists who laid the foundations of economics were engaged in a struggle for enlightenment. The neo-classical economists who have taken their place are not contributors to any such genuine research. Their aim is to frustrate intelligent enquiry. The student must make up his or her mind about this. The principles set out above are strictly followed throughout this book. They are deliberately abandoned in the orthodox texts.

The use of graphs to portray the price relation is examined at greater depth in an Appendix.

The field of "philosophy cum economics" is barren in my view, but for an alternative viewpoint and a good survey of the relevant writers, see **Redman, D.A.** (1991) *Economics and the Philosophy of Science.* Oxford University Press.

Part One

A price network is a dynamic relation between a relatively large number of people. For study purposes, this number may be reduced to about ten or even five, but the single individual can never be studied as a typical representative of the group, any more than a boxing contest can be simulated with only one boxer. The buying and selling network must always be visualised as a multi-sided interchange where producer/sellers constantly change places in order to act as their own buyer/consumers. The first task therefore is to create an enclosed network of dependencies where everybody is using money to buy and sell the goods that they jointly produce. No other beginning is possible.

The next step, after this simple money-based economy is in active operation, is to introduce the differentiation between wages and profits, all the while maintaining the daily repetition of buying and selling alongside a production/consumption cycle that maintains the general living standard for society as a whole. The interdependence of the various parts must be clearly demonstrated, so that the goods produced, the actual prices paid, and the incomes earned are coherent and self-sustaining, linking every member of this society with every other member, in their respective roles as either a worker earning and spending wages or an employer earning and spending profit.

The final step in this Part One is to introduce the banks, who administer the money stock on behalf of society as a whole. The income for the banks is called interest. The three basic elements of a capitalist society are now displayed in a dynamic presentation that re-generates itself day after day, the money flowing in a continuous stream from one pocket to another as goods are bought and sold in accordance with the relative demand and the available supply. The diagrams portray this network in realistic terms. Everybody's financial situation is specified to the last penny (rounded to whole pounds) and the diagrams maintain their arithmetic integrity as they evolve from one stage to the next.

1

The transition from barter to money

The price mechanism is a process that has defied analysis for two thousand years or more. Some effort is needed therefore, to understand it. But like many puzzles it is essentially quite simple when solved. We will develop a model with very elementary specifications and bring it to life so to speak as a market economy with "real" exchanges and "real" prices.

Imagine a community of fifty working people. They produce collectively five different commodities which are sufficient to sustain life and which they freely exchange among themselves according to their needs and preferences. Our task is to create a price network which enables them to do this, in other words, to create a money-based system of buying and selling, capable of matching supply to demand, with a specified price for every commodity. Precise details are shown in Figure 1-1, which represents one day's output.

1	2	3	4	5
number of workers	output per worker	total output	bulk value in gold	income per worker
10	80 grms gold	800 grms	800 grms	80 grms gold
10	16 pies	160 pies	800 grms	80 grms gold
10	8 shirts	80 shirts	800 grms	80 grms gold
10	30 eggs	300 eggs	800 grms	80 grms gold
10	4 chairs	40 chairs	800 grms	80 grms gold

Figure 1-1

Taking each of the columns in turn, we note first that an equal number of workers is employed in the production of each commodity. This is a temporary assumption which will change as we proceed. The outputs per worker, in the next column, are determined by the production efficiency of this particular society. The magnitudes chosen here are arbitrary. The total outputs in the third column are obtained by straightforward multiplication. The bulk values in the fourth column are simply the current output of gold placed alongside the other outputs. Gold has been adopted as an intermediary and its rate of production serves as an index for the rate of production of all the other commodities. In practice this means that everyone needs to carry a float or reserve of gold, to act as a physical exchange medium through which goods can be bought and sold in terms of a common standard of valuation based on the rate at which gold is being produced. Any commodity could serve as an index, but metals that are relatively scarce are the best choice because money must be durable, portable and divisible. These qualities are found in gold, silver and (generally) copper, which are hard-wearing, conveniently proportioned in weight for large, middling or low value transactions, and easy to melt and weigh with accuracy.

We assume in Figure 1-1 that the rate of production of all the commodities is continuous and stable. This means that gold (or any other selected commodity) is being produced and consumed at a daily rate which can serve as a measure of the daily production/consumption rate of every other commodity. In this way, gold (or some other choice) becomes a universal equivalent and commodities acquire a scale of value expressed in gold, which allows them to be exchanged against gold in proportions that correspond to their production rates. We now need to visualise Figure 1-1 as a dynamic equilibrium. Each day goods are brought to the market and sold at these prices. Everybody earns the same income, namely, 80 grams of gold per day. This income is spent every day. The goods are regularly produced, exchanged and consumed, but although gold flows through the market and is regularly consumed just like any other commodity, the gold that acts as money is not consumed in any sense at all. It simply travels back and forth along reciprocating pathways that are endlessly repeated. Money is continually being earned and spent, but it has no destination, no position of rest. Sale and purchase are simultaneous acts, but every person is sequentially a seller and then a buyer, so the same money hops back and forth between them. The whole market network consists of people who buy other people's goods at prices that create incomes just large enough to enable their own goods to be bought. Figure 1-1 is a poor representation of this dynamic interdependence, but the price network must be visualised in these terms, as a process where every part sustains every other part. This is the first main difficulty that has impeded the analysis of price down the centuries.

Figure 1-1 gives us a clearly specified set of prices. A pie sells for 5 grams of gold, shirts are 10 grams each, eggs are 32 grams per dozen and chairs are 20 grams each. Every commodity has its gold price. The total value of all the goods produced in one day is 4000 grams of gold, and the total income of all producers in one day is 4000 grams of gold. So these people earn just sufficient income to buy all their goods. But we can say much more than this. These goods are being produced in the precise ratios needed to satisfy aggregate demand. In short, demand and supply are balanced in Figure 1-1.

To repeat, this society is producing goods in exactly the relative proportions that its members require. How can we be so sure of this? Well suppose these goods are not being produced in the proportions that this society needs or prefers. For example, let us assume that buyers want more eggs. If so they will

1	2	3	4	5	6
number of workers	output per worker	total output	bulk value in gold	bulk price in gold	income per worker
9	80 grms gold	720 grms gold	720 grms	648 grms	72 grms gold
9	16 pies	144 pies	720 grms	648 grms	72 grms gold
10	8 shirts	80 shirts	720 grms	720 grms	72 grms gold
14	30 eggs	420 eggs	720 grms	1008 grms	72 grms gold
8	4 chairs	32 chairs	720 grms	576 grms	72 grms gold
		totals	*3600 grms*	*3600 grms*	

Figure 1-2

try to buy more, and competition between them will force the price up. If egg prices rise, the incomes of egg producers will rise above the income level of other producers. But there is no such disparity in Figure 1-1. All incomes are equal, so supply and demand *must* be in balance. If supply and demand were not in balance, then the respective incomes would be different. In this kind of elementary economy, where buyers and sellers are the same people, and where they exchange their goods with each other by means of a universal equivalent called money, the decisive element that stabilises the balance between demand and supply is equality of income. There are in fact two equilibrium systems in operation here. One is the balance of demand and supply. The other is the equality of everybody's income. These two equilibrium systems articulate with each other throughout the price network.

Figure 1-1 therefore portrays an equilibrium set of prices which correspond to a balance of supply and demand. Let us trace exactly what would happen if demand were to alter. The first effect will be that some prices will rise and some will fall. Then some incomes will rise and some will fall, in step with the altered prices. The next effect will be that those producers with lower incomes will switch to the production lines that give a higher income (we assume open competition free from impediment) and a new equilibrium will be established when all incomes are equal again. This is the mechanism that adjusts supply to demand. It is quite easy to modify Figure 1-1 to illustrate this sequence of events, though the changes are far-reaching.

Figure 1-2 shows the new equilibrium, following a change in demand. We have assumed that relative demand for eggs has increased (necessarily reducing the demand for other goods) and this has set in train the sequence described in the previous paragraph, leading to a new equilibrium of equal incomes. Supply and demand are balanced again. But several compensating factors have been involved. The new range of prices which is just sufficient to bring about the required re-distribution of the workforce (to match the new demand pattern) is derived not only from the values determined by the rate of gold production, but also from the number of workpeople in each production line. As a result, some commodities have a price which is above their value, and others have a price which is below, although the sum of the prices is still equal to the sum of the values. Only a commodity produced by the average number of workers, such as the ten workers who make shirts in Figure 1-2, has a price which corresponds exactly with its value. There is nothing mysterious here and no complicated arithmetic. Every commodity acquires a ***relative value*** determined by its own production rate and the production rate of gold, but the ***price*** of any given commodity is higher or lower than this value according to the proportion of the communal workforce employed in its production.

Figures 1-1 and 1-2 demonstrate how detached groups of producers who attend solely to the production of their own respective commodities are able to adjust the combined pattern of production of all commodities to match the aggregate social pattern of relative demand, without the need for any shared knowledge between the detached groups. The price network automatically adjusts itself to achieve this end, operating entirely on the basis of competitive self-interest, yet it is responsive to the needs and preferences of every single individual. The only restraints in this process are the natural limits of the production processes themselves. Assuming that nothing impedes the free choice of individual producers to switch to any other production line that gives better returns, then the people in this kind of society are always maximising their productive efforts in the best interests of themselves as a caring social group. This is the benevolent "invisible hand" that Adam Smith identified, and although his understanding was mainly intuitive he clearly recognised the enemies of this inherent benevolence and was outspoken in his condemnation of governments or combinations of businessmen who sought to interfere with the free operation of the pricing system for their own ends.

Before moving on, let us cover this ground again, step by step, starting with commonplace knowledge and threading our way forward to present conclusions. Whoever wants more of a particular commodity, say commodity **A,** will simply buy more, at its current price. But if there are other buyers who also want more, then existing supply will be insufficient to satisfy demand and the current price will rise to a point where nobody will pay more money to obtain a greater share. At this price the market will clear. But demand and supply are not in balance for society as a whole. The elevated price creates a higher income for the producers of commodity **A**, and (assuming no impediment to free competition) producers of less lucrative lines will switch to the production of commodity **A**. This switching procedure is in constant operation for all commodities. Thus a "profile" of prices, with peaks and troughs, extends across the entire market. These prices are sensitive at all times to the least variation in demand, and as they rise and fall every producer is continually checking whether his income is comparable to the income of other producers, or whether he should transfer his production to a commodity that gives a better income. This rather laboured description may seem to state the obvious, but a special sequence of cause and effect is present here. The dependency order can be traced from equality of income for all producers. This the key that locks together a set of prices that in turn lock together supply and demand for all commodities in the market. The price is an *outcome*, the final adjustment that continuously varies to balance equality of incomes against aggregate demand. Figures 1-1 and 1-2 illustrate this process in action, in a model community of fifty people, producing five commodities with hypothesised production rates. All incomes and all prices are specified, and a similar model can be constructed for any size community producing any number of commodities.

If you refer to Figure 1-1 you will see that the price of a chair is 20 grms of gold. The price of a chair in Figure 1-2 is 18 grams of gold. The price of chairs has dropped slightly. Why? The answer seems complicated when the variables are looked at superficially. Forty chairs were formerly being produced by ten people, whereas now only eight people are producing thirty-two chairs. Incomes have also changed from 80 grams to 72 grams of gold per day. The reduction in the demand for chairs, the changed value of money, the re-distribution of the workforce, and the attendant modifications to all outputs (except shirts), are all counterbalancing influences that combine to determine the new price of chairs. Without a clear understanding of these intersecting elements, together with data about actual production rates, the price of chairs is a total mystery. The notion that the price depends on "supply and demand" is just empty parrot-talk, and the text-books that pretend to explain prices in the jargon of marginalism offer nothing but circular logic in place of real knowledge. Yet the relationships portrayed in these two diagrams involve only simple arithmetic. All the connections are quite easy to follow.

The only form of money considered here is gold. The evolution of a paper currency is dealt with in Chapter 3, but it is possible at this early stage to see why a paper currency is needed. There is an obvious anomaly in Figure 1-2 above. Gold, in its commodity form, by which we mean gold intended for use, is being produced at 720 grams per day. But the bulk price for this quantity is 648 grams of gold. This implies that gold, as the consumable metal itself, can be exchanged for a different weight of itself as money, which is quite absurd in practice. How can a certain quantity of money, congealed so to speak in the form of a precise weight of metal, be used to buy and sell different weights of itself? This problem is solved by a paper currency that carries an invalid or non-operational promise. The signed statement printed on the paper says in effect "I promise to pay the bearer one gram of gold", (or some other amount) but such exchange is prohibited. This prohibition enables a piece of paper carrying such a promise to be exchanged for gold in any number of varying ratios, regardless of the fact that these ratios directly contradict the ratio of exchange expressed in the promise. In this way, 720 grams of gold can acquire a price of 648 paper notes, or any other number of notes, each of which carries a stamped value of one gram of gold. The stamped value is never redeemed, and the anomaly in Figure 1-2 above is effectively removed. This anomaly, and its cure through the adoption of a *non-convertible* paper currency, are the key factors for any understanding of the so-called Gold Standard, and its historical abandonment in the inter-war years. Non-convertibility is in fact a very important landmark in the development of a stable currency. We will examine this feature more closely in the analysis ahead. Meanwhile, we need to enlarge our present understanding of the price network as depicted in Figures 1-1 and 1-2, and two aspects of this process deserve special attention.

Note first that the unit price must always be distinguished clearly from the bulk price. A commodity's bulk price reflects the demand for that commodity relative to other commodities. When the bulk price for one commodity changes then the bulk prices of other commodities are affected. Bulk prices co-determine each other, and operate at the level of the market as a whole, as shown in Figures 1-1 and 1-2. But the unit price is a form of expression that can change without any change in bulk prices, and vice versa. For example, the bulk price for a thousand ties at £2 each is £2000, and the bulk price for two thousand ties at £1 each is similarly £2000. It is important to grasp that a change in the unit price may or may not affect the bulk price, and vice versa. These two forms of price, the bulk price and the unit price, are linked to each other via the bulk quantity. There are three entities here, all formally quite distinct. The bulk price expresses a *pairing or match* between quantity of goods q and quantity of money m, determined for the market as a whole. This match changes whenever q or m alters at aggregate market level. The unit price is the *ratio* between q and m, expressed in terms of a never-changing unit of goods, meaning that only the money side of the expression is altered when the bulk pairing changes. The goods amount stays permanently fixed at some convenient unit

Figure 1-3

Relation between demand, supply, bulk price and unit price.

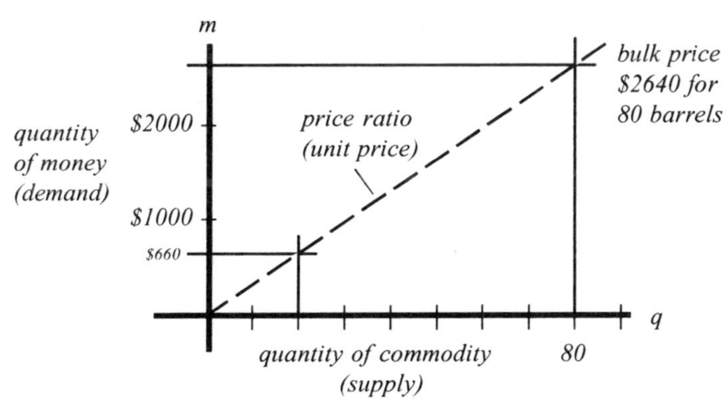

1 When supply is constant,

(a) the bulk price rises and falls when the demand rises and falls.

(b) the unit price rises and falls when the demand rises and falls.

2 When demand is constant,

(a) the bulk price stays constant.

(b) the unit price falls when supply rises, and rises when supply falls.

3 When demand and supply rise in step, bulk price rises but unit price stays constant.

4 When demand and supply fall in step, bulk price falls but unit price stays constant.

5 Nothing specific can be deduced from the behaviour of the unit price on its own.

of measurement. The money side of the expression is therefore a response to alterations in *two* variables, m and q, neither of which can be distinguished from the other in the expression of the unit price. Put simply, the bulk price is the decisive factor, and the unit price is a mere corollary. Although this relationship is awkward to describe in words, the distinction is quite simple in practice, as shown by Figures 1-1 and 1-2. The bulk prices are obviously the key factors in overall relation to each other, while the unit prices are just contingent division sums. Thus the bulk price for a commodity is a significant piece of information, alongside other bulk prices, but unit prices and their variations explain nothing. Anybody who tries to explain how demand and supply are related to price without clarifying the important distinction between bulk price and unit price, is hopelessly lost. In the orthodox text-books, simple graphs are used to illustrate how supply and demand are supposedly correlated with unit price. Such graphs are false both in their assumptions and in their perverted mathematical procedures, (see the appendix), but a graphical technique is of course not defective in itself. The graph in Figure 1-3 (already discussed in the Introduction) shows the correct relationships between supply, demand, bulk price and unit price. Apart from this example, and in Appendix A, graphs based on correlations are not used in this book because we remain always at the level of specific magnitudes.

Note second that bulk prices are the sole source of incomes. The bulk selling price is identical with the gross income of the sellers, which common sense would suggest. In fact we need to recognise a triple identity here. Total income earned is equal to total bulk prices, and total bulk prices are equal to total incomes spent. In terms of Figure 1-2, the total income earned is 3600 grams of gold, and this income is spent on goods that sell for 3600 grams of gold. It is impossible for this three-sided unity to be broken. The significance of this will become apparent as the analysis advances, but for the present we must understand that the price network does not simply set prices. It determines incomes as well, both earned and spent, because "bulk price" and "income" are just two names for the same thing. To study price movements while holding incomes stationary, as the textbooks do, is an absurd contradiction, every bit as silly as studying the change in the "speed" of a moving object while its "velocity" is presumed to be constant.

To consolidate our elementary level of understanding we need to grasp the following logical steps and verify them carefully against the circumstances portrayed in Figures 1-1 and 1-2.

(1) The bulk production rate of gold is expressed by some convenient number which denotes a particular weight of the metal produced in a particular time, and this creates an index which can be used to measure the comparative value of all other commodities, on the basis of bulk quantity produced in the same time. In this way every commodity acquires a relative value.

(2) These *relative values* are then converted into a set of *equilibrium prices*, which are adjustments to the value-form to ensure that all producer incomes

are equal when they supply goods in proportions that match supply to demand. Some values rise while other values fall, in mutual reciprocation. These reformulated values are the bulk prices that dominate the market.

(3) When demand changes, bulk prices alter, some rising and some falling. The equilibrium is lost because incomes cease to be equal, giving producers an incentive to switch to more lucrative lines of production. This search leads to a new equilibrium of equal incomes with its attendant set of prices, thus restoring the balance of supply and demand.

(4) The motivation among producers is simply to acquire the highest possible income. This motivation is sufficient to ensure a continuous automatic adjustment of supply to satisfy the fluctuations of demand, whether such fluctuations arise from change in preferences or variations in supply. In terms of Figure 1-2, the dynamic pricing mechanism operates by altering the distribution of resources in column 1 to preserve equality of incomes in column 6 whenever demand calls for fresh preferences in column 3, or supply capability alters in column 2.

(5) All that is necessary for the pricing system to operate as described is an index that evaluates all commodities on the basis of their rates of production. The numerical magnitude of the index is immaterial. In a gold-based system the magnitude of the index is determined by the output of gold, but in a paper-money system the index has no fixed magnitude. These matters will be fully explained in the chapters ahead, and need not detain us now.

Two important definitions can be emphasised here. **Values** are the bare relation of equality between bulk quantities that are produced in the same time period, as expressed by the quantity of gold produced in that time. On this basis the total value of all commodities produced in a particular time is equivalent to a certain quantity of gold, which is obviously the summation of all the respective bulk values. This sum is redistributed by the price mechanism, in the form of new bulk **prices** for all the commodities. The sum of the bulk prices is always equal to the sum of the bulk values, neglecting the effect of time lags.

Where does barter fit in? Barter is an exchange relation based on goods alone, without an intermediary to act as a universal equivalent. Clearly no intermediary is called for when just two people exchange their goods with each other. But when three (or more) people exchange their goods, a special relationship is created, in which an intermediary could operate. Let us try to evolve this intermediary, step by step, using the hypothetical barter exchanges set out in Figure 1-4, which we may regard as a monthly production/consumption cycle to give a realistic basis to output rates and exchange ratios.

There is no sign of a price network in Figure 1-4. If we interpret the bartered ratios as "prices", then one cow is equal to 10 bushels, 10 bushels are equal to 20 sheep and 20 sheep are equal to 3 cows. It is clearly absurd to equate one cow with three cows. Nevertheless these barter transactions, and a great many other possible variants, are all perfectly feasible as private arrangements between any pair of these farmers. Hence the first point to note is that barter ratios can certainly achieve practical reality even though they contradict each other, but such ratios are not prices.

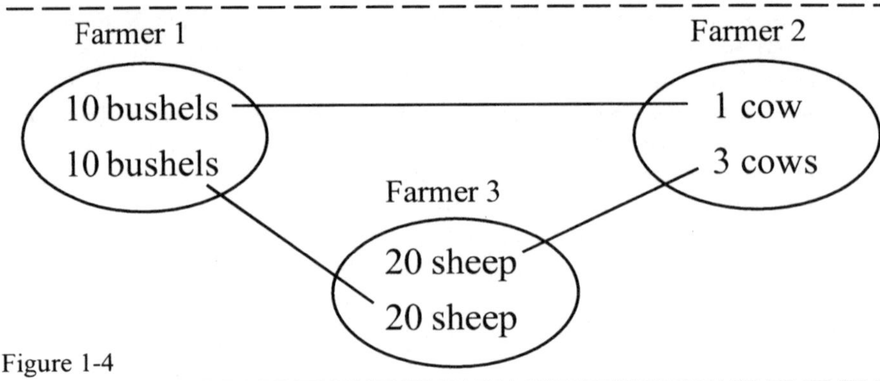

Figure 1-4

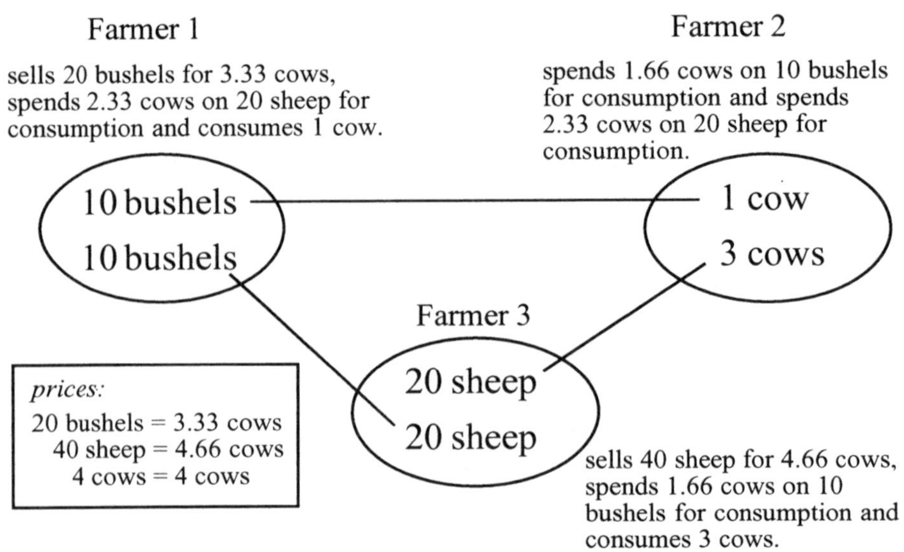

Figure 1-5

Nevertheless, if we carefully study Figure 1-5, we can confirm that a set of self-consistent prices is indeed present in the barter arrangement, concealed, so to speak, in the very ratios themselves. If we choose cows as money, then the prices are as shown in the rectangle.

These prices (obtained by calculation, using simultaneous equations) can now replace the barter transactions. It is obvious that if all three farmers buy and sell according to these prices, as detailed in Figure 1-5, they will obtain exactly the same quantities of goods that they would have obtained by direct barter. Hence we may conclude that hidden inside every multi-sided barter system is a potential money-based system by means of which goods can be bought and sold in perfect harmony with the barter exchanges. This means that as soon as a small-scale barter system is in operation, a money system stands poised alongside it, waiting in the wings so to speak, ready to take over with its own totally different set of exchanges. These different exchange arrangements are entirely consistent with the original barter deals as far as the actual transfer of goods is concerned. In Figure 1-6 this new exchange system, based on money, is displayed in the form of a table like those at the start of this chapter. The prices in column 5 are the money prices that lie concealed in the barter arrangement of Figure 1-4, and which are brought into full view in Figure 1-5.

1	2	3	4	5	6
number of workers	output per worker	total output	bulk value in cows	bulk price in cows	income per worker
Farmer 1	20 bushels	20 bushels		3.33 cows	3.33 cows
Farmer 2	4 cows	4 cows		4 cows	4 cows
Farmer 3	40 sheep	40 sheep		4.66 cows	4.66 cows
		totals		*12 cows*	

Figure 1-6

But how could this money-based price system become a practical reality? It is not supported by any discernable self-interest. There is nothing to tempt these farmers to exchange their goods in this way. The fact that there are two alternative exchange systems, one based on direct barter and one based on money is of no interest to these farmers. They simply barter their goods in ways that satisfy their own requirements, and they will feel no need to seek out an alternative system that would require consultation and supervision, wasting their time to no purpose. Each farmer is keen to barter with the other two, but has no interest in any bartering that these other two may arrange between themselves. So although we have devised a set of money prices that *could* operate between all three farmers, we have demonstrated only a theoretical possibility, nothing more. The step from barter to money cannot be accomplished by these three producer/consumers. Even if they did adopt the money-based exchange system shown in Figure 1-5 and Figure 1-6, they would evaluate their respective incomes in terms of the universal equivalent (cows in our present example) and the higher income of Farmer 3 would induce the other two farmers to switch their production to sheep. This means that Figures 1-5 and 1-6 are potentially unstable even though the exchange of goods still corresponds to the original barter preferences. But now consider Figure 1-7, where there are many more farmers, proportioned between the three farms to ensure that they all earn the same individual income.

Now we can introduce the notion of competitive self-interest, within a freely mobile economic community of 36 independent producers. The three farmers in the original barter arrangement were essentially monopolists. Each was the sole supplier of a particular commodity. In Figure 1-7, we have replaced these

1	2	3	4	5	6
number of workers	output per worker	total output	bulk value in cows	bulk price in cows	income per worker
10 (Farm 1)	2 bushels	20 bushels		3.33 cows	0.33 cows
12 (Farm 2)	0.33 cows	4 cows		4 cows	0.33 cows
14 (Farm 3)	2.86 sheep	40 sheep		4.66 cows	0.33 cows
		totals		*12 cows*	

Figure 1-7

monopolists by a multiplicity of suppliers, all in competition with each other. At the same time we have introduced a notional standard of productive capability, which is a given datum in all societies at a particular historical stage of development. The production capabilities which we have chosen (in column 2) ensure that the incomes of all 36 producers are equal when the outputs they achieve (in column 3) are exactly sufficient to match the original barter exchanges. The community of Figure 1-7 is now in a state of equilibrium. No producer can improve his income by switching to another line of production. Supply and demand are in balance, and if the demand pattern should change, or the productive capability be improved (or reduced), the causal sequence previously described will come into operation. The first effect will be respectively higher and lower prices, as a result of which incomes will respectively rise and fall, and producers will then be attracted to enter other more rewarding production lines, and by doing so the uniformity of incomes will eventually be restored, alongside a new balance of supply and demand.

In summary we may say that we have introduced the concept of a *numeraire* into the direct barter network of Figure 1-4, by choosing the production rate of one of the bartered goods to serve as a scale of comparison which enables the other goods to acquire a relative value. But as already stated this is merely a mathematical exercise. The barter network is not influenced by any such calculations. A numeraire cannot just announce itself and expect to be obeyed. It cannot achieve reality unless it is linked in some way with tangible self-interest. A direct barter network between relatively few people cannot transform itself into a money-based system, because such people are in effect monopoly suppliers of their own particular goods, and their self-interest extends no further than the quantity of goods that they personally acquire in their own barter transactions. But as soon as a multiplicity of suppliers is present, the money-based exchange values that lie dormant in every multi-sided barter network become feasible in practice, because these exchange values embody a new universal form of self-interest, namely, a money income, which comes into view when a particular commodity is adopted to serve as as a convenient intermediary. This new trading procedure based on money will be adopted haphazardly and transiently at first, but when its advantages (in comparison with the restrictions imposed by barter) are recognised, its use will spead. The acquisition of goods for consumption will cease to be the prime objective of selling. Henceforth the legitimate purpose of trade will be to acquire money. This change of focus in no way alters the final outcome. On the contrary, the barter exchanges are preserved intact within the buying and selling nexus, though they are completely hidden from view. The barter exchanges go underground, so to speak, where they operate in conformity with supply and demand, though the buyers and sellers are completely ignorant of this fact. The buyers and sellers are liberated from the severe restrictions of barter, and no further reasoning is deemed to be necessary to explain the emergence of money, which is looked upon simply as a convenient invention. The link to antecedent circumstances is lost. Everybody's trading maxim is to buy as cheap and sell as dear as possible within the limits of a money income, and such collective behaviour endows money with a mysterious regulatory power which is quite genuinely benign. Every producer/consumer in a freely competitive closed market enjoys the fruits of an optimum match between social supply and social demand. Money operates as a guarantee of collective welfare for everybody in a society of freely associated individuals who buy and sell their own goods, even though they regard each other as rivals, and do not understand how their own monetary network functions, or how it came into being.

We have now set forth the basis on which the money network operates. There are three interlinked procedures in constant fluctuation. First is the rise and fall of prices, which is a response to rise and fall in demand. Second is the re-distribution of producers, to take advantage of higher incomes made possible by variation in prices. Third is the equalisation of incomes, which establishes an equilibrium that will hold until the pattern of demand or supply capability alters in the course of time. The only suppositions we make are that the producers in this society are in mutual competition to maximise incomes, and that they work in free association with each other, switching between the various lines of production to achieve the best returns. They never bother about production times. Their sole aim as individuals is to maximise income. Nevertheless, production times are the basis on which they collectively act. Thus we may say that only prices are real, but values have a virtual existence, providing a kind of theoretical under-pinning similar to scientific laws. Column 4 is left blank in Figure 1-7, because nobody consciously assignes a value to these commodities on the basis of a universal equivalent, such as (in our example) cows. But column 4 can be completed in exactly the same way as in Figures 1-1 and 1-2, namely, by ascribing to each commodity a *relative value* which is identical with the quantity of the money-commodity (cows in this instance) produced in the same time. This leads us to Figure 1-8 overleaf. We have transformed a simple bartering group of three people into a money-based community of thirty-six producer/consumers, and our analysis reveals that the barter exchanges contain a money-form in embryo, capable of realisation at some historical point by any relatively large group of freely competing suppliers who act as their own buyers.

1	2	3	4	5	6
number of workers	output per worker	total output	bulk value in cows	bulk price in cows	income per worker
10 (Farm 1)	2 bushels	20 bushels	4 cows	3.33 cows	0.33 cows
12 (Farm 2)	0.33 cows	4 cows	4 cows	4 cows	0.33 cows
14 (Farm 3)	2.86 sheep	40 sheep	4 cows	4.66 cows	0.33 cows
		totals	*12 cows*	*12 cows*	

Figure 1-8

From this point on, we can take forward an understanding of the pricing process under two complementary aspects, theoretical and practical. Goods produced in a particular time period acquire a value expressed in the quantity of gold (our universal equivalent from now on) produced in the same period of time, and this value-form is then modified for each commodity to produce a range of prices which ensures that all incomes are equal when supply and demand are balanced. That is the theory. The actual practice that sustains this pricing mechanism has nothing to do with calculations or comparisons involving production times. It simply depends on the desire by producers to earn the best possible money-income by supplying the goods that people want. If the producers behave in this way, then in the course of buying and selling their own goods among themselves in a closed community, they will unconsciously maintain the theoretical linkage between prices, values and production rates.

In very general terms we may say that gold is transformed into money, barter exchanges are converted into prices, and goods become saleable commodities, by human trading activity over the centuries. These three transformations are interdependent aspects of the same historical process. Barter is the germ-form which contains these three presuppositions within itself. Money is not explained by describing it as an invention that solves the problems associated with barter, any more than the oceans are explained as devices that solve the problem of where to store all the rain. Such statements are mere justifications, and do not really explain anything. Of course both of these statements are confirmed by everyday experience. But an explanation that increases knowledge and understanding is more than just a stringing together of shallow truisms.

2

The goods exchange interface

The rate at which goods can be produced in any given community is the foundation of its economic existence. Every production process has technical limits which govern output, and all economic choices must comply with those limits. Rate of production is therefore the most fundamental of all economic concepts. It is the starting point from which a cooperative pattern of work between humans can evolve in historical reality, or can be understood in theoretical analysis.

This starting point, for a community of producers who exchange seven different commodities between themselves, is set out in Figure 2-1. All that is shown is their output capability, expressed as technical rates of production in column 3.

Figure 2-1

1	2	3	4	5	6
workdays per day	*commodities*	*output per worker*	*quantities*	*bulk price*	*daily income per worker*
	gold	1 ounce			
	ribbon	10 metres			
	whisky	3 litres			
	bananas	6 crates			
	hats	8 hats			
	bicycles	2 bikes			
	leather	15 hides			

We now need to specify a demand pattern and a corresponding supply response. Using the rates in column 3 we can allocate the working days of this community to suit any pattern of relative demand. This allocation, in column 1, enables us to specify a range of actual quantities produced per day, in column 4, and thus we arrive at Figure 2-2. We are presuming a community of 100 producers who consume their own goods after buying them from each other using money.

The equality of incomes for all producers, shown in column 6, confirms that this pattern of supply is in balance with the relative aggregate demand for all

Figure 2-2

1	2	3	4	5	6
workdays per day	*commodities*	*output per worker*	*quantities*	*bulk price*	*daily income per worker*
12	gold	1 ounce	12 ounces	£10.08	£0.84
33	ribbon	10 metres	330 metres	£27.72	£0.84
12	whisky	3 litres	36 litres	£10.08	£0.84
4	bananas	6 crates	24 crates	£ 3.36	£0.84
14	hats	8 hats	112 hats	£11.76	£0.84
16	bicycles	2 bikes	32 bikes	£13.44	£0.84
9	leather	15 hides	135 hides	£7.56	£0.84

total £84

commodities. We assume that there are no obstacles to open competition, and hence all producers are free to switch to any alternative product line that gives a better return. The information set out in the first four columns of Figure 2-2 is sufficient to determine the equilibrium bulk prices in column 5. The paper notes that circulate as currency in this society carry a promise in the usual form, namely, "I promise to pay the bearer on demand one ounce of gold". In other words, the monetary scale is based on one-ounce notes. The respective unit prices of these goods can be calculated by simple division. (This society would no doubt have its own symbol to represent money, but we retain the familiar pound sterling sign, which comes from the days when the promise referred to one imperial pound weight of sterling silver, and we will also adhere to the metric system in which one penny represents a hundredth of a one-ounce note).

As already explained, these prices, which correspond to an income of £0.84 per day for each individual producer, are in equilibrium for two reasons. First, no producer can improve earnings by switching to an alternative product (earnings would fall for any producer who did so), and second, when every consumer has spent his income according to his relative preferences, all goods are regularly cleared from the market at the rate at which they are being produced. A change in demand would alter these prices and create opportunities for producers to earn more by switching from a lower to a higher priced product, resulting in a new set of equilibrium prices. In such a case, Figure 2-1 would not change, but a new distribution of the hundred working days per day would give us a different version of Figure 2-2. Changes in demand never produce any alteration in Figure 2-1, which simply expresses the current level of production capability in a given society. This level of technical expertise steadily improves as time goes by, in almost every line of production, but this source of alteration in Figure 2-1 is quite separate from the great variety of demand/supply patterns that may appear in Figure 2-2. In all cases the equilibrium prices of commodities are determined by the relation between technical production rates, relative demand and social production rates. The latter depend on the allocation of simultaneous working days. Assuming no impediment to free competition, equilibrium prices stay constant until there is a technical change in production capability, which alters Figure 2-1, or until there is a change in relative demand, which skews prices and offers opportunities for better returns by switching to more lucrative lines, thereby altering Figure 2-2. Skewed prices are present during the change from one set of equilibrium prices to another, and are bound to appear in a real market as a result of time-lag in the adjustment of supply to match demand, or vice versa.

As can be seen from Figure 2-2, the unit price of gold in our model society is £0.84 per ounce. This means that 84 hundredths of a one-ounce note will buy an ounce of gold. The incongruity between the market price of gold (84p needed to buy an ounce of gold) and the promise on the paper note (100p convertible into an ounce of gold) is harmless in our model society because the paper currency, based on one-ounce notes, is inconvertible. In other words the promise is void. No bank or treasury or other authority or person will honour the promise to "pay the bearer on demand one ounce of gold", and nobody is issuing such notes in return for an ounce of gold. Whoever made such a promise in the past no longer exists in our present self-sufficient community, which comprises one hundred working people producing goods which are sold to each other before consumption. We will describe the origin of these promises in Chapter 3.

The dynamic equilibrium illustrated in Figure 2-2 is a system of interlocking dependencies. Once the production/consumption cycle is up and running, so to speak, it sustains itself by constantly restoring the conditions for the next cycle. There is a transfer of goods from point of production to point of consumption, but there is no such transfer of money in the reverse direction, despite the fact that all goods pass from the producers to the consumers in exchange for hard cash. Producers and consumers are the same people in this society, and the only thing that passes between them is goods. This seems to be a perverse assertion, but in essence a moneyed economy is really just a bartering economy with a sophisticated interface. The bartered goods change hands. The money in the interface appears to change hands, but it doesn't. It is always in the hands of the buyers, because the buyers and sellers change places when the money is transferred.

If we move stepwise through the cycle in slow motion we will uncover these polar interactions, where cause and effect not only produce a sequential outcome but also regenerate their point of origin at the same time. Imagine a situation where all the goods are piled up for sale in the market and the first producer enters, now in the role of a consumer, with 84p to spend. At this stage we must envisage the 84p as a float that enables the cycle to start. This consumer moves through the market, buying whatever he wants till all his money is spent. The next producer/consumer does the same, and the next follows suit, and so on till all the goods are sold, and all their money is spent. But though all the money is spent, it is also true that none of it has been spent. Everybody can now leave the market with his original float of 84p, even though they have all bought whatever goods they wanted (to the limit of their income) and the markets are all cleared. The fact that they all buy and sell from each other makes this outcome inevitable. Money travels from one pocket to another, but expenditure by the buyer is income for the seller, and hence the money is always returning to somebody every time it leaves somebody. The float is needed at the outset, but is thereafter absorbed into the system, allowing cash in hand to rise and fall for some people as it falls and rises for other people. The actual prices are transacted through a self-compensating network which needs no money supply. Incomes are generated by the sales that the incomes are spent on.

We need to grasp the dynamics of this double transformation as concretely as possible. Suppose all the goods produced in our society are bought and sold in a supermarket, where customers freely select what they want from the shelves in the usual way. But the customers also supply these goods, so each customer is responsible for stacking one particular product on a section of shelf that belongs to him. Seeing that all goods are being handled in this way, the point of sale is located at the shelf itself, where goods are selected and money handed over. Each customer obtains money at his particular shelf when his goods are sold, and then transfers this money to other shelves to buy other goods. As long as all goods are regularly replenished, every customer receives a regular flow of money, which is regularly spent. But the money never goes anywhere, and never comes from anywhere. It just remains on the shelves all the time, (or on standby in somebody's pocket), and its sole function is to circulate constantly from one location to another. The only throughput is the goods themselves, and the only exchange is in ownership of the goods, while the money, strictly speaking, belongs to nobody, except temporarily. If we freeze this dynamic interchange at any given moment, some people will be buying goods with money obtained from earlier sales, and some people will be stacking the shelves with goods in anticipation of sales which will provide money for future purchases. This situation never changes, but the people themselves move through an alternating cycle in which they become disbursers of money at one point in time and receivers of money at a later stage, in balanced reciprocation with each other. The same money passes backwards and forwards between them. In this imaginary supermarket, the shelves represent a goods-exchange interface where money and commodities continually change hands, the goods entering and leaving the interface in a continuously replenished stream, while the money circulates inside the interface with no need for replenishment apart from wear and tear caused by repeated handling. Of course in real terms this interface is not located in any particular place. It is spread throughout society wherever commodities are bought and sold.

It is most important to grasp the fact that the money that passes between these seller/buyers can be any size at all without the ratios of commodity exchange being affected in the least. The money needed for the buying and selling transactions comes from the buying and selling transactions themselves. If every week I give you £1000 for your goods and you in turn give me £1000 for my goods, then a float of £1000 is obviously needed to start this cycle, but once the cycle is in regular operation, it supports an income of £52,000 a year for each of us. The same float, passing successively between five people every week would support five annual incomes of £52,000, prompting the question where does all this money come from? If the cycle speeds up from weekly to daily, the same float of £1000 will support five incomes of £365,000 per year. If the float for some reason shrinks from £1000 to just £10, still being used to transfer goods successively between five people every day, then the corresponding annual incomes would shrink down to £3,650 respectively, and we may ask again where has all this money gone? Throughout all these changes, in which the bulk prices of the goods exchanged would be either £1000 or £10, and in which one set of incomes would be a hundred times bigger than the other, the amount of goods consumed would remain at whatever level they were being produced. And anyone who wants to know where such money comes from, or where it vanishes to, is asking a silly question. There is no source that such money comes from.

But the float comes from somewhere. It is the money that is needed to get the system up and running. When the float is too small, everybody is obliged to wait for earlier transactions to obtain money for present purchases, and only by using small sums very quickly can the throughput of goods be maintained. A float of adequate size allows transactions to proceed smoothly and conveniently, which means that quantities bought and sold can be big or small and at a frequency to suit the convenience of the transacting parties, unaffected by the size and frequency of purchases and sales with other people before and after, within reasonable limits.

Hence our preliminary assumption that a float of 84p per producer would get the system up and running needs to be revised. This bare minimum of 84p requires all producers to spend their daily income every day, and never to spend more or less. In practice, the float needs to be much larger, allowing people to do their regular spending every week, or every month, or at varying intervals, in accordance with personal convenience, and in keeping with the type of commodity they are buying. How large should the float be to give reasonable flexibility along these lines? An income of 84p per day is the limit imposed on them all, and this amounts to just over £306 per year, or roughly £25 a month. Perhaps the average amount kept on stand-by in our model society is three month's income, about £75. No doubt some people would wish to hold more than this in reserve, while others may live hand to mouth with no reserves whatever. Some might be saving for a future big purchase, while others might be spending such savings accumulated from the past. These would all balance each other in the long term, so an average of £75 could be a reasonable estimate. On this reckoning, the float in this society of 100 people would be about £7,500, and it would be in physical existence in the form of paper notes and coin. This float would support one hundred incomes of £306 per year. We can now distinguish between the total amount of tangible banknote money in this society, namely, £7,500, and the total annual income of society, namely, £30,600.

Before continuing, we must deal with two misconceptions that may cause difficulties at this stage. Everybody in this community buys and sells through the goods-exchange interface, and this is where money incomes are generated. Everybody must have worked to produce these goods in the first place. But nobody pays them for this work. Their productive activity simply makes them the owners of fresh stocks of goods which they must sell at the interface as before to acquire an income. *There is no source from which money comes.* (The category of wage-earner belongs to a later stage of analysis, not dealt with here). Even the notion that money comes from the sale of goods is, strictly speaking, an illusion. The seller acquires money by selling, but in this very same act, the same sum of money is being spent by the buyer. In a closed circuit, these gains and losses nullify each other. Therefore in essence, goods are exchanged for other goods, not for money. Money is just a system of gates or valves that regulate the proportions in which goods flow from producer/consumer to consumer/producer.

The fact that money can change hands between any two people at any time for any purpose whatever, gives rise to the second misconception. Such transfer of money can certainly be a source of income for one party, but only to the extent that it is a loss of income for the other party. No fresh income is generated thereby. Incomes are created solely at the goods-exchange interface. For instance, a professional musician may be very highly paid, but every penny of his fee already exists in the form of goods that his patrons can buy whether his performance takes place or not. When they pay to hear him, they pass their entitlement to these goods over to him in return for musical performance. Such exchange, whether to mutual satisfaction or otherwise, plays no part whatever in the determination of prices or income generation at the goods-exchange interface. Similarly, taxes, donations and gifts, fraud and extortion, bribery and blackmail, gambling, auctions of rarities, all services performed for a fee, and many other apparent sources of income, are nothing but the transfer of ownership of money. Such money is already in existence as an integral part of the goods-exchange interface, which is in continuous operation and dominates the entire field of economic relationships. Hence we need to distinguish two basic types of income, namely a primary income which originates at the goods exchange interface and becomes an income for its first owner, and a derivative income, which is not new but is simply a pre-existing income passed from the first owner to a second, third, perhaps a fourth owner and so on, before being spent on commodities. (In studies of national income it is important to avoid multiple counting in respect of these two categories.)

With these misconceptions set aside, we can resume our examination of money in our society of a hundred people, buying and selling seven commodities, using paper notes, with a suitable float to avoid cash flow problems. This society has all the money it needs, and this money has nothing to do with living standards. If everybody in this community works long hours to produce goods that are barely sufficient to sustain life, then these people are very poor, and they regard their incomes as very low, and they produce and buy mainly necessities, in frequent small amounts, and cash in hand is relatively small. By contrast if their daily workload is very light and they produce commodities in abundance, then these people enjoy a high living standard, and they can afford to transfer incomes between themselves to pay for teachers and sporting facilities and medical services and pensions and museums and research institutions, etc. Such a community is rich (in economic terms) with high incomes. But typical incomes (generated at the goods exchange interface) in either case may be £10 a week, or £1000 a day, or in fact any arbitrary sum at all. Money is simply a mechanism that regulates ratios of exchange. It has no other numerical reference point. (This is the reason why a physical commodity such as gold cannot meet the specification for an ideal form of money. Gold imposes a numerical reference point in the shape of its own value as a commodity. It is impossible for this value to keep its own identity in a set of relationships, and to act at the same time as a coefficient of some sort derived from those relationships, just as it is impossible for an unknown such as x in an algebraic equation to have a predetermined magnitude alongside the magnitude it acquires when the equation is solved. An original piece of paper with the authorised signature of a very trustworthy person who faithfully promises something which will be worth whatever the going rate is, in other words, an inconvertible banknote, is the only form in which money can exist and function properly without internal contradictions).

A critical distinction arises here in the behaviour of a gold economy compared with its paper counterpart. Let us make our model society Figure 2-2 much richer by multiplying all the rates in column 3 by say ten. Let us also assume no change in relative demand, which means that everybody is satisfied to consume ten times the quantities of their preferred goods in the same proportions as before. Column 1 will therefore stay the same, while all the quantities in column 4 will increase tenfold. What will unit prices be now? The answer depends on whether money is a physical substance or a paper promise. In a community that uses gold or pelts for money, unit prices will not change. The price of gold for example, which used to be £10.08 for 12 ounces will now be £100.80 for 120 ounces, which is simply the same unit price of 84p an ounce. The same rule applies to the other commodities. There is no change in unit prices in a community with a price network based on gold or some other physical substance which is bought and sold as a commodity, as long as gold output is rising as part of the general improvement in productivity. But our model community in Figure 2-2 uses inconvertible paper notes as money, and when the quantities in column 4 rise tenfold, all commodity prices expressed in paper notes will fall to a tenth of their former magnitude. A one-ounce banknote will now buy ten times more of any commodity. Of course the final outcome will be the same for either of these communities. Living standards will be ten times higher, because living standards depend on actual rates of production, not on prices or any other numerical link with money. (The notion that more money can make a particular person richer is true because others become correspondingly poorer, but more money cannot make an enclosed society richer).

What happens to incomes when production is increased tenfold? Again the answer depends on whether a commodity like gold or pelts is being used as money, or whether a paper currency is in operation. In a gold-based price network, incomes (in weights of gold) will be ten times greater, while unit prices stay constant. But in our model community with its inconvertible paper currency everybody will earn the same income (in banknotes) while unit prices fall to a tenth. The distinction to be grasped here is that where money takes the form of a physical substance like gold or convertible banknotes linked to gold, the production rate of gold dominates the price network and sets its level. All commodities acquire a price which expresses their actual rate of production in terms of the actual production rate of gold, and if production rates of both the gold and the commodities increase by ten, their relative proportions stay the same and therefore unit prices do not change. But when money takes the form of inconvertible banknotes, the price network is released from the domination of gold. Banknotes are unaffected by the tenfold increase in commodity production rates, so the same value of banknotes continues to express the same set of ratios, shown as bulk prices in Figure 2-2, and these ratios remain the same whether they are multiplied by ten or twenty or any other number. For this reason, the bulk prices will remain as they are, but they now apply to ten times the quantity of commodities, and hence unit prices will be ten times cheaper. To repeat, the general price level in a gold-based economy stays constant when general output rises, while incomes increase. The general price level in an inconvertible bank-note economy falls when general output rises, while incomes stay the same.

We may summarize all the foregoing as follows. In the kind of community we have looked at so far, the relation between technical production rates, aggregate demand, and social productivity rates determines the actual prices of commodities. The regulator that governs the equilibrium between supply and demand is equality of income for all producers. A minimum float is needed to start and maintain this reciprocating interchange, and if this float is more than the minimum it will provide a flexibility which releases the individual exchanges from rigid sequential dependence on each other. The money needed for this "adequate float", which is called pecuniary accommodation, consists of all the money on "standby" awaiting the call to participate in a buying transaction, and its quantity is determined by the need for cash in hand, to act as a reserve or cushion to maintain cash-flow. For individual sellers and buyers, this reserve is constantly being augmented by sale of goods, and constantly being depleted by purchases, and hence the typical person in our model community regards his own reserve as no more than a sensible precaution to meet emergencies, or as a form of saving for the future. But the combined float of a whole community is an important structural element in the monetary system, and it cannot be understood from the shallow perspective of the ordinary individual.

We have now isolated the concept of pecuniary accommodation in the sense that it has no direct link with any of the other variables. If the accommodation is adequate, then prices, incomes, aggregate demand, technical production rates and social production rates, will all mutually take care of themselves. But what happens if the accommodation alters, and how does the accommodation get there in the first place? In our model society (and in the advanced nations of the world at large) this accommodation, or "float" as we have termed it, takes the form of printed promises on paper notes. Where did these paper notes come from? Who made the solemn promises that are inscribed on these notes? Why are these trustworthy people no longer present in our model society?

3

Paper money

We stated earlier that rates of production define the capabilities of any given society of producer/consumers, and such rates are therefore the foundation on which a communal standard of living depends. So we can visualise our model society in its simplest aspect as an assemblage of people who through specialisation and cooperation can regularly produce goods at high output rates and need to devise some method of exchange. How does a price system evolve in such circumstances? We are now thinking in historical terms and our theorising needs to be consistent with practical reality. In point of fact, the expansion of the American western frontier during the 19th and early 20th centuries gives us a close approximation to these conditions. Townships sprang up overnight, especially where gold deposits were found, creating an urgent need for a speedy and dependable currency.

The essential trading medium for people in these circumstances is a physical money-commodity. No physical substance is entirely satisfactory, but any frequently traded item can serve, as long as it possesses a widely acknowledged use-value which doesn't deteriorate too quickly. Gold has the advantage that its desirable qualities are permanent and recognised throughout the world, but dividing it into tiny fractions is difficult. A pinch of gold dust between finger and thumb could once buy a drink in a Californian saloon. Pelts, furs, sea otter skins, beeswax and tallow were also accepted as currency in Missouri and Kansas in the early 1800s. But these expanding populations were well acquainted with paper money in the form of banknotes issued by eastern banks, and they wanted the same facilities, namely, a printed declaration of value on a paper certificate signed by a widely trusted authority. There was a desperate shortage of such currency in the burgeoning towns of the frontier states.

This shortage is at first puzzling. If gold and many other substances can serve as money, why should a certificate of indebtedness, expressed in terms of one of these substances, be so difficult to provide? All that is needed is a warehouse, where (say) pelts can be stored and guarded. If everybody deposits their pelts at the warehouse and obtains a receipt, then paper money comes into existence and all buying and selling becomes so much more convenient. Security for the pelts is easier to provide in one central heavily guarded spot, instead of everybody having to lock away and guard their own reserves, while the paper certificates themselves can be safeguarded on the person, or deposited as a drawable account at the warehouse. Given that the warehouse owner, who is really a prototype banker, is an honourable and widely trusted member of the community, the advantages for everybody are obvious. Why was this arrangement not promptly adopted in the frontier states?

One superficial reason is easy to find but it only deepens the mystery. In many western states there were laws against the creation of any such banking facilities. At one time or another during the 1800s, banks were banned by law in Kansas, Minnesota, Illinois, Wisconsin, Iowa, Arkansas, Texas and Nebraska. In other states, for example, California, where gold strikes created a surplus of gold alongside a severe shortage of currency, there were laws which allowed banks to do business, but would not permit them to issue notes. (We are studying banks only under their role as issuers of notes. Provision of loans is a separate topic not considered here). Postage stamps were used for small change in Wyoming. In Nebraska, bankers were classified among criminals. It is puzzling to account for such hostility against note-issuing banks in territories where they were so obviously needed.

The general banking history of the USA up to the 1930s presents the same puzzle in rather a different light. There were 28,000 banks by 1914, mostly independent units serving a small locality, so legislative hostility was no obstacle to their growth. But there were very good reasons why they were so distrusted. They failed with astonishing frequency. All kinds of regulations, including minimum capitalisation requirements, cash reserve limits, deposit insurance schemes, prohibition of branching, state appointed examiners, and a federal reserve banking system, were introduced by the various states and by the US central government but none was effective. There were bank panics throughout the 1800s, for instance, as the century closed, in 1873, 1877, 1893 and a serious crash in 1907. In the decade after the first world war, bank failures were widespread, and in 1929 the US banking system crashed spectacularly. From this viewpoint, the puzzle is, how does a banking system that is so obviously defective, and deeply distrusted, and shackled by legislation, still manage to survive and grow, all the while repeatedly destroying the assets of depositors on an ever increasing scale? These historical details provide a background to our analysis.

Our model community of 100 producer/consumers (at the start of Chapter 2) has a specified set of production rates for seven commodities and a price network corresponding to a given demand pattern. We know that this network will operate smoothly with a suitable float, and this float is already present in the form of one-ounce notes that promise to reimburse the bearer with an ounce of gold. Somebody in the past must have offered warehousing facilities for gold, and issued signed receipts of indebtedness to the people who deposited their gold holdings for safe keeping in this warehouse. We must examine what happens next.

The signed certificate, with florid elaborations and artistic styling, is obviously intended to be instantly recognisable as the genuine article, to promote speedy transactions and prevent counterfeiting. With such an assurance, it can serve as "legal tender", which means that ownership of the ounce of gold in the warehouse passes legally to whoever is the owner of the paper promise. In this way, the ounce of gold stays safely protected in guarded premises, which we shall now call a "bank", while the paper promise travels between successive owners, any of whom can call at the bank at any time and redeem the promise, giving back to the banker the latter's own signed certificate, and receiving in return, without quibble, the stated quantity of gold.

Although these signed certificates come into existence as simple "warehouse receipts", it is obvious that wherever gold circulates as money, the paper promise can take its place. So gold no longer circulates directly as money. As fast as it is produced, it is deposited in the bank, in return for certificates of indebtedness which are far more convenient. At this stage, there are two exchange ratios for the gold, one at the bank, and one in the market where gold as a commodity is bought and sold, because in a paper-based economy the people who consume gold will use paper money to buy it, and this market price of gold is determined in just the same way as any other price is determined. A glance at Figure 2-2 will confirm that the price of gold in our model society is 84p per ounce.

Nobody in their right mind would try to obtain gold from a bank by redeeming the paper promise, if gold can be bought at 84p per ounce in the market. And no gold producer in his right mind would sell gold on the open market at only 84p per ounce, when the bank will issue a full one-ounce certificate for every ounce. So the gold producer and the banker have a very close relationship, and in fact, the selling of gold on the open market (at 84p per ounce) is best handled by the banker. (Or alternatively, the gold producer could set up in business as a banker). In circumstances like these our model community would have a very stable monetary system. Everything would be in equilibrium. But consider how fortunate the banker is, in such a situation. His certificates of indebtedness circulate as money, and he guards an amount of gold in his reserves corresponding to the certificates he issues, and he is scrupulously honest. Nevertheless, if he prints a signed certificate of indebtednes for an ounce of gold, he can use this certificate to buy an ounce of gold in the market, and this ounce of gold can be placed in his reserves to "cover" for the certificate. But his purchase of an ounce of gold will only cost him 84p. He thus acquires an excess of 16p quite legitimately, because the note he has printed is fully backed by gold. In fact this arbitrage advantage can be exercised by the banker whenever he accepts an ounce of gold for safe keeping. He can charge a fee for this service, which will mask the 16p excess by appearing to be a fee for time and effort, but its real source is the arbitrage advantage. We may conclude then, that times would have been good for bankers in the early days of our model community. But those days are gone. Note-issue is now forbidden in our model community. Gold is traded only by a gold producer. Our model community has all the money it needs, and no bankers.

The fact that gold was once needed to serve as so-called backing for the note issue calls for closer examination. There is no such hoard of gold in our model community now, but at the initial "warehouse" stage, a bank such as we have described could come into existence only on the strength of an absolute guarantee that its paper promises could be redeemed. Nobody would accept a mere written promise in place of real goods, unless that promise had cast-iron certainty. So the first bankers were well known and highly respected merchants, often but not always traders in gold, with high standards of integrity and ample reserves of wealth. Yet they were playing a clandestine role, quite unconsciously. In open view, they were agents acting on behalf of people who needed a convenient certificate to use as money, but at the same time they were acting as agents on behalf of an embryo currency system that needed a float. The gold or pelts that they accumulated at the "warehouse", and the notes of indebtedness that they issued in return, had a one-to-one correspondence in the beginning, and could be redeemed instantly, on the solemn word of the banker. But from the moment that such receipts began to be used as money, they were earmarked for a different purpose. They were absorbed into the price network to provide a float, and once absorbed, they were beyond recall.

All is well in the beginning for a bank that issues such notes. A bank will generally prosper at this early stage. But a point is reached, sooner or later, when all the notes have been absorbed and no more float is needed. At that moment the bank's situation is altered fundamentally. Nothing reveals this on the surface. In fact, this moment occurs when the bank is at the highest point of its prosperity, judging by the accumulation of its reserves. But from this point on, the bank will either fail or it will abandon its original role as a supplier of gold-backed notes and become an entirely different institution.

The reserves of a note-issuing bank (we assume that it conducts no other operations) belong to its depositors, and in theory, the depositors could return all the banknotes to the bank and reclaim their gold or pelts or whatever, at par. But such action by all depositors at once would deprive the currency of its float, and destroy the price network. The float is relatively small compared to the incomes that would no longer successively sustain each other. Recalling our earlier example, if my income of £1000 a week sustains your income of £1000 a week then a float of £1000 is transferred back and forth between us every week. Remove this float, which is just a single sum of £1000 in real banknotes, and two annual incomes of £52,000 disappear. Any attempt to withdraw the float from the currency produces catastrophic consequences. Long chains of mutual dependency are wiped out. This kind of damage is inflicted by a bank panic.

But why should this happen? As long as the goods themselves continue to flow from producer to consumer, all is well. The notes enjoy the best possible confirmation of reliability by the steady maintenance of everybody's standard of living, and by the fact that improvements in output automatically produce a rise in living standards, so why should there be any loss of confidence in the monetary system? Why should paper money suddenly be distrusted?

The stability of paper money lies in the fact that the paper promises are no longer valid. The banknotes are inconvertible. Even though these promises had to be real in the beginning, a time comes sooner or later when they must be repudiated universally, by strict legal enactment. The reason for this becomes plain when we examine the circumstances in which the float first appears. Once an adequate float is in existence, no more is needed. If the exchange medium is a physical money-commodity like gold or pelts, then all further supplies of the money commodity beyond this point are not money but simply commodity for sale and consumption. But if the exchange medium is banknotes, issued as described above, the further supply of such money, after the adequate float is created, devalues the entire price network. All prices rise. This is not harmful to anyone in a community of producer/consumers. In fact the reciprocal relation between pecuniary accommodation and price level is a normal part of the price mechanism, and such adjustment is automatic. There is no such thing as a shortage or surplus of money in a price network based on banknotes, except by massive abuse such as destroying notes in thousands by burning, or printing them in vast quantities. Even then, it is the scale, rather than the action itself that causes the damage. Printing need be no more than for the purpose of replacement for wear and tear. This point needs special emphasis. The general price level for all commodities, including the former money-commodity, (gold or pelts etc), rises and falls automatically as the need for pecuniary accommodation falls and rises. In other words, prices rise when banknotes are issued in excess of that required for accommodation, or when the need for accommodation falls in respect of a pre-existing float, and vice versa. This alteration in prices, brought about by the need for a float which is adequate but no larger than adequate, harms nobody (if it is gradual), as long as bank-notes are inconvertible.

But in the early days of an embryo currency, bank-notes depend on their convertibility to prove that they are trustworthy. Nobody anticipates that this arrangement must be ended at a critical point. These paper promises must be put in circulation for only a relatively brief period, namely, until the float is adequate. If note issue continues beyond this point, (or if the need for accommodation falls in respect of a previously established float) the general price level will rise, including the paper-price of gold. As long as the price stays below a one-ounce note per ounce of gold, times will be good for bankers in our model community. But when the float is adequate, the gold price will adjust to its market level, and if notes exceed accommodation, or accommodation falls below notes, for whatever reason, this price level will rise. The arbitrage advantage which was initially favourable to the banker will turn against him. Depositors will be keen to redeem their paper promises when the market price of gold rises above the rate expressed in the promise, and the gold producer will switch to selling in the open market. When this happens the bank is in serious trouble. But this fact is hidden from the bank because the drain of gold appears alongside an increase in note holdings, and these can be used to buy more gold on the open market, so there is no immediate problem.

All that the bank needs to do, to avoid its pending difficulties (always supposing that it had any inkling of trouble ahead) is to stop redeeming banknotes for gold. But no bank can contemplate such action. Any hint that it can no longer support its own notes will harm its reputation and damage public confidence. In any case, the bank is oblivious to what lies ahead. The bank observes that its reserves seem to have reached a peak, and then they begin to decline. Loans are called in to maintain solvency. But the drain continues. If a rumour spreads that the bank is in difficulties, there will be a stampede to withdraw deposits. The bank must hang on, pretend that nothing is wrong, borrow funds to keep going, and hope for the best. The historical record leaves no room for doubt about the outcome. The bank will fail, or will be taken over by a bigger bank with a reputation that restores public confidence.

A note issuing bank is essential for the evolution of an economy based on money, because it provides a much needed paper currency which in turn creates a stable price network, but this task is accomplished once the float is adequate. From this point on, the tide of business turns against the bank, which will be ruined sooner or later by the inevitable drain on its gold holdings. This drain causes no harm to anyone else, and the economy can operate as normal while the bank (as a note-issuing institution) passes out of existence. Its gold reserves, maintained as long as possible by buying gold with its own notes, will discharge all its obligations (more or less, depending on the arbitrage deficit) and the float of paper notes in the monetary network will be maintained. Meanwhile the gold being returned to its owners will be sold by them at an arbitrage profit, and once the bank has vanished the economy will have accomplished a transition from a gold based system to a paper-based system. But in practice this smooth transition will be prevented by two very likely events. A bank known to be in trading difficulties loses the confidence of depositors, and it is they who then destroy the bank by demanding withdrawals on a vast scale, which the bank cannot meet. Assets of its customers will be destroyed, causing the collapse of dependent chains throughout the economy. The other event is the struggle by the bank to stay in business. It will borrow to stay solvent, or negotiate a rescue package by another bank.

When a bigger bank rescues a smaller one, the problem is merely postponed. Sooner or later the bigger bank will be in financial difficulties, and its impending collapse will have more serious consequences, calling for intervention by the biggest banking firms. Eventually the whole banking system is threatened, and the inability to redeem their own notes alongside the perceived obligation to honour future promises forces the leading banks to devalue the notes and start afresh on a new basis. In America during the 1800s the currency value varied between 14 and 16 dollars to an ounce of gold. In 1921 it was officially set at 21.67 dollars to the ounce. In 1933 the official rate was set at 35 dollars to the ounce, and it remained at that nominal price for nearly forty years. So strictly speaking, the american dollar has been convertible throughout that time. But in the New Deal introduced by Roosevelt in the early thirties, it became illegal for any american citizen to trade in gold, and everybody, including the banks, had to surrender their gold stocks to the US government (at the old rate of 21.67 dollars per ounce). This compromise, which meant that on the one hand the american dollar was still officially redeemable in gold at 35 dollars per ounce while on the other hand no american citizen was allowed to conduct transactions in gold, is inconvertibility in all but name. (At the time of writing, the US dollar is trading against gold at somewhere under 400 to an ounce, so its convertibility at 35 dollars to the ounce long ago became meaningless, together with the prohibition on trading in gold. The prohibition was lifted in 1971, when the international convertibility of the dollar was also terminated.

Hence we may say that the failure of a bank is its natural destiny, whether this "failure" takes the form of a total repudiation of its paper promises (inconvertibility) or a losing battle to maintain convertibility and survive as a business. It is the struggle to survive that damages the economy. If the bank simply allowed its gold stocks to dwindle, managing its debts till they were all finally discharged, maintaining total secrecy to avoid panics, then its business days as a note issuing institution could come to an end and nobody would be harmed. But if its customers hear tell of financial difficulties, a run on the bank may be triggered, causing immediate collapse of the bank, and some customers, perhaps most, will lose their deposits. If a bigger bank intervenes it can discharge all debts, perhaps even at par, (though usually at a percentage loss), and restore normality. But the stage is set for the next crisis on a bigger scale.

Our conclusions may be summarised thus. When a bank creates a currency in its own notes it will sooner or later find that the tide of business turns against it. This occurs at or near the point when an adequate level of pecuniary accommodation has been reached. If all note redemption stops at this point, then the bank can continue in any other role, as say a source of loans, or in the management of depositors' accounts. But if public suspicions are aroused at this transition stage, the bank may suddenly be called upon to redeem all its notes simultaneously, and such a task is quite impossible. The bank will collapse, and most of its customers' deposits will vanish into thin air. This is the evolutionary path that all prototype banks are obliged to follow. Their paper receipts must be linked to gold at the outset, but no bank is safe that issues notes redeemable on demand. Only when this link is broken, by legal declaration that such notes are inconvertible, does a stable monetary system become possible.

As stated earlier, our model economy of a hundred producer/consumers has no banks, but banks must have existed at some earlier time in order to create a paper currency. They are needed no more, once an adequate float has been established. This float is quite flexible, and is simply the sum of all cash in hand, in tills and pockets and purses, or any other form of hoard which people or institutions keep on standby for regular buying and selling. It consists exclusively of banknotes and coin, and it constantly passes from one owner to another, and is constantly being replaced by new notes or coin as the old ones wear out. In conditions of perfect competition, all commodity producers in this society will have the same primary income, but a proportion of these incomes may be transfered to other non-producers as payment for services, or to support dependent groups, or to pay taxes, etc, or as a result of theft or deception. Such derivative incomes may be relatively high or low.

The first role of a bank begins when it opens as a place where gold or pelts are accumulated in return for warehouse receipts. At some later stage this process ends, and the bank (after many crises on the way) continues in its second role as an institution where inconvertible bank notes are accumulated and managed as a combined communal asset. In other words, the float for the whole community becomes concentrated in one central spot, and it is disbursed to depositors as they need it. Customers withdraw money from the bank to buy goods, and the sellers of these goods, who are the same people in a closed economy, return the money to the bank. The bank keeps track of the fluctuating balances in its customers' accounts, which are self-compensating. As money flows out, the same money flows back in.

The price of gold in paper notes is then determined in a straightforward fashion, just as for any other commodity, while the general price level for all commodities moves up or down according to the relation between the total of bank-notes in circulation and the demand for pecuniary accommodation. We will examine this relation later.

In our model community there are no banks which fulfill this second role. We have presumed that banks were dispensed with when the float became adequate. This assumption allowed us to study the circumstances under which banks first appear, and to isolate the role that they played in the creation of a paper currency, a role which sooner or later must come to an end and be followed by a declaration of inconvertibility. By adopting this approach we obtain a proper insight into the rules that govern a paper currency. Of course, as soon as banks appear, their various roles come into operation alongside each other. They are kept separate in this analysis and treated sequentially for purposes of exposition.

Not a single bank in the entire modern world now issues redeemable notes as a form of currency. In all currency domains, such as the dollar, the pound sterling, the franc, the yen, the mark, etc, only one central bank is still responsible for *printing* notes. But this printing activity is entirely different from the note-issue described above, which belongs to the formative years of the banking system. We will examine the printing of notes in later chapters.

All historical references in this chapter are taken from:

Doti, P.L. and Schweikart, L. (1991) *Banking in the American West: from the Gold Rush to deregulation*. Norman, USA. University of Oklahoma Press.

4

Modelling a simple economy

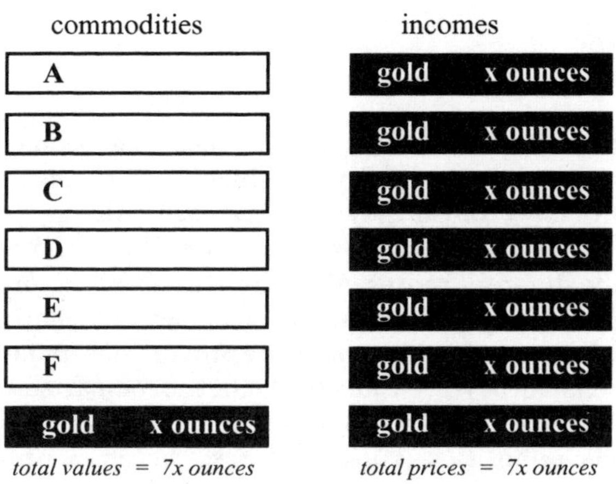

Figure 4-1

The basic model for a money-based economy is shown above in Figure 4-1. We already know that the bulk prices for the seven commodities are bound to be exactly the same as the incomes obtained from their sale. But the information missing from the diagram is the number of people who jointly produce these commodities. If commodity A sells for the amount of gold indicated in the diagram, this income will be shared between the producers of commodity A, and the same applies to the other commodities. Obviously, the situation portrayed can be a continuously stable equilibrium only if every commodity is produced by the same number of working people, thereby creating a situation where each of them has the same regular income. Figure 4-1 is therefore a special case. Nevertheless, this diagram lies at the root of our understanding about all price systems in a closed economy. Although it does not specify the price that a commodity sells for, it sets the operational limits within which the technical production rate, the social production rate and the equilibrium price can rise and fall in relation to each other.

Now examine Figure 4-2. The workforce is shown in precise numbers, and a value is specified for the x ounces of gold. These two pieces of information are all that is needed to determine the prices on the right, because these prices rest

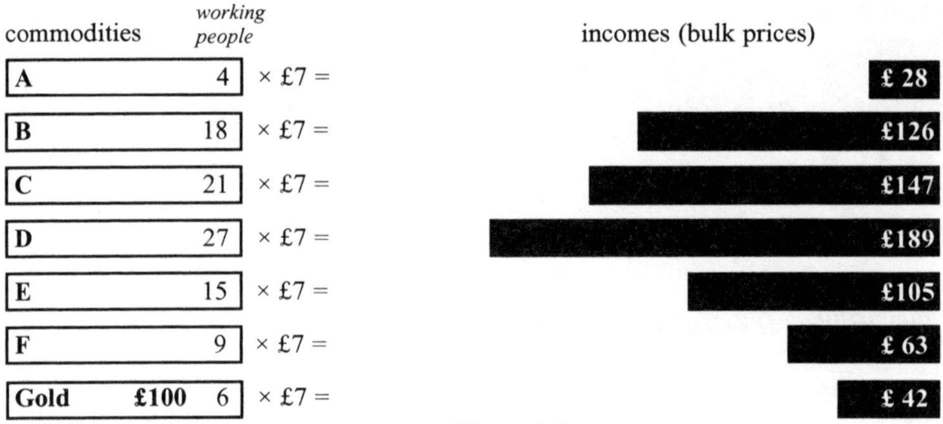

Figure 4-2

on the assumption that every worker earns the same income. The arithmetic is quite simple. Consider commodity A, which is produced by 4 workers. The commodity sells for £28. So they earn £7 each. All the prices on the right correspond to an income of £7 for every worker. This is the daily average, if we assume that the diagram represents a daily production/consumption cycle.

The fact that no physical quantities are specified confirms a point made earlier, that bulk prices are determined by proportions and not by magnitudes. These proportions can be traced only throught the comparison of bulk quantities. Once price is expressed merely as a ratio, (oil at 33 dollars a barrel, for instance) the link to bulk quantities is lost and price becomes unintelligible. But if information about bulk quantities is known, all the relationships involved are quite straightforward, as shown in Figure 4-2. Whatever the physical outputs are, they sell in bulk for the prices shown. If commodity A is 28 axes per day, then each axe sells for £1. If output is 10 axes per day, then each axe sells for £2.80. Thus, price and income adjust themselves to a particular distribution of the workforce which in turn corresponds to some hypothesised pattern of aggregate demand.

If there were no paper currency here, and gold was the physical money-commodity, then the physical weight of gold produced in one day (assuming that the diagram represents one day's production) would be the basis for the incomes shown, which would be expressed as weights of gold. But we are assuming an inconvertible paper currency whose current value stands at £100 for one day's production of any commodity. In this self-contained community, supply and demand are balanced, and each producer is earning £7 per day. The total value produced is £700 and the total of all incomes is £700 per day. The bulk prices of the commodities are as shown, and are identical with the incomes, as they must be. But the unit prices of the commodities depend on actual quantities per day, which are not specified. Any other distribution of the workforce, to suit any other pattern of demand, would be just as easy to model, with fully specified prices for all bulk quantities.

All the variables that play a part in the determination of prices are present in Figure 4-2. The currency can assume any value. If for instance it changes from £100 to £173, then incomes will be £12.11 per day and all bulk prices will be multiplied by 1.73. Nothing else in the layout will change (and living standards will remain as they were). The actual production rates for all the commodities, including gold, may be any magnitude whatever, and once they are specified, the corresponding unit price ratios, expressed in terms of the currency value, can be calculated by simple arithmetic. As production rates increase, unit price ratios go down, meaning that goods become cheaper per unit, but incomes and bulk prices (which are just two names for the same thing) stay the same, and therefore the layout of the diagram will not alter. Any variation in aggregate demand will alter bulk prices, causing a redistribution of the workforce which will modify the layout to produce a new equality of incomes, thereby establishing a new equilibrium with a new set of bulk prices and unit prices. Changes in productivity per worker will also change the layout in ways that are quite easy to follow. This simple model of the price mechanism is the foundation for any understanding of a money-based economy.

What determines the currency value? Its original magnitude (in any nation of the real world) is a historical datum, namely the total face-value of a particular quantity of notes relative to output at the moment when gold was replaced by paper. From that point on, it rises or falls according to how much pecuniary accommodation its citizens want. We have suggested in our current models that an average of three month's income per person may be a plausible estimate. In that case, 100 people earning £7 daily income for 90 days = £63,000, and as long as banknotes to this value are present in pockets and purses throughout the community, the currency value will be stable. Similarly, for a currency value of say £200, daily incomes for these hundred people would be £14 and the total float would be £126,000 in tangible banknotes. (These banknotes would exist in random hoards throughout the community. The creation of a monetary base is a banking operation that we will examine later, in Chapter 11). Thus the currency value of a given total face-value of the notes in circulation varies according to the level of pecuniary accommodation, or as we may describe it, the float. If the float is too large (meaning that the need for pecuniary accommodation has fallen), prices rise and vice versa. This adjustment is entirely automatic and is a normal part of the price mechanism. In fact, it is more sensible to see this adjustment in the currency value as a compensation that continuously balances the float against production so that the float always answers the need for whatever pecuniary accommodation is required. The printing of banknotes is an entirely separate inflationary influence that drives the currency value up, and prices with it, because the new notes increase the total face-value of the notes in circulation.

There is an important point to be made here concerning stability of prices over time. As the general level of productivity improves, unit prices fall, caeteris paribus, while incomes and bulk prices stay the same. This is the normal condition. By contrast, the effect of printing banknotes is to raise the general level of prices, caeteris paribus. If banknotes are printed at a certain critical rate that just offsets the fall in prices caused by increased productivity, then unit prices will stay constant, and incomes and bulk prices will rise instead. The effect of this, on the community as a whole, is simply that everybody will have more money to spend on more goods whose prices remain steady. Whether new notes are printed or not, the standard of living for the community as a whole always rises as productivity improves. But when banknotes are printed to keep unit prices steady, two important side-effects occur. First, a new income appears on the scene, namely the income embodied in the newly printed notes, an income for nothing, as any counterfeiter will confirm. We will investigate what happens to this income later. The second side-effect is to create an impression that "normality" is a condition of steady prices. This view is false. The normal operation of a money economy based on an inconvertible paper currency is for incomes to stay constant and unit prices to fall as general productivity improves. But the printing of banknotes is very convenient from a business point of view. Incomes from selling rise, while fixed incomes fall in relation to the social average. In other words rich people get richer, while poor people become relatively poorer. (Fixed incomes are for instance wages or pensions, neither of which has appeared at our present stage of analysis). In all the leading nations banknotes are printed in a regular stream because they are allegedly required to maintain banking liquidity. This matter will be thoroughly investigated in the chapters ahead. For the present we merely note that the normal outcome of rising productivity is a fall in unit prices, but the printing of banknotes counteracts this cheapening effect by reducing the purchasing power of money, and hence the net response is that prices stay constant, with an appearance of normality that hides the interplay of two opposed trends.

Returning to Figure 4-2, the total value produced per day is £700. Multiplying by a notional 365, we obtain a total annual value of £255,500. Total incomes per year are similarly £255,500, or £2555 per person. The float, consisting of the real banknotes needed to sustain this expenditure, can be roughly estimated at about £63,000, as stated above. These calculations are valid for the kind of community portrayed, where everybody is a producer/consumer, and a seller/buyer, with access to a float of inconvertible banknotes, kept on the person or conveniently at hand. As already stated, there is no banking system here to centralise the float by providing deposit accounts, or to lend money. These features will be introduced later.

It is important to understand that although a money economy such as described above lies at the heart of a capitalist economic system, it takes precedence over that system, and operates entirely on its own account. Thus we are not yet describing anything that is specifically "capitalist". Neither money, nor a printed paper currency, nor the early banks that issue "warehouse receipts", have any necessary relation to capitalism as an economic system. We will take the first step into a capitalist system in the next chapter.

Nevertheless, the economic arrangement shown in Figure 4-2 has a natural affinity with a capitalist system, in two respects. Consider first the basic logic of the price mechanism. All the bulk prices (which are identical with incomes) on the right hand side are derived from the distribution of the workforce and the currency value of £100. The £100 tells us that the total daily value of the seven commodities is £700. This £700 is redistributed across the seven commodities according to the proportion of the workforce involved in each commodity. The causal agent that brings about this redistribution is the incentive to maximise income, and a position of rest, or equilibrium, is reached when all incomes are equal. So much for the logic. But in historical terms, the simultaneous interlacing of these various strands, dependent as they are on the context of a closed economy, is far more haphazard and protracted than a strict formal analysis would suggest. The global trading network that links all humans in a web of mutual dependency has been slowly evolving for several thousand years. During recent centuries, with the rise of the capitalist firm, this process has accelerated. The operating basis which sustains all mass production systems and links them to a shared mass market is the turnover of money, and as these huge systems spread across the world, a closed global economy is brought ever closer. This closed economy is ruled by the price mechanism and its inexorable logic. Thus the capitalist system may be said to provide an environment in which the price mechanism, operating quite autonomously, is able to fulfill itself.

The other natural affinity between the price mechanism and the capitalist system is the inverted logic that entwines them. Once we understand how the bulk prices on the right hand side of Figure 4-2 are arrived at, we can follow how these prices become incomes, and how these incomes are then divided between the producers. In terms of commodity A, a bulk price of £28 is first of all generated at the goods-exchange interface, and this is the income for 4 producers who receive on average £7 each. This is the intrinsic logic of the process. But anyone who lacks this understanding may well "explain" the price of £28 as £7 multiplied by 4, as if the four producers had said "It is because we have paid ourselves £7 each that our commodity sells for £28". Using the same logic, I can divide a cake into four equal portions, and if each portion weighs seven ounces, then I can explain the weight of the cake by multiplying seven ounces by four. Such an explanation is quite silly, not because it is untrue but because it is an obvious tautology. The weight of the cake exists prior to its division into four equal parts, and it must therefore have a prior explanation. But an approach which uses this tautology appears very plausible, particularly to a capitalist owner but also to everybody else, because it "explains" prices as the sum of wages, raw materials, equipment upkeep, profit, etc, in perfect accord with the surface appearance of such things. On this basis, the owner can argue a case about "fair" wages and "fair" profits, and the debate looks genuine to other parties even though they are all at sea. The textbooks dutifully follow this line, which we shall examine in the next chapter.

It would be useful at this stage to illustrate how an actual price list would operate in the economy of Figure 4-2. We will invent a set of production rates for all seven commodities, as shown in Figure 4-3.

Any alteration in the bulk output column will alter the unit price, but the bulk price will not change, because bulk prices are controlled by the goods-exchange interface, as set out in Figure 4-2. The interface responds to a change in

Figure 4-3

commodities	bulk output	bulk price	unit price
Axes	53	£ 28	52p per axe
Books	341	£126	37p per book
Cups	370	£147	40p per cup
Dolls	940	£189	20p per doll
Eggs	456	£105	23p per egg
Forks	28	£ 63	£2.25 per fork
Gold	8 ounces	£ 42	£5.25 per ounce

demand, which disturbs prices and sets in train a re-distribution of the producers, who seek a fresh equilibrium of incomes by switching to other more lucrative lines, as already explained. The outcome is a new set of equilibrium prices. No doubt any change in bulk output rates will also trigger an alteration in relative demand, and a multitude of effects will be set in motion simultaneously, causing changes which will mystify the superficial observer. But each of these effects can be traced independently, in either Figure 4-2 or Figure 4-3, and their mutual interaction is not really complicated at all.

An overall improvement in the above productivity rates will result in a general fall in unit prices. But if, as we suggested above, banknotes are being steadily printed at the same time, then the general fall in prices will be offset

Figure 4-4

commodities	bulk output	bulk price	unit price
Axes	58.3	£ 28	48p (52) per axe
Books	375.1	£126	34p (37) per book
Cups	407	£147	36p (40) per cup
Dolls	1034	£189	18p (20) per doll
Eggs	501.6	£105	21p (23) per egg
Forks	30.8	£ 63	£2.04 (2.25) per fork
Gold	8.8 ounces	£ 42	£4.77 (5.25) per ounce

by a counter-tendency for prices to rise. If these opposing tendencies balance each other, the net outcome will be that prices will hold steady. We can examine this effect, using the price list in Figure 4-3. Suppose that productivity levels are all improved by 10%. The new unit prices will be as shown in Figure 4-4.

It is obvious that the standard of living in this society has now risen by 10%. Bulk prices are still the same, and therefore incomes are still the same, but unit prices have fallen. (The old prices are shown in brackets). Let us now print some banknotes and inflate the currency value by the same percentage. The outcome is shown in Figure 4-5.

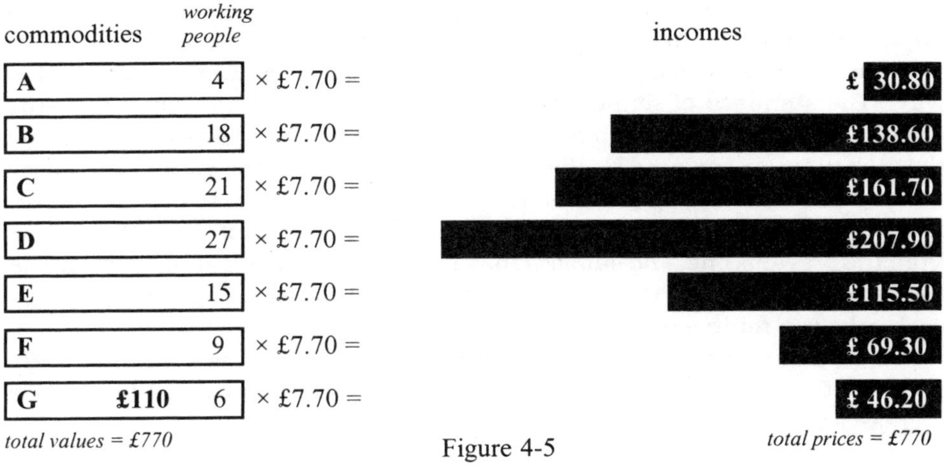

Figure 4-5

The currency value has risen from £100 to £110, an increase of 10%. As a result, all the bulk prices on the right are also 10% higher, and incomes for the hundred producers are £7.70 each. With no great mental exertion we can see that when these new bulk prices on the right are installed in Figure 4-4, the old unit prices will be restored.

But how did we raise the currency value by 10%? By printing banknotes. When the currency value was £100, the float was £63,000. This sum was based on an estimate of three month's income for everybody, when daily incomes were £7 each. Daily incomes are now £7.70, so, using the same estimate of three month's income, the new float will need to be 100 ´ £7.70 ´ 90 = £69,300. The new float is larger than the old one by £6300, an increase of 10%. This sum is the value of the extra banknotes that must be printed to keep prices constant when general productivity rises by 10%.

Let us probe this price-stabilising manoeuvre a little further. What kind of an income is provided by this printing of banknotes? In our example, a sum of £6300 is printed, which compares with an annual income of £2810 for every individual producer in our model community, using 365 as a notional multiplier for the daily income of £7.70. On the assumption that production efficiency rises steadily at 10% per annum, and banknotes are printed at a rate which expands the float by 10% per annum, then an income of £6300 per annum will be created, while prices remain constant. Who benefits from such an income? If the extra notes are forged by a private individual, who spends them on himself, the answer is obvious. The forger gains and the community loses. If the notes are printed by a government agency and the money is spent on freely used roads or free medical services or free education, or some other free provision, then the community suffers no loss, broadly speaking, though the same effect could be achieved by straightforward taxation of incomes, open to public scrutiny. But in fact this income is not targeted in any such way. It vanishes into the banking system, where it merges into the "money supply" that the banks provide in the form of loans. The borrower of these funds is the person who eventually "spends" the printed banknotes as income. There are no banks in our model so far, so we will trace this important development later.

What happens to standard of living, when prices are held stationary in this way? The standard of living still rises for everybody at the same rate, (as determined by the general improvement in overall output) even if we assume that the notes are printed by illegal counterfeiters. But the gain to the latter means that the 10% improvement is based on nine-tenths of the output. Imagine a series of cakes baked at regular intervals, each of them 10% bigger than the previous one, and suppose that 10% of each cake is eaten by mice. The remainder of each cake is still part of a series that increases by 10%, although each cake is a tenth smaller than it ought to be.

We can summarise these various effects as follows. If notes are regularly printed at a rate that counteracts the fall in unit prices caused by regular increases in production efficiency, then

1 an income is created for whoever spends these notes
2 unit prices stay constant
3 bulk prices, which are the same as incomes, rise
4 the value of money, comparing the present with the past, falls
5 standard of living still rises at a rate corresponding to the rate at which output is rising.

The general rate of productivity improvement in a large community, and its downward influence on unit prices, are very difficult to forecast. The printing of banknotes to forestall this downward effect on prices cannot be anything but a hit-and-miss affair. There is no indicator other than the overall rate of currency depreciation, which is not easy to assess. The popular view is that in a well-behaved economy with relatively constant prices, the printing of banknotes to maintain liquidity where it is needed needs to be kept within limits that do not devalue the currency too steeply, but otherwise a moderate amount of inflation does no harm. Such reasoning is superficial, but it is accurate as far as the practical outcome is concerned. In the kind of society we have analysed so far, the printing of banknotes at a rate which is not only sufficient to offset any fall in prices due to productivity improvements but is slightly higher, so that prices steadily rise, does no harm to society considered as a whole. The overall rise in standard of living is not affected. Confirmation of this comes from the common historical experience of all the leading nations. In broad terms, without differentiating any particular social group, the overall standard of living steadily rises, prices steadily rise, and money steadily loses its value. As we add more detail to this general picture, we will modify our assumption that the printing of banknotes is needed to keep prices steady. There are sources of extra banknotes other than the printing press.

5

The wage/labour contract

A slave-owner may be said to be responsible for the upkeep of his slaves. He himself, and even his slaves, may regard this cost as an exchange for the work they do. But no-one is really deceived by such logic. The slaves do all the work, and receive a portion of their own output as subsistence. The remainder belongs to the master, because he already owns everything. There is no exchange.

A feudal landowner can argue a more plausible case. He grants land to serfs who in return must work on the lord's land. A fair exchange it could be said, by which both sides may conceivably prosper. But again, no-one is really deceived. The serfs do all the work, producing a harvest from their lord's land and from their own tenancies. Their subsistence comes from the latter, while the former belongs to the master, because he already owns everything. There is no exchange.

The above two economic arrangements, chattel slavery and land-owning serfdom, are based on a direct allocation of physical goods, an allocation dictated by the will of a master. If money is introduced into the relationship between the parties, two things happen. First, the will of an individual master ceases to be omnipotent, because money creates a network of prices linked automatically to each other throughout the entire currency domain, and

commodities	*working people*	*wages*	*profit*
A	4	× £6 = £ 24	£ 4
B	18	× £6 = £108	£18
C	21	× £6 = £126	£21
D	27	× £6 = £162	£27
E	15	× £6 = £ 90	£15
F	9	× £6 = £ 54	£ 9
G £100	6	× £6 = £ 36	£ 6

total value £700

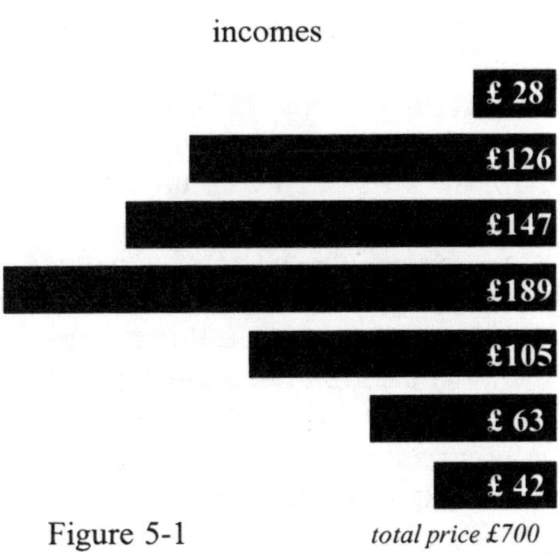

Figure 5-1

second, the notion of a fair exchange becomes very plausible indeed. So plausible that it is accepted as true. In fact, a written legal contract can be drawn up between the master and the labourer, specifying the rate of remuneration, hours of work, and all manner of terms and conditions, affecting both sides. "A fair day's work for a fair day's wage" thereby acquires a commonsense validity, and the two sides can take up positions depending on how they interpret the word "fair". We will now take a close look at this notion of contractual equality between employer and employee by modelling such an arrangement, in Figure 5-1, based on our earlier model, Figure 4-2.

The groups of cooperating specialists that produce the seven commodities are now closer to the economic concept of a firm. Adopting this definition, we can see that the first firm employs four workers, paying them £6 each. Total wage bill is now £24, leaving a profit of £4 for the firm's owner. Similar profits are shown for owners of the other six firms. The respective incomes for all workers used to be £7 per day. All worker incomes have now dropped to a wage of £6. This is the only change, and it produces a surplus which is a source of income ranging respectively from £4 to £27 daily for seven owners. Nothing else in the layout needs to be altered in the transition from Figure 4-2 to Figure 5-1. Supply and demand are still in balance, and prices remain as they were. Note that the rate of profit is the same for all firms. The rate of profit is the amount of profit expressed as a percentage of the amount "invested" by the owner. Taking the first firm as an example, £24 has been paid in wages, and no other costs are present, so total investment is £24, which yields a profit of £4. This rate of return is 16.66%. All seven owners enjoy this rate of profit.

There is clearly a reorientation of viewpoint in Figure 5-1, compared with Figure 4-2, even though the changes (in terms of mere arithmetic) are slight. In Figure 4-2 the match between supply and demand depended upon equality of income between the producers. In Figure 5-1 the equality of income between the producers (now viewed as a workforce earning wages) can be assumed beforehand, and on this basis, equality in the rate of profit becomes the factor which stabilises the match between supply and demand. In other words, for firms that pay equal rates of wages, the price mechanism in a closed economy produces a balance of supply and demand, with an appropriate set of prices (some of which are above, and some below their values), when the rate of profit for all firms is equal. (This is a discovery that Marx made in his middle years, but which he withheld until the intended publication of the third volume of *Capital.* This third volume was published by Engels more than a decade after Marx died).

We stated above that the owner's will is no longer omnipotent when a price network appears. Some of the limitations on his power can be seen in the model. The owner is part of a collective group. He cannot reduce wages unless the other owners do the same, otherwise his workers will switch to another employer if the labour market is fully mobile. If he expands production the increased supply may exceed relative demand and gross revenue from sales will fall. His fortunes are dictated by the market. The wage-earners are also part of a collectivity. By moving freely between the different firms, they tend to equalise the wage rate.

But is there an exchange relationship here, or at least an appearance of such? The slave-owner provided subsistence in return for work. The feudal lord granted land in return for work. What does the firm's owner give in return for work? Nothing can be found in the diagram that answers this question. Yet an answer is clearly specified in all written contracts of employment (and in all the text books) and is on everybody's lips. The owner provides "wages". But it is obvious from the model that he does no such thing. The wages are already provided by the bulk prices on the right hand side. Taking the first firm as an example, £28 is the bulk selling price of commodity **A**. This is set by the market in the ways we have explained. Four people have worked to produce this commodity and its selling price gives them a possible allocation of £7 each. This allocation can be reduced to a wage of £6,or less, but its original source is always the revenue from sales. It is not provided by the owner or anybody else. Look at commodity **D**. Twenty-seven people produce this commodity, which sells for £189 and hence they could receive £7 each. If this amount is reduced by the owner to £6 each, how can he be said to be paying this wage himself? Such a claim is clearly false.

It is important to distinguish the economic logic here, and keep it separate from any argument based on "fairness" or "natural justice". The owners of these firms may have sound reasons to extract a share of the revenue from sales, and their workers may be happy to earn a daily wage of £6 instead of £7. Such circumstances have no bearing on the matter. *These owners do not pay wages in return for work*. There is no such exchange. They may handle the money and claim that it is their own property when it passes through their hands. A deduction may conceivably be in order, as just stated. But the money is received in one hand and is passed on with the other. Nothing comes out of the owner's pocket. The money comes from the selling price of the goods. All disbursement of money, whether in the form of wages or profit or payments in respect of any costs whatever come from the selling price of the goods. The legal contract between employer and employee is therefore not based on an exchange of any kind. The wage-earner in a capitalist economic system is in exactly the same position as the slave and the serf in former times. The master owns everything and dictates terms, while the labourer does all the work necessary to keep himself and the master. Even if the owner works alongside his workforce, perhaps harder than any of them, he is no different from a slave-master or feudal lord who might do the same. The work provided by the owner may be an essential element in the total productive output of his firm, in which case he could justifiably claim a larger wage. But we are not concerned with justifications. We are establishing where the wages come from. They do not come from the owner. They come from the sales revenue. And if there is a residue called net profit after all costs have been met, this residue does not form part of any so-called "exchange". It is simply an undistributed surplus.

In this chapter we have used the term "investment". This term is part of the special vocabulary called into being by our changed orientation. The arrangement portrayed in Figure 4-2 naturally focussed on the producers of the commodities. There were no other players on stage, so to speak. But the owners of seven firms have now appeared in Figure 5-1, and they play a commanding role. Part of that role is to distort the truth in their own interests. Their main subterfuge is to represent themselves as the source from which wages are paid in return for work. The notion of "investment" is part of that subterfuge.

The initial advance of wages may well come from a wealthy individual or group. In addition, he or they may advance funds to pay for land, buildings, equipment, raw materials, heating and lighting, and so on. These funds must be provided at the beginning to get a new enterprise on its feet. But once the new firm is "paying its way", the initial expenditure by the wealthy investor is soon paid back, and thereafter he enjoys a steady income, which he is quite happy to represent as a return on so-called investment. This notion of "investment" is strictly an illusion. It may seem to be present in Figure 5-1 in the form of wages but no concept of investment is present in Figure 4-2, where the self-same cycle of production, exchange and consumption takes place alongside an identical network of stable prices. The transition to Figure 5-1 does not disturb this basic continuity. The only change is a reduced income for the producers, a reduction which is clearly the source of the new owners' incomes, though for obvious reasons this fact is best kept hidden, under a palaver about investments, and "creating jobs". But every businessman knows that his so-called investments provide an income that costs him nothing. He would not "invest" otherwise.

The transformation of Figure 4-2 into Figure 5-1 shows how profit and wages come into existence simultaneously when a group of co-operating specialists becomes a firm which is legally the private property of a designated owner. The specialists become a workforce earning wages and the owner becomes an employer extracting profit. Nothing is thereby introduced that could conceivably be described as "investment". A proportion of the gross revenue from sales is allocated to *wages* and the remainder is an allocation called *profit*. These allocations are two respective segments of the gross sales revenue, just as an apple can be cut into two segments with a knife. No other economic concept is

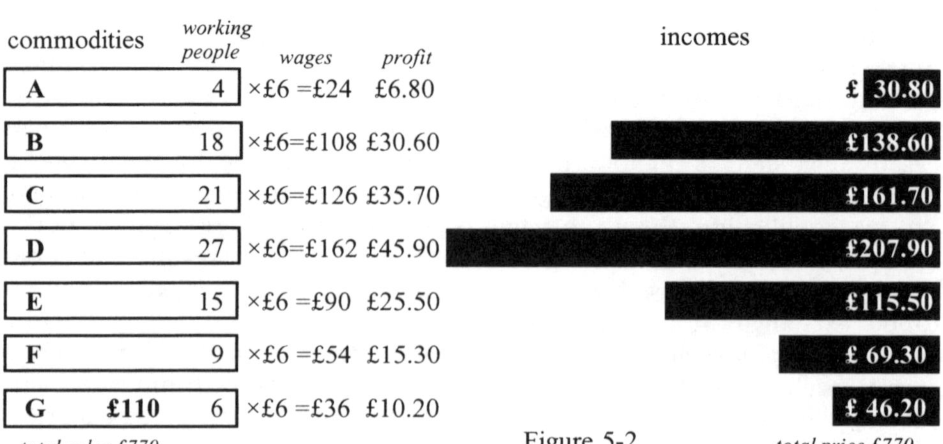

Figure 5-2

present, at this stage of our analysis. The gross sales revenue is the source from which wages and profit are extracted.

But we will greatly enlarge our understanding of the capitalist system if we now introduce a 10% improvement in productivity accompanied by a 10% rise in the currency value. In all societies a steady improvement in productivity occurs over time as a result of greater technical expertise, or discoveries, or better organisation, etc, and a steady rise in the currency value can be brought about by printing banknotes to keep unit prices stable in the manner described in the previous chapter. Figure 5-2 shows the outcome.

As can be seen, wages are not affected at all. The contract between employer and worker stipulates the wage rate, and this rate cannot be changed except by agreement between the two sides. But the income for the owner, namely the profit, rises automatically whenever the currency value rises. Here lies a powerful incentive for capitalist governments to print banknotes at a rate corresponding to what is judged to be an acceptable level of inflation. Let us go over this reasoning again.

In Figure 5-2, the increase in the currency value from the former £100 to £110, would, on its own, cause prices to rise. But as already explained there are two simultaneous effects here which neutralise each other. The productivity increase is 10%, and notes have been printed to 10% of the value of the float. Hence unit prices will stay the same. More goods are being produced at lower unit prices, while the bulk price stays constant, but these lower unit prices are offset by the falling value of money. The general appearance will be that inflation is zero, because unit prices stay the same. In reality inflation is present at a rate of 10%. In Figure 5-2, the profits for all firms have risen, and the true source of this rising prosperity is the 10% improvement in productivity, which flows automatically into profits but leaves wages where they were. As can be seen, profits have increased. The rate of profit has risen from 16.6% to 28.3%. Unit prices stay constant all the while, and the value of money steadily falls. The rich get richer, at a considerable rate, while the poor keep the same living standard, because they are tied to a fixed wage and prices are constant.

At first sight, it may seem to be an equitable and "fair" proposal that wages (or any other preset rate of remuneration) should rise in proportion to the perceived inflation of prices. But the effect of such a proposal is to defraud wage-earners out of any benefit from improved productivity, all of which goes to profits. A wage that merely keeps pace with perceived inflation means that a worker's standard of living never falls or rises in absolute terms, and hence it steadily diminishes compared with the rising social average. Standard of living for wage-earners improves, in absolute terms, only when wage rates increase more than the perceived rate of inflation. Even then, the workers' standard of living never rises in step with the standard of living for society as a whole.

The previous analogy with the cake is useful again here. In a slave-owning society, the slave receives a subsistence portion of the cake and nothing more. The harder he works the bigger the cake but the slave's portion never increases. All of the increase goes to the master. The slave's situation is quite transparent. There is no betterment for him unless the master's share is reduced. Similarly, the lot of the wage-earner cannot improve unless the employer's share (profit) is reduced. Where else could the improvement come from? But what we hear from the pundits is quite different. The wage-earner is deemed to be forever demanding more, which forces employers to raise prices, while for his part the employer just wants improved efficiency, to lower costs and keep prices down. And the government prints banknotes because they are needed as money supply for the rising output of goods. The villain of the piece is obviously the wage-earner, who ought to understand that irresponsible demands for higher wages simply lead to a "wage/price spiral" from which everybody will suffer.

All this so-called reasoning is bogus in every particular. The facts are these. Prices rise when general productivity falls, or when banknotes are printed, or when banknotes which have become superfluous remain active in the monetary network. These are the only influences that can cause an overall rise in prices. A general increase in wages simply means a corresponding decrease in profits. The only disturbance to prices that may follow from this (and only if the wage increase is considerable) is a reduced demand for dearer goods and an increased demand for cheaper goods.

More hokum is preached about inflation than any other topic in economics. The official view is that wage increases must be moderate to keep inflation down. If this is true, then it is also true that profits must be moderate for the same reason. Why is this second view never heard while the first is regarded as gospel? Because both statements are false but the first expresses the self-interest of the employer, who is opposed to wage rises because they reduce his profits. A specious theory is concocted that the economy has a certain level of "demand" determined by output, and that spending by workers can easily exceed this prudent limit, whereas rich people abstain from spending and "save" their incomes, thereby helping investment and creating jobs. When the prudent limit is exceeded, there is "too much money chasing too few goods" and hence prices rise. This notion of a prudent limit that can be exceeded if demand becomes excessive is just crafty word-spinning. The only limit on consumption is the achieved level of production, plus any goods that are supplied from reserve stocks, minus any goods that are added to reserve stocks. The wage determines the worker's share and the profit determines the employer's share. When the wage rises the profit falls and vice versa. Nothing in this reciprocal relationship can give rise to an excessive demand (whatever that may mean). As for the notion that the rich prefer to invest rather than spend, who but a fool would believe that rich people voluntarily abstain from enjoying their wealth? People in all classes can postpone present spending in order to spend more later, but "later" is always arriving in the present for as many people as those who are restricting their present spending in order to splash out in the future, so the net effect of saving (or so-called abstinence) on consumption is zero for society as a whole. Self-interest, not self-denial, is the dominant motive for all classes in a money-based economy. The reality about investment, abstinence, saving and inflation will be closely examined in the chapters ahead.

6

The wage/price/profit relation

All the different influences that combine to maintain an equilibrium network of prices in the kind of closed community that we have considered so far, are represented in Figure 6-1 below, which is based on Figure 5-2, except for a change in the pattern of aggregate demand. This change is introduced merely to illustrate the price mechanism in action. As always, we assume that producers can switch without hindrance from one line of production to another. This means that two groups of people are seeking maximum income gain, namely, the workers whose wages will thereby be equalised, and similarly the employers whose rates of profit will be equalised. When this latter condition is fulfilled, supply and demand will be in balance.

commodity values		*unit price list*	*number of workers*	*wage bill @ £6 each per day*	*profits*	incomes (bulk prices)
90 Axes	£110	60p per axe	7	£ 42	**£11.90**	**£53.90**
341 Books	£110	41p per book	18	£108	**£30.60**	**£138.60**
350 Cups	£110	44p per cup	20	£120	**£34.00**	**£154.00**
636 Dolls	£110	23p per doll	19	£114	**£32.30**	**£146.30**
339 Eggs	£110	25p per egg	11	£ 66	**£18.70**	**£84.70**
35 Forks	£110	£2.42 per fork	11	£ 66	**£18.70**	**£84.70**
20 ozs Gold	£110	£5.39 per ounce	14	£ 84	**£23.80**	**£107.80**
total values £770						*total prices £770*

Rate of profit for all firms is 28.33%.

Figure 6-1

The new aggregate demand pattern for these commodities is shown by the altered outputs which result from the redistribution of the workforce. For instance, in Figure 5-2, dolls were being produced by 27 workers at a rate of 940 dolls per day (refer to the table in Figure 4-3). In Figure 6-1 this workforce has been reduced to 19 and output is correspondingly lower. But the relation between production times, whereby all quantities produced in a given unit of time are equal in value, is the fundamental basis of adjustment for these or any other new quantities, and all that is needed is a mere number to provide an index which then expresses these relative values. This index was once provided by gold in its physical body so to speak, and from that origin came paper promises expressed in gold, as described in Chapter 3. But gold is no different from any other commodity when paper notes become inconvertible. The currency value in Figure 6-1 is £110 for one day's production of any commodity.

Hence the currency value is just a passive indicator that shifts its position whenever banknotes are printed, or when there is a change in the need for accommodation. For society as a whole this shift is immaterial, but it has serious consequences for anyone whose income is based on calendar time.

The bulk prices in the black rectangles and the unit prices are determined by three factors, namely the distribution of the workforce, the actual outputs that result from this distribution, and the currency value. Each commodity is sold at a bulk price which corresponds to an equal rate of profit for all firms. The rate of profit is equalised by competition between firms to maximise income, and when this equilibrium is achieved, the total aggregate demand for all commodities is balanced with the supply. The operating leverage so to speak comes from the buyers, who express their wishes by altering the "price profile" across the market, thereby altering incomes and disturbing the equal profit rates of individual firms, who then compete to restore this equality. By this means, the buyers get the goods they want in the proportions they want.

In Figure 6-1 wages and profits are shown *outside* the black rectangles that represent commodity incomes, because they play no part in the determination of prices. As already explained, wages and profits are mere derivatives or subdivisions of the bulk selling prices. The inverted logic that *adds all costs together to arrive at the price* gives an answer which is correct because it is a tautology. The bulk price exists prior to its division into its various parts. At the present stage of our analysis, these parts consist of wages and profits. Other costs such as raw materials, equipment replacement, maintenance, heating and lighting and so forth, will be considered in due course.

The unit price list for these goods is shown. If productivity rises, these unit prices will fall, caeteris paribus, and everybody's standard of living will rise, although neither wages nor profits will be changed. If productivity stays constant, and banknotes are printed, unit prices will rise, the currency value of £110 will rise, and profits will rise, but wages will stay the same, and worker living standards will fall. If productivity rises and banknotes are simultaneously printed to hold unit prices steady, profits will rise but wages will still stay the same, and living standards for workers will stay the same. We have already covered this ground, but we can now show these effects better in Figure 6-2.

commodity values		unit price list	number of workers	wage bill @ £6 each per day	profits	incomes (bulk prices)
99 Axes	£121	60p per axe	7	£ 42	**£17.29**	**£59.29**
375 Books	£121	41p per book	18	£108	**£44.66**	**£152.46**
385 Cups	£121	44p per cup	20	£120	**£49.40**	**£169.40**
700 Dolls	£121	23p per doll	19	£114	**£46.93**	**£160.93**
373 Eggs	£121	25p per egg	11	£ 66	**£27.17**	**£93.17**
38.5 Forks	£121	£2.42 per fork	11	£ 66	**£27.17**	**£93.17**
22 ozs Gold	£121	£5.39 per ounce	14	£ 84	**£34.58**	**£118.58**

total values £847 *total prices £847*

Rate of profit for all firms is 41%.

Figure 6-2

To interpret these changes we need to compare Figure 6-2 with Figure 6-1. We observe that the currency index has risen to £121, a rise of 10%, and outputs have also increased by 10%. Unit prices have remained as they were, and profits have increased dramatically. No benefit has filtered through to wages, and in fact, from the point of view of the wage-earner, nothing has changed, except that he or she is working harder or longer or with increased efficiency. But from the employer's viewpoint, the economy is thriving. The rate of profit has leapt from 28.33% to 41%. From an all-embracing standpoint, the standard of living in this society of one hundred and seven inhabitants is rising by 10% (over what period is not specified) but all the benefit flows exclusively into the incomes of seven owners.

Note that it is the printing of extra banknotes that diverts all benefit away from the workforce and into the pockets of the employers. If these extra notes were not injected into the monetary network, unit prices would fall when productivity rose, and the improved standard of living would be spread throughout the community. The typical employer's incentive to raise productivity in his own firm is actually based on a delusion (but see below). He thinks that if his workforce increase their output rate, he will get richer from increased volume of sales. But this increased volume, viewed from a social standpoint, merely lowers the unit selling price. If all employers do the same, none of them will get any benefit from increased productivity. To capture the social benefit of lower unit prices and divert it into profit some means must be found to stop unit prices from falling when productivity rises. Hence the printing of banknotes (or some other means of creating surplus banknotes) is an essential part of a capitalist economy. By this means, the wage-earner is reduced in economic reality to the level of a slave, who works harder only to improve the lot of his master, while the truth of his position (which was always clear enough to the slave of old) is concealed under the fiction of a "negotiated" work contract.

We must introduce an important caveat here. All our diagrams so far have represented the market network in its totality. Necessarily so, because the origin of money and the price mechanism itself cannot be understood without this comprehensive overview. The result is that the "firms" we have identified are really "spheres of production", and the supply variables we have employed in our analysis are the total outputs of the commodities passing through the market. Individual firms, in their hundreds and thousands, which are the constituent parts of every sphere of production, are not represented as such, and these firms operate in quite different competitive circumstances. The owner of such an individual firm quite correctly assumes that by improving efficiency he can increase revenue from sales and enhance his profits. But these increased sales come from the loss of business suffered by his rivals. He gains the profits that they lose, while the level of prices remains untouched, unless economies of scale bring improvements in productivity. It is natural for the firm's owner to assume that these competitive conditions are to be found throughout the entire market, and that the only difference between himself and the big operators is size. It follows from this restricted view that under "free competition" the insignificant individual is wholly dominated by market forces whereas under "monopoly conditions" an all-powerful giant can distort the market to his own advantage. This distinction is real enough, but there is another difference of great theoretical significance. As the giant gets ever bigger and approaches complete control of an entire sphere of production his competitive circumstances change. He cannot capture more business from others whose market share is no longer significant, hence any improvement in productivity will simply reduce unit prices, as explained above. He is now completely dependent on the printing of banknotes alongside his rising output rates to ensure that his profits continue to rise in step with rising profitability elsewhere. This is exactly the picture portrayed above. Figure 6-2 takes an all-embracing view of the economy, in which firms (we will continue to use this term for the present) are really spheres of production.

In Figure 6-2 the improvement in outputs, compared with Figure 6-1, is assumed to be exactly 10% in all lines of production. What would happen if this change in outputs was spread in varying degrees across the commodities of Figure 6-1, including a possible fall in output? Figure 6-3 shows the outcome. We assume a 10% rise in the currency value, as before. The percentage improvements (or reductions) in productivity are listed at the left of the diagram, and the old prices are shown in brackets in the price list.

The first thing to notice in Figure 6-3 is that the 10% rise in currency value (as compared with Figure 6-1) is wholly responsible for raising the rate of profit,

change in output	commodity values		unit price list	number of workers	wage bill @ £6 each per day	profits	incomes (bulk prices)
+10%	**99 Axes**	£121	60p(60) per axe	7	£ 42	**£17.29**	**£59.29**
nil	**341 Books**	£121	45p(41) per book	18	£108	**£44.66**	**£152.46**
–10%	**315 Cups**	£121	54p(44) per cup	20	£120	**£49.40**	**£169.40**
+20%	**763 Dolls**	£121	21p(23) per doll	19	£114	**£46.93**	**£160.93**
+10%	**373 Eggs**	£121	25p(25) per egg	11	£ 66	**£27.17**	**£93.17**
+10%	**38.5 Forks**	£121	£2.42(2.42) per fork	11	£ 66	**£27.17**	**£93.17**
nil	**20 ozs Gold**	£121	£5.93(5.39) per ounce	14	£ 84	**£34.58**	**£118.58**
	total values £847						*total prices £847*

Rate of profit for all firms is 41%.

Figure 6-3

which is exactly the same, at 41%, as in Figure 6-2. In those commodities where productivity has increased by a corresponding 10% (axes, eggs and forks) the unit price has remained constant. Productivity above 10% (dolls) has reduced the unit price, and productivity less than 10% has raised unit prices (books, cups, and gold). What is the change in cost of living when different commodities are affected in different ways? In our model, axes, eggs and forks are the same price per item, dolls are cheaper, while books, cups and gold are dearer. Some kind of calculation based on a representative sample of goods is generally adopted to provide a very rough measure of perceived inflation, expressed as a "cost of living" index, rising or falling as may be.

For an economist, the rise shown above in the unit price of books, say, does not lead to the conclusion that the demand for books is rising. The relative demand for books has not altered. Fewer books are being cleared from the market at a higher price, but the total amount of money spent is the same. The demand for books cannot be interpreted from unit prices, but only from bulk prices. The distinction between bulk price (on the right of the diagram in the black rectangles) and unit price (in the middle) is vital for any theoretical understanding. It might be useful at this point to restate in Figure 6-4 the basic tenets of elementary price theory. These have been explained in the Introduction, and in Chapter 1, using the same graph as shown.

Figures 6-1, 6-2 and 6-3 take no account of possible changes in demand which would lead to a redistribution of the workforce. And as stated earlier the rate

Relation between demand, supply, bulk price and unit price.

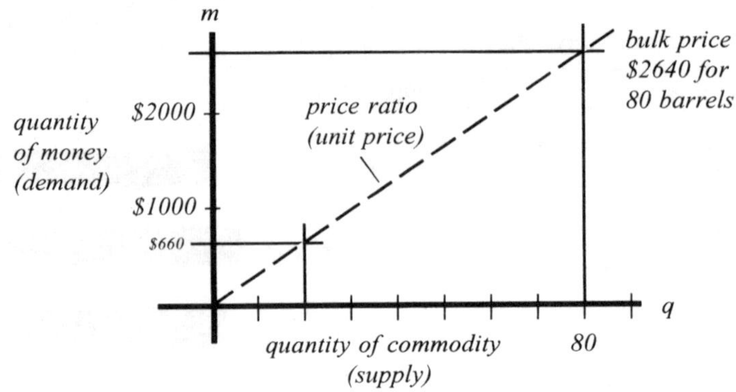

Figure 6-4

1 When supply is constant,
(a) the bulk price rises and falls when the demand rises and falls.
(b) the unit price rises and falls when the demand rises and falls.
2 When demand is constant,
(a) the bulk price stays constant.
(b) the unit price falls when supply rises, and rises when supply falls.
3 When demand and supply rise in step, bulk price rises but unit price stays constant.
4 When demand and supply fall in step, bulk price falls but unit price stays constant.
5 Nothing specific can be deduced from the behaviour of the unit price on its own.

of profit is over-simplified because no factor markets are present to provide raw materials and intermediate products. Only the finished goods market is shown. In addition, these diagrams are stationary on the printed page, so to speak, even though they represent a continuous process of buying and selling, repeated every day. Simplification along these lines is a hindrance, but at the same time essential, just as the parts of an engine must be visualised at rest in various positions before the dependency order of the piston, connecting rod, valves, spark, etc can be brought into overall comprehension. The working of the stationary engine must be understood at two levels, so to speak, the static and the dynamic, and then at a higher level when the vehicle is moving. Similarly with price networks.

So our next step is to view this equilibrium of internally self-compensating elements as a process operating through time. Figure 6-5 shows how changes in productivity and currency value influence wages, prices and profit in the course of a 6-year time period. Each society is the same simple market economy of a hundred producer/consumers, all working as wage-earners for seven employers. These seven employers are the legal owners of all the goods produced by their own workers, and they sell these goods to everybody else. The wage earners never sell goods. They spend their wages and the owner spends his profit.

In each diagram the black columns represent total output of one day, displayed on a horizontal time scale at yearly intervals. Any change in daily

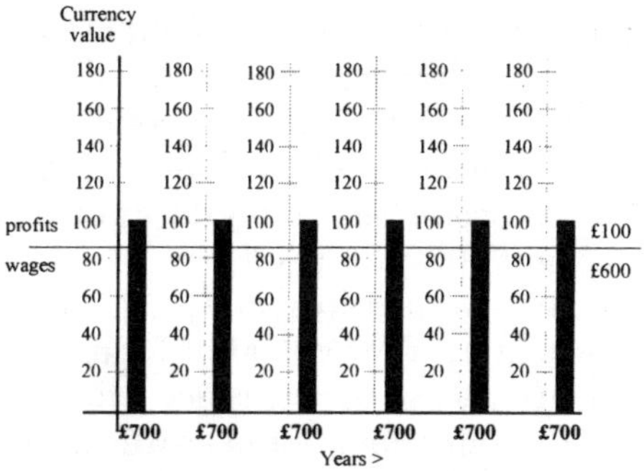

Society A

Productivity constant. Currency value constant.
Prices constant. Standard of living constant.
Real inflation nil. Perceived inflation nil.
Worker pay throughout 6yr period - £6 daily.
Employer profit at start of 6yr period - £14.28 daily.
Employer profit at end of 6yr period - £14.28 daily.

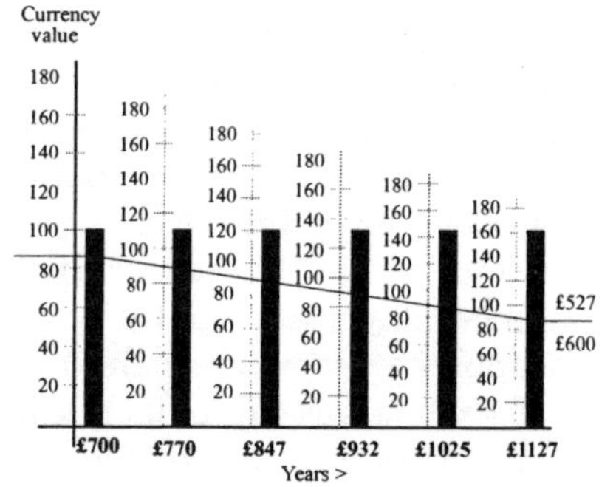

Society B

Productivity constant. Currency value rising 10%.
Prices rising. Standard of living constant.
Real inflation 10%. Perceived inflation 10%.
Worker pay throughout 6yr period - £6 daily.
Employer profit at start of 6yr period - £14.28 daily.
Employer profit at end of 6yr period - £75.28 daily.

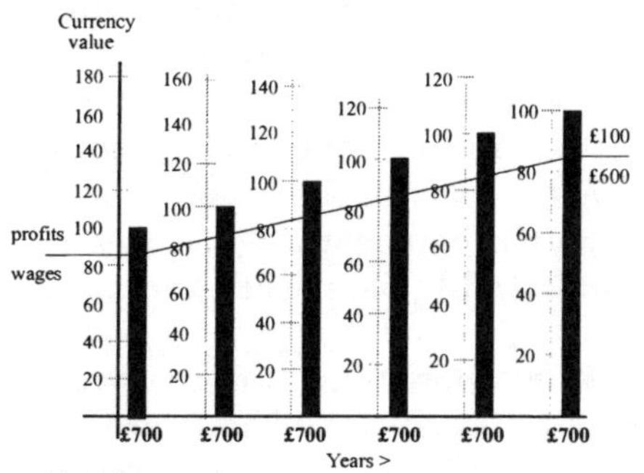

Society C

Productivity rising 10%. Currency value constant.
Prices falling. Standard of living rising.
Real inflation nil. Perceived inflation nil.
Worker pay throughout 6yr period - £6 daily.
Employer profit at start of 6yr period - £14.28 daily.
Employer profit at end of 6yr period - £14.28 daily.

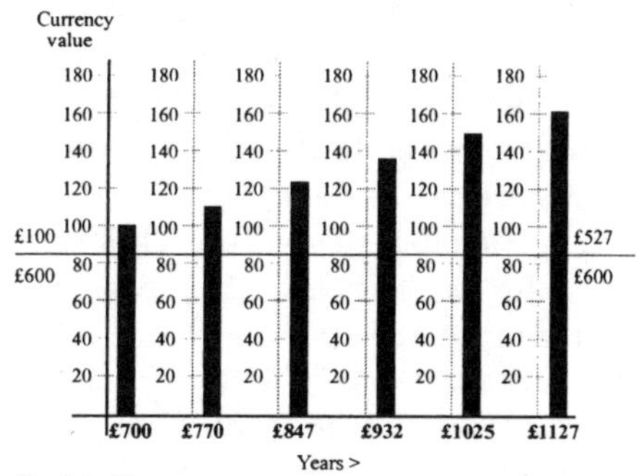

Society D

Productivity rising 10%. Currency value rising 10%.
Prices constant. Standard of living rising.
Real inflation 10%. Perceived inflation nil.
Worker pay throughout 6yr period - £6 daily.
Employer profit at start of 6yr period - £14.28 daily.
Employer profit at end of 6yr period - £75.28 daily.

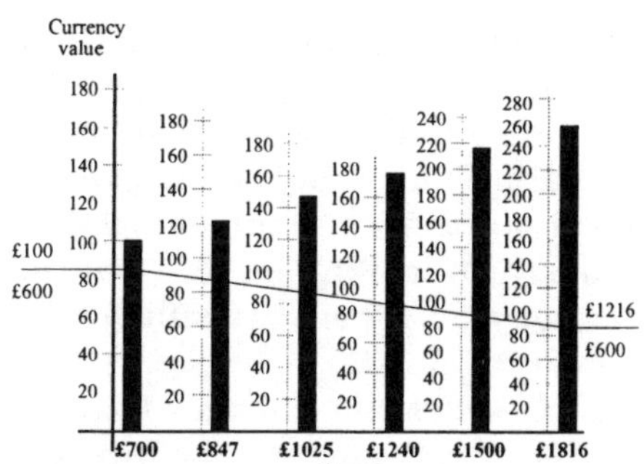

Society E

Productivity rising 10%. Currency value rising 20%.
Prices rising. Standard of living rising.
Real inflation 21%. Perceived inflation 11%.
Worker pay throughout 6yr period - £6 daily.
Employer profit at start of 6yr period - £14.28 daily.
Employer profit at end of 6yr period - £173.71 daily.

Figure 6-5
The relation between output and inflation.

output during the six year period is shown by a rise or fall in the height of these black columns. The vertical scale shows the currency value. As already explained, the currency value is an index linked to production of any commodity per day. *It is not linked to a particular quantity of commodity.* Understanding this fact is very important. A change in quantity produced per day does not alter the currency value. If the currency value is £100 per day then 10 apples produced per day are worth (in value) £100. If 20 apples are produced per day then 20 apples are worth (in value) £100. The value of the apples has fallen from £10 to £5 each as a result of increased productivity but the currency value has not changed. It is still £100 for one day's production. Values are always anchored to a fixed time because they express equality of output rates in terms of an equal time period.

In the light of this, we must be perfectly clear how the currency value is displayed in Figure 6-5. *When the black column rises the currency value must rise alongside, keeping its own magnitude.* The reference point for the currency value is the top of the black column, wherever that may be. In other words the black column rises whenever there is an increase in quantity produced per day, and the vertical scale expands at the same time to ensure that the currency value stays locked to this daily level. In yet other words, the black column has its own vertical scale of physical output, not shown on the graph. The scale shown is the currency value. This relationship is demonstrated clearly in the diagram for Society C. In this society, output steadily rises, while the currency value remains at £100.

Now turn to Society A. Where does the £700 come from? It comes from the £100 currency value that every commodity possesses. There are seven commodities. Hence the black column represents £700 in value produced every day. Of course, relative demand and prices may alter in all manner of ways in this society (as earlier portrayed in Figures 6-1, 6-2 and 6-3) but such changes will make no difference whatever to the the diagram. Society A is obviously in steady state equilibrium. Neither the overall level of output nor the currency value is changing.

Refer now to Society B. Output is steady, but the currency value in respect of that output is rising from £100, to £110, to £121, to £133 and so on, a regular increase of 10% inflation per year. Moving on to Society C we observe that there is no inflation, but output is rising steadily by 10% each year, whereas in Society D both productivity and currency value are rising by 10%. In Society E, the rise in productivity is likewise 10%, but the currency value is rising twice as fast, by 20% per year. (These two influences compound each other and produce a net inflation rate of 21%).

A graph with a vertical scale that expands and contracts may seem odd, but we cannot show the interaction between output and currency value in any other way. These two variables are uniquely related. When output changes, they both move conjointly, as partners so to speak, rising and falling together. The changed output keeps the same currency value. This means that the currency scale must expand and contract. But when banknotes are printed, the currency value inflates on its own, and establishes a new reference point with output.

When both rising productivity and inflation are present, the response is partly partnership, partly separation, and both effects must be combined together on the graph.

We can now check the values at the base of each black column. The top of the column gives a reading on the vertical scale. This reading is the currency value. Multiply this reading by seven to obtain the total value of the seven commodities produced per day.

Changes in output and currency value are combined in various ways in this series of graphs, enabling us to study the effect on prices, incomes, standard of living and the perception of inflation. Standard of living for instance, for the community as a whole, is dependent entirely on output. It has no link with money (as commonsense would suggest). And unit prices rise only when currency value rises faster than productivity and vice versa. (Hence if the currency value is constant any rise in productivity lowers unit prices). When currency value and productivity alter by equal percentage amounts, there is no change in the general price level, and no perception of real inflation (or deflation). These are general observations from studying the black output columns and their related scales.

We turn now to the wage/profit line that crosses all the output columns. In year one, for every society, the starting position is £700 of value produced in a working day. This is divided into £100 of aggregate profit for 7 owners, and £600 in wages for 100 workers, as explained in chapters 4 and 5. We are working with exactly the same model as before, examining what happens when output and currency value change over a six year period.

Clearly there is no change in Society A. In Society B, the currency value has risen each year by 10%, and at the end of the 6-year period, profit has risen to more than five times its former magnitude. Prices have risen by 10% per year, but there is no change in productivity, and no change in wages. Although the standard of living for society as a whole has not altered, the living standard of all workers has fallen because of rising prices. The sole beneficiary from inflation is the employer.

In Society C the yearly rise in productivity benefits the whole community, through falling prices. There is no inflation, and everyone's income stays the same. In Society D both productivity and inflation are rising, but the inflation is completely hidden because unit prices stay constant. Wage is also constant, so worker living standards are the same from year to year. But profit increases by a multiple of five. It is clear that the rise in currency value is the means whereby an improvement in communal standard of living is diverted into the pockets of the employers.

This view is confirmed when we come to Society E. With productivity rising alongside a currency value that is rising even faster, the workers' standard of living deteriorates rapidly while the profit for the employers is multiplied twelve times over. Society E is typical of capitalist societies in general. We will examine these typical circumstances more closely in the next chapter.

7

The capitalist wages system

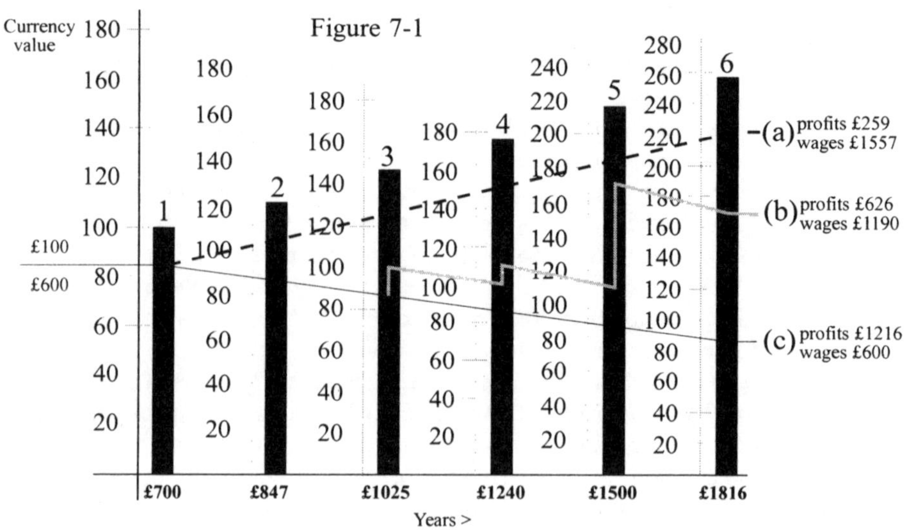

Society E Productivity rising 10%. Currency value rising 20%.
Prices rising. Standard of living rising.
Real inflation 21%. Perceived inflation 11%.
Worker pay throughout 6yr period - £6 daily.
Employer profit at start of 6yr period - £14.28 daily.
Employer profit at end of 6yr period - £173.71 daily(c).

Our analysis is at the stage where we can distinguish clearly between two economic classes, a working class and an employing class, and now we need to make their relationship precise. All the means of production are owned by the employing class in the form of private firms. The working class have no such possessions. In these circumstances, the employers are the legal owners of all goods produced for sale, and the money from such sales belongs to them. This money is used to pay all costs associated with each firm, including a payment to the working class called wages. The remainder after all costs are cleared is the employer's income called profit.

The relation between worker and capitalist owner is made plain, in economic terms, by Figure 7-1. In this society there are no costs other than wages, which is quite unrealistic. But we are simply treating wages as the first deduction from bulk sales, to be followed later in the analysis by other deductions. There is no suggestion at this stage that the wage-cost has any special priority. We are examining the various costs as they arise, to clarify how the revenue from gross sales is apportioned. The position of the employer can only be clarified when all costs have been deducted. By proceding in this way, we steadily improve the theoretical model and bring it closer to reality.

The economic situation of the 100 workers at the start of the 6-year period is represented by an aggregate daily wage of £600 in a society where £700 will buy the total production of one day. The residue is £100, which, for the present, we regard as the net profit for seven employers. This situation is indicated in Figure 7-1 by the thin black line entering from the left. If we assume that this wage contract is never re-negotiated, then the wage for each worker will remain fixed at £6 per day throughout the 6-year period. By following the thin black line leading down to point (c) we can judge how the worker's position alters both in absolute terms and in relation to society as a whole. In absolute terms he or she becomes steadily poorer, because prices are rising. In relative terms his deterioration is immense.

The broken line rising to point (a) shows how the worker's pay would rise if he maintained his position relative to society as a whole. The grey line leading to point (b) shows the effect of three pay rises, in the years 3, 4 and 5 of the 6-year period. The first rise lifted the aggregate wage from £600 to £700, an increase of 16%. The second rise lifted wages from £700 to £770, an increase of 10%, and the third rise lifted wages from £770 to £1190, an increase of 54%. Nevertheless, despite these substantial increases (the third quite unbelievable for a modern workforce, though not unusual for company directors and the like) worker living standards still stay well below the broken line that denotes parity with society as a whole.

The worker's position is permanently undermined by the fact that he is paid at a fixed rate per unit of working time. Even if he secured a pay rise that took him to the broken line, the steadily rising inflation (which is effectively hidden, partly or entirely, by his own rising productivity) ensures that his relative living standard will always be downwards from that point on. By contrast, the employer's living standard is always rising, interrupted only when wage rates increase. We can repeat here a point made earlier, and illustrate it exactly in Figure 7-1. A level of pay that rises automatically because it is linked by contract to the *perceived* rate of inflation would produce a horizontal wage/profit line on the graph, corresponding to a stationary living standard for the worker, with no benefit from increased productivity.

It is clear from Figure 7-1 that so-called wage bargaining between a workers' side and an employers' side is a confrontation that is settled on the basis of the relative power of the two sides and not on some notion of fair entitlement. However civilised the bargaining process may be in a modern democracy the analogy with the slave of old retains its validity. In a dictatorship the power of the employer is exercised as undisguised force against the wage-earner. No trade unions are allowed. Agitation for democratic rights is forbidden. The employer's attitude is brutally plain. Why give bargaining rights to a slave? *But our workers are not slaves*, say the employers in the democracies. *We provide a contract of work with the right to terminate by either party. Every citizen has voting rights to elect a government based on consensus, and access to knowledge is freely available. Informed decision-making by the majority is everywhere our policy, and politicians and the press are free to organise and comment as they please.* These fine words are true, but they do not tell the whole truth. Undoubtedly the work contract is an important form of protection, and voting rights are an important form of participation, and access to knowledge within a forum of free debate is an important form of legitimation, preferable by far to police batons. But reduced to its bare essentials, the worker's case at the negotiating table is a plea to the employer to reduce the intensity of exploitation or mitigate its circumstances. The two sides never directly negotiate on such bald terms because the exploitation operates at systemic level, behind their backs so to speak, not at the level of the individual firm. Both sides aim for a compromise which seems to balance their respective interests. But any improvement for the worker means a less severe rate of relative decline, and any concession by the employer means a less frantic accumulation of profit. Slave and master are still present, although the master is not embodied in the personality of the employer, as of old.

Words like "slave" or "exploitation" have an emotional connotation which is inappropriate in a factual analysis. Such terms are justifiable only when the intrinsic meaning accurately expresses the facts of the case. Hence, to remain objective, we should examine our reasoning with particular care at this point where the notion of slavery within democracy is alleged.

If we retrace our steps to Figure 5-1, in Chapter 5, we see there the first appearance of an employer paying wages and deriving an income from the remainder. Such an employer springs into existence at the moment when the bulk sales on the right no longer belong to the associated producers. All money from bulk sales passes into the hands of the owner, and he then allocates wages of £6 per day to his workers, keeping the remainder for himself as profit. Is this the essential transformation that brings a capitalist society into being?

When gold serves as money, the answer is yes, but in a paper-based economy the answer is qualified. We need a special manipulation of the monetary system as well, to convert the employer into a capitalist. The bare relationship of private owner and wage-earner can be seen in each of the five societies of Figure 6-5. It is present in the first year of the six-year period for all of them. But Society A is not a capitalist society, nor is Society C. There is no capitalist exploitation in either of these societies. The wage-slave is present only in Societies B, D and E.

In all five societies the worker's wage is £6 per day and the owner gets a much higher income, but this is no different in principle from a ship's captain being paid more than the crew. The captain is a qualified person, with skills and experience, and carries higher responsibilities. If an ordinary member of the crew is paid much less, but has opportunities to acquire similar skills and can look forward to the possibility of becoming a captain himself no-one would argue that such a pay differential was inherently exploitative. In the same way, the owner of a firm has supervisory and other responsibilities and he may work hard and contribute in large measure to his firm's success. The fact that he is better remunerated than any of his workers does not make him a capitalist. This point applies particularly to Society A and Society C. All the employers in these two societies seem to have taken no advantage of their powerful positions as private owners. Consider how poor their income (profit) is at the end of the 6-year period compared with the income of the employers in the other three societies. So something more than the mere power of ownership is involved.

The essence of the matter is that in Societies B, D and E *the power of ownership acts in conjunction with the activities of a third party, the central bank.* In these societies, the employer simply hires the worker at the going rate and from then on the employer gets richer and the worker gets poorer. The price network is "managed" by the central bank (we will examine this management role later) to keep unit prices constant or rising slightly, and by this means the worker is defrauded (another emotive word but correctly employed here) of any benefit from improved productivity, all of which goes to the owner, without the latter lifting a finger, and regardless of whether the owner is a "good" employer, paying better than average wages, or whether he runs a sweatshop. As already explained, the worker can maintain a steady living standard in absolute terms only if his wage is regularly adjusted to keep in step with perceived inflation. Whether this happens or not (most likely not) his living standard in relative terms is *always falling.*

So in answer to our earlier question we may say that private ownership of firms is an essential feature of a capitalist society, but a central bank is also needed with a special role. The activity of the central bank transforms the private owner into a capitalist, whether he is aware of the fact or not, whether he boasts a social conscience or not. Observe how poorly the owners in Society C fare, by having no central bank to "manage" the economy and send their profits soaring. In passing we may note that during the early days of a capitalist society the worker and employer are in confrontation at the level of the workplace, but not so later. The reason is partly because firms are small at first, and their owner/managers are more conspicuous, but there is a deeper cause which appears after the transition from a gold-based to a paper based economy. Confrontation is absorbed into the system and loses its personal character. The firm is no longer controlled by an identifiable master but by a bureaucratic hierarchy in which accountants and financial advisors act as intermediaries linking the firm to the banking system. A new set of masters operates from afar.

Before we continue, an important point can be made here. Society A in Figure 6-5 shows a situation where output is obviously constant year by year. But productivity may in fact be rising. A constant output with rising productivity can mean only one thing. The hours worked must be falling. In this case the benefit from an overall increase in productive efficiency results in a shorter working day, allowing more free time, an important component in a worker's living standard. This possibility exists in any of the five societies but it creates havoc with the activities of a central bank. Reducing the working day while output stays constant means that unit prices stay constant of their own accord. Hence there is no need to print extra banknotes to "manage" the economy by holding prices steady. But the mechanism that churns out ever increasing profits needs these extra banknotes, otherwise it comes to a standstill. For this reason, a general reduction in the working day is strenuously resisted by employers in a capitalist society. Increase in output is an essential element of profit-making. The more the output is increased, the more the currency value can be inflated to prevent unit prices from falling, and the more the currency value is inflated the bigger the profits. From the employer's point of view, increased efficiency must never be wasted by reducing the hours of work. The employer explains this to himself by supposing that rising output, whether this comes from an extension of working hours, or an increase in the intensity of work, or better equipment, increases his market share at the expense of rival firms. But it is the mainly concealed inflation injected by the central bank (or coming from some other source yet to be identified) that steadily swells the profits of all successful firms.

We resume our analysis by asking the question, is the arrangement shown in Figure 7-1 satisfactory to the central bank? Have extra banknotes been printed in the right quantities? The situation portrayed in the diagram seems to be ideal, and in fact if more banknotes were printed to push the currency value higher still, the employers would reap even more profits. Why not do so? Because when prices rise rapidly, the effects are: (1) regular buying and selling is continually disrupted and the future becomes uncertain, (2) social unrest is caused among workers and others on fixed incomes, (3) exporting firms cannot compete in overseas markets, (4) the government (in a democracy) is accused of failure on all sides. Hence the central bank is an institution with special responsibilities. It has close ties with the government, which wants to please the electorate with a record of good economic management. The watchword here is caution, keep inflation modest, and do not pander to boardroom greed. It also has close ties with the employers, whose individual viewpoint is the opposite, since they all want high profits. But there is no clear watchword here, because domestic firms benefit when the currency value is raised, but exporters experience difficulties related to currency exchange rates. The central bank must juggle with these conflicting interests and hence is always in a dilemma. (Its global responsibilities in respect of currency exchange rates cannot be included here).

But despite this ever present dilemma, one thing is certain. *Whenever output is raised, either by increased productive efficiency, or by longer working hours or by greater effort, or by all three, the bank's problems are solved.* Because the more output rises, the more notes can be printed without pushing prices up. All domestic firms will benefit, and overseas markets will not appear be harmed. There will be no visible inflation, and the government's record will be outstanding. All this improvement, just for working a bit harder. These benefits are always just round the corner. The extra effort is needed *now*, to usher in a general era of prosperity *tomorrow*. So we may have to wait a little while, but a great future lies ahead . . . . . The familiar clap-trap of the politicians does not of course include any enlightenment for the worker about the role of the banking system. The politician's duty is in fact to make sure that the real connections between worker, politician and the banks stays out of sight. The empty rhetoric sets a populist agenda for mock combats at election time between puppets whose strings are all pulled by the same master. Most intelligent people are aware that the party political system is largely a sham, but it flourishes as democratic window dressing because it is (rightly) judged to be better than dictatorship, in a society where the general population has no understanding of its own economic relationships.

A truthful portrayal of the worker's situation is presented in Figure 7-1. His only defence against a capitalist wages system is to press continuously for higher wages by any means that lie in his power. If he manages to achieve point (b) then his standard of living in absolute terms has improved slightly over the six year period, and it is perfectly possible for some groups of workers to achieve this level or go even higher, if their particular skills are scarce. Hence there is normally a gradation in wage levels between skilled and unskilled sectors of the working class. But the diagram is intended to show wage levels as an average for all workers. In some countries, the worker's position may deteriorate well below point (c) particularly when there are no democratic checks on government activities, and political power is harnessed to serve the reckless greed of the big employers.

There are no economic arguments that justify any sort of a limit on wage levels. If wages rise then the rate of profit-making falls. There are no other consequences. Production continues as before. Prices are unaffected, though there may be a temporary rise if the need for accommodation falls. The effect on profits is to reduce the rate of acceleration. Profits still accumulate, but less rapidly. The worker's standard of living, in relative terms, deteriorates less steeply, and may actually rise in absolute terms. But the real situation of particular workers does not necessarily conform to these facts as stated. When competitive circumstances are the same for all firms in a given sector, a firm that pays high wages while workers in other firms are paid less may go bankrupt, and the argument that the high wage has caused the firm's failure can be correct both in theory and in practical effect. But this is an instance of low-level theory and narrow practical effect. The survival of firms in competition against each other in a given market sector, where more or less identical goods sell for the same price, depends on the differences in their cost liabilities. The wages they pay can be high for all of them, or low for all of them, without affecting survival chances in respect of each other. But when wages differ between similar firms, in circumstances where there are obstacles to labour mobility, an advantage accrues to the firm that pays less. In these circumstances the worker is dependent on cooperation from fellow workers in rival firms to keep the general wage level as high as possible. The employer is opposed to this kind of cooperation for obvious reasons, and will justify low wages by economic arguments that are always bogus, though these arguments have a limited truth in the narrow instance, and the worker who disregards them may lose his job. This possibility of job loss is constantly being preached to the worker, and cooperation between workers is everywhere limited by legislation, with very severe penalties in some countries.

The more freely workers are able to migrate between firms is search of better wages, the more uniform the wage level for any particular type of work. Higher wages in formerly restricted sectors or distant regions tend to fall as workers circulate more freely. Reduction of high wages is welcomed by employers and resented by workers, who blame the fall in wages on the new arrivals. This resentment is understandable, but such reasoning is a further instance of the narrow application of low-level theory. The low-level theory states that wage levels are set by the number of workers competing for jobs. This is false as a general principle, but it contains a limited truth. The general principle is that wage-levels are set by the proportionate division of proceeds from sales. A portion of these proceeds goes to the workforce and a portion goes to the employer. The portion that goes to the workforce is divided among the individual workers and hence if there are many workers the wage is small. But at this point we need to recall the analysis in Chapter One, with particular reference to Figure 1-2. The distribution of the total workforce across all commodities is determined by the aggregate social demand pattern. Producers move from one sphere of production to another in search of the best returns, and equilibrium in a freely competitive market is reached when all incomes are equalised. This is the how a money network operates. Equality of incomes is built into the system. It comes about automatically, in any market that is truly competitive, and has nothing to do with capitalist arrangements. But the division of the sales revenue into a *fixed rate* for the workforce and the *remainder* for the employer, is an essential part of capitalist arrangements, with no equalising principle at its root. If the wage-rate for each worker declines because their numbers are growing, they will tend to blame the newcomers and not grasp the fact that the gross wages for all of them is an allocated portion set by the employer from gross sales, and this allocated portion could be made bigger by reducing the employer's portion. Such action does not harm the firm at all unless the firm is superfluous within the sphere of production that it belongs to. In that case it needs to move elsewhere, and is merely hanging on to its place by paying sweatshop wages. It is always in the interests of workers *as a whole* to test this situation, but a particular group of workers may be harmed thereby. Some sweatshops are destroyed, and workers lose their jobs. But workers in other sweatshops are placed in a position where their wages could be raised to the level that prevails in the sector as a whole. This will reduce their employer's surplus profits, without necessarily jeopardising their firm's future. It is obvious that plenary co-operation between all workers in a particular sector is needed to give this kind of protection. Trades unions (where they are allowed) would seem to offer this essential unity, but in practice their role is to negotiate small concessions in return for peace and quiet. They act to accommodate a very uneven power relationship and (quite sensibly in most cases) do not challenge it.

The presence of jobless workers actively seeking employment is a very reassuring scenario for the employer. Wage levels can be kept low without much resistance. In poor countries a destitute population surviving in decayed feudal or tribal conditions provides an ideal nurturing environment for new capitalist enterprises. In advanced countries with welfare programmes, where lack of jobs is an election issue, the unemployed have an economic identity as a taxation burden. We cannot deal with either unemployment or taxation until our models include a large service class with derivative incomes.

There is a possible source of misunderstanding in the interpretation of Figure 7-1 that we need to guard against. The process represented is a self-sustaining dynamic equilibrium. The black vertical columns represent consumption as well as output. The price/wage/profit network for each column is a co-dependency that allows no leaks. As it appears to the eye, the diagram shows a daily earning and spending pattern which is rigidly sequential in the span of one day. The mechanism that allows a relaxation of this rigid dependency is the float, or to use the older term, the pecuniary accommodation, consisting of the reserves that everyone in this society carries in pocket or purse or similar resting place. It is a serious error to suppose that anyone in this society can save his or her income in the form of a hoard. A hoard can certainly be accumulated, but the incomes shown can *never* be extracted from the network. They are always spent every day. They all depend on each other. All this has been explained in Chapter 2, but we need to keep this understanding uppermost in our minds at all times.

In other words, there is *no such thing as money-savings in this society*, taken as a whole. The only form that savings can take for a whole society is stockpiling of goods, which may or may not be a sensible practice in any given circumstances. These stockpiles can be produced by reducing consumption of goods while still continuing to buy them. Thus demand stays constant, and supply stays constant, but a surplus of goods is steadily accumulated. The notion that people could save a little of their income each week until everybody had sufficient for a rainy day is shallow thinking. All incomes depend on a maintained spending level. Individual saving for all sorts of purposes is indeed possible, but past savings being spent today are a counterbalance for today's savings which will be spent tomorrow, and in a large community with a myriad of spending and saving decisions, the net effect is zero, even though people can accumulate large savings which are perfectly real for them as individuals. Hence no money savings can ever exist for society as a whole. If the net effect is other than zero, the float is affected and the price level adjusts automatically to restore this zero position.

Although the origin and functioning of the float have already been explained, it is worth recapitulation at this point, because it is essential to theoretical understanding. The float must not be envisaged as a mere standby reserve. It acts in this fashion for individuals but it is much more than that. Imagine that all producers of goods face each other in a circle. This is the supply situation. The goods have been manufactured and they now await distribution into the hands of consumers, who are the same people. Now imagine that one producer, on his own, travels round the circle and distributes his goods to everybody else in the proportions that they require. When he returns to his place he will have nothing left. Then the next producer does the same. Then the next, and so on round the circle until all the producers have distributed their goods. Everybody's identity has now been changed from producer to consumer, and they all have the goods they want.

Now bring money into play. When the first producer travels round the circle he cannot just give his goods away without an equivalent of some kind, something that represents value. If we call this equivalent "money", then he will arrive back in his place without any goods, but he will have gathered a stock of money as a substitute. This means that everybody must have a stock of money to start with. When the other producers travel round the circle in turn, they will also acquire a stock of money, but a second process will have started. The first producer, who has returned to his place with an accumulated stock of money, will begin to lose that money, as he hands it over to later producers. In fact all the producers, as each in turn adopts the role of consumer, will steadily hand over money to the later producers who follow them round the circle. By the time the last producer has travelled round, all goods will have been transfered to the consumers who want them (who will be themselves) and the stock of money that they each possessed at the beginning will be restored as if it had never left them. This is what we have refered to above as zero position for the money.

Now bring the float into play. If everybody's stock of money is large enough, there will be no need to wait for producers to travel round the circle. Goods can be bought and sold as need or fancy dictate. The money acts as a temporary stopgap, something to tide over over the shorter or longer period that may intervene before acquiring the goods that are the real point and purpose of the exchange operation. Hence goods are exchanged for other goods. The money merely acts as a sophisticated interface to match buyer and seller without the need for synchronisation of time and place. In a closed market community, the total money stock needed to achieve this flexibility is called pecuniary accommodation, or as we have termed it, the float. This float is an integral part of buying and selling operations that are bound to be in balance with each other. The totality of goods is being exchanged for the same totality of goods. Therefore the proportions in which they exchange must express an essential unity, per day, per month, even per minute, even though the people in the market are free as individuals to buy and sell whenever they like. This unity is embodied in a price network which operates in conjunction with a float. Although money seems to enjoy a completely liberated existence, *it exists only as a counterpoise, so to speak, for the commodities that are continually passing from production to consumption. Money can never act as an agent on its own.*

Once we fully understand that no "leaks" are possible from the price network, we can allow the possibility of "loops" in any number and any size. Money can be "spent" for any purpose whatsoever. It can be donated to a charity, pooled in a lottery, gathered in taxes, stolen by thieves, invested in a Rembrandt, lost in a wager, deposited in a bank, in short transferred to other hands for any conceivable reason or no good reason at all. But the money in all these transactions always loops back to the goods exchange interface that it originated from. Otherwise the system is forced to correct itself by a change in the currency value. The buying and selling of commodities involves a unique form of "spending" that to the ordinary view seems just like any other money transaction between two parties, but such spending at the goods exchange interface is utterly different from any other money-based activity. Incomes may be spent in all manner of ways, but money that buys commodities is bonded inseparably with the money that is earned by selling commodities. It is fatuous to suppose that money can exist independently of this two-sided identity. The float provides a cushion between two interlocked elements. It does not separate them from each other.

This essential understanding is encapsulated in the odd-sounding comment that *banknotes are real but incomes and savings are fictitious*. Banknotes can be extracted from a buying and selling network and they will make a heap of paper on the floor. But the face-value of these paper notes bears no resemblance at all to incomes. The incomes exist only when the process is in operation. And savings exist (in self-cancelling form) only when incomes are being generated. These facts are strikingly confirmed in periods of severe monetary crisis. A community that tries to convert all its savings into real banknotes will find that its savings do not exist, and if it tries to hoard banknotes then incomes will not exist. These vanished savings or incomes cannot be restored by printing more banknotes. There is only one effect that follows from printing banknotes. The currency value rises. There is only one source of incomes. The buying and selling network. And there is only one source of savings. The delayed expenditure of the saver in balance with the overspend of the dis-saver.

This digression has taken us away from the capitalist wages system as such. But it is essential to understand the float and to expose all illusions about the origin of incomes. Money that takes the form of wages does not originate in some mysterious way from the work contract, as if labour itself had a price. Such a notion is ridiculous. Wages are a proportion of bulk sales, just as profits are. But when wages are falsely defined in terms of time worked, a veil is drawn over the true relationships. Bulk selling prices can be enhanced by inflation, making profts rise as a proportion of bulk sales, while the wages proportion falls. The worker is defrauded, even though his pay stays constant alongside unit prices that also stay constant if output rises in step with the inflation. This is the secret of capitalist exploitation. We can now turn to consider the banking system, and explore how the inflation is introduced and controlled.

8

The banking system: part 1

The basic structure of the banking system is shown in Figure 8-1. The central bank accepts securities from the local bank in the transition from phase 1 to phase 2. These securities are merely a form of backing, a guarantee of solvency for the central bank, if the local bank should fail. They are not a loan and they do not generate interest. The central bank is now prepared to loan money to the local bank. This loan must be paid for by a certain rate of interest, shown in phase 3 as 5%.

The local bank can now lend money to other clients, and if the interest on these loans is greater than 5%, the difference will provide an income for the local bank. There are regulations about minimum reserves that the local bank must follow, but otherwise the local bank is free to conduct its own affairs. This situation is shown in phase 4, where a possible interest rate of 9% is suggested.

Moving to phase 5, we now see this relation repeated for other local banks who are all satellites so to speak of the central bank. Thus at the hub of the monetary system there is a central bank, which sets an interest rate for loans to a wide range of financial intermediaries, who in turn set a second interest rate for everybody else. This basic arrangement is found in all capitalist countries, and a great variety of financial organisations grow within this framework. For modelling purposes we must simplify matters by including all financial intermediaries under the heading of "local banks", who in practice can charge any interest rate they like, as long as they can make an income for themselves, and still maintain their debt repayments to the central bank.

It is obvious that the central bank must not loan funds to all and sundry at the 5% rate or the position of the local banks will be undermined. The central bank stands behind the local banks so to speak, and it is the latter who supply funding for the economy at large. The interest rate set by the central bank therefore has a special significance. It dominates and controls all the other rates. In addition, the central bank can exercise its power by buying and selling financial assets of any kind, at the going rate, just like an ordinary participator in any financial market. Such open market operations can increase or reduce the total banknote value in the monetary base. A slight degree of control can also be excercised by varying the reserve requirements of the local banks. These are the basic features about banking that are found in the standard texts. We will now look at the central bank's role in more detail.

Figure 8-1

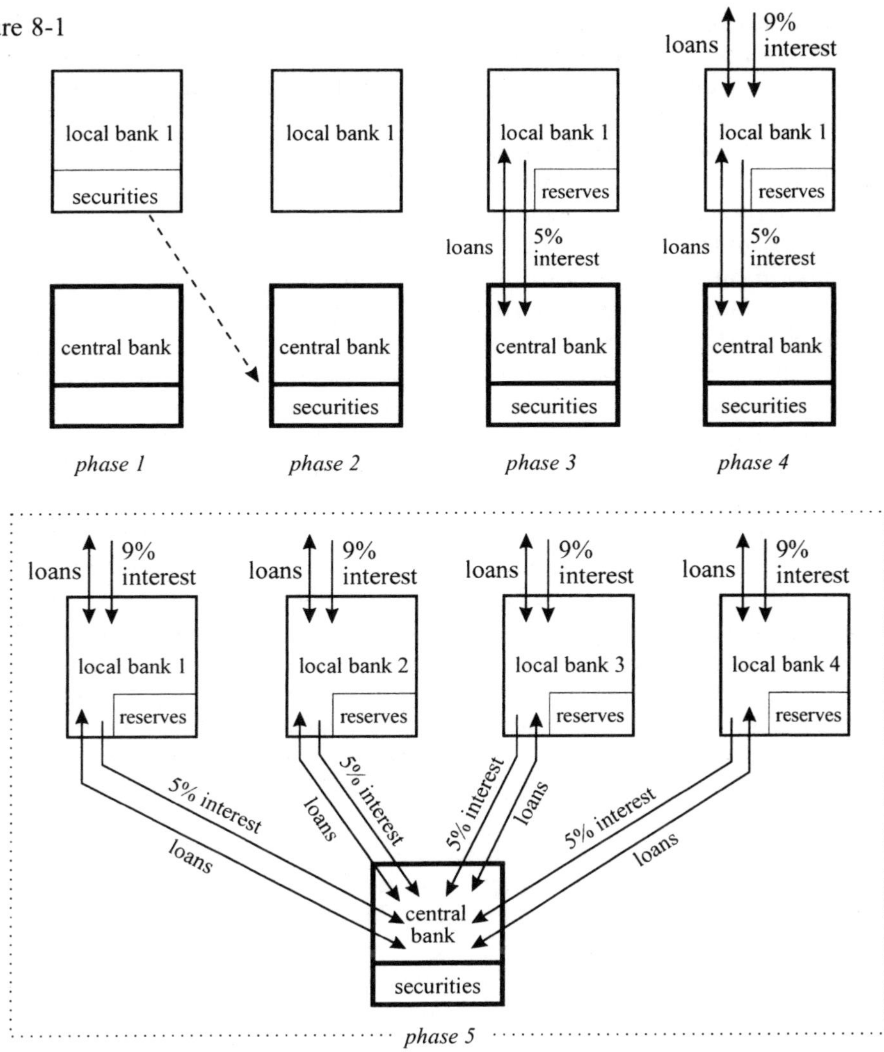

The superficial view is that the central bank provides the money that is needed for all the financial activity of the economy. Money passes from the central bank to the local bank and then to businessmen who pay wages and other costs to become the owners of commodites which are sold to obtain a revenue. From this sales revenue all costs are reimbursed and interest on loans is deducted, leaving disposable income that is spent on goods and services and so the money finds its way, together with the money-wage that the workers spend, back to the bank. The banknotes that fill the economy are busy travelling round the eddies and loops of this circuit. By adopting some hazy notion along these lines we enter a fairytale world where money is the prime mover of all things, and the first question to be answered before a pipeline is laid, or a field is sown with corn, is *where will the money come from to pay for these things?*

This question is real enough, but the fairytale world is created by ignorance. Everybody knows that for a brief moment in its life the winning ticket in a lottery is a valuable item. It has no intrinsic worth, but when the owner presents it he receives the prize-money in return, and the ticket has served its purpose and can be thrown away. Nobody attributes magic properties to the winning ticket, even though, for its owner, it embodies the power to materialise a vast sum of money. Similarly, a game of tennis is always played with a standard white ball, and the point of contact between the ball and the defined court area is the deciding factor in awarding points. But the ball is not venerated in any way, even though all eyes are fixed on it when the game is being played.

The money that threads its way through the economy likewise attracts everybody's attention but it has no magic properties. It is just an allocating device. Whoever owns a sum of money can exchange it for a proportion of the current output of goods. It passes from one owner to another for all sorts of purposes. Eventually it is exchanged for goods in the act of buying a commodity for consumption, and at that moment, for the buyer, it vanishes for good. Yet in this very same moment it is restored as money for someone else, the seller. This is the heart of the system. This is where money in the form of incomes is generated, at the goods exchange interface. Nowhere else. Money is continually flowing from the buyers of commodities to the sellers of those commodities, and the buyers and sellers are constantly change places, thereby keeping the money forever hopping between them while freshly created goods continually change owners and are consumed. The hopping backward and forward creates these owners' incomes. We already have this system up and running in our models so we already know where money incomes originate. Now we need to integrate the banking set-up displayed in Figure 8-1 into the main analysis.

The actions of the central bank seem to result in a supply of money into the economy. But a modicum of thought will confirm that any such notion is quite silly. Moneylenders do not supply money. Moneylenders are administrators of a large fund which is loaned piecemeal to various clients who, as individuals, receive big amounts that they can spend at once. But the clients themselves maintain the fund because the money flowing in, which consists of the repayment of loans plus interest, is always greater than the money flowing out, which consists solely of loans. If this differential were not present where would the income of the moneylender come from? Moneylenders enrich themselves at the expense of their clients, and banks do the same when they lend money. Any student of economics who is unaware of this fact needs to stir his or her wits, and break free from the nonsense peddled in the textbooks about a supposed "money supply". In Figure 8-1 all loans are shown with double-headed arrows because the combined effect of many loans is simply an outward flow of money that is exactly balanced by repayments of the loans. The only net movement of money is the additional interest payments from the clients to the banks.

Admittedly the banking system is more than a simple moneylending business. To investigate this process in detail we need to start from an earlier beginning. Imagine that Mr Neat and Mr Tidy are bicycle makers in an enclosed economy. Both work a ten-hour day in partnership, producing one bike a week which sells for £100. Hence the proceeds from sales is £100 a week. Costs are £40. So £60 a week is their joint weekly income, which divides into £30 each. Mr Neat then volunteers to take over entire responsibility for the business, and offers to pay Mr Tidy £30 a week for ten hours work per day. Mr Tidy agrees. They both now work hard every ten hour day and by dint of practice and ingenuity their output of bikes rises. Assuming that all other producers are also improving their productivity, we can now reason as follows.

All outputs are rising, and if the people in this community continue with their same relative preferences, happy to consume the goods they want in ever increasing quantities, bulk prices will not change. But unit prices will fall. This means that two bikes will sell for £100, and three or more bikes will sell for £100. The price of each bike will sink to £33 or less. How will Mr Neat and Mr Tidy be affected? If the intensity of work has not altered, and the working day is still ten hours as before, their standard of living in every respect will be rising. Prices are falling everywhere, and each of them has a steady income of £30 a week. The future for both of them is good. (These circumstances were portrayed earlier in Society C, Figure 6-5).

On the basis of our analysis so far, we can recognise what is missing in this economy, from Mr Neat's point of view. He would welcome a little inflation. If only someone would print banknotes to raise all bulk prices, then total bike output would sell for more than £100. If these extra banknotes were sufficient to hold unit prices steady, one bike would sell for £100, two for £200, and three bikes would sell for £300. In this last instance, he could pay Mr Tidy his usual £30 (or perhaps £40), and after deducting fixed costs of, say, £150, Mr Neat would have £120 for himself (or £110 if he raised Mr Tidy's wages). So on the one hand we have Mr Tidy who may be quite content with this arrangement because working conditions remain the same, and prices are constant, while his standard of living would continue as before, or perhaps be improved by a substantial pay rise, from £30 to £40. His future would be very satisfactory. On the other hand we have Mr Neat, whose future would be transformed.

But where will this inflation come from? A counterfeiter? Hardly. The scale of operation is too large. A steady fall in prices across the whole economy (caused by rising production rates) cannot be arrested by some furtive operation in a back street basement, though every little helps. No doubt there are many other owners of businesses in the same situation as Mr Neat. What they need is a legal, large-scale system of some kind that ensures a steady rate of inflation. (Always bear in mind the fact that "inflation" in the context of our analysis is the printing of banknotes to hold unit prices steady when they would otherwise fall in consequence of rising productivity). So let us note at this point that all employers like Mr Neat would benefit greatly from *a legal, large-scale device or manoeuvre that would automatically ensure regular inflation of the currency.*

Of course Mr Neat is not consciously aware of any such requirement. His viewpoint is simply that he could certainly use some more money to improve his manufacturing capability. He is continually replacing worn tools and installing better equipment. Perhaps he hopes to employ another workman in the future alongside himself and Mr Tidy. At present he must use his profits to pay for costs like these, and his income suffers. Why not borrow the money? He could re-equip his workshop at a stroke without touching his income. But Mr Neat is a sensible businessman. He knows he will be burdened with interest rates on any such loan, and he does not want to fall into the clutches of a moneylender. He believes in paying his way.

So Mr Neat and employers like him are not much attracted by the idea of borrowing money just to burden themselves with debts. But this reasoning is correct only for someone with a modest fixed income. If Mr Neat's income is rising, then he has more leeway. In fact, if his increase in income is sufficient to meet the interest repayments, he may as well go ahead and borrow on the strength of his rising prosperity. But as a cautious businessman, Mr Neat needs to be reasonably sure that his future income will cover the interest payments, so that the present scale of his business will not suffer, before he decides to negotiate a loan.

We can pause here for some general observations. To be dependent on a money-lender is not normally a desirable state of affairs. Such a situation may arise as a temporary expedient, but the sensible view is to avoid debts and interest payments, which are always a source of impoverishment. If this is so, then a very natural question arises. Why are the finances of great nations handled perpetually by money-lenders? Why are such debts not paid off at the earliest opportunity so that industry and commerce can proceed in the normal way under a sensible pay-as-you-go arrangement albeit with extended credit if necessary? Why is a businessman always borrowing money, always re-negotiating loans with a banker?

We have just given the answer, or so it might seem. A businessman like Mr Neat borrows money in the hope that it will improve his business and bring rising profits, which will more than compensate for the interest payments, and in this way the banker also obtains a share in these rising profits. The two tables opposite illustrate the situation. Table A shows why Mr Neat's instincts are sound when as a general rule he keeps clear of banks that want to lend him money. A loan of £200 for 9 months could be repaid in eight instalments of £25 each, with interest added at say £6 per month, leaving him with £69 per month. This means that his income, expected to be £900 over a nine-month period, would fall to £852, a loss of £48, which would pass into the hands of the money lender. But now consider Table B. Mr Neat's income is rising by roughly 2% per month and the total for nine months (income 1b) is now £972. He still surrenders £48 to the moneylender, leaving £924 for himself, but clearly this loan is quite sensible. It enables Mr Neat to re-equip his business without dipping into his income, which in fact rises from £900 (income 1a) to £924 (income 2b), and also provides an income of £48 for the lender. They both benefit. This is why the banker is needed. Mr Neat may well find this line of argument very persuasive.

But Mr Neat's viewpoint is necessarily restricted to his own circumstances. From the wider perspective of the economy as a whole, we already know two things that have great significance here. *First,* when productivity rises, goods become cheaper, but nobody's income is improved. *Second,* moneylenders do not

Table A

months	1	2	3	4	5	6	7	8	9	totals
income 1a	£100	£100	£100	£100	£100	£100	£100	£100	£100	£900
loan	**£200**									
principal		£25	£25	£25	£25	£25	£25	£25	£25	
3% interest		£6	£6	£6	£6	£6	£6	£6	£6	£48
income 2a	£300	£69	£69	£69	£69	£69	£69	£69	£69	£852

Table B

months	1	2	3	4	5	6	7	8	9	totals
income 1b	£100	£102	£104	£106	£108	£110	£112	£114	£116	£972
loan	**£200**									
principal		£25	£25	£25	£25	£25	£25	£25	£25	
3% interest		£6	£6	£6	£6	£6	£6	£6	£6	£48
income 2b	£300	£71	£73	£75	£77	£79	£81	£83	£85	£924

supply money to their clients. On the contrary, they take money away from their clients. These two truths need to be included in any responsible analysis of Mr Neat's situation when it is generalised for society as a whole.

So let us re-organise the facts to show their true causal relationships. Mr Neat's income is rising steadily because inflation is being introduced in some way. He is not responsible for this inflation and is unaware of it. It signals its presence only by the steady fall year by year in the value of money. But we noted earlier that all employers would benefit from a legal, large-scale inflation of the currency, and if this inflation is present, Mr Neat's rising income is already guaranteed. All he needs to do is sit tight and let regular doses of inflation push his profits up. He actually has no need for moneylenders who will only steal part of his income. This is quite true, but if Mr Neat sits tight and does not improve his productivity, other bicycle firms will put him out of business. The policy of just coasting along while inflation lets extra profits fall in your lap is reserved only for a firm that comprises the whole sphere of production of a given commodity. For firms that are surrounded by competitors in the same line of business, the higher productivity is part of the competitive struggle. The firm that survives has borrowed sensibly, introduced high-tech equipment, worked harder, economised more, adopted superior managerial practices and so on. This firm survives because its goods maintain a certain quality but are still the cheapest in the market. The reward for all this increased efficiency is to triumph over the competition, to be the firm that stays in business and makes higher profits. The natural conclusion is that these higher profits come from the improved efficiency. But this impression is false. Improved efficiency (as a generalised effect) merely makes goods cheaper. The higher profits come from the inflation. In other words the higher profits are already waiting for whichever firm happens to survive, because they are guaranteed in advance by the inflation that keeps unit prices constant. Competition between rival firms in the same line of business forces them to use a money-lender for rapid large-scale expansion, without having to finance this expansion from their own flow of profits. From the ordinary view, it is natural to suppose that the banker steps in to provide the necessary funds. This may be technically true for the individual firm, but the big picture is quite different. The rising prosperity that comes automatically to the employer originates in the systematic inflation, and the banker diverts a portion of this prosperity into his own pocket by lending money at interest. The employer is forced to use the moneylending facility (if he has no funds of his own) to stay ahead of competitors. This is the reality that we must examine in detail.

We can now resume the thread of our analysis. The fairytale world described at the beginning of this chapter seemed to show that money is supplied in the form of loans, which flow into the economy and are paid for by interest levied at a certain rate on the loan. There is no such flow. An accumulation of money in the hands of a potential lender is the start of the process. This money already exists in the float. It accumulates in the hands of one owner simply because it has not been spent by that owner. He has saved it (or obtained it somehow). If such savings continue to grow and lie fallow, they will become large enough to reduce the float significantly and the general price level will start to fall. (Pumping banknotes into the float sends the price level up; withdrawing money from the float in the form of a hoard sends the price level down). Long before that stage is reached, the money is available for lending. When it is loaned, it is simply transfered to a new owner, who can now spend it, and such money is no longer lying fallow. There is no mystery here, because no new money has been created. Existing money has merely passed into the hands of a borrower. If this borrower is Mr Neat he will re-equip his business and steal a march on his competitors, hoping that such action will bring higher profits. But whether Mr Neat is successful, or whether he loses out to a rival firm, the winner's higher standards of production efficiency will engender no higher profits to boost income and cover repayment debts on the loan. The winner's higher profits come from the inflation. The proof of this is displayed in Figure 6-5.

A clarification is needed at this point to avoid confusion between the narrow perspective of the firm and the holistic overview of the objective economist. There is a crucial theoretical distinction between the individual firm and the average firm. The individual firm operates in a competitive setting where gains and losses are made. But the average firm in any particular sphere of production is of course a generalisation derived from them all. Improvements in efficiency may lead to higher profits in certain cases when firms are considered in relation to each other, but these higher profits do not affect the average firm in that particular sphere. Higher profits for the average firm can come from only three sources, namely an increase in demand, a reduction in costs, (neither of which can apply here because we are holding such things constant) or from inflation of the currency, which raises the profits of all firms throughout the entire

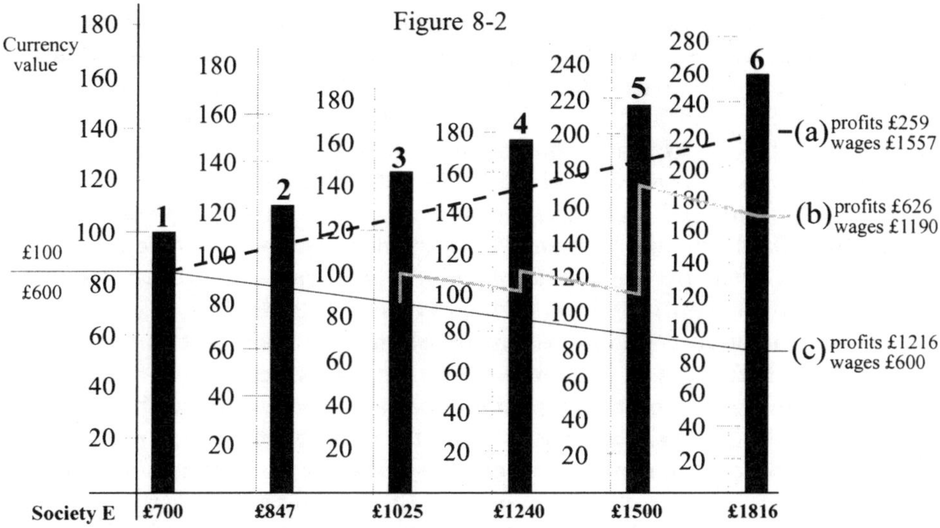

Figure 8-2

total value per day	£700	£847	£1025	£1240	£1500	£1816
float value (90 days)	£63,000	£76,230	£92,250	£111,600	£135,000	£163,440
inflation (21%)	£13,230	£16,020	£19,350	£23,400	£28,440	£34,440

economy. This latter effect is our present concern, because Mr Neat's situation corresponds to the average employer negotiating with a banker to borrow money to expand his business. If Mr Neat's efforts are successful, he will enjoy higher profits either because (a) he is more efficient than the average firm and (b) his profits are due to rise in any case as a result of inflation entering the system. We are concerned only with (b). The differentials between individual firms are self-cancelling from our standpoint of the economy as a whole.

Hence, in preparing our models for the introduction of a banking system, we need to show two quite distinct processes in action alongside each other. One of these is the lending operation, and the other is the "inflationary" operation. Figure 8-2 gives us some preliminary information about the latter. If we assume that the float is three months average income for everybody (merely to obtain a specific amount for calculation purposes) then we can state precisely how much extra value must enter the money network to produce a given rate of inflation. In the model, the real inflation rate, year by year, is 21%, and on this basis the amounts shown in the bottom row are the "inflationary increments" needed each year.

It is certainly wise for a progressive firm to borrow funds, particularly for large expenditures that would otherwise cause a big drop in current profits, with attendant damage to its market position. But there is always a risk involved, which poses a dilemma. A firm that is too cautious with its borrowing plans will lose ground against a bolder competitor. If the firm decides to go ahead and the gamble succeeds it will increase its income. But the future cannot be foreseen. Figure 8-2 shows a progression in time, displayed with hindsight so to speak. In the transition from year 1 to year 2, employer income has risen from £100 to £247, an increase of 147%. In such a case it is certainly sensible for these employers to consider borrowing money at a 9% rate of interest, or at a higher rate. But they are involved in an unfolding sequence of events that cannot be foretold, and hence they negotiate on the basis of expectation. The size of the loan, the rate of repayment and the interest levied will depend on an assessment of risk by the parties involved. The rate of interest on loans therefore is always entirely fluid. It bears no calculable relation to anything.

A newly introduced business venture cannot immediately compete with other established firms. It cannot at first meet its own costs, and is therefore dependent on a source of money that will be repaid sometime in the future, if all goes well. The banker's professional activity is to assess the future profitability of any such proposed venture, balancing risk against possible rewards, and to negotiate a deal with the client which gives them both an expectation of profit. The client cannot proceed without the banker, unless he has funds of his own. The banker cannot stay in business unless he finds clients who need to borrow money. Such collaboration throughout the entire commercial world powerfully reinforces the illusion that money is the foundation on which all economic activity depends. But the money is not the starting point for anything. We banish this illusion when we view the exploitation system in its entirety. This system allocates a portion of the proceeds of sales to the workforce as wages for time worked, leaving the remainder of the proceeds as profit, to be enhanced by systematic inflation alongside rising productivity. The central bank provides the systematic inflation, (in ways which we are about to examine), and the employer squeezes higher productivity from the workforce. In this way, the bank and the employer, (but not the workforce), both become richer by a process that stays hidden from view. This is the authentic starting point.

The true originators of all wealth in commodity form, as everyone in their right mind knows, are the organised groups of working people whose labour produces an ever-increasing flow of products for markets throughout the world. Such wealth is not brought into existence by negotiations with a banker. The banker's signature on a cheque for say a million dollars *must* acquire its exalted status from a linkage of some kind between the banker and the true originators of wealth, and the object of intelligent inquiry is to lay bare the nature of this linkage, in other words, to explain how the former is able to congeal in a signature the wealth created by the latter. But this line of inquiry is nowhere in evidence, least of all in the standard textbooks. The widely disseminated view is that money itself possesses a sort of power, that it can be "invested" to generate a yield of some sort, that it can be a creator of wealth in its own right, and this seems to be what the banker himself believes, because he certainly wants everybody else to believe it. Such belief means that intelligent inquiry is abandoned and mere appearance is taken for the truth. But this is not of course an abandonment of intelligence by the banker, as it is for everybody else. The banker has good reason to keep the truth hidden.

9

The banking system: part 2

It is important to trace the origin and destination of all monies, to counteract the deep-rooted illusion that money is a free agent with magical properties of its own. Mr Neat's basic situation is that he must pay a wage of £30 per week to Mr Tidy, and meet all other costs as well, out of his gross revenue. But he is now quite happy to meet all costs including the wage by borrowing the money required, and then paying the agreed interest on the loan by regular deductions from his sales revenue. This interest is a transfer of income from Mr Neat's firm to the lender. But note that this money is only a transfer, it already exists as part of the system, and it stays inside the system because it is merely spent by whoever makes the loan instead of being spent by Mr Neat.

The central bank and all other financial intermediaries earn the money to pay their own wages, salaries and profits from the interest payments that they collect as a money-lending institutions. This money comes from the commodity-producing firms who have taken out the loans. As just stated, the firms that make these interest payments do so by deductions from their sales revenue, so this money is at all times part of the existing price network.

The money for the loan is also part of the existing price network. It has been saved by the lender and is spent by the borrower. The entire loan-and-interest package is a mere transfer of existing money between different owners. No additional money is supplied from out of the blue by these operations. There is no miraculous expansion of money. A large quantity is acquired all at once by the borrower, and is then paid back in small amounts, while interest so-called is deducted from gross sales to pay for this service. The interest therefore has no necessary connection with the size of the loan. The interest is simply payment for a service. Someone (the lender) has abstained from spending, thereby accumulating a quantity of money, which has passed into the hands of someone else (the borrower) who spends it. Both the loan and the interest payments consist of money that is generated at the goods exchange interface and is returned to the interface. There are no leaks and no injections. Money unspent by one owner is spent by another.

Of course the lending operation itself suggests otherwise. The superficial appearance implies a linear progression, with an entry point for the money and a process that terminates in more money. To the ordinary view (and according to the text-books) Mr Neat is borrowing funds, at say 9%, to meet all his business costs. He uses these funds to pay wages and perhaps everything else. Then his workers set to work, making goods that sell for a profit. Out of this profit comes a debt repayment with added interest at 9% and the rest belongs to Mr Neat, who has taken on this debt and its risks and is entitled to his rewards as a successful entrepreneur and job provider, helped of course by whoever loaned the funds. In orthodox parlance Mr Neat and his banker are "wealth creators", who start with a certain quantity of money, spend it in all directions to get the production process rolling, and end up with commodities that can be sold for a greater quantity of money than they started with, sufficient to recompense them for all the money spent, settle any debts, and still leave them with a surplus in the form of profits. The truth is quite different. The wealth is created by a group of working people who produce a quantity of commodities which are then sold, at a particular bulk price in the market. This bulk price provides an income which is split into two portions, one for the workforce, as a wage for time worked, and the remainder for the employer. The borrowed money enables the firm to operate on an extended scale, producing more goods in a shorter time. The only direct effect of this heightened production rate is to lower prices, but inflation, entering the system from somewhere else, prevents prices from falling, with the result that profits rise, making the employer much richer and the workers relatively much poorer. Out of these new riches, the employer deducts repayments to the lender, called interest.

We can therefore distinguish two types of capitalist whose incomes are derived from the exploitation system. These are the industrial capitalist who is typically the owner/employer, and who extracts profits from his own firm, and the financial capitalist who lives on interest extracted from the profits of the industrial capitalist. They work hand in glove to gather all the increase in value that corresponds to increased output. But it is necessary to add that they may well not understand the exploitation process that they benefit from, because they are not the source of the inflation that the exploitation depends on, and in any case all or most of this inflation is hidden from sight by the false assumption that constant prices denote normality.

The loan package negotiated by the employer seems to be an essential component of the firm's rising prosperity, and in a sense this is true, but only because the loan acts as a carrier so to speak for the interest. The loans are made by a huge range of financial intermediaries, many of which have no particular ties with the central bank, but simply use their own funds to lend money and obtain an income from interest payments. But all these money-lenders depend on a regular injection of money into the float to prevent prices from falling as output increases. Hence in all capitalist countries there is an association of large banks with one powerful bank at the centre, and this central bank has two exclusive features. It can print currency, and it can write cheques against itself. By open market operations this central bank can also buy and sell high value securities as it considers necessary. If, when buying, it uses accumulated reserves of banknotes acquired from earlier sales, there is no long-term change in the total money stock and no long-term inflation. Money that is injected or withdrawn in this way produces temporary changes in the float which raise or reduce the general price level. But if the central bank uses its power to issue self-cancelling cheques that in effect are drawn on nobody, then the currency is inflated permanently. New deposit accounts that are created in this way (when such cheques are presented at the banks) eventually result in a raised demand for bank-notes as the new money finds its way to normal retailing levels. (This raised demand reduces the stocks of notes in the banks, an outcome we will examine at a later stage).

The power of the central bank to control inflation appeared when banknotes ceased to be convertible. Prior to that time, the central bank had no such power. The price network was controlled by a physical money commodity, namely gold, and the production rate of gold was the pivot round which bulk prices rose and fell for all commodities. The float consisted of a quantity of gold, kept on standby for all buying requirements, just as we have described for a paper-based economy. Gold entered the system freely from the very mines themselves. Banks had no control over this process. In fact as described in Chapter 3, the banks were helpless victims of the instability that is inherent in any economy based on a physical money-commodity. Controlled inflation of a paper currency is impossible while that paper currency is convertible. Printing redeemable banknotes in a gold-based economy leads to one of three outcomes. Briefly, either the banknote issue ceases at a certain point and the notes are withdrawn in return for full or part value, or the notes steadily devalue by general repudiation and become worthless, or the issuing bank is destroyed, as they were in their thousands in the United States during the Great Depression. But from the moment that banknotes are declared inconvertible by law, controlled inflation by the printing of banknotes becomes possible.

Does this mean that inflation is impossible when a "gold standard" is in operation? Strictly speaking, the answer is yes. The physical output of gold from the mines dictates the behaviour of the general price level. But there is a source of inflation which arises simply from the continual improvement in banking efficiency in its widest sense. Any procedure that economises in the use of gold (or banknotes) by avoiding transfers that are mutually self-cancelling, and any form of certification that is accepted as a substitute for gold in circumstances where gold was formerly required as a guarantee of value, reduces the need for pecuniary accommodation. The gold (or money in the form of banknotes) that is thereby "released " from standby duties is surplus to the requirements of the float. The effect of any such surplus is to raise the general price level, just as if the gold had come out of a gold mine, (or new banknotes had been printed). The cheque system is one obvious example of an efficiency innovation that reduces the need for money as a physical presence. Throughout the 19th and 20th centuries, the float has steadily decreased from these causes, resulting in a general upward trend in the price level. To be precise, this upward trend of prices in a gold-based economy necessarily reduces the price of gold at the same time, and its consumption as a commodity therefore increases. This removes gold from the float (by increased consumption) as fast as it becomes surplus to the float (by improvements in banking efficiency) so the general price level is not permanently disturbed and would cause no

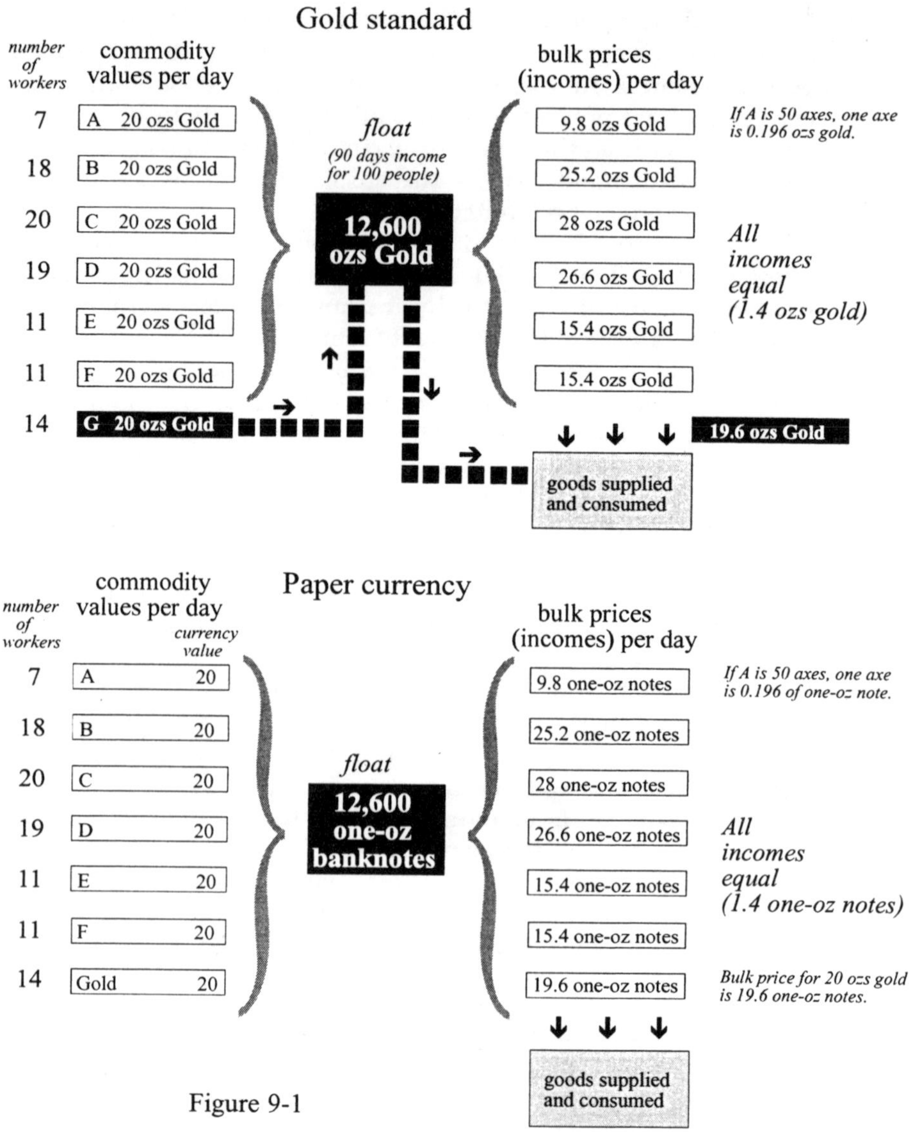

Figure 9-1

fluctuation at all but for inevitable time lags. In this way, gold remains "in charge" of prices so to speak, and inflation from improvements in banking efficiency is never more than a temporary rise and fall about a central position. But with a paper-based economy, extra banknotes always raise prices to a new level which is stable in its own right. When the gold standard was abandoned in the 1920s and 30s, improvements in banking efficiency thereafter produced a regular general upward trend in the price level that had not been present during the reign of gold.

But whether a general upward trend reveals itself as such is dependent on other trends that may be operating at the same time. We already know that unit

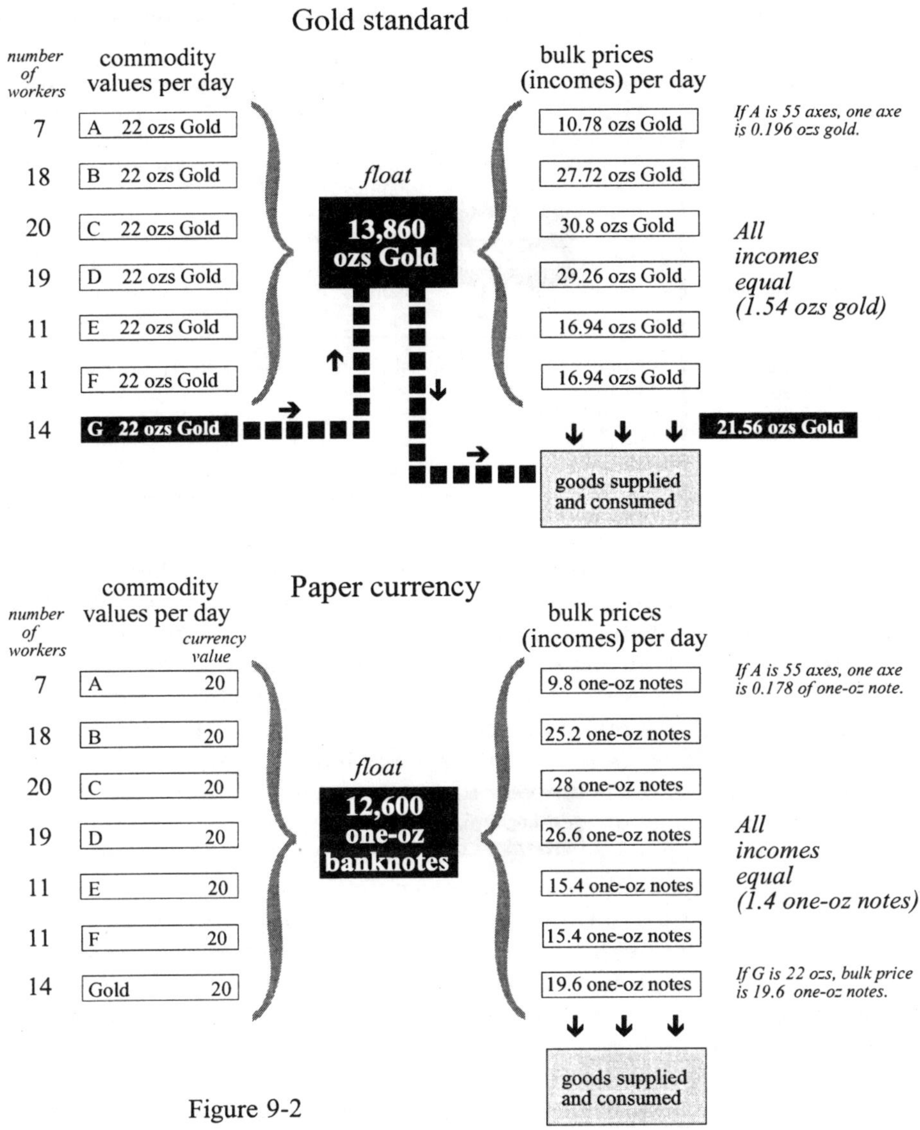

Figure 9-2

prices stay constant in a gold-based economy, as general output rises, but in an inconvertible paper economy the unit price level falls as output rises. Thus, a condition of steady prices in a paper-based economy does not imply an absence of inflation. On the contrary, inflation *must* be present if prices stay constant while output is rising. We need to pause therefore at this stage, to gather together these various aspects of the phenomenon known as inflation, and make sure we understand it properly. Figure 9-1 shows how gold behaves compared with a paper currency, at a given level of output in the type of community we have studied so far. Gold flows continuously into the float and is continuously consumed as a commodity. A constant quantity is thereby

Figure 9-3	Gold alone as money	Gold plus convertible banknotes	Inconvertible banknotes
Gold output rising steadily. All other outputs constant.	**1** Prices rise. Incomes rise. (Minting gold coins is profitable).	**2** All prices rise but gold price in banknotes falls. Incomes rise. (Banks prosper).	**3** All prices constant. Gold price falls. Incomes constant (including gold producer).
All outputs rising steadily including gold.	**4** Prices constant. Incomes rise.	**5** Prices constant. Incomes rise.	**6** All prices fall. Incomes constant.
Gold output constant. All other outputs rising steadily.	**7** Prices fall. Incomes constant. (Melting down gold coins is profitable).	**8** All prices fall but gold price in banknotes rises. Incomes constant. (Banks fail).	**9** All prices fall. Gold price constant. Incomes constant (including gold producer).

maintained in the float which regulates the supply of gold-as-money within the community. (Note the discrepancy which is always present when money is a physical commodity and is therefore required to express its own price). At the prices shown, demand and supply are in balance for all commodities, because incomes are equal. Unit prices are not specified (except as an example for commodity A) because we do not know the actual production rates.

If gold were replaced instantaneously by a non-convertible paper currency, the situation would be as shown in the lower half of Figure 9-1. There is no change whatever. Of course in real life, the change to paper, even if it were instantaneous throughout society, would not produce a paper float that was an exact counterpart of the gold float. During the gold-based period a steady stream of convertible bank-notes has been entering the system and successive crises and devaluations have brought about a wide divergence of the paper currency from its face-value correspondence with gold. But we neglect this technicality because it has no bearing on our present analysis. We may therefore say, at present, that the only change in moving to paper from gold is the substitution of an inconvertible certificate in place of the physical entity.

But Figure 9-2 reveals that this change which appears to be so slight has in fact far-reaching consequences. A general increase of 10% in output for all commodities has been introduced and we can see how a gold-based currency reacts to improved production compared with a paper-based version. Incomes rise and unit prices stay constant in a gold-based regime. But incomes stay constant and unit prices fall in a paper-based economy. The float in a paper economy is not affected by changes in output. It responds to only two influences, namely, the need for accommodation and the introduction of superfluous notes. These latter come from a printing press or from some other source.

Prior to the 1930s, the leading capitalist nations operated a gold-based system which automatically ensured a general rise in incomes, as long as there was a steady rise in gold output as part of a general improvement in productivity throughout industry as a whole. In these circumstances, the standard of living improves for society in general, in the form of rising incomes alongside constant prices, as illustrated by comparing Figure 9-1 and Figure 9-2. But the situation is different after the 1930s, when the leading nations left the gold standard. Improvements in productivity still implied a rise in living standards for the community in general, but in a paper economy the float stays constant, incomes stay constant, and unit prices fall, as Figures 9-1 and 9-2 indicate. The only counterbalance to falling prices in a paper-based currency system is the steady reduction in the need for pecuniary accommodation, the effect of which is to push prices up as the required float level shrinks. Thus when peacetime normality was resumed after the second world war, the leading capitalist nations had to operate their financial affairs on a different footing. A regular source of inflation was now needed. Otherwise prices would fall, and the profit-making mechanism would no longer deliver steadily expanding profits.

This regular source of inflation can be provided by the surplus banknotes that are squeezed out of the financial network by more efficient operations. But let us set this effect on one side for the moment, and concentrate on the basic determinants of the price level as summarised in Figure 9-3. Each numbered compartments describes a possible arrangement of our model community. We will refer to them as Models.

All the information in Figure 9-3 can be verified by suitable adaptation of Figures 9-1 and 9-2, which, as they stand at present, illustrate the middle row of the table opposite, specifically Model 4 for a gold-based system and Model 6 for a paper-money system. With different data the other numbered models can be represented. Moving from the middle column to the right-hand column is analagous to the changeover from gold to paper in the 1920s or 30s.

Figure 9-3 may be easier to follow if we set out the basic principles involved. Manipulating each variable in isolation (while other variables are constant) produces the following effects:

In a gold standard economy

If gold output rises, incomes increase and prices rise.
If gold output is constant, incomes are constant and prices are constant.
If gold output falls, incomes fall and prices fall.
If other outputs rise, unit prices fall. No effect on incomes.
If other outputs are constant, unit prices are constant. No effect on incomes.

In an inconvertible paper-money economy

If gold output rises, gold price falls. No effect on incomes or prices.
If gold output is constant, gold price is constant. No effect on incomes or prices.
If other outputs rise, unit prices fall. No effect on incomes.
If other outputs are constant, unit prices are constant. No effect on incomes.

The combined effect of gold output and commodity outputs varying together can be judged from the above lists, and checked against Figure 9-3. These effects can never be observed in practice as they are shown here, namely as isolated phenomena, because changes in output alter the demand pattern of society and an entirely separate sequence of price and income adjustments is set in motion simultaneously. But we are holding the demand pattern constant so that distribution of the workforce is not disturbed.

The point we have reached in our analysis is represented by Model 5 and Model 6 in Figure 9-3. In Model 5 prices stay constant and incomes rise. These are the circumstances in which a wage for time worked, deducted from bulk sales, will stay constant, while the remainder called profit will rise steadily, because such profit contains all the increased value from rising productivity. The wage-worker is here a victim of fraud. No inflation is needed to bring about this effect. It is a natural outcome arising inevitably from the fact that the output of a physical money-commodity is steadily increasing. But in Model 6 this natural effect is absent. A wage paid for time worked does not in itself mean that the worker is being defrauded. Inflation must be injected into the system to produce this effect. Thus prior to the 1930s, the capitalist system could plausibly be defended as part of a natural order in which exploitation (if such a word were justified) was inherent and therefore inevitable, with personal consequences that could be described as a kind of social darwinism. But after the Second World War, the capitalist system became a managed arrangement susceptible to manipulation by the central bank in order to maintain the fraudulent basis of profit-making. Such intervention demolishes the argument that profit-making is part of a natural economic order. All that now keeps the capitalist system alive is the hidden inflation that prevents unit prices from falling in response to rising productivity, and the marginalist drivel in the text-books, which prevents the mass of the population from understanding their own economic relationships.

The bare essentials of the banking system are relatively simple. Money-lending never creates money. It is an operation that simply moves money from one owner to another, just like a gift. If I lend £100 and it is paid back in five instalments of £20 each, then a debt was created and discharged. But no money was created. If I lend £100 and it is paid back with added interest, then a debt was created and paid back and I acquired an extra sum which someone else, the borrower, forfeited from his own assets. Again no money was created. But when money is transferred in this way, to create a debt between different owners, it can appear to grow (or diminish) if a time period intervenes during which the value of money changes. For example, I may lend £100 to someone who buys a diamond ring worth £100. Suppose then that money falls to half its value and the ring is sold for £200, its true worth, and my loan is returned together with an interest of £50. I now have £150 and the borrower has £50. The loan appears to be responsible for the creation of new money, because the original £100 which I loaned has come back to me with an added £50, and the borrower is also better off by £50. Without the loan the borrower could not have bought the ring, nor subsequently have sold it with a gain of £100. Without the loan I could not have acquired the extra £50 derived from this gain.

Nobody who examines this situation is misled by such superficial reasoning. The gain of £100 comes not from the selling of the ring, nor from the loan transaction, but from the fact that non-money assets such as the ring appreciate in value if the value of money falls. There is no net gain or loss for society as a whole because the asset owner's gain and the money-owner's loss necessarily cancel each other.

If loans cannot in themselves provide a source of increasing value, how does a banker cooperate with a capitalist employer to make them both rich? We have already covered this ground. The banker lends money to the capitalist who buys a valuable asset, not a diamond ring as in the above example, but a team of workers who produce commodities. These workers are paid for their labour-time at the going rate. The employer manages the enterprise while the banker supplies the cash. The workforce of a capitalist commodity-producing society is typically employed in such an arrangement, producing goods in ever increasing quantities and as a result the unit price of these goods is bound to fall as the supply increases, other factors remaining constant. But other factors are not constant. The value of money is steadily falling as the central bank injects banknotes into the float. So the trend of falling unit prices is prevented. Prices stay constant (or perhaps rise). Wages stay constant. Profits soar. The employer discharges the loan, plus interest, and the magical transformation of money into more money is accomplished by two apparently clever people, the capitalist owner and the banker. This conjuring trick works because everyone's eyes are fixed on the money earned by the firm and the banker. Nobody pays any attention to the role of the central bank. The increasing stream of commodities produced by the workforce are assets that rise in value relative to the depreciating currency. Output and bulk value rise together, instead of output rising against a bulk value which stays constant, while unit prices fall. Ten carrots per hour worth 10p become twenty carrots per hour (because productivity has doubled) worth 20p (because the value of money has halved). If the carrot producer is paid 10p an hour, a surplus of 10p accrues to whoever sells the carrots for 20p. But this surplus of 10p comes from the inflation, which has pushed the price of 20 half-penny carrots back to one penny each. The carrots sell all the time at one penny each not because their price is unchanged, but because during the period when output increased from 10 to 20 carrots an hour, the value of money fell by one half.

The increased value arising from the inflation requires a time interval to produce its effects, and the presence of the banker is required not to supply funds as such but to circumvent the time interval and thereby obtain a competitive advantage. To the superficial view the banker appears to perform a miracle, by making funds of the future available today. In a sense this is true, because it is through the banker's activity that a society based apparently on individual self-interest finds a way to abstain from present enjoyment and engage in productive activity which will bear fruit in the future. The banker claims to be the means through which this "investment" process is made possible, because whoever lends money has clearly abstained from spending it on present enjoyment. But when the whole process is unravelled, the banker's claim is shown to be false. A capitalist society is not based on individual self-interest. It is an exploitation system based on class interest. Self-interest is promoted for one group but not for another. The banking system is certainly the means through which present enjoyment is sacrificed in order to release funding for investment purposes. But the sacrifice of present enjoyment is borne by the wage-earner. All our analysis so far, and the carrot illustration above, make this plain. The wage earner continues to buy carrots at one penny each and his wage has not changed. So he notices nothing and his standard of living remains steady. But carrot productivity has doubled, and the monetary value of this improvement passes exclusively into the employer's pocket.

However, the above analysis needs an important modification to accommodate the inflationary effect that arises from efficiency improvements that are constantly being introduced into the banking system itself, an effect that we temporarily set on one side (page 97). As already explained, this inflationary effect does not appear until inconvertible paper money takes the place of gold. We may therefore state that the various numbered Models in the first and second columns of Figure 9-3 are historically accurate. In other words, Models 1, 4 and 7, and Models 2, 5 and 8, display conditions that correspond in broad terms to real developmental stages in the growth of a money-based society. But Models 3, 6 and 9 are not accurate in this sense. Three related factors need to be introduced. The first, as just stated, is the inflation caused by more efficient monetary procedures. The second new factor is that inflation from some quarter is now essential to keep the profit-making machinery in operation. Such inflation was not needed during the gold-based period. The third new factor is that the central bank now acquires an importance in respect of inflation that it did not formerly possess.

We accommodate these three new factors, which affect only Models 3, 6 and 9, in Figure 9-4. Inflation caused by efficiency improvements has been introduced in column 2. But this effect is impossible to measure in any way. It may be large or small. So we have assumed that it is sufficient to counteract the tendency for prices to fall as a result of rising productivity. In fact, we face the same dilemma as the central bank when we try to estimate the magnitude of this effect. For instance, Model 6, in the first column, shows prices falling and incomes constant, but nobody knows in advance how much output will rise and nobody knows how much inflation will enter the price system as a result of efficiency improvements. By assuming that these two effects counterbalance each other, we can specify that the outcome will be as shown in column 2, but this outcome is only one of several possibilities. Nevertheless the illustrations in column 2 are historically sound, because they are developmental stages that correspond to reality, either as they stand, or with simple modifications which we can now describe.

The outcomes in respect of gold are no longer important because we are in a paper-based economy. Gold is present here just to maintain continuity with the previous Figure 9-3. It serves as an example for any commodity that may behave differently from the rest, but otherwise gold can be ignored. So for our present purposes, there is no distinction between Model 6 and Model 9. The matter in hand is the presence of inflation in the price network. We want to know where it originates from, how large it is, and what effects it produces.

Figure 9-4	*column 1* Inconvertible banknotes	*column 2* Inflation entering from somewhere	***Comments on column 2***
Gold output rising steadily. All other outputs constant.	**3** All prices constant. Gold price falls. Incomes constant (including gold producer).	Prices rise. Gold price constant. All incomes rise.	***Inflation is visibly present in the general price rise, but not visible in respect of gold.***
All outputs rising steadily including gold.	**6** All prices fall. Incomes constant.	All prices constant. All incomes rise.	***Inflation is completely hidden.***
Gold output constant. All other outputs rising steadily.	**9** All prices fall. Gold price constant. Incomes constant (including gold producer).	All prices constant. Gold price rises. All incomes rise.	***Inflation is completely hidden, except for gold.***

Each numbered Model in Figure 9-4 now has two versions, column 1 and column 2. Column 1 supposes no inflation (extra banknotes) from anywhere, while column 2 supposes that extra banknotes are entering the system. The ideal situation for a capitalist economy is represented by Model 6 in the column 2 version. Assuming that general output is rising steadily, then if the inflation necessary to move Model 6 from column 1 to column 2 comes from efficiency improvements alone, (as assumed in Figure 9-4) the central bank has no role to play in the profit-making mechanism. Wages will stand still, unit prices will remain constant, and profits will grow, as if by a pre-ordained natural order. If the inflation from efficiency improvements falls short of this necessary level, there is a role for the central bank, to make up the deficit by injecting some extra inflation. If it does so with moderate accuracy, the outcome will be effectively as shown in Figure 9-4. Hence, the role for the central bank is, in essence, to top up the inflation caused by efficiency improvements, or, when this inflation is too great, to reduce it. In other words, the bank must keep a watching brief on the rate of inflation and keep it in step with rising output. Note that inflation must be present to maintain a steadily rising rate of profit. In Model 3 for example, wages and profits stay constant unless inflation brings about a move from column 1 to column 2. This move creates a set of circumstances in which money wages will fall in real terms while profits grow. But unit prices rise steeply from such inflation when there is no productivity rise to hold them in check. Rapidly rising prices are harmful to all classes, though in different ways. In these circumstances it may appear to the onlooker that the central bank should act to reduce inflation by (say) selling securities. But such action is contrary to its basic aim, which is to boost profit-making. This aim is ideally realised when two conditions are present simultaneously, namely, rising productivity and a compensating rate of inflation which holds unit prices constant. If productivity stays constant for whatever reason, inflation will certainly boost profits but such inflation is plain for all to see in the escalating prices which the central bank is expected to control. The central bank is hamstrung in these circumstances. But if rising output is present, the bank can act to curb excessive inflation, (resulting from its own earlier misjudgements or from efficiency improvements) by, say, selling securities. Hence, any competent interpretation of rising prices, when such rise takes the form of an overall general trend, must be based on a critical judgement whether (1) production is no longer increasing but inflation is entering the system from somewhere (2) production is rising but the needful inflation to hold prices steady is being exceeded. Model 3, column 2 in Figure 9-4 illustrates the first case, and Model 6, column 2 illustrates the second case, if we assume that the inflation is excessive. In the first case the central bank is in an insoluble dilemma. In the second case it can act to reduce the inflation. By contrast, where output is rising, but inflation is absent or too small to prevent prices from falling, the central bank can always act to increase the inflation to its "proper" level, by, say, entering the open market to buy securities. Seeing that the central bank's role is to increase the deficit or reduce the excess in respect of an inflation rate that may or may not be forthcoming from efficiency improvements, and that if and when such inflation does appear the deficit or excess to be corrected depends on rising production rates that are similarly unpredictable, it is little wonder that the central bank has no clearly stated policy and merely awaits events with a kind of stoic calm, easily mistaken for inscrutable wisdom. No criticism is implied by such a description. For most of the period after the second world war till recently, this has been the reality of the situation, as far as control of inflation is concerned.

In Figure 8-2 we tabulated the inflationary increments necessary to maintain a thriving capitalist society in which profit-making is very successful, but which suffers from a high perceived inflation rate of 11% per year. We have explained how this state of affairs may arise, and the options open to the central bank to reduce this level of inflation, if it should wish to do so. All that remains at this stage is to show how the financial capitalist fits into such a society. There is no need to alter the diagram in any way, to show transfers of money. The banker is simply a money-lender, parasitic on the industrial capitalist, but justifying his role by enabling the latter, his client, to stay ahead of competition from other firms, and acquire an advantage that is inherent in borrowing when prices rise through inflation. Figure 9-5 therefore, as it stands, is all that is necessary to illustrate the two essential elements of the banking system, the inflation that has both hidden and visible components, and the lending operation that is always beneficial to any employer at any time during the six years.

The details of the lending operation can be explored using a realistic example. There are seven different firms in Figure 9-5, but the same argument applies to them all, so we can treat them as if they were combined into just one composite owner. At the start of year 1, this capitalist owner pays wages of £600 per day and receives a total sales revenue of £700 per day, leaving £100 daily for himself. He wishes to expand. His proposed scheme is to build new premises and install new equipment, an operation estimated to take one month. His total

Figure 9-5

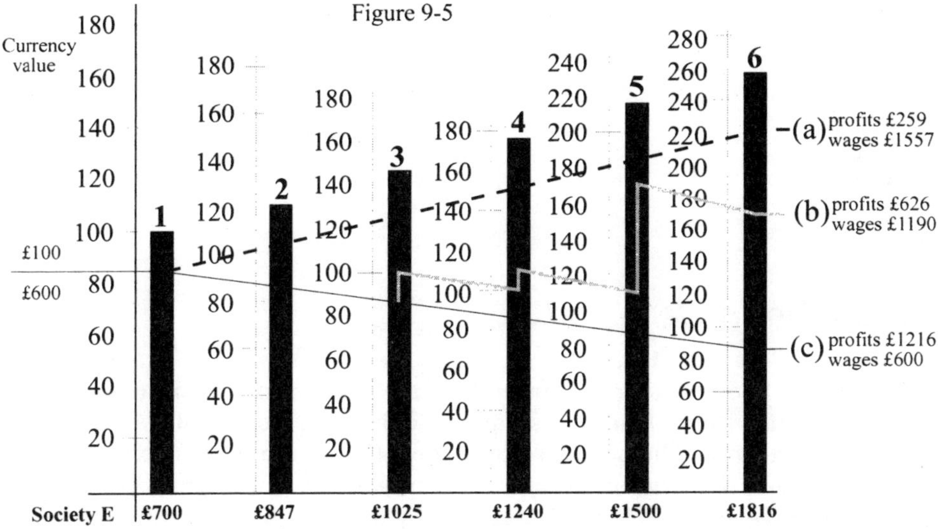

total value per day	**£700**	**£847**	**£1025**	**£1240**	**£1500**	**£1816**
float value (90 days)	**£63,000**	**£76,230**	**£92,250**	**£111,600**	**£135,000**	**£163,440**
inflation (21%)	**£13,230**	**£16,020**	**£19,350**	**£23,400**	**£28,440**	**£34,440**

income during this first year will grow from £100 per day to £247 per day. So his entire year's income will be notionally £173.50 multiplied by 365 = £63,327. Perhaps the proposed scheme will cost £20,000. Should he wait till he can save this sum, at a rate of say £1667 a month for twelve months, or borrow the money, commit himself to monthly repayments, and start his project at once? A loan at 9% over a year will raise total cost to £21,800, to be repaid in 12 monthly instalments of £1817. His year's income will be reduced by £20,000 if he saves, but the reduction will be £21,800 if he borrows. Why should he forfeit this extra £1800? For two reasons. First, to keep his firm ahead of competitors. Second, the value of money is falling, and hence if he waits for a year, the cost of his project will rise from £20,000 to £22,000. For these reasons, it is sensible for him to join forces with a banker, and allow the latter to share some of his rising income.

This clarifies the role of the banker, but leaves us with a problem. Efficiency improvements in the banking system reduce the size of the necessary float. Our diagrams show no such thing. Inflation is making the the float get bigger and bigger. This apparent anomaly needs to be explained.

10

The banking system: part 3

According to our analysis so far, efficiency improvements in the monetary system inevitably lead to a smaller and smaller float. This is consistent with historical data. The pay packets that contained real banknotes and coin, and which were distributed every Friday to workers throughout the land in times past have long ago been superseded by pay slips that merely record the details of payments made into bank accounts. Cheque books are now in use everywhere. Even in day to day retailing, a banker's card is increasingly being used for relatively small sums in place of banknotes and coin, and in all financial institutions computerised processing has streamlined monetary transactions in a multitude of ways. The result has been a massive reduction in the use of "real money" during this last half-century. In order to understand the significance of this change we need to recall an illustration used earlier in our analysis.

We imagined a situation where all producers sat in a circle and, one after another, distributed their goods round the circle. Everybody had a store of money, which was augmented when they travelled round the circle as a distributing producer or seller, but which was depleted when they sat as buyers while someone else travelled round the circle. Although everybody's store of money was increased by a sale and diminished by a purchase, a steady quantity of money remained in everybody's possession, since no money can ever go astray by such mutual trading. The prices at which goods change hands may vary, but such variations are bound to be self-compensating. The money in the group regularly buys the goods on offer at the rate at which they are being supplied. This mental picture enables us to visualise a group of producers who are their own buyers and sellers. In other words we are visualising an elementary closed economy, and everything must be explained from this starting point.

Now we need to introduce the notion of a float. As formerly explained, this float must be large enough to liberate these producer/consumers from rigid sequential dependence on each other. Nobody need wait for a sale in order to buy. The float introduces a leeway or breathing space that allows short or long intervals of time between individual buying decisions. This leeway, in conjunction with reserve stocks that the sellers carry, enables the production cycle and the consumption cycle to proceed in tandem, the former setting its own rate of progress and the latter keeping in step as an aggregated response, all the while leaving individuals free to buy as they please without cash flow problems, within reasonable limits. We have suggested that a float consisting of three months average income for everybody is a plausible assumption in the model societies we have constructed.

The next step is to introduce a banker into our circle of producer/consumers, not in the role of a money-lender, but in the important social role of manager of the float. We have tacitly assumed so far that everybody's float is in their personal possession, carried in pocket or purse or kept in a till or cash box or some secure place at home or in supervised premises. But now let us assume that everyone in our circle of producer/consumers hands over their reserve of three month's income to a trusted individual for safe keeping, on the understanding that money can be withdrawn for spending purposes as and when necessary. We now have a banker whose clients have their own deposit accounts. When banks appear in this role, as managers of the float for the whole community, the float acquires a second identity so to speak. It still continues in essential existence as the float, but its tangible form becomes a monetary base in the care of the banker.

The trusted individual, or banker, will possess at first a relatively large sum that can be defined quite specifically as the float. But the banker does not need all this money to meet his obligations to clients who from time to time draw money out of their account or put money in. A much smaller quantity will serve, and it is this smaller quantity which henceforth distinguishes itself as the monetary base. The banker can spend the surplus, (we will reconsider this later) which is obviously the difference between the float and the monetary base. If he does so, his spending will have an inflationary effect. The price level will rise. Such money, once spent, vanishes into the float. From then on, there will be two important determinants of the quantity of money circulating in the economy. One of these is the float, but it now appears in the form of savings, which is the quantity of money that people choose not to spend at present, but to keep in reserve. This is exactly the same as our old definition of the float, but in this form, as explained earlier (Chapter 7) it is fictitious. The other is the monetary base, which consists of real banknotes and coin. Whoever needs cash to buy something, obtains money in notes from their bank account, and when such cash is spent it passes into the hands of a seller, who returns the cash to the bank, possibly within a day, where it is ready to be used by somebody else who wants cash. Thus the same cash, which may for example be only £100, is in sequential use for a never-ending stream of people whose rate of spending may be £1000 a month. From the point of view of the account holders, the bank seems to be supplying this £1000 every month, from their respective deposit accounts. But it is only supplying the same £100 every two or three days. The fact that a small monetary base can sustain a much larger float introduces a new concept called *the velocity of the currency*. This concept is quite simple. With a float of £1000, the monetary base could be £500, or £100, or £50. The velocity would be 2, or 10, or 20, and so on.

This division of the float into a fictitious form (which is still present as an operational determinant) and a real monetary base which sustains the float in practice, appears when local banks take on the role of managers of the float for society as a whole. The "efficiency improvements" that were discussed in the last chapter continually reduce the size of the monetary base. A smaller monetary base is not harmful in any way, but the cash that becomes surplus whenever the monetary base shrinks has an inflationary effect on the price level. Hence Figure 9-5, which tells us a lot about the expansion of the float, gives us no information at all about the monetary base. The latter may indeed be steadily shrinking, but if so, all we can say at this stage is that some of the inflation shown will be attributable to the surplus squeezed out of the float by such shrinkage. The efficiency improvements may be uneven, in which case the inflationary effect will be present in some years but not at other times. The inflationary effect may even be present but hidden for a while, because extra banknotes, whether originating from a printing press or from a shrinking monetary base, can be absorbed by the float with no change in prices if society as a whole is increasing its level of savings at the same time.

The actual amount of money that the banker handles may diminish more than usual when several clients want large sums simultaneously. A generous reserve is therefore needed to meet such emergencies. But this money always comes back, so in the long run, the grand total never gets bigger or smaller. It just travels in small portions out of the bank and back again, from one person's account to another. In fact, if the clients use cheques for all their purchases, no money need ever leave the banker's premises. He just receives signed cheques every day and adjusts his clients' accounts accordingly.

But the float remains exactly the same as it was, and continues to function as normal regardless of whether the monetary base is large or small. The average person in our closed economy has deposited (and regularly maintains) three month's income with the banker, and this determines the leeway within which the community's average spending power must be confined. More importantly, the incomes that people earn are unaffected by the presence of a monetary base. Substitution of cheques for money has no effect whatever on the operation of the price network, as long as a banker is supervising the float in the form of deposit accounts. Nobody can spend beyond their income. The

Figure 10-1

	1	2	3	4	5	6
total value per day	£700	£847	£1025	£1240	£1500	£1816
float value (90 days)	£63,000	£76,230	£92,250	£111,600	£135,000	£163,440
inflation (21%)	£13,230	£16,020	£19,350	£23,400	£28,440	£34,440
velocity of currency	× 6	× 7	× 8	× 9	× 10	× 11
monetary base	£10,500	£10,890	£11,531	£12,400	£13,500	£14,858

banker will note when an account is overdrawn, and suspend the account. Sellers of commodities will pay all the cheques they receive into their accounts, which will rise accordingly, but every cheque comes from a buyer, and seeing that they are all the same people, the accounts will simply rise and fall in balanced reciprocation exactly as before when banknotes were circulating. But there is an important difference. As the monetary base shrinks, the techniques at the disposal of the central bank for controlling inflation become more effective. Influencing a huge float by open market operations is impracticable because buying and selling operations would need to be on a vast scale to have any effect. This was the situation immediately after the second world war. But the float can be controlled by open market operations if the monetary base is small and its velocity high. Selling or buying securities of relatively modest value can withdraw or inject banknotes into the monetary system on a scale that significantly influences a small monetary base. Thus, the central bank is nowadays more powerful in discharging its mission. It is no better placed for estimating what action is needed. But once the decision is taken, be it right or wrong, then extra inflation can be injected or excess inflation removed much more effectively than in the past.

We have now introduced a general clarification which enables us to show how four things, the float, inflation, the monetary base, and the velocity of the currency, are all related to each other. In Figure 10-1 the data from Figure 9-5 is brought forward and the notion of a monetary base is introduced, simply on the assumption that in year 1 the monetary base is a sixth of the float, and in successive years it decreases to a seventh, then an eighth, and so on. As just explained, the monetary base decreases whenever people cease to use cash as a customary means of payment, and instead make regular use of cheques, or a banker's card, or a similar substitute. The bottom line in Figure 10-1 shows how a monetary base that is getting proportionately smaller year by year, (shrinking from a sixth to an eleventh when compared with the float) is in fact getting larger in absolute terms because the float is inflating at a faster rate.

What is causing the float to inflate? As already explained, some of the inflation comes from the shrinking base itself. Let us assume that a float is in existence operating in conjuction with a much smaller monetary base, as shown for example by the data displayed under year 1, in Figure 10-1. The process that brings about a reduction in the monetary base during the year is the drift away from cash to substitutes like cheques etc. This releases cash in the banks, who find that their reserve of notes is increasing. When this surplus is spent it causes inflation, which we can now identify as the first contribution to whatever inflation is needed to hold unit prices steady, against their tendency to fall in response to rising output. The central bank now enters as a second contributor, injecting whatever extra inflation is needed to bring about this desired stabilisation of unit prices.

This sequence can be traced in terms of the data shown for year 1. The float is operating with a monetary base of £10,500, which is a sixth of the float's value. But this base will fall to a seventh of the float's value in the course of the year, a reduction from £10,500 to £9000. The surplus of £1500 can be spent. It will add £1500 × 6½ = £9750 to the float, assuming a mid-way currency velocity for the year as a whole. The specified inflation of 21% corresponds to a float increase of £13,230, as shown. We have just calculated that £9750 will be supplied by the surplus from a shrinking monetary base, leaving £3480 to be contributed by the central bank. Thus the central bank will need to inject about £535 into the monetary base, (by buying securities of this value), which at a velocity of 6½, will inflate the float by £3480. If the central bank made no contribution at all, the float would expand by £9750 from £63,000 to £72,750, entirely as a result of the velocity increase from 6 to 7. This is a real inflation rate of 15.5%, but seeing that this inflation rate occurs alongside a rise in output of 10%, only 5.5% of this inflation is visible in the form of rising prices. The rest is all hidden. The central bank may be content with this level of 5.5% visible inflation as representing a satisfactory compromise between higher profits and excessive price rises. In this case the central bank will take no action. But if 5.5% is considered to be too high, the central bank could sell securities and take a quantity of bank-notes out of the system.

Although we analysed the money-lending activity associated with banking in the last chapter and our conclusions need no revision (for the present), there is an observation to be made about lending, in the light of the above. The surplus that accrues to the bank when the monetary base shrinks is not spent by the bank as if it were an income. It takes the form of excess reserves of banknotes which pass quite naturally into the loans that the bank makes, as part of its regular income-earning business. Hence the loans are essential to bring about the inflationary effect, even though the loan package itself does not manipulate money in any self-expanding way, and nobody is printing banknotes. The loans simply act as hidden carriers for the inflation. At this point we can refer to our earlier comment that when the central bank issues a cheque against itself, the new deposit account so created will eventually reduce the reserve of notes in the local banks. But these reserves, as just explained, may be steadily rising as the monetary base shrinks. So any such cheque issued by the central bank may well call for no additional printing of banknotes. There is already a surplus of notes in circulation that will pass into the newly created accounts as and when necessary, instead of into the local banks' loans. Either way, the inflation effect is still transmitted to the general price level.

To the ordinary view, it seems inescapable that money comes from bankers, because by the time the deal with the banker has run its course, the banker's client is richer, the banker himself is richer, output is rising, prices are stationary or not increasing by much if visible inflation is moderate, wages continue to be paid at a rate settled by negotiation and compromise, all within a framework of free competition and equal opportunity. How can exploitation exist in such an open and fairly rewarded society? Such are the delusions on which a modern political democracy is built.

The task of understanding the complexities of a democratic capitalist society is addressed by two categories of people, the genuine investigator, (represented typically by Petty, Smith, Ricardo, Mill, Marx, and many other lesser lights in the classical period and earlier), and by modern economic advisers to governments, who nowadays possess the immense advantage of detailed statistical information, and the electronic means to process such information quickly and accurately. The names just quoted were genuinely independent thinkers, but the latter group reach their high positions via a career-dependent route which destroys critical detachment. Academics are similarly placed, as well as newspaper and television commentators on economic affairs. Their role is to inform and elucidate, using powerful means, but they work within an imposed orthodoxy which requires their continuous allegiance, if they are to keep their jobs. They are the great pretenders, impressively equipped to explain the facts of economic existence, but in reality empowered to do no such thing.

Nevertheless, they are forced to address the real world and make some sense of it. Hence at these supposedly expert levels of economic interpretation, the concepts we have so far identified in our analysis are all to be found, namely, the monetary base, the level of savings, inflation, the velocity of the currency, the monitoring duty of the central bank, the investment role of the banking system, and so on. Economics specialists employed by governments, banks, universities and the media make what they can of these matters and some of them write or speak with candour, respect for the facts, and with due humility towards their own depth of understanding, but always with unwavering commitment to the capitalist system as a whole. The result is pseudo-knowledge, an amalgam of fact and fable endlessly sifted and stirred with scholarly zeal, but held together by shared loyalties not by a sound theoretical core. The absence of a theoretical core is fairly obvious, and is admitted sotto voce by leading academics. In fact disquiet on this matter is present in the literature throughout the entire neo-classical period. From time to time the malaise is plainly stated. Hayek wrote in 1935:

> *The task of monetary theory is a much wider one than is commonly assumed. Its task is nothing less than to cover a second time the whole field which is treated by pure theory under the assumption of barter, and to investigate what changes in the conclusions of pure theory are made necessary by the introduction of indirect exchange.*

At an international economics seminar held at Queen's College, Oxford, from 1979 to 1981, attended by eighteen professors and lecturers, Desai presented a paper on the above quotation. It is reproduced in Advances in Economic Theory, ed. Baranzini, 1982, Blackwell Publishers Ltd. Desai concludes that the task is no nearer to accomplishment at the time of writing than in Hayek's time. McCloughry also examines the notion of monetary equilibrium in the same context, with similar conclusions. Cencini, also in the same publication, attacks Walras and neo-classical price theory, suggesting that the theory should be abandoned, and quoting an earlier comment by Samuelson:

> *Indeed we still lack in 1972 a really adequate theoretical structure that encompasses the foundations of a money economy.*

Similar views can be found in the literature today. No thinking person can feel comfortable with the standard textbook expositions. A sensible analysis of economic relations necessarily progresses from simple dependencies to increasingly complex groups. The textbook approach is to convert commonplace assumptions into symbols, manipulate them in dubious graphs and dress them up in algebra to give an appearance of profundity. The phenomenon of price is a good example. It is never examined in a realistic setting. Its link with barter is ignored. It is severed from its own operational circumstances and reformulated as a mental concept, supposedly familiar to everybody, with supply and demand correlations that any dimwit can grasp. Mathematical deceits invest these simple-minded notions with theoretical complexity and an impressive labyrinth of "knowledge" is created in the style of the old philosophical quest for a logical blueprint that "explains" everything. Such so-called explanations lead nowhere, and never have any practical application. They are a godsend to the governments of capitalist democracies.

There is continual criticism of orthodox economics even, as we have seen, among its own representatives, who are vaguely (if not fully) aware that their position is untenable. But it would be a mistake to suppose that the body of mock learning known as neo-classical economics is now crumbling under attacks from its critics. The critics are an essential part of the act. They raise a fuss because the old routines need to be patched and refurbished to keep the show on the road. The emperor wears no clothes but his tailors and dressers are always busy.

Of course our analysis is still deficient in many respects. There are no income-earning services in our models. Everybody is either a wage-earner, a capitalist owner, or a banker. These three basic classes exist in codependent unity, and constitute the kernel of a commodity-producing exploitation system. When a service class is introduced, the incomes earned by the three basic classes are not all spent on commodities, but are spent in part on a service of some kind, which means that such spending power is transferred to a new type of income-earner whose spending at the goods exchange interface substitutes for the spending of the person who buys the service. A large so-called middle class comes into existence in this way. The models also lack the distinction between factor-producing firms, and firms that produce finished goods. We also need to consider the class of commercial capitalists who act as wholesale and retail intermediaries between production and consumption, and who, in simplistic terms, derive an income by buying cheap in order to sell dear. When these features have been introduced, our models will be more realistic, and we can examine the procedures that enable the central bank to inflate the monetary system and control unit prices. These developments will be introduced in Part Two using working models similar to those we have used so far.

11

Summary

The **value** of a commodity is its rate of production, (measured as output per calendar time), expressed in terms of some other commodity's rate of production. This other commodity serves as a chosen standard which enables all commodities to express their values relative to each other. In times past many physical substances have been used in this way, as a universal equivalent, but gold and silver are the most suitable. "Magnitude of value" for a particular commodity is the quantity by weight of the universal equivalent which corresponds to the quantity of the commodity produced in the same time, designated by weight or length or volume or unit number. Thus in the British system, an imperial pound weight of sterling silver was the original standard unit of value, and the value of an ounce or a foot or a gallon or an item of commodity could be expressed as a particular weight of silver. By this system, weights of silver became the negotiating medium for buying and selling of commodities, and the relationship that determined the magnitude of the respective weights was derived from the production times of the commodities. In this way, all commodities are exchanged for the universal commodity on a commensurable basis, despite the infinite non-commensurable nature of commodities as bundles of use-values.

But the value of a commodity is not its price. The price of a commodity is governed by the relation between its supply and intensity of relative demand as expressed through a money income. These two influences, the supply and the demand, must be carefully identified. The supply is always governed by the technical capability of a given society at a given time. All commodities therefore have *fixed* rates of production for a given mix of productive resources, although the rate of production per time period *can vary widely*, according to the resources allocated. Any particular pattern of relative demand across the entire economy can be satisfied by an appropriate allocation of resources. Thus the flow of commodities as rates per day through the market can be controlled to suit the pattern of relative demand, if some means exist to adjust the allocation of production resources. The value system described above is the means by which this adjustment takes place. Although the value of one commodity compared with another is always determined by its production rate, society can raise that production rate relative to other commodities, by paying more for that commodity (and correspondingly less for other commodities) thereby creating a value-form which rises above (or below) the actual value of any particular commodity. This departure from basic "production rate" values is not an independent movement because the sum of the new value-forms is always equal to the sum of the basic values. The new value-form is called **price**. Every commodity has a price which is automatically linked (through incomes) to all other prices, thereby providing a mechanism for the adjustment of its production rate relative to the production rate of other commodities. The price of a particular commodity considered in isolation is not linked to its own production rate in any way whatever.

The **equilibrium price** is the outcome when supply is so adjusted that intensity of relative demand is the same for all commodities in the market. In such circumstances, demand is demonstrably satisfied because nobody will pay more to obtain more of any commodity in preference to any other. In theory, intensity of *absolute* demand may be assumed to be without limit for all commodities, but in practice the effective demand for goods is subject to two restrictions, namely, the finite level of production capability in any given society (at a certain stage of its historical development), and the fact that production resources allocated to a particular commodity can never be increased or reduced without a corresponding loss or gain to other commodities. (We presume a closed and freely competitive economy, as always). In other words, speaking generally, society has limited productive resources that can be allocated in a multitude of ways, and each particular allocation has a corresponding price network that can clear the market in conjunction with a particular pattern of demand. How is the appropriate allocation selected by the price mechanism? For the answer we need the next definition.

Primary incomes are generated by selling commodities. An active price network generates aggregate incomes which are identical to the **bulk selling prices** of all the commodities, but the only stable price network is one in which incomes are *equal*. All other price networks are unstable because a better income can be found by switching production from a low earning commodity to another with higher returns. This variation in money income is an integral part of the price mechanism. Competition between producers brings about equality of their incomes alongside a particular set of prices which enable current demand to be satisfied. If demand is not satisfied at these prices, competition between buyers produces a different set of prices, and then competition between producers for equality of incomes begins again. Thus the search is for an income level which is equal for all producers and which simultaneously produces a range of prices that satisfy demand. This three-way dependency means that the demand pattern is not a freely chosen set of preferences, even in a freely competitive market. The demand pattern is forced to comply with equality of incomes and in this way the achievable production rates of a given society at a particular stage of its historical development exert their ultimate domination. In circumstances where market choice is free, and the allocation of productive resources is entirely flexible, the price mechanism allocates resources in such a way as to equalise all incomes when (1) the pattern of relative demand is satisfied by (2) a particular flow rate of goods which is consistent with (3) achievable output rates per unit mix of resources. Hence variations in **relative demand** (1), modify the **social production rate** (2), according to limitations imposed by the **technical production rate** (3), to produce a dynamic nexus in which a closed society of producer/consumers can compete for maximum money incomes and thereby obtain the best possible match between their aggregate consumption needs and their combined output capabilities. This explanation is wordy because three interdependent factors are involved, but the mathematics is quite straightforward. Several working examples are shown in the early chapters.

There is no source, other than sale of commodities, from which a money income can be created, although an income so generated can pass into the hands of a new owner, who may well regard such money as an income just like anybody else's. But such a **derivative income** must always be distinguished from the primary incomes generated by the sale of commodities. Derivative incomes, which are a means of livelihood for all who provide a paid service, are not examined in our analysis so far.

Primary incomes, derived from sales, are split into two portions, one for the workforce called **wages** and the other for the firm's owner called **profit**. Wages are falsely identified as a payment for time worked, which conceals their true origin, but net profit is correctly identified as the money remaining after all costs such as raw materials, maintenance, debts, lighting and heating, etc, have been paid. The appearance is that all such costs, plus wages, are met by the owner from gross revenue, leaving a net profit which is his income. But it would be just as true to say that all such costs, plus net profit for the owner, are met by the workforce, and the remainder is wages. The sums tally in both cases. Either description may be regarded as correct. But deception is introduced by the **bogus work contract** which determines wages as a rate linked to calendar time, as though actual labour itself had a price. If the employer's profit was determined as a rate linked to calendar time then positions would be reversed. Whoever is paid on the basis of time worked is condemned to a relative standard of living that falls automatically while the overall social standard of living rises with increased productivity. This last statement is true of a gold-based society. In a paper-based society the statement is true only if a source of **inflation** is present, alongside rising output, to prevent unit prices from rising. In either case, the growing divergence between these two living standards, one falling for the worker and one rising for society as a whole, manifests itself in a rate of profit which grows rapidly. The only check to this exploitation process is the struggle for higher wages. There is no inflation strictly speaking in a capitalist gold-based society. Inflation is essential in a capitalist paper-based society.

In a paper-based economy, when rate of output rises for all commodities, unit prices fall while bulk prices are unaffected. This cheapening effect raises the standard of living for the entire community. An economy based on paper money would normally operate in this manner but interference arises from an external source of inflation caused by improvements in the efficiency of the monetary system such as cheques and credit cards. These devices dispense with the need for cash, and as a result, the monetary base shrinks. The cash that thereby becomes surplus to requirements enters the money network and inflates prices, with the result that the fall in unit prices that would normally follow from increased output is arrested, partly or wholly (and unpredictably). The **central bank** constantly tries to estimate two related trends, the future growth in output, (which will reduce unit prices) and future inflation (which will counteract this fall) in order to intervene as necesary to prevent unit prices from falling. Such intervention (at this stage of our analysis) takes the form of buying securities to inject cash into the monetary system, or selling securities for the opposite purpose.

The concept of **hidden inflation** is essential for any understanding of the profit-making process. When output rises, inflation of the currency is needed to prevent unit prices from falling. This required inflation may be considerable, if the rise in output is relatively large. But to the ordinary view, even this considerable level of inflation would be nowhere visible (except in the falling value of money) simply because unit prices would stay constant. In these circumstances, primary incomes rise rapidly. Seeing that wage-rates are negotiated on the basis of calendar time, the worker sees no change in his or her circumstances because the weekly wage is unchanged and prices are unchanged. But the rapid increase in average earnings for the whole of society means that the worker is being left behind. He or she is responsible for the increased output but is automatically excluded from the circle of beneficiaries. The capitalist wages system embodies this devious but highly effective form of exploitation.

Banks are essential in the early days of an economy based on money to provide a **paper currency**. This paper currency is originally convertible on demand into a gold (or silver) equivalent. When banks print and issue paper money beyond the requirements of the necessary monetary base, the general price level rises, including the paper price for gold. Instead of paying a high market price for gold, the owner of paper money can present such notes for redemption at the bank of issue and obtain the face value equivalent (or a proportion thereof) which was set when gold had a lower price. The bank is now vulnerable to a drain on its gold reserves that it cannot meet at short notice, if at all. The history of banking is a record of repeated bankruptcies from this cause, which arises from a combination of currency inflation alongside convertibility. When the leading nations left the gold standard between the two world wars, this source of massive instability was removed from the banking system. But an automatic mechanism essential to profit-making was lost at the same time. In a gold-based system, when general output rises, unit prices stay constant while incomes increase. Not so in a paper-based system. Unit prices fall and incomes stay constant, when general output rises. Unless some means of inflation can be found to counteract falling prices when output rises, profit-making is curtailed and the capitalist exploitation system loses its momentum. The central bank acquires a special mission to ensure that this needful inflation, most of it hidden from view as already explained, is forthcoming.

The amount of inflation that the central bank must provide is complicated by the fact that inflation steadily enters the monetary system as a result of cheque payments and the like which dispense with the need for cash, as described earlier. Moreover, the money stock exists in two forms, the **savings** that a community chooses to hold in reserve (which are fictitious) and a **monetary base** that is much smaller (but consists of real banknotes). The monetary base has a **velocity** which links it to the savings reserve, and this velocity rises as the monetary base shrinks. Cash that is surplus to the shrinking base percolates out and is absorbed into bank loans. Savings, the monetary base, the velocity, and hidden inflation are all interlinked in perfectly understandable theory, but they vary in unpredictable ways in the real world. Hence the central bank never has any clear idea what it is doing.

The essential concepts for understanding a capitalist economic system are briefly summarised above. The first task is to deal with the rubbish in the standard textbooks. In an appendix the **perverted misuse of graphs** to explain prices is examined closely. Anybody who is duped by supply and demand curves has no hope of understanding economics. A **veiled official purpose** is thereby neatly realised, since the main political problem for freely elected rulers in an open democracy is how to maintain the facade of deception and lies that prevents a literate population from discovering the truth about how the capitalist system works.

Theoretical understanding is tested by the use of models. These have been continuously presented alongside the developing analysis, to provide concrete illustrations. Figure 11-1 is the most important for understanding the economic concept of price, which is a relationship between three variables, namely, the pattern of aggregate demand, the social production rate, and the technical production rate. The reader can supply exemplary values to complete the diagram, confirming for him-her-self how prices arise and how they alter as these variables change. Basic assumptions are seven commodities, a closed community of 100 producer/consumers, and a daily production cycle. The three variables are introduced in the following manner. We will deal with a gold economy first.

(1) Choose the output rates that correspond to the aggregate demand pattern. Three hundred golf balls, eighty-six pies, thirty-seven umbrellas and so on. These are listed in the boxes on the left under the heading *commodity values.* The seventh of these must be gold, expressed like the others as a quantity (weight) produced per day. Once these boxes on the left are completed the aggregate relative demand for the whole community is expressed in terms of the daily production rates required.

(2) In the vertical column under *number of workers*, assign to each commodity the appropriate number that corresponds to this society's production capability. Ten workers to produce 100 golf balls, seventeen workers to produce 86 pies, twenty-one workers for 37 umbrellas, and so on, for all seven commodities. The total number of workers must add up to 100. Relative demand is now expressed in terms of the technical production rate (quantity per worker per day) and the social production rate (quantity produced by simultaneous working days).

(3) All factors that determine both the bulk prices and the unit prices are now present. Each of the seven commodities has a value equal to the value (the stated daily weight) of gold. This stated daily weight, multiplied by seven gives

Gold standard

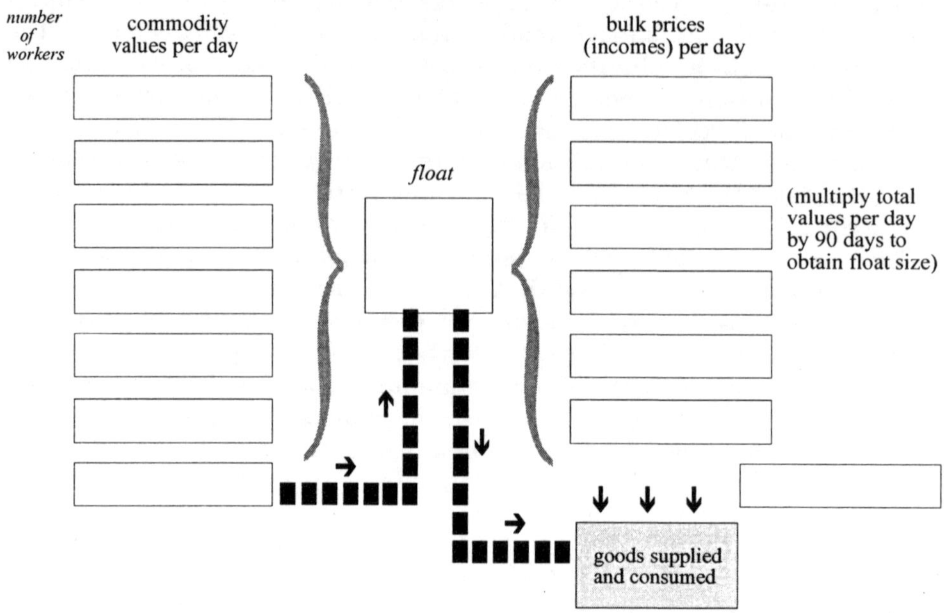

Paper currency

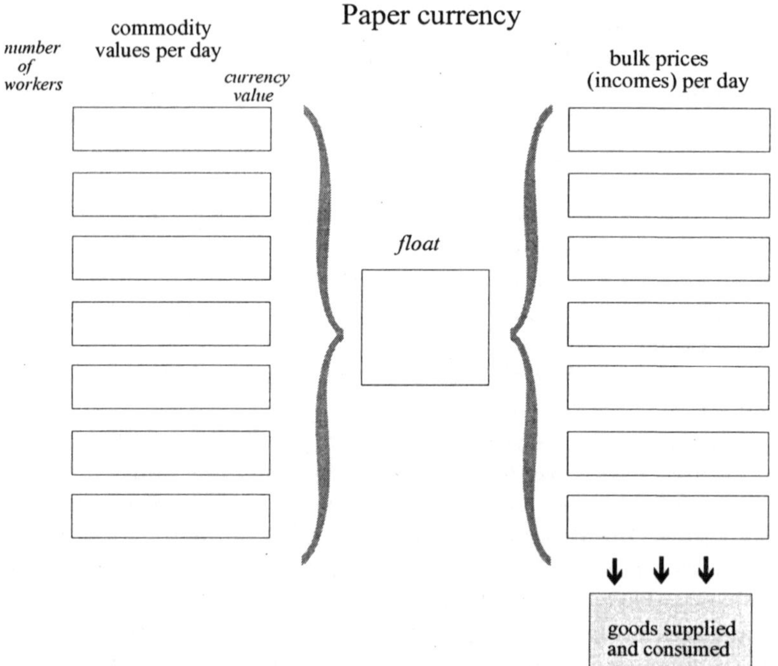

Figure 11-1

the total value produced each day. Now allocate this total value in the boxes on the right in such a way that every worker receives the same income. The total of the values on the left will necessarily be equal to the total of these new bulk prices on the right. Demand that corresponded to a particular aggregate supply is now satisfied by a set of prices that are stable.

The procedure is exactly the same for a paper economy. But instead of the stated weight of gold, a **currency value** must be specified. Any number will serve. Historically, this number is the paper-price for a day's production of gold at the moment that inconvertibility is declared, but from then on this number is free to move to any other magnitude, depending on the size of savings or the size of the monetary base. We will examine these movements later. For the present, an arbitrary currency value will suffice. This value is multiplied by seven to give us the total daily value, from which bulk prices can be derived as before. Once this price determination mechanism is understood, in respect of a gold-based society or an economy based on inconvertible banknotes, the three variables may be altered at will, either singly or simultaneously, to verify how they jointly interact to produce a price network. The arithmetic is quite simple:

[Output of gold per day] × **[number of spheres of production]** = **[sum of all bulk prices per day]** = **[sum of all primary incomes per day]** = **[total output value per day]**

or currency value

We now turn from **the price network** as a process that balances achievable supply rates against the pattern of relative demand, and move on to consider how **the general price level** is determined. If gold is the exchange medium, then the output rate of gold sets the general price level in the manner already described. But in a paper-based system, the general price level for all commodities can move up or down according to the relation between the currency value, the level of savings and the monetary base, as depicted in Figure 11-2. A currency velocity of 6 is adopted, and we presume a savings level equal to an average income of three months (90 days) for every person earning a primary income. In our model community, all the workforce of 100 and the 7 capitalist owners earn a primary income. If a financial capitalist or banker is present then he earns a derivative income. Primary incomes are generated at the goods exchange interface by the buying and selling of commodities. Derivative incomes pass from one owner to another in return for a service of some kind.

[total daily output value] × 90 days (***accommodation***) = [float (savings)]

[monetary base] × 6 (***velocity***) = [float (savings)]

The float is fictitious. Only the monetary base is real.

Figure 11-2

The float is fictitious whether the currency is gold or paper notes. (A real float is possible only when everybody keeps their savings on the person or in some secure private location). Money (as gold or banknotes) is paid into a bank and ownership of that money is registered in a deposit account. This ownership is strictly safeguarded, but the money (gold or notes) merges into the float that the bank manages on behalf of the community as a whole. The bank retains only sufficient to act as a reserve, large enough to meet unusually high withdrawals. It may appear that the bank obtains funds from the mass of deposits, seeing that only a sensible reserve is kept on hand and the surplus can be utilised. But this surplus is absorbed into the loans that provide the bank's income.

The bank lends money that can be used to pay wages. The work performed to earn those wages produces a continuous stream of goods whose unit price steadily falls as productivity improves, alongside the steadily falling unit price of all other goods produced in ever greater quantities by other wage-earners. This steady fall in unit prices would inevitably reduce the general price level but such outcome is prevented by a fall in the purchasing power of money. This fall (we summarise the causes in a moment) means, in specific terms, that if £700 could buy today's output, £770 is needed at a later stage. Thus a 10% price inflation is present, while (say) a 10% improvement in output is also present, and the net effect is that unit prices stay constant (and the 10% inflation stays hidden) during the period when productivity and inflation are rising in step together. Constant unit prices accompanied by rising output means higher and higher bulk selling prices, and all of this enhancement flows exclusively into profits. These enhanced profits are used to repay the banker's loan, with interest, and still leave a healthy profit for the capitalist employer. The interest repayments are the banker's income, and this income after deduction of operating costs, salaries, upkeep etc is the source for further loans.

Figure 11-3 demonstrates the dynamic relation between the float and the monetary base, and shows how this relationship affects the banker. The illustrations are quite simple but are needed to dispel the widespread illusion that banks supply money to the economy. In January the bank opens a deposit account for a client who is saving £100 every month. When £500 has been saved the client withdraws the money and spends it. On the next line is a similar account, opened one month later. Six successive accounts are opened, which the bank supervises, paying out monies on demand as the accounts rise and fall. These withdrawals are shown in bold type. It is clear that all the money received by the bank is handled with scrupulous honesty. It is accumulated and then returned to the client. But in June, July, August and September, the bank pays out only £500 per month, while total deposits rise by £600 per month. During this time the reserve of banknotes rises. But in October the bank pays out £1000, while total deposits fall from £2000 to £1000, and the essential reserve of banknotes falls from £1000 to £500. This example illustrates how the float and the accommodation period can rise together and fall together, creating a surplus or a deficit in the vault cash of the banks, and lowering or raising the general price level. But all these changes are *trend-stationary*, meaning that such changes must return to their point of departure, when the savings have

	Jan	Feb	Mar	Apr	May	Jun	Jul	Aug	Sep	Oct	Nov	Dec	Jan	Feb	Mar
	£100	£200	£300	£400	**£500**	£100	£200	£300	£400	**£500**	£100	£200	£300	£400	**£500**
		£100	£200	£300	£400	**£500**	£100	£200	£300	£400	**£500**	£100	£200	£300	£400
			£100	£200	£300	£400	**£500**	£100	£200	£300	£400	**£500**	£100	£200	£300
				£100	£200	£300	£400	**£500**	£100	£200	£300	£400	**£500**	£100	£200
Figure 11-3					£100	£200	£300	£400	**£500**	£100	£200	£300	£400	**£500**	£100
						£100	£200	£300	£400	**£500**	£100	£200	£300	£400	**£500**
size of float						*£1600*				*£2000*					
size of monetary base						*£500*				*£1000*					

	Jan	Feb	Mar	Apr	May	Jun	Jul	Aug	Sep	Oct	Nov	Dec	Jan	Feb	Mar
	£80	£160	£240	£320	£400	**£480**	£80	£160	£240	£320	£400	**£480**	£80	£160	£240
		£80	£160	£240	£320	£400	**£480**	£80	£160	£240	£320	£400	**£480**	£80	£160
			£80	£160	£240	£320	£400	**£480**	£80	£160	£240	£320	£400	**£480**	£80
				£80	£160	£240	£320	£400	**£480**	£80	£160	£240	£320	£400	**£480**
Figure 11-4					£80	£160	£240	£320	£400	**£480**	£80	£160	£240	£320	£400
						£80	£160	£240	£320	£400	**£480**	£80	£160	£240	£320
size of float						*£1680*				*£1680*					
size of monetary base						*£480*				*£480*					

been spent, because nothing can ever be spent from savings unless those savings have been accumulated beforehand. The irregularities of a rising and falling float, alongside falling and rising prices, and rising and falling reserves of banknotes, are bound to be self-compensating over time. In terms of Figure 11-2, the 90 days accommodation is reduced when savings are spent, and the 90 days are extended when savings accumulate. But all the effects that flow from these movements are merely oscillations about a fixed point. In short there is no accumulation of money here that would generate a so-called money supply, any more than a lake formed by damming a river can become an extra source of water. Neither the banks as lenders of money, nor the central bank with its printing press, can create extra spending power for society as a whole.

The essential interdependencies are displayed in Figure 11-5. The production consumption cycle may be daily as shown, or expressed in terms of any other time period. Similarly, the money saved from one day and spent on the next day, may be spent two days later or a month later or after any other time period, synchronised or not with the production cycle. Sooner or later all savings are spent, and the general outcome is that the equalities shown in the boxes remain undisturbed, or rise and fall about a central position. This central position can of course alter as a long term trend, but this provides no source of money.

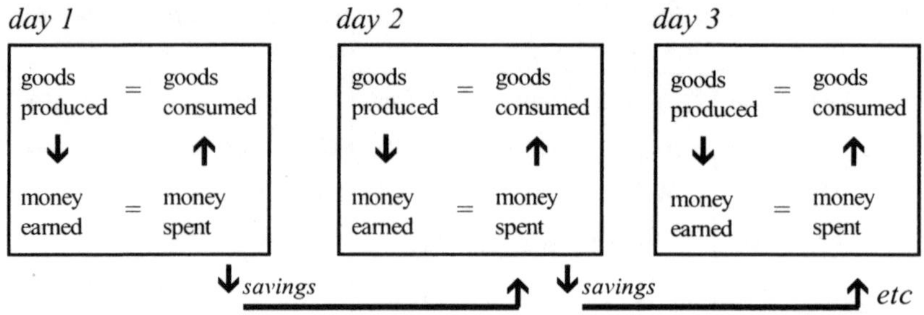

Figure 11-5

Of course the deposit accounts shown in Figure 11-3 are highly contrived. The randomising effect of high numbers cannot be represented by just six accounts. If we work on the assumption that the savings pattern for a large community will be infinitely variable between the different members, then the regularity produced by such randomness when numbers are huge can be imitated by a representation like Figure 11-4, where every variable is reduced to an average that is constant over time. The average amount being saved every month is £80 per person, the average amount being spent every six months is £480, and all such deposits and withdrawals will necessarily form a regular time sequence. The total of all deposits is constant at £1680, and the monetary base that the banker must maintain is £480, operating at a velocity of 3½. The cash difference between deposits and the monetary base is available to the banker, but only once. In any case, if these accounts are instant access, and pay no interest to the depositor, it is unlikely that they will be allowed to grow so large. Depositors will switch such funds into time deposits of one form or another, which will yield an interest. In this way the money becomes part of the bank's loaning business. No manipulation of Figure 11-5 can create a source of money for anybody which is not already there to start with. Monies accumulated at a central point on the understanding that they can be reclaimed on demand, or after an agreed period of notice, can never be a source of surplus funds. Huge amounts of money can of course be accumulated and spent. But if the accumulated money is all returned to the original owners together with more money, then extra money from somewhere else must have been added, either by transfer from other reserves, or by the printing of extra banknotes, or by reduction in accomodation. Money cannot miraculously reproduce itself to provide extra income, except in fairytales or dreams or the official textbooks.

The final important clarification in this summary concerns Figure 11-2. The total daily output value does not change when output changes. No matter how the general level of output may rise and fall, the total value produced in one day is constant, because these goods are matched to a particular money stock spread through society as a whole. Outputs may alter as they please, but nothing will alter in Figure 11-2. For all lines of production, **outputs in a given time have the same value.** So the currency value does not need to have any particular magnitude. It just needs to be the same for all commodities. That is why, up to the present, we have simply chosen an arbitrary number to represent the currency value and manipulated all relationships on this basis. But we must now take a holistic view, and make all the numbers we are using fully accountable. This brings us to Figure 11-6, where all relationships are transparent because they are linked by straightforward mathematical operations. We can now state the exact relationship between pieces of paper that have numbers printed on them and the production rates of commodities:

> **The sum of real banknotes, muliplied by the velocity, is equal to the total physical output during the period of accommodation, and this sum, divided by the spheres of production, gives a currency value for each sphere's output during that period.**

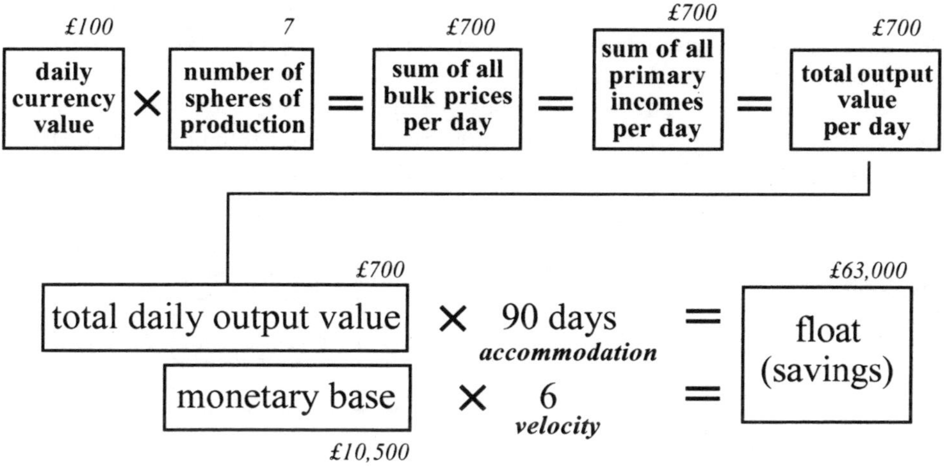

Figure 11-6

The bulk value of each sphere's production per unit of time is the important reference point that determines unit prices for each commodity. This reference point is identical with the currency value, which may be expressed in terms of a day or a week or a year, etc. Nothing related to demand or supply has any effect on the currency value. If output rises dramatically, then unit prices fall dramatically, but there is no alteration in the currency value or in the bulk value. The currency value is responsive only to the quantity of banknotes that serve the need for accommodation. If the number of banknotes rises, caeteris paribus, the currency value rises. All goods become dearer. If the need for accommodation rises, caeteris paribus, the currency value falls. All goods become cheaper. This effect is entirely automatic, and is not in itself harmful to the community as a whole, because living standards depend solely on outputs, and not on any manipulations involving money.

The entire set of relationships is shown in Figure 11-6, where all variables can be identified and their dependency order examined. Formerly we would have said that any number can serve as a currency value, and once this is specified for a given community with its own particular spheres of production, then the sum of the bulk prices, the sum of all primary incomes and the total output value are determined, while individual commodity prices are determined in accordance with Figure 11-1. Now we reverse the approach and say this. An accommodation period will be adopted by any given community which will create a float of banknotes with a total value equal to the goods produced during that period (say 90 days), whatever the actual output in that time may be, and whatever size the float of banknotes may be. This float supports a price network operating according to Figure 11-1, in which a value system regulates the exchange of goods on the basis of equal values for equal production times. The magnitude of this value, which has no intrinsic significance, depends on whatever sum is expressed by the banknotes that form the float. This monetary system is ingenious and foolproof, and completely stable as long as the quantity of banknotes remains constant. In these circumstances a currency value appears for each line of production, as shown in Figure 11-7. Seven spheres of production are shown. Each of them has the same currency value, which is a seventh of the float. The actual goods produced by each sphere during the accommodation period now acquire their values. The relation between the float and the quantity of real banknotes depends on the actual quantity of the

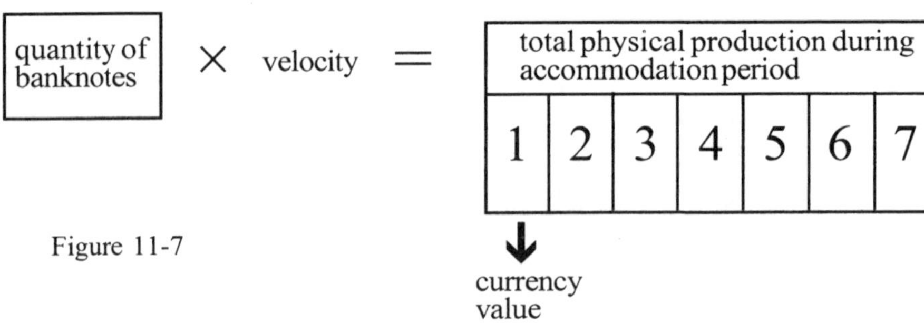

Figure 11-7

printed notes themselves, the size of savings that the community retains as a reserve, namely the accommodation, and the turnover velocity of the notes in proportion to the transactions in which they need to be present.

The float as thus described initially appears as the sum of all monies that members of society keep on hand as their own private reserves to allow flexible buying and selling within the constraints of income. The monetary base and the float are identical at this point, and therefore the velocity under these circumstances is **one.** When these hoards are centralised by a banking system, the same flexibility of buying and selling can be ensured by a much smaller monetary base, with a velocity of say three, or four or higher. The centralising process in itself causes no immediate change in prices or incomes or the currency value. The banknotes formerly scattered in hoards are simply gathered in one spot. But in the form of a shared pool, most of these banknotes become superfluous, and they enter the monetary system through the loaning operations of the bank, causing the currency value to rise to a new position of stability, and prices and incomes all rise accordingly.

The currency value is locked to a particular magnitude at the moment when inconvertibility becomes operational, and from then on, it adjusts to match the output of a particular accommodation period to the total value of banknotes in the monetary base, thereby confering a value in terms of goods on a set of numbers, contrary to the usual impression that the numbered notes confer their own value on a quantity of goods. This adjustment consists of two quite separate processes in simultaneous action. The first process relates to the variables shown, which are all linked to each other by the simple mathematical operations of adding and multiplying. The second process relates to the banknotes that become either surplus or deficient, in respect of the monetary base, whenever a change occurs in the accommodation, or in the monetary base and its velocity. The first process is essentially the interaction of supply and demand, and it determines the prices of commodities in relation to each other. The second process affects the general price level. Roughly speaking, the centralisation of private hoards may last for three or four decades but it must come to an end sooner or later, and the inflation it causes will also subside. The central bank then acquires its role as the agent in charge of inflation.

Anything that makes the monetary base shrink, results in a superfluity of banknotes that in turn makes the currency value rise, and vice versa. This outcome masks the fact that the currency value is the fundamental pivot on which the entire system rests, not as a particular magnitude, but as an expression of equality for all outputs of all spheres of production when compared with each other on the basis of an equal production time such as a day. The standard economics textbooks are quite ignorant of any such concept as the currency value. The falling value of money as a secular trend is recognised (who could ignore it?) but left wholly unexplained.

The relationships shown in Figure 11-6 are very simple in themselves, and their combined effects in practice are not difficult to disentangle, though they look quite puzzling from surface appearances. For example, the monetary base as shown is one sixth of the float. If it shrinks to one seventh, (because people are using cheques more) a surplus of £1500 will be "ejected ". These surplus notes are no longer required, but they remain operational, and obviously they are a source of inflation, just as if they had been freshly printed. If the accommodation period simultaneously expanded from 90 days to 105 days, the float would rise to £73,500, and all of the surplus notes would be "recalled to duty" so to speak, at a new velocity of 7. None of the other values would alter, including the currency value, which would remain at 100. Thus two substantial changes could occur simultaneously, but, so far, they cancel each other, with no effect on prices or incomes at first. But the banks would notice a change. Their reserves of banknotes would grow considerably, because deposits would rise as the 90 days grew longer, while the proportion needed for the monetary base would fall. This extra money causes no inflation until it is introduced into the system through loans made by the banks. As these loans filter down to retail levels, the currency value would begin to rise.

If, by contrast, the required monetary base increased to say a fifth, (because people were using cash more), the banknotes in circulation would be insufficient.

If, in addition, the accommodation period fell, thereby reducing the size of the float, none of the other values would alter, just as in the previous example. But the bank's reserves of notes would fall considerably, because withdrawals would be increasing while a larger proportion of notes would be needed for the monetary base. The banks would need to sell assets and/or call in loans.

None of the diagramatic models in this summary are capable of illustrating the exploitation system known as capitalism, until they are conceived as processes operating through time, as in Figure 6-5. In the form of stationary models they illustrate the normal working of a money-based economy, whether of gold or paper, with co-dependent parts that repeat the same arithmetic operations over and over. Once this dynamic motion is under way, the exploitation system called capitalism makes its formal appearance at that historical juncture when the wage-slave appears, the worker whose livelihood is disconnected from the income creation process and made dependent on a wage-contract which specifies a rate of payment for duration of working time. This disconnection occurs in a gold-based economy, and in such circumstances nothing further is needed to ensure that rising living standards made possible by improved productivity will flow exclusively into profits. In a paper based economy, where falling prices are the means through which the whole community benefits from improved productivity, the wage-contract alone will not ensure this fraudulent expansion of profits at the wage-earner's expense. Hidden inflation must be present alongside rising productivity to ensure that unit prices do not fall. At first no action need be taken to bring about this required inflation. It is already being generated automatically, during the decades immediately following the change from gold to paper, because private hoards are being converted into bank accounts, and cheque systems and the like are dispensing with the need for banknotes, which remain in circulation and steadily reduce the value of money.

Hence inconvertibility is a crucial historical turning point for two reasons. It solves the severe instability that is inherent in a gold-based system, and it removes the circumstances in which the wages system is an automatic instrument of exploitation. Hidden inflation must now be present, or the exploitation process will not operate. Much of this needful inflation is provided at first not by capitalist manipulations but by the settling down of an inconvertible paper-based system to its equilibrium level, with a stable monetary base and a cheque system (or equivalent credit devices) in full swing. When this equilibrium is eventually reached such self-generated inflation will disappear. Of course this equilibrium does not imply constant prices. On the contrary, it implies steadily falling unit prices that the capitalist system must always find the means to prevent, if it is to survive. If the capitalist system for some reason fails in this requirement, in other words fails to maintain the hidden inflation that keeps unit prices constant or gently rising while output rises, then the wage-slave will no longer exist. A contract based upon time worked has no inherent disadvantages for the worker when the currency value is stable. We have already illustrated these circumstances in Society C, Figure 6-5.

Part Two

The transformation from theoretical value into operational price has been clearly shown in all our diagrams so far, from the first chapter, and the calculations involved have never been more than an adjustment of ratios to compensate for the uneven distribution of producers across the various spheres of production. This equalisation of incomes for producers became an equalisation of profit rates for firms when the wage/profit distinction was introduced in Chapter 5.

So far we have not examined the concept of costs (other than so-called wage costs). Firms have simply allocated their sales revenue between wages and profit, as if no other costs were present . As a result, the adjustment from value to price has been no more than simple arithmetic. But in Part Two we will introduce factorial costs, ancillary costs, and retail discounts. The financial circumstances of each firm are now more intricate, and the transformation of values into prices in order to maintain a uniform rate of profit, is no longer a simple adjustment of ratios. We pursue this convoluted process in diagrams that look rather complicated, but the principles are easy to follow, and the arithmetic is still elementary, despite the variety of compensating factors that modify each firm's conception of its own rate of profit.

Once a fully operational model is up and running, so to speak, with detailed specifications in respect of factorial inputs, ancillary services and a separate retail function, we explore the banking sector in greater detail and then create a composite diagram that merges all the main strands of a modern capitalist economy, consolidating our theoretical understanding at this stage, and providing a convenient vantage point to glance briefly at the theoretical development of economics during the twentieth century.

The short Introduction that follows is intended to guide the reader through some modifications to the layout of the diagrams. At the same time it serves to recapitulate the concept that runs consistently through all our investigations, the equalisation process.

Introduction

We now resume our analysis with the kind of model developed in Part One, Chapter 6. We will build the model afresh from basic assumptions, demonstrating how the value/price relation operates in a simple economy, and making our groundwork secure before moving the analysis forward. Figure 1 displays the production process in its bare essentials. A workforce of 100 people produces a range of seven commodities in quantities that satisfy relative demand, meaning that this society has allocated its productive resources in the proportions required to maintain a steady flow of goods that satisfy their joint needs and preferences. One day's production is shown, and our task now is to devise a price network that will enable these goods to be bought and sold in the bold rectangle. The first thing we need is a currency value, and once this is specified, a set of prices will emerge if we follow the logical steps that have already been described in detail in Part One. The currency value can be any number as long as it is the same for every commodity. Let us suppose that the currency value is £121. Figure 2 shows the currency value in place. All these commodities now have a relative value, but two further operations are required before they have a price.

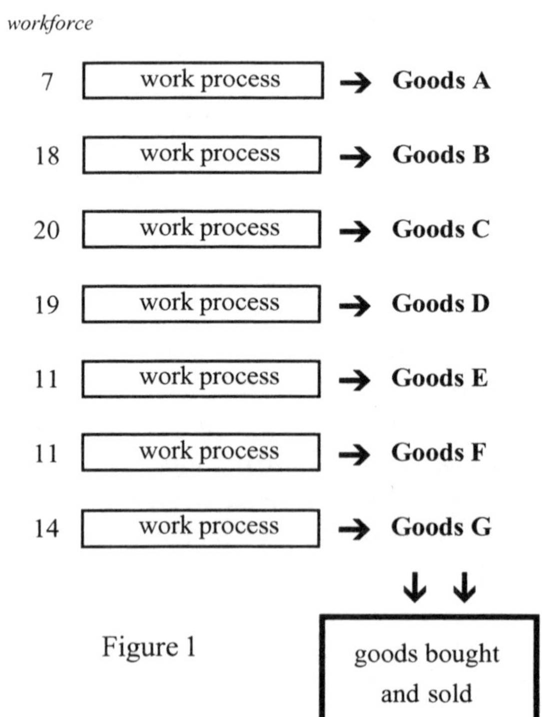

Figure 1

If these goods simply realised their values when they were sold, the shared incomes for the producers would be very different. The twenty workers in Firm C would earn £121,

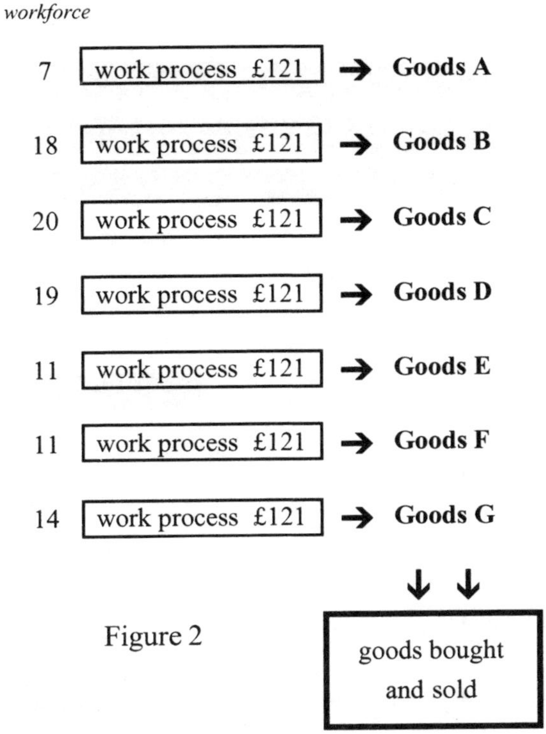

Figure 2

only £6 each, compared with £17 each for the seven workers in Firm A. So the next step is to equalise the wage rates. This can be done at several levels, but we will choose a wage rate of £6 per worker, leaving a residue in each case that we can identify as profit. The result is shown in Figure 3, overleaf.

The layout has been altered slightly to bring all incomes to the right of the diagram. And the wages for the workforce are shown outside the open rectangles because they are not part of the value creation process which takes place inside. The wages are a deduction from the value that is newly created every day, and when this deduction is made, the remainder is the profit shown on the right. As can be seen, the total value created is £847, and the goods themselves travel to the bold rectangle to be bought by the incomes on the right, which also, wages and profits, add up to £847.

Every firm's trading situation is very clearly shown. The workforce needed to produce the goods is paid at the same daily rate per worker in all the firms, in accordance with the assumption of a freely competitive market. (Graded rates of wages will be introduced in the next chapter). But the profit rates for the individual firms are all different. Our initial hypothesis is that this particular distribution of the workforce results in a mix of outputs which satisfies aggregate demand, so all that is missing in Figure 3 is the particular network of prices that will equalise the rates of profit for all firms. Once this price network is in operation, no firm will have an incentive to switch to another line of production. The appropriate prices are shown in Figure 4.

In Figure 4, the goods produced each day have prices that harmonise with three objectives, all of which must be present to ensure a stable equilibrium in a closed and freely competitive market. Wage levels are equal, rates of profit are equal, and the sum of all incomes created every day is equal to the sum of the prices of all goods produced per day. (The goods are no longer shown because their presence is clearly implied, and the diagram needs to be free of unnecessary clutter).

The fact that prices diverge so significantly from values is explained by the dynamic interplay of the competitive marketplace. The slightest mismatch of

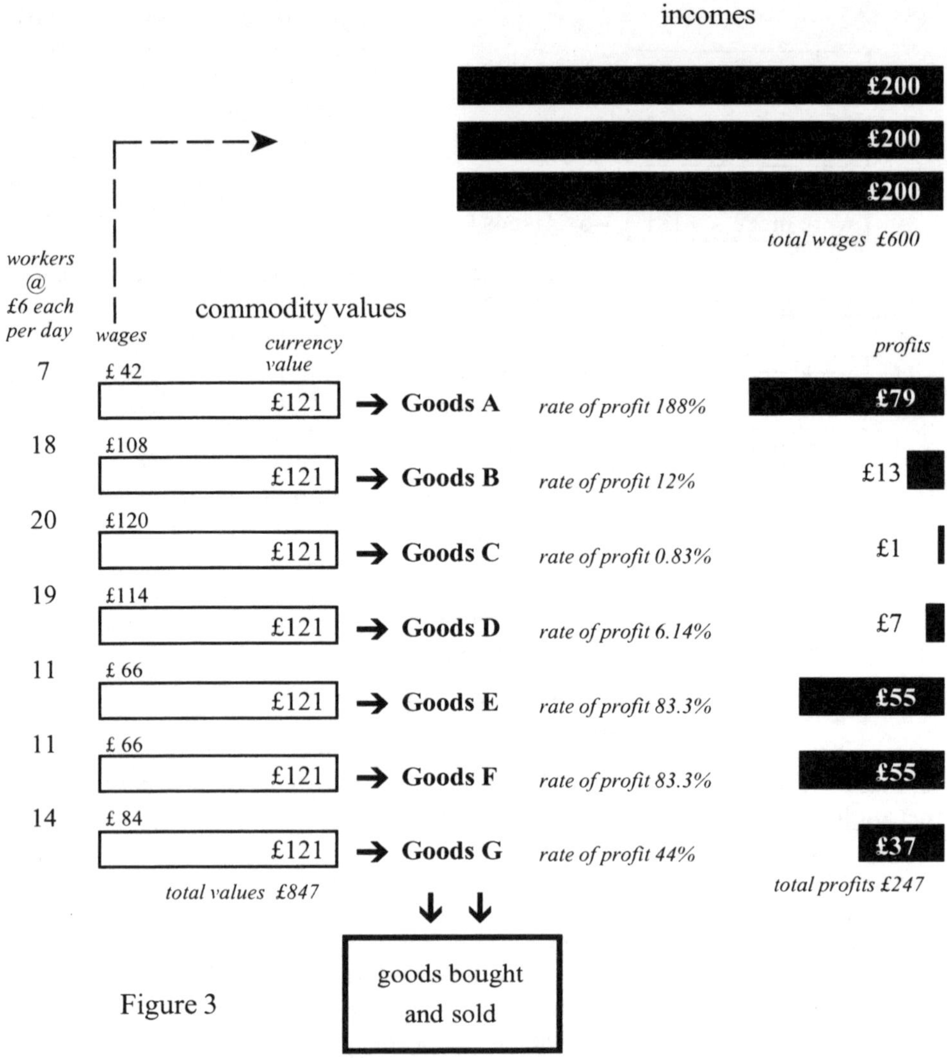

Figure 3

supply to aggregate demand will create a relative shortage of a particular commodity, and this commodity's price will rise, while some other price(s), in a closed market, will fall. The former equality in rates of profit will be disturbed and firms will switch production to restore this equality. Thus demand is always setting the pace, so to speak, by pitching the price now high now low and competition forces firms to respond by altering supply as necessary to equalise their profit rates. When the profit rates are equalised the mix of outputs must correspond to aggregate demand (neglecting the effect of time lags). So the uniform profit rate is the balance point that the price network continually seeks. The price therefore has nothing whatever to do with the use-values of any commodity, and it is a delusion to seek to explain variations in price on the basis of utility or need or any property that a commodity may possess as part of its nature. The achieved production rate of a commodity is the sole determinant of its value, measured in relative terms alongside the achieved production rates of all other commodities, and this value appears in the market in the form of a modifiable price which rises when buyers want to increase the supply and vice versa. All prices stand still when the buyers get the goods they want in the proportions they want, because all suppliers' incomes are equalised. The dynamic balance of supply and demand corresponds to this triple equilibrium. All so-called supply and demand curves that purport to show how the magnitude of price is fixed are a delusion and a perversion of mathematical logic. It is impossible to derive magnitudes from correlations, and the supposed correlations are bogus on several counts. (The graphical representation of supply, demand and price is examined in an Appendix).

Figure 4

To summarise, Figure 1 illustrates the physical outputs of the production/ consumption cycle. Figure 2 shows how the currency value is linked to these outputs. Figure 3 shows how equality in wage rates is related to profits, and Figure 4 shows how bulk prices are formed by the modification of values to ensure equal rates of profit. These bulk prices operate in the bold rectangle where goods are sold on the basis of unit prices that vary according to actual quantities.

To simplify even further, consider Firm A in Figure 3. The firm pays £42 in wages. Goods are valued at £121. The corresponding profit is £79 and the rate of profit is 188% as shown. But the rate of profit for other firms is far less. In such circumstances they will switch to producing commodity A and the balance of supply to demand will be lost. Now consider the same firm in Figure 4. Wages are the same and the quantity of goods produced is the same, but the goods actually sell for £59.29. The rate of profit is 41%, and this is the profit rate for all other firms. So the price network is stable. This particular model is the same as the model in Figure 6-2 and 6-3 in Chapter 6. But our new presentation is more open and will lend itself better to the complexities that lie ahead. We can now move on to Chapter 12.

12

Factor costs: part 1

In our diagrams so far, the only costs shown for a typical firm have been wages. We can now take a step closer to reality by including the other two main sources of cost, namely, raw materials and maintenance of equipment. At the same time, we can introduce differential levels of pay in the workforce. These changes are incorporated in Figure 12-1.

The different pay scales for the workforce are self-explanatory. The categories chosen, *skilled / unskilled / supervisory / clerical*, can plausibly represent the different types of labour inputs required by a typical firm. The currency value is shown as £1000 per day. This specifies the value in banknotes of one day's bulk production of any commodity. There are five firms (which are really spheres of production but we will call them firms for convenience) producing five commodities. So the total value produced per day, by these five firms, is £5000. But all of these commodities carry two additional values, which are the costs that must be made good in respect of raw materials and upkeep of equipment. The latter is shown under the heading *instrument*.

Thus if we check the situation portrayed in respect of Firm C, we note that the workforce consists of 22 unskilled workers, 5 skilled workers and 4 supervisory & clerical, each group earning respectively £220, £250 and £80. Instrument costs are £185 and raw materials are £177. The newly created value per day is £1000, and the total value of the finished goods is the sum of all the amounts *inside* the rectangle, namely £1362. The value of the goods does *not* include the wages. The value of £1362 is realised by the sale, and the wages are *a deduction* from this realised value. A profit of £450 remains when all costs have been met. Hence the wages (and the profits) are *outside* the value rectangle, because they play no part in the formation of value. We have already covered this ground in Part One.

When the costs of wages, raw materials and equipment upkeep are all deducted from the bulk selling price of £1362, the amount left over is the profit of £450 per day, shown in the black rectangle on the right hand side of the diagram. The firm's owner confronts the necessity of paying all these costs regularly, and his view of the value-creating process leads him to think that his costs plus a fair profit determine the selling price of the goods. As we know, this view is quite false. We have analysed the price mechanism in Part One and we know that commodities acquire their exchange value from their production

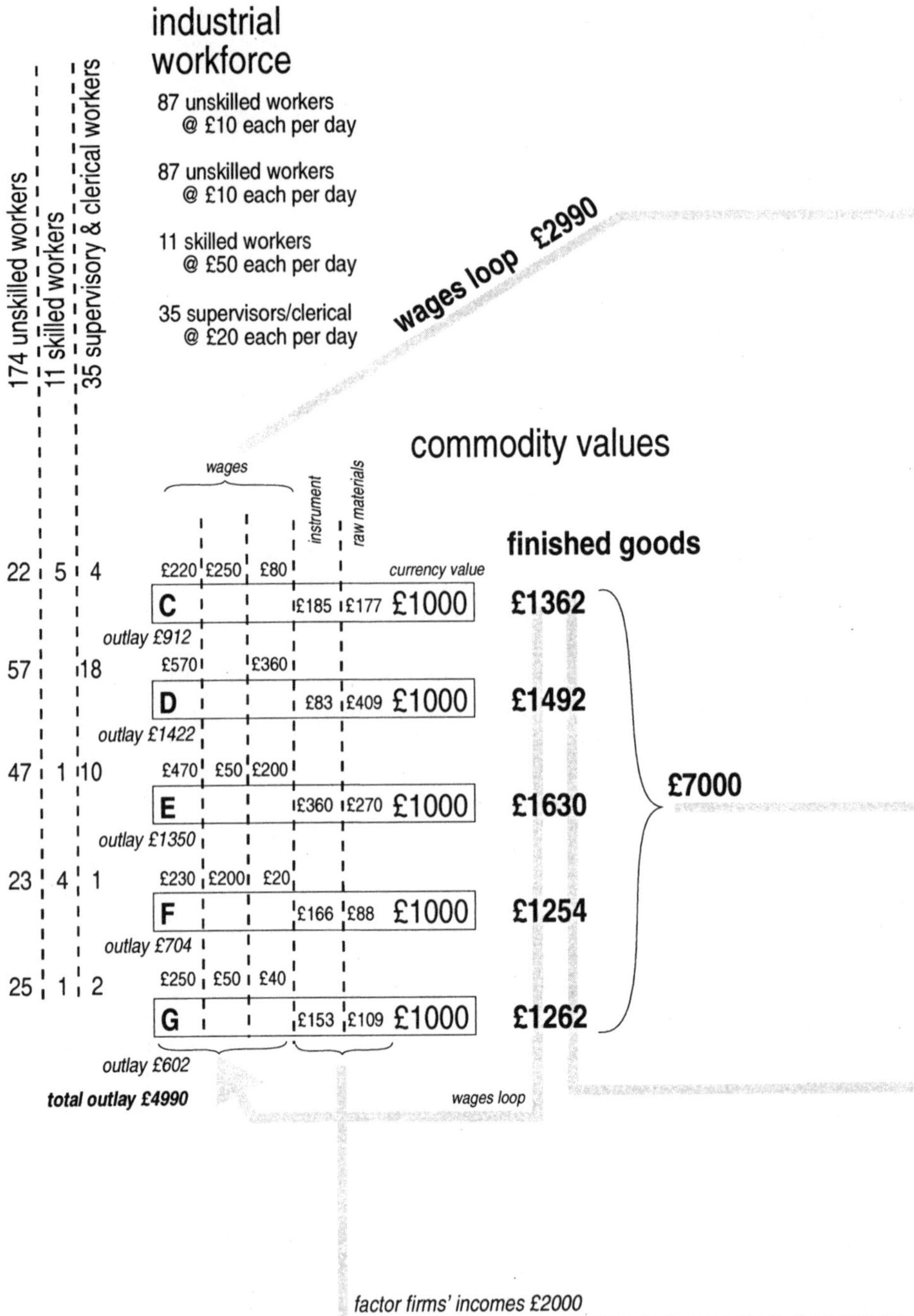

Figure 12-1 (both pages)

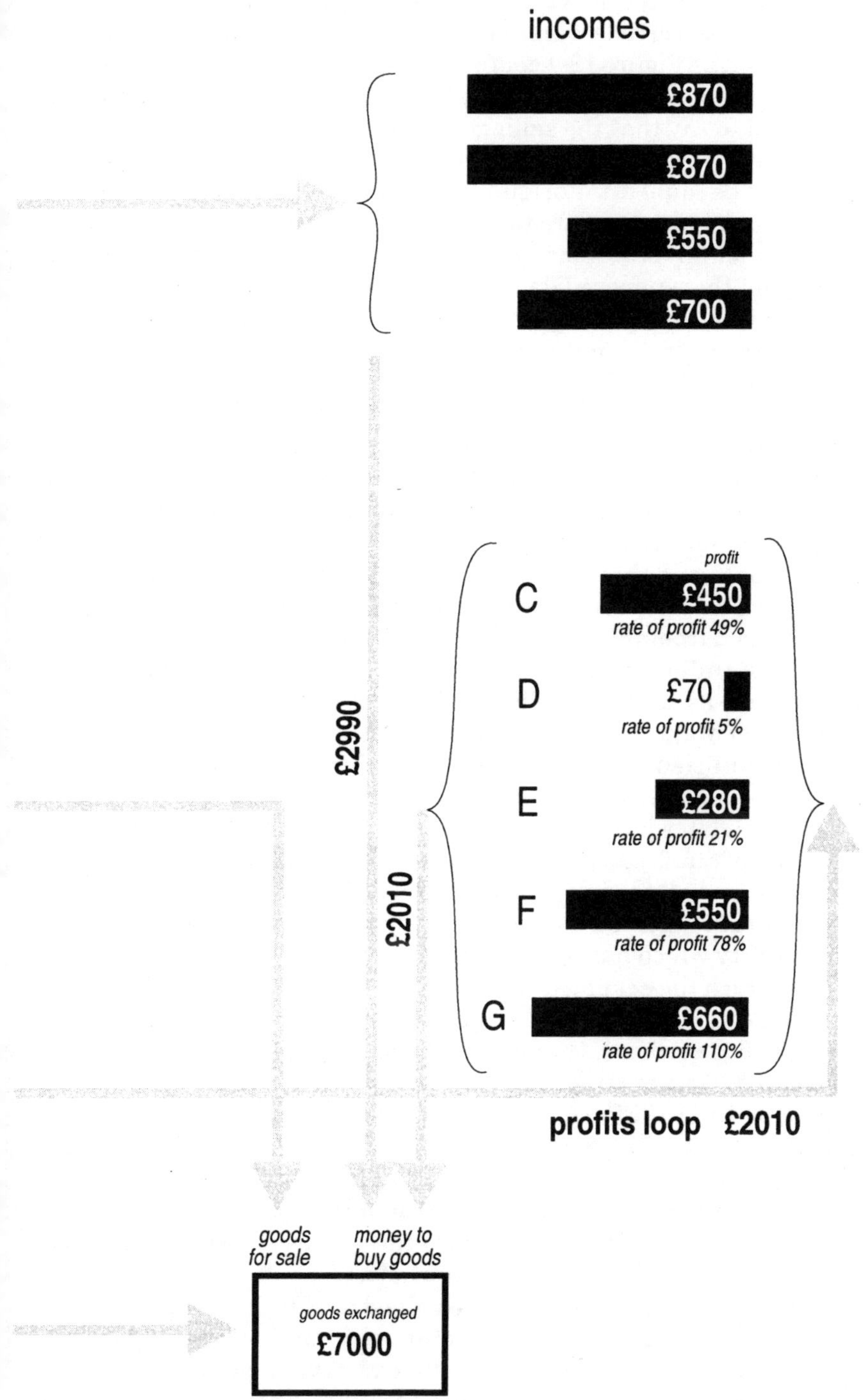

Figure 12-1 (both pages)

rates, expressed at first in terms of a universal commodity equivalent, and then later in terms of inconvertible banknotes. But the false impression carries considerable weight, as Figure 12-1 confirms. The outlay for Firm C is £912, as shown, and when the goods sell for £1362, the remainder of £450 is the profit. So it seems logical to say that the selling price is the sum of the costs and the profit. Likewise, if a piece of string is cut into three lengths, the sum of these three lengths must be equal to the original length of string before it was divided, and so it may seem logical as before to say that the original length is obtained by adding the cut lengths together, inferring that the former depends on the latter. The proof of this supposed dependency can be furnished very easily in real terms by anyone with string and scissors. Such a line of reasoning is obviously quite nonsensical, but this is the logic presented in the textbooks, and it looks plausible to the ordinary view because it is always true, and it corresponds to the narrow practical outlook of individual firms within a particular sphere of production. This kind of inverted logic, where an outcome is used to explain its own antecedents, can always be substantiated by proofs galore drawn from real situations, and even the genuine investigator can easily be misled by seemingly irrefutable evidence into a cul-de-sac of ignorance where empirical data and theoretical conclusions link themselves together in empty tautologies. During the so-called classical period, the fledgeling discipline of economics escaped from this cul-de-sac, and the foundations were laid for a scientific understanding of all phenomena connected with money, an understanding that was fundamentally hostile to ruling class interests, explicitly so in the writings of Marx, but also clearly present in other non-revolutionary writers who had sufficient integrity to stand by their own research findings. John Stuart Mill is a good example of an independent investigator who posed no subversive threat but who expressed views that were disturbing to the ruling powers. A blanket of dumb subservience replaced this independent tradition of genuine research, and all the advances of the classical period were lost, when Jevons, Walras and Menger led the way back into the cul-de-sac with a very old concept called utility which has no objective dimensions (because it is entirely subjective), but which they claimed could be measured by a new breakthrough in analytic wizardry called marginal analysis, a contortion of logic widely employed in orthodox economics but never adopted by any other discipline. We will examine this conjuring trick in a moment.

In Figure 12-1, the workforce, the wages, the instrument costs, the raw material costs, the bulk selling price and the profit are shown for all five firms. The total value produced per day is £7000. We do not know what the unit values are for any of the commodities, because actual quantities are not specified. But whatever these quantities are, they acquire the values shown. We can now consider the coherence of the diagram as a whole.

The goods produced by the five firms are valued at £7000 and each day they travel to the goods exchange interface represented by the bold rectangle at the bottom. The money to buy these goods is provided by the wages and the profits that are generated each day. (The wages for the 174 unskilled workers are shown as two blocks of £870 simply to align all incomes on the right hand side while the value creation process is kept on the left). Incomes from wages and profits are £2990 and £2010 respectively, making a joint total of £5000. We face the fact that the goods are valued at £7000, but only £5000 is available to buy them. Where is the missing £2000?

The missing amount is not difficult to find. These five firms have paid out money for raw materials and upkeep of equipment, so there must be other firms in the community who supply these services. These other firms and the money they earn need to be introduced into the model. But these firms do not make finished goods, so we keep them separate for the moment. For present purposes we simply note that these other firms earn incomes which are necessarily identical with the costs shown in the instrument and raw materials columns in the diagram. These costs do indeed make a total of £2000 (chosen quite arbitrarily to keep the arithmetic simple). Although these other firms are not shown, we can now confirm that Figure 12-1 contains a coherent values network. The total value of the goods produced in one day is £7000. The incomes generated to buy these goods is made up of wages at £2990, profits at £2010, and earnings at £2000 for other firms, not shown, who provide factorial services in respect of instrument upkeep and raw materials.

These other firms are not shown because we need to proceed step by step. They will be introduced in the next chapter. Meanwhile, we still have a further operation to perform. Although Figure 12-1 possesses a coherent value system, it does not have a set of stable prices. Prices are stable only when the rate of profit is equal for all firms, because otherwise, in a freely competitive market, firms will always switch to the production of any commodity that gives a better return. So our train of reasoning is as follows. If the present distribution of the workforce produces the particular mixture of goods that corresponds to the pattern of aggregate demand, then everybody by definition will be satisfied. How can this particular mixture of goods, regularly produced each day, be stabilised to ensure such an outcome? Clearly not by the values that are shown. We need a set of prices that correspond to equal rates of profit for all firms, thereby removing any incentive to switch to another commodity. The required price network is shown in Figure 12-2.

In the previous Figure 12-1 the overall rate of profit, derived from a total outlay of £4990 and a total profit of £2010, for all firms considered as a whole, is 40.28%. In Figure 12-2, prices are adjusted so that all firms achieve this rate of profit. The former coherence expressed in values is now expressed in prices. This conversion to prices means that some commodities have a price which is higher than their value and vice versa for other commodities (values are shown in brackets). But the sum of the prices is equal to the sum of the values, so whether as values or prices the total purchasing power is the same in respect of exactly the same output of goods. The change from values to prices has no effect on production. All the goods are still produced and purchased in the same proportions. But the price-form is a modification of the value-form to bring about an equal rate of profit, which in turn ensures that these production rates stay constant, thereby matching supply to aggregate demand. (Marx is the economist who discovered this relation between values and prices).

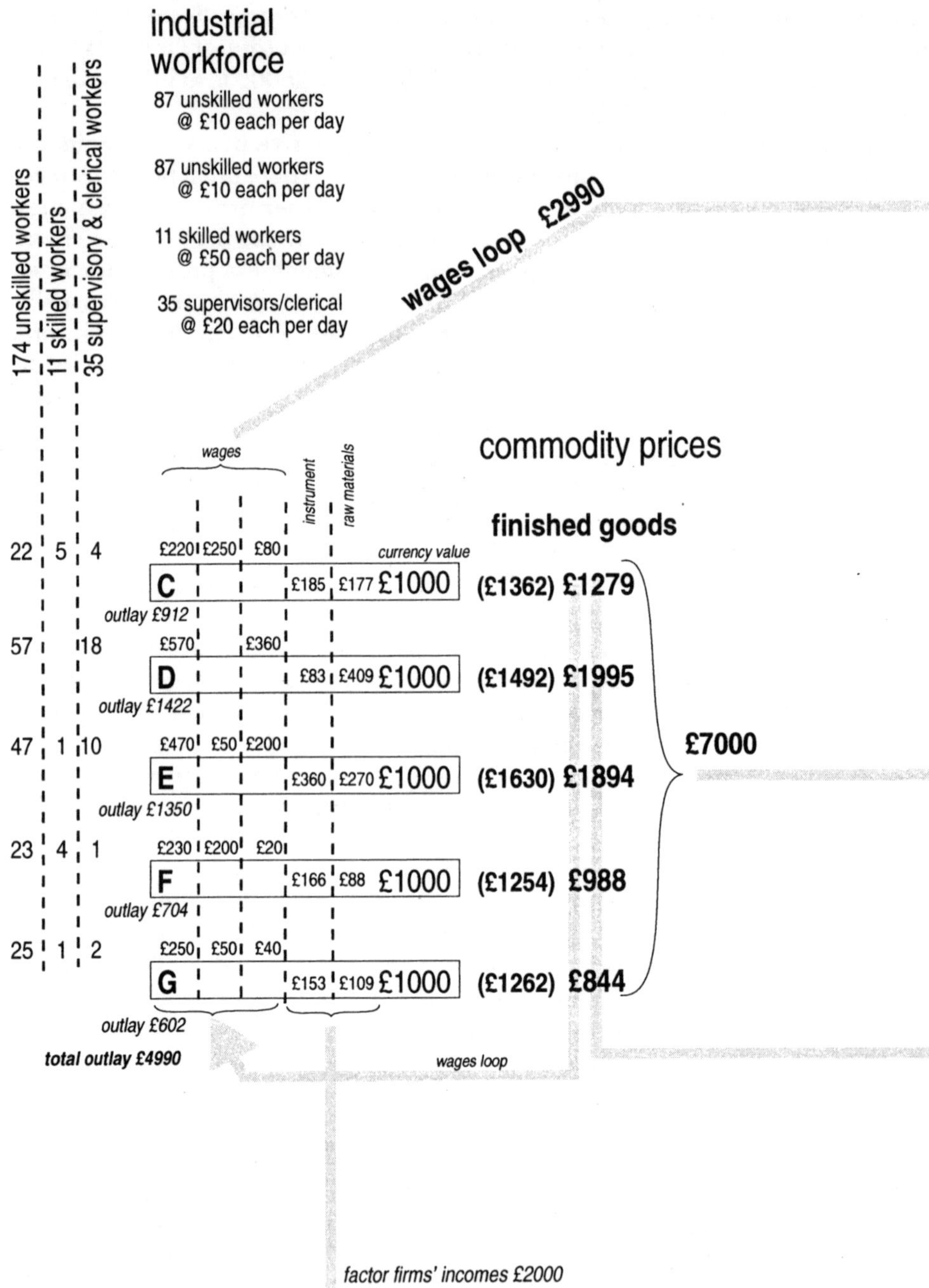

Figure 12-2 (both pages)

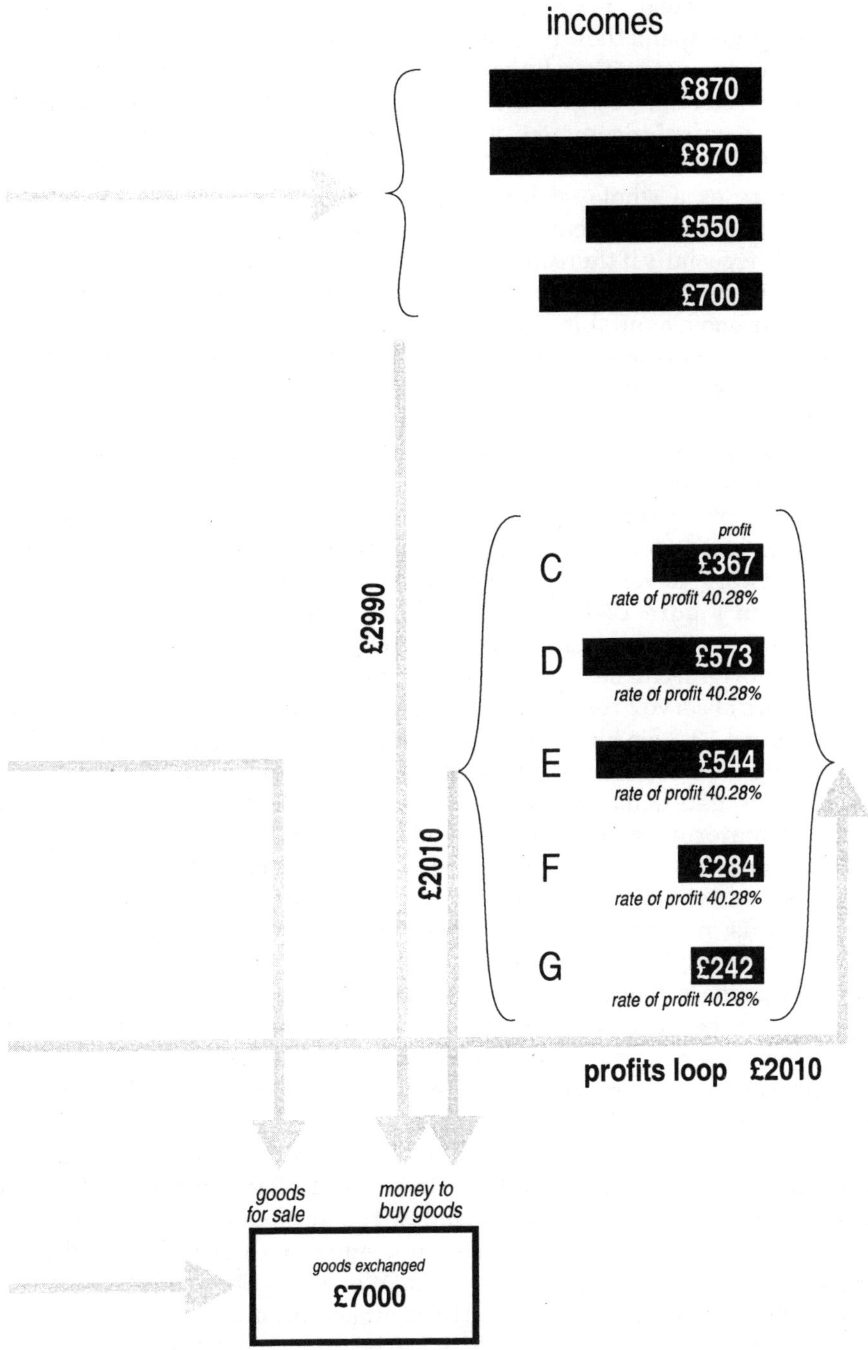

Figure 12-2 (both pages)

Of course nobody is performing the kind of calculations described here. People simply spend their incomes according to need or preference. If they want more of a commodity they buy more, and spend less on some other good. This freedom is exercised by everybody, and much of it is self-compensating. I want more of a particular commodity today but less of it tomorrow while somebody else wants the reverse. Such individual variations may be quite large, but in the community as a whole with millions of buying transactions they are quite random and therefore cause no appreciable change in the general level of demand, especially if there are reserve stocks to absorb minor fluctuations. But when demand by a significant number of buyers rises simultaneously for a particular good, available stocks will sooner or later be exhausted and buyers come into competition with each other. The price then begins to rise. In a freely competitive economy, the higher selling price will attract other firms and the supply will increase. We have rehearsed this sequence of events many times. The price network is now moving to a new equilibrium which will be reached when equality in the rate of profit is restored for all firms. This movement of prices and profit rates from one equilibrium to another is continuous and is simply the normal sequence of events in a freely competitive market. Hence the price network never takes the form of a values network, as portrayed for instance in Figure 12-1. It exists only as a prices network like Figure 12-2. Values are never on parade, so to speak, only prices. But the behaviour of prices, and their origin, can be deciphered only if the value-form is understood. Figure 12-2 is the observed reality and Figure 12-1 is the theoretical underpinning.

In Figure 12-2 we have a stable price network, an equal rate of profit for all firms, and a distribution of the workforce which enables production outputs to match aggregate demand. We are assuming that the money spent on instrument and raw materials will eventually find its way to the goods exchange interface. On this basis we can affirm that goods to the value of £7000 are being produced each day, and that incomes are being generated simultaneously each day to buy these goods, namely £2990 in wages, £2010 in profits, and £2000 earned by firms providing factorial services. So the model is in equilibrium. Supply of finished goods is balanced against social demand. But Figures 12-1 and 12-2 are incomplete, because some participating firms are missing. The omission of these firms is a departure from the rigorous standard we have followed till now. We have always portrayed the entire economy. These factorial firms must now be incorporated into the model.

Before continuing however, we have a good opportunity at this stage to consider how the information shown in Figure 12-2 is presented in the standard text-books. (Readers who wish to follow the main analysis should move on to the next chapter). A model of sorts, in keeping with orthodox wisdom, can be constructed as shown in Figure 12-3. We retain the same layout to assist comparison. Note that there are three important differences.

First, the currency value, which links the number of banknotes in circulation to the physical output of goods produced during the accommodation period, and thereby provides the basis for all the magnitudes shown, is missing. (The textbook fumblings in this area are known as the "quantity theory of money").

Second, the coherence of the model now depends on the kind of logic that explains the length of a piece of string by cutting it into several pieces and adding them together. In other words, the price is explained as the sum of all costs, including wages, plus the profit. We can now claim to be on very secure ground. Answers to economic questions are bound to be correct because they are locked in tautologies. Where does the profit come from? It is the remainder when total costs have been deducted from gross sales. Where do the wages come from? They are a cost deducted from gross sales. Where does the selling price come from? It is the sum of all costs, including wages, plus an increment added called profit. Why do these prices or wages or profits alter? Because the demand or the supply in regard to labour or goods or outlay have altered, causing some magnitudes to rise and others to fall. And so on. Thus everything explains everything else, and an equilibrium is achieved by reciprocal dependency that has no exogenous foundation, as in a famous exploit by the great Baron Munchausen, who tells how he leaped over a lake on horseback, wrapping his immensely strong legs round the horse's belly to keep it in the air, while he in turn was kept aloft by the horse, till they both landed on the other side.

Third, and very important, is the fact that this model is no longer part of a developing series. There is no evolutionary progression from earlier to later stages that could offer insights into historical change in the real world, (and thereby obtain the confirmation that all theoretical reasoning depends upon). The model just comes into being from nowhere and endures as it is, infinitely adaptable to the fluctuations of supply and demand, which exist side by side in self-compensating harmony. In other words, the model is perfect on its own terms. It may be over-simplified as it stands, but this can be corrected by progressive elaboration to include more and more of the features that are present in a real economy. This is the general approach of the standard textbooks, and an important corollary follows. The model's perfection is, in the orthodox view, an inevitable limitation on the scope of economics as an applied science. We are all endowed with free will, so the argument goes, and the real world is the complex outcome of desires and deeds that cannot be modeled in any sense. Economics is a scientific pursuit, dealing with facts, not opinions and chance encounters. It studies the outcomes of certain economic decisions, but the decisions are the responsibility of those who make them. Here we meet the much trumpeted distinction between a normative approach to economics, which is unscientific because it rests on a commitment of some kind, political or utopian or humanitarian or similar, and the superior approach of the textbooks, where economics is allegedly studied as a pure science, free from value-judgements.

This alleged distinction between normative and positive economics is an important theoretical issue. Let us carefully examine the grounds on which the textbooks make their claim to be value-free.

When two or more variables interact with each other, an outcome of some kind is produced. This outcome must be clearly distinguished as a dependent response, meaning that it is later in time and in logical sequence than the variables which act as causal agents. All knowledge depends on the correct identification of variables and outcomes in these terms. We create mental concepts that distinguish (and give names to) particular causal agents and we place them in the correct sequential order relative to the outcome, an order in which time and logic are combined. An equilibrium, therefore, is not fully understood when (1) its variables are recognised and (2) the relationship between them and the outcome is expressed as mere reciprocation, while (3) the dependency order is unclear or ignored. For instance, a hot air ballon will tend to rise when the enclosed air gets hotter, and it will tend to fall when the total weight of balloon and cargo increases. The causal agents are temperature and weight. The outcome or resultant is altitude. These correlations can be tabulated for a particular balloon, and such data can be tested in practice to prove their accuracy, thus confirming that the interaction between the variables has been accurately understood by whoever compiled the tables. The tables can be used to show all manner of possible combinations between temperature, weight and altitude. Altitude can even take precedence as a conceptual variable, while the other two variables are speculatively adjusted according to the tabulated information. But even though it is quite sensible to use the tables in this inverted fashion, the altitude variable can never take precedence in reality or in explanatory logic. The weight and the temperature assert their influence on the altitude, never the other way round. Of course in this particular example it would be stupid to think otherwise. But in the conventional economics textbooks this cart-before-the-horse logic is standard practice.

What advantage is gained by such subverted reasoning? The advantage for purveyors of humbug is considerable. In terms of our balloon example, if weight and temperature are correctly defined as causal agents acting on the altitude, and if the balloon's altitude is also defined as a causal agent acting on the weight and the temperature, then we need seek no more for any further knowledge about the balloon's behaviour. We have a complete theoretical framework supported by masses of empirical data. No balloon could ever behave inconsistently with this framework, which is quite value-free, so our scientific credentials will be superb. We need not bother about a theory of gravitation, or a molecular theory of gases, or any other topic of common dispute and speculation. Such matters lie outside the pure theory of balloon behaviour. No doubt the people who fly balloons will concern themselves with such things, but that is their own affair. We stand above any such normative preferences, which belong to the domain of democratic free choice, and we are totally opposed to people who would interfere with this freedom by advancing their own pet notions under the guise of scientific theory.

Anyone arguing along these lines with regard to balloons would soon be recognised as a fool. The reversal of logic is too obviously silly. An event in real time cannot be explained by logic that nominates the outcome as a cause. Logic must conform to a temporal order. Keeping this in mind, compare Figure 12-2 with Figure 12-3. In the former there is a distinct causal pathway. Goods produced in a specified time period acquire a currency value which is added to instrument and raw material costs to create a value-form which then interacts with other value-forms throughout the market as a whole to create a selling price which then splits three ways into wages, costs in respect of instrument and raw materials, and profit. Every day (or week or year) this pattern is repeated. The causal sequence moves comprehensively forward both in logic and in real time. Now look at Figure 12-3. The overall causal sequence, based on real time, has vanished, and in its place any variable can masqerade as a cause, or be treated as if it were an outcome. The linkages remain true, and the arithmetic is correct. But all the magnitudes in Figure 12-3 are promiscuously co-dependent, bound together in tautological loops, like a spider's web in which all the strands are linked to other strands and none is anchored to any support. Explanations can now be perfect, because they are interlinked truisms. All that is needed is a style of explanation to hide the silliness, a form of words and an appropriate vocabulary, a method of explaining things that allows us to make positive statements that are ultimately self-referencing, with no dependence on external support, and we can then claim that they are value-free.

This explanatory style, with a technical vocabulary of its own, is called marginalism, and it enables us to study variables in a rather peculiar way. In any competent research project, variables are identified and studied in relation to their effect on other variables. Each variable thereby becomes part of a causal chain, moving through time, and this causal chain, once discovered, is the explanation for the outcome, whatever that outcome is. The same course is followed in marginal logic, but the causal chain, with its link to time, is not regarded as the explanation. The last increment added to the magnitude of a variable is held to be the explanation for the outcome. An example will clarify this distinction. If a pack-horse carries what may be described as its optimum load, then the animal is neither over-burdened in terms of its strength and endurance, nor under-employed in terms of an efficient means of transport. Thus we may sharply observe that as a light load is made progressively heavier, the returns improve, till at the optimum load the returns reach a peak, while any further increase in loading becomes counter-productive and results in diminishing returns. The progressive augmentation of the load brings to light a critical margin of maximum efficiency, from which come two notions, first, the perfectly sensible notion of the optimum load, which is measured and explained by some criterion of efficiency, and second, the notion of the marginal load which is measured and explained by the fact that it possesses the last added increment that just enables it to achieve optimality. In this second notion, the efficiency criterion is not regarded as the explanation. The last incremental addition to the variable is highlighted as the causal agent.

The study of an equilibrium by incremental increases in one of its variables is a perfectly reasonable procedure and no-one could quarrel with the pack-horse example as just described. And whether the most efficient load is described as "optimum" or "marginal" is neither here nor there. But note that the causal pathway, the chain of logical and temporal reasoning, is quite clear. The horse is *first of all* loaded and it performs its work *afterwards*, and then the goods can *subsequently* be consumed, sold or utilised in some way. A certain load gives rise to a certain performance, which results in certain returns, not

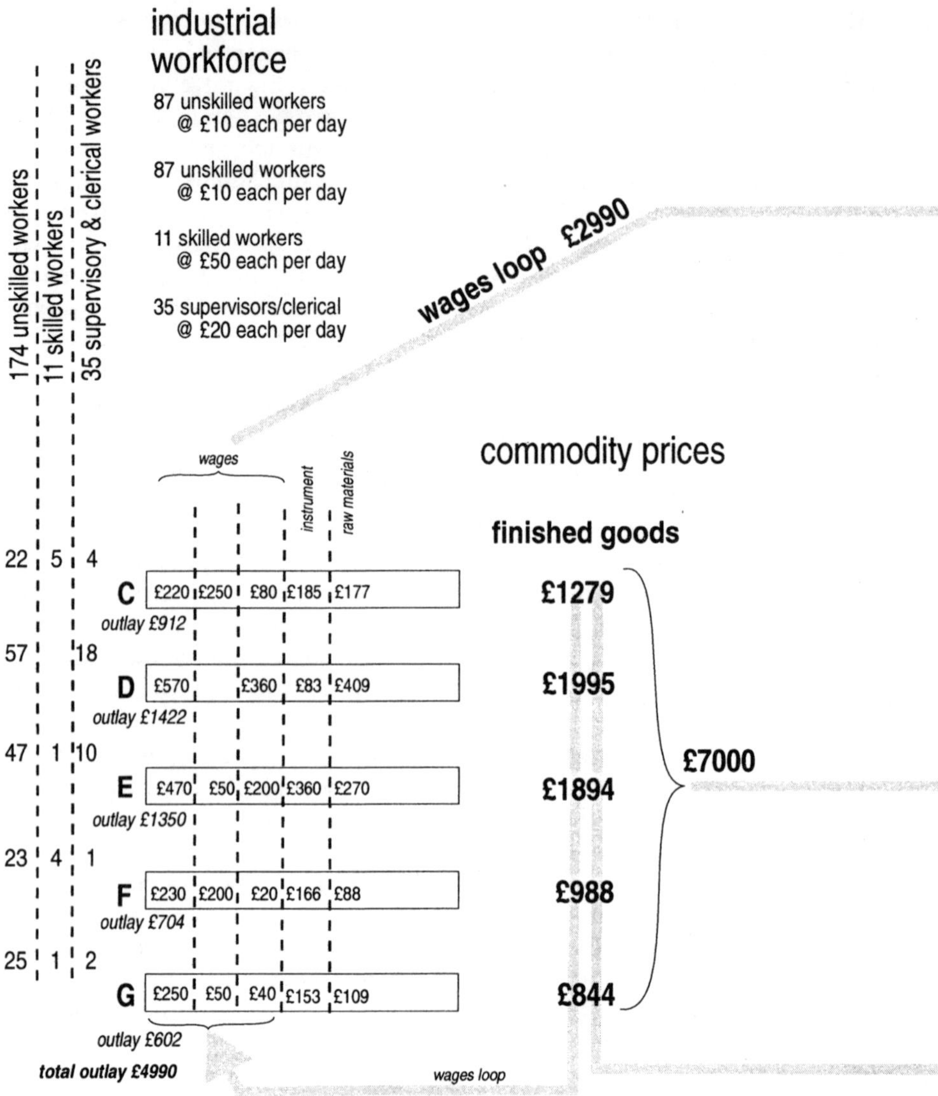

Figure 12-3 (both pages)

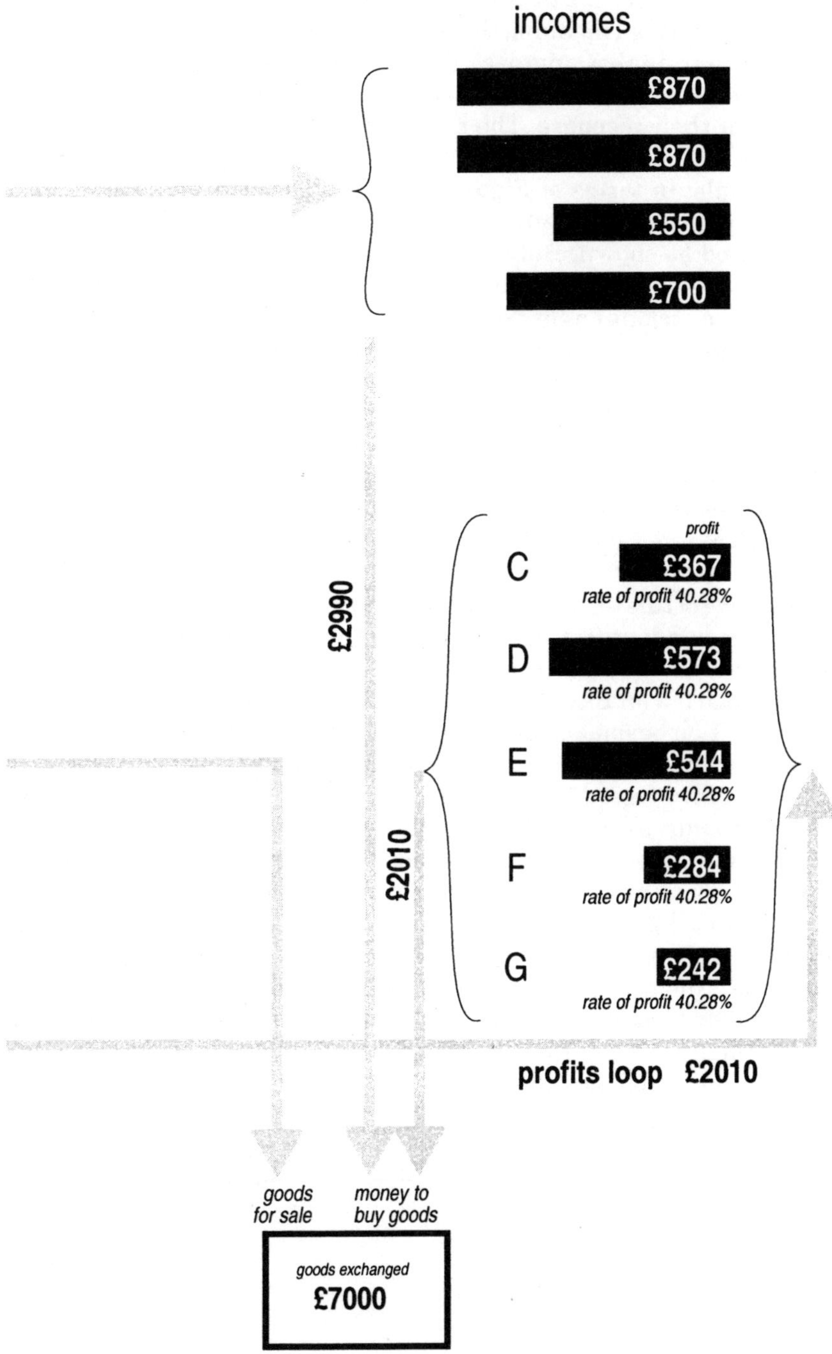

Figure 12-3 (both pages)

the other way round. But if the relationship between variables is treated as mere reciprocation, meaning that cause and effect are allowed to change places, then this marginalist approach degenerates into mere trickery. Any part can be defined as a "variable"and altered incrementally, while the other parts are studied for their response. The procedure seems eminently reasonable, and in fact there will be plenty of empirical evidence to support such circular reasoning. For example, in terms of Figure 12-3, it is quite obvious that a good deal of accurate information is present. Wages and operating costs and profits are all interrelated as shown. But nothing can be explained at overall level because outcomes are not distinguished from their antecedent causes. The reasoning is trapped in a vicious circle. No further progress is possible until the circularity is broken by discovering the developmental order. In such a situation as this, marginal theory comes into its specious own, because it bars the way to further enlightenment by offering authoritative explanations which are in fact devoid of content. The marginal price can be identified, and marginal profits and marginal costs and marginal everything else, with a wealth of empirical data that fits perfectly. But all these fine marginal truisms are a cover to hide the tautological ignorance.

The essence of this technique, reduced to the simplest possible terms, is to make reality its own justification by proving that it cannot be otherwise than it is without becoming something else. Thus if I walk from my home to the post office, which is a mile away, I must not walk more than a mile or less than a mile, otherwise I go beyond or fall short of my destination. I will arrive at the post office only when my walking reaches that incremental limit which corresponds to the distance I need to travel to get there. This explains why the post office is exactly a mile away. No other distance will fit the incremental optimum, and the explanation is scientific because it is verified by experience and it is independent of any value judgements. This explanation is always true for journeys to all post offices everywhere. Here beginneth and here endeth the gospel according to marginalism. It is no surprise that despite its "scientific" posturing, this doctrine enjoys no vestige of credibility anywhere outside the discipline of economics, even though the study of variables and equilibria is found in many other fields of learning. Marginalism is invaluable as a language of deception. It has no other worth.

13

Factor costs: part 2

The models in the preceding Chapter 12 were incomplete because factorial firms were missing. Only the finished goods market was shown, with hypothesised costs in respect of intermediate goods and services. The complete economy is shown in Figure 13-1 overleaf. Firm A provides a maintenance and replacement service for all tools and equipment, and Firm B supplies raw materials. This model is coherent in all its magnitudes. All costs, all values and all incomes are specified. The production process, final and intermediate, creates a flow of commodities and services at the values shown, from which incomes arise in the form of wages and profits, and these incomes in turn enable those self-same goods and services to be bought. But, as already explained, Figure 13-1 is only a *values* network. Values never appear in the market as such. Values must be converted into *prices* to acquire a real existence. Hence this diagram is only the first half of an interlocked duality. It is suspended in mid-air so to speak, awaiting resolution, in the same way as Figure 12-1 needed its twin version Figure 12-2.

Let us consolidate our understanding before moving on. Although the values shown in Figure 13-1 are not stable, the diagram has a solid practical and theoretical base which will be preserved when these values are transformed into prices. The distribution of the workforce will not change, and our fundamental supposition is that this distribution ensures that finished goods are supplied at rates which satisfy aggregate relative demand for this group of 270 workers and 7 owners. The collateral demand for intermediate goods and services (supplied by Firms A and B) is also satisfied by this arrangement. Once the workforce distribution is defined in these terms, with a fully specified example as in Figure 13-1, the finished goods output rates (whatever they are) can be indexed by any arbitrary number that is the same for each respective line of production. We have chosen the arbitrary number £1000 to serve as a currency value, which, as we know, is linked to the total face-value of real banknotes in the monetary base. This linkage is traced through the size of the accommodation period and the velocity of the currency in ways we have analysed in Chapter 11.

Figure 13-1 incorporates all this information and also takes two further steps, first into the determination of wages as a payment for working time. Once again we choose an arbitrary figure, denoting a particular apportionment of

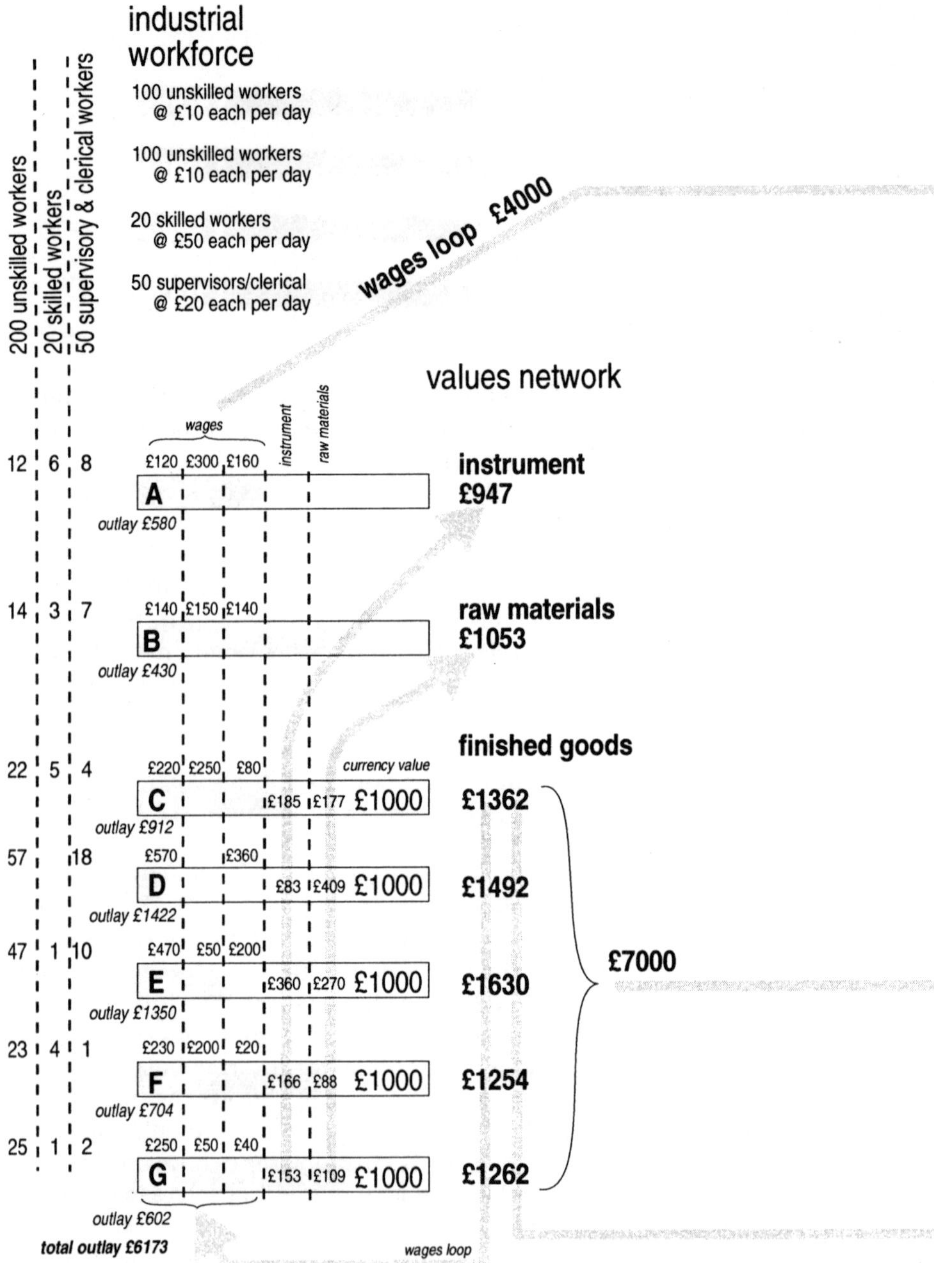

Figure 13-1 (both pages)

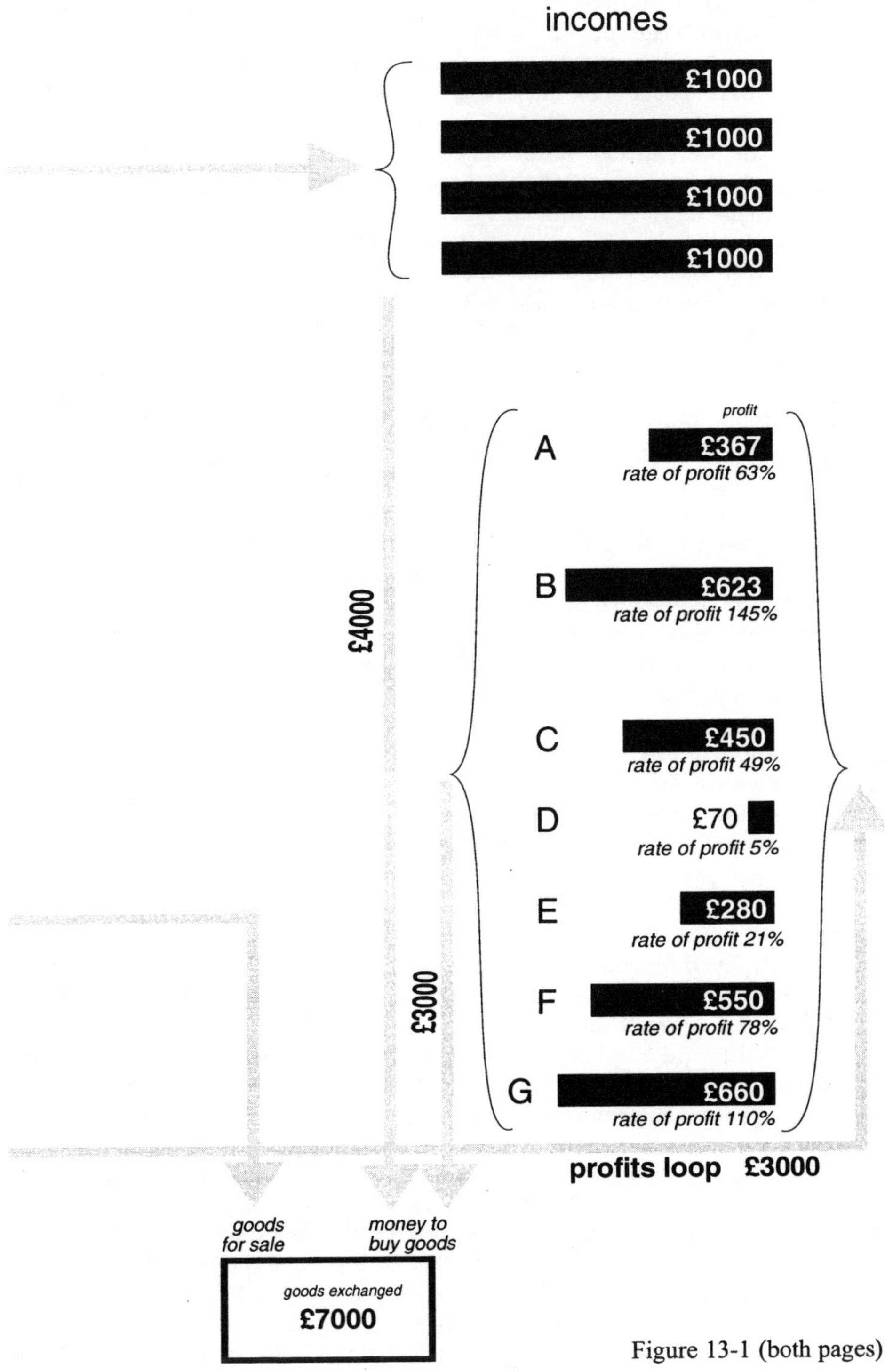

Figure 13-1 (both pages)

sales revenue between wages and profits, and we merely presume that different skills will earn different pay rates, while the rates themselves will be the same in all firms because labour is freely mobile. The second step is to show the costs for all firms in respect of raw materials and upkeep of equipment. These costs, added to the currency value of £1000, give the total values of the finished goods, and from this we can calculate (speculatively, because these values never appear in the market as such) the corresponding profit and rate of profit for each of the five firms C, D, E, F and G. The two factorial firms A and B earn their incomes not by any direct involvement in the goods exchange interface (where only finished goods are traded) but by external transactions which impose costs on any firm that uses their services. Thus there is a lot of factual information in Figure 13-1, grounded in clearly stated suppositions and strict arithmetic operations.

We must now convert the values network of Figure 13-1 into a stable prices network, in the same way as we converted Figure 12-1 into Figure 12-2. But we need to be clear about the status of the magnitudes displayed in our present model, Figure 13-1. The finished goods acquire an overall value of £5000, plus an extra value in respect of costs for instrument maintenance and raw materials. The £5000 is fixed but the extra costs, £947 and £1053 were arbitrarily chosen. We selected these magnitudes to give a nice round figure of £2000, but this can be no more than a dummy value. The real value will be "set by the market", to use a common phrase. Remember that the value-creation process confers a value only on *finished goods,* because it is the relation between the respective production rates of *finished goods* that endows the circulating banknotes with their value. In other words, although the notion of "value" may be loosely applied to all sorts of things, in economic theory the term "exchange-value" applies strictly to finished goods and nothing else. There is no "value" as such for raw materials, no value for maintenance services, no value for any factorial element or ancillary activity, regardless of how important these things may be to the productive process. The only fixed magnitude (in respect of money) in Figure 13-1 is the £5000 derived from the currency value, and this, to repeat, attaches itself only to finished goods. Every other magnitude is an *outcome* wholly dependent on the network of prices in the market. The significance of such a rigorous definition of exchange-value will become clearer as we move the analysis forward.

The procedure we must now follow can be described thus. The average rate of profit is calculated for the finished goods firms, CDEFG, as if they were an aggregated group, using the dummy values that (for the present) stand for raw material and maintenance costs. This average rate is then adjusted upwards or downwards by reducing or increasing the dummy values, which are the earnings acquired by A and B for their services. These adjustments in turn have the effect of raising or lowering the rates of profit for A and B. An adjustment that increases the rate of profit for CDEFG will reduce the rate of profit for A and/or B, and vice versa. Thus an equilibrium point can be found where all rates of profit are equal. At this equilibrium point, the overall costs for raw material and equipment maintenance are determined, and the particular costs for each separate firm in CDEFG can now be calculated from this overall cost. The bulk prices of the finished goods is the sum of these costs plus the currency value of £1000. Thus for Firm C, the bulk price of its goods per day is £185 + £177 + £1000. The currency value remains totally unaffected by any of these operations. It acts as the fulcrum round which all other magnitudes rise or fall in an equalisation process that determines the uniform rate of profit for every firm in the entire market.

There is nothing especially difficult about the arithmetic involved, but it is long-winded and tedious. In fact the adjustment process as described is exactly the same as the operation of the market in real life. No firm can fix the price of its products arbitrarily (we take for granted that there are no monopolies) and therefore every firm's general objective in a freely competitive economy is to maximise profits, and this urge constantly equalises the rates of profit between them. On this basis the prices that balance supply and demand are brought into existence. In theory we neglect the effect of time-lags. In practical reality, there will always be continual realignment and disturbance about a mean position which itself alters in the longer term, as a result of technical improvements or changes in the pattern of demand. Such oscillations and swings do not invalidate the theory. On the contrary, the existence of a potentially stable equilibrium is the basis for explaining the deviations.

But we are not concerned with any deviations. We are engaged in understanding the equalisation process in its essential integrity, in order that we can transform Figure 13-1 into a viable prices network. Nevertheless, following from the above observations, we now have a reorientated view of Figure 13-1. Figure 13-1 is simply a network of possible prices which do not coincide with an equal rate of profit for all firms. The arrangement portrayed is perfectly viable if we allow the presence of monopoly conditions in one form or another throughout the economy. As long as the total income created per day is equal to the total value of finished goods produced per day, then the resulting price network is internally coherent, and all goods are cleared from the market at the same rate as they are being supplied. There are a great many coherent price networks that will balance aggregate supply with aggregate demand. But among this range of coherent price networks there is only one that will *also* ensure an equal reward to all producers. This particular price network with its three-sided compatibility (supply balanced with demand, daily incomes equal to daily value of goods produced, and a uniform rate of profit for all firms) is ferreted out so to speak by competition. The trouble with Figure 13-1 is not that it needs transforming into a prices version, but that it conflicts with our basic assumption of a freely competitive market. The dummy values that we have postulated for raw materials and instrument costs are inconsistent with free competition. When we converted Figure 12-1 into Figure 12-2 we were in effect allowing "market forces" to operate as they normally would, given no impediments. An equal rate of profit is the outcome, alongside a set of prices that no longer correspond to the original exchange values. The latter just vanish from view. But these original exchange values are the key to any understanding of price formation. Without this key the whole process remains a mystery.

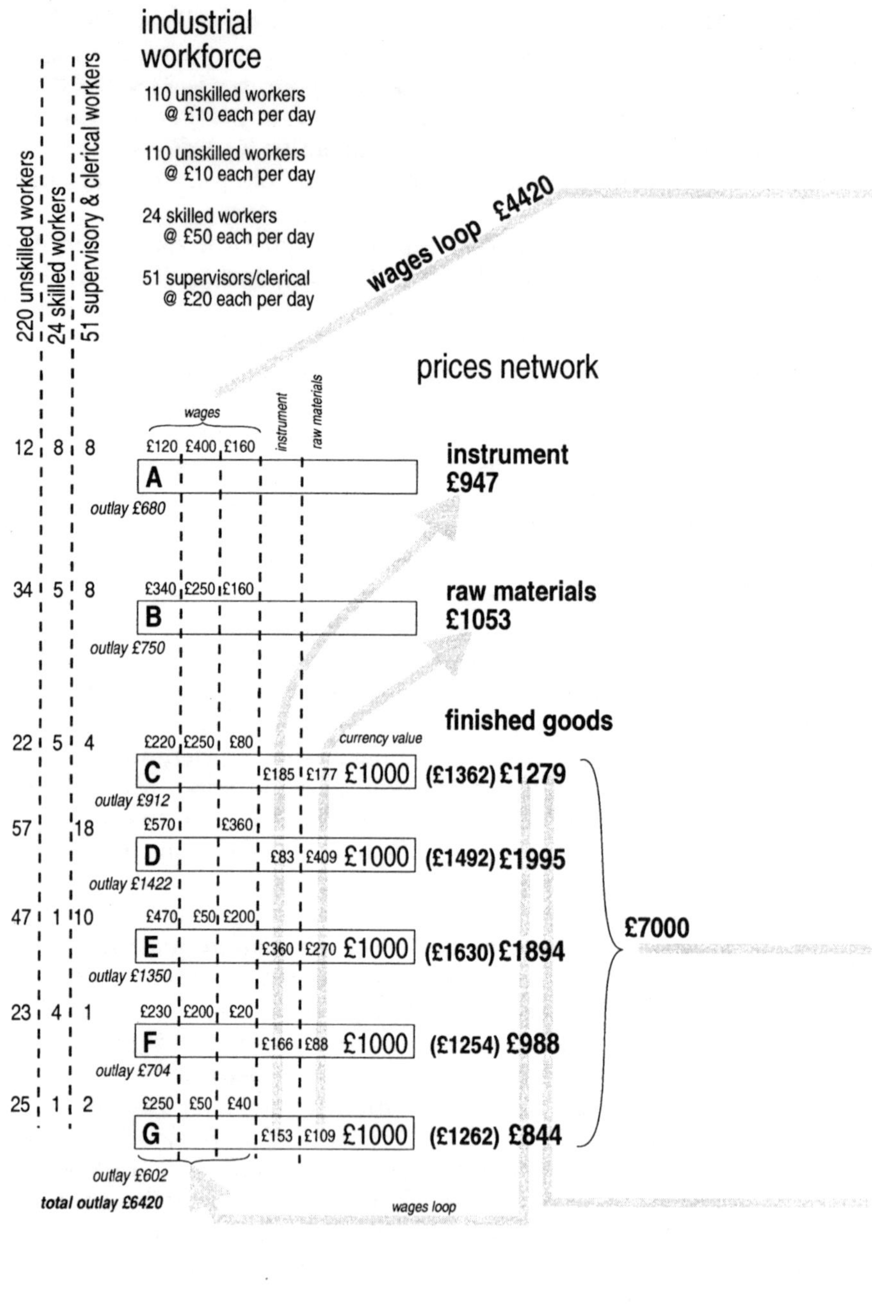

Figure 13-2 (both pages)

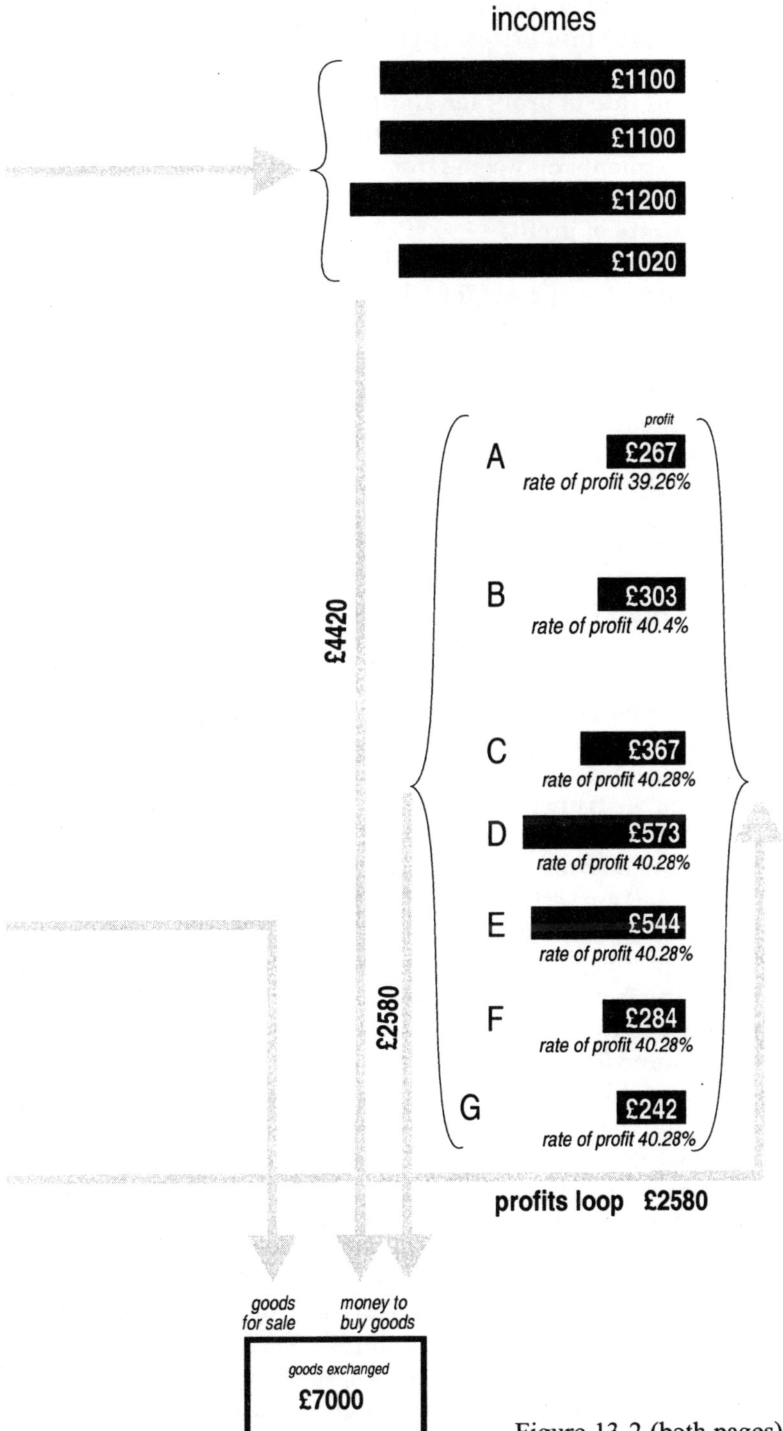

Figure 13-2 (both pages)

We now have a wider understanding of the equalisation process that converts values into prices. It is simply the ever-present response of a freely competitive economy to any change, no matter from what source, that disturbs the uniform rate of profit for all firms in the market. Any imbalance in profit rates sets in train a series of adjustments that tend to restore the balance, and these adjustments may come from different sectors of the economy. Even with a simple economy like Figure 13-1, there is more than one way to bring about a uniform rate of profit.

The method we will use is as follows. If we fix the incomes of A and B as given, so that the factorial costs for CDEFG are also fixed, (because these costs are identical with the incomes for A and B), we can calculate the average rate of profit for CDEFG (which we already know to be 40.28% from Figure 12-2), and we can then make the rate of profit for A and B equal to 40.28% by suitable adjustments to the wages and profits of A and B. The rate of wages can stay as it is if we vary the wage costs by altering the number of workers employed. Wage costs plus profits for A and B must always be equal to the respective incomes we have fixed for them, but within this restraint they can be adjusted to give a profit rate of about 40%, give or take the incremental effect of a whole day's wage, which is £10. In effect we are hiring or firing workers as necessary to bring the profit rates for A and B into line with the prevailing profit rate in the rest of the economy. The result is portrayed in Figure 13-2. Observe that the workforce for A and B has expanded, compared with Figure 13-1.

Of course our original assumption that finished goods are being supplied at a rate that satisfies aggregate demand still holds good. And we are now adding a further assumption that the outputs of Firms A and B satisfy the demand by CDEFG for instrument maintenance and raw materials. This is a secondary demand, so to speak, a kind of subsidiary market that can alter independently of the finished goods market, although it is ultimately governed by the latter. There is a certain technical requirement for factorial services in the production of nearly all finished goods. Leather for footwear and steel for automobiles are obvious examples. If natural leather was displaced by synthetics and steel by plastics, the factorial market would alter drastically. Prices for factorial goods and services may therefore be subject to all kinds of variation quite independently of the demand for finished goods, and quite independently of the general wage level. Figure 13-3 is an example. The two factorial costs, for instrument upkeep and raw materials, have been halved compared with Figure 13-2. The output of finished goods is the same as before, and wage rates are the same. The workforce in firms A and B is reduced in Figure 13-3, but nothing else has changed for the entire workforce throughout all firms. The prices of all goods have fallen, the general rate of profit has risen from 40% to 50%, and standard of living has risen for everybody because of the lower prices, but the improvement in productivity (halving the factorial costs) has flowed mostly into profits, while the workers discharged from A and B have lost their livelihood.

The levels of adjustment that progressively modify the original values and convert them into final prices can be listed as follows. The basic position is established by the physical production rates of finished goods that acquire their relative exchange values directly from the currency value (£1000 in our present models). The first adjustment is the addition of value (indeterminate at this stage) corresponding to factorial inputs. The next adjustment balances the profit rates between firms producing these finished goods (between CDEFG respectively), and then comes the adjustment that balances the profit rates between the finished goods sector and the factorial sector, (between CDEFG as a group and the group A/B). At this stage the factorial costs are determined. Next is the adjustment that balances profit rates between all the foregoing firms and every other ancillary firm that contributes to the production process in any way, no matter what that contribution may be. A cost for a service, of any kind whatever, is real for the firm that pays such costs, and is a factor in the series of modifications that transform value into price. No ancillary firms are shown as yet in our analysis, and there is a further adjustment process in respect of retailing which also lies ahead. Four sectors of the economy are thus distinguished by this series of adjustments, namely the finished goods sector, the factorial sector, the ancillary sector and the marketing sector. Only two of these are shown in our models so far, namely the finished goods sector and the factorial sector.

But what is already quite plain is (1) a profit equalisation process dominates a money-based economy, (2) this equalisation process rests firmly on the original exchange values that finished commodities acquire from their relative production rates, and (3) all prices, either of goods or services, throughout the entire enclosed economy, are interlinked in a network that harmonises the original exchange-values with an equal rate of profit for all firms. The general level of wages, and hence its counterpart the general level of profits, is not affected in any way by this equalisation process, which just distributes the same total of profits in different proportions between all the firms.

We can re-emphasise here that no form of exploitation is necessarily present in any of our models considered in isolation. The profit that provides an income for the owner of any firm shares a common origin with the wage of a workman, no matter how great the quantitative disparity between them. If a hundred men produce goods that are sold for £1000, then this £1000 is the source of all wages and profits that accrue from the transaction, and there is no natural law which decides how this sum should be divided between the producers, nor, if we exclude all ethical criteria, between themselves and any other interested parties. If each producer receives £8, then a surplus of £200 remains which may serve as an income for an owner or lord or ruling body. The producers may decide that such money is sensibly allocated, possibly on the grounds that the ruling body provides a service of some kind such as administration or protection. There is no formal definition of human freedom that would disqualify such an arrangement, given that no coercion or deceit is present. Exploitation cannot be alleged merely on the basis that some people are rewarded more than others. The ethical dilemmas that arise when the fruits of co-operative labour need to be distributed play no part in economics as a distinct field of knowledge with its own domain of facts and consequences. How people manage their social relationships is a matter for the people involved.

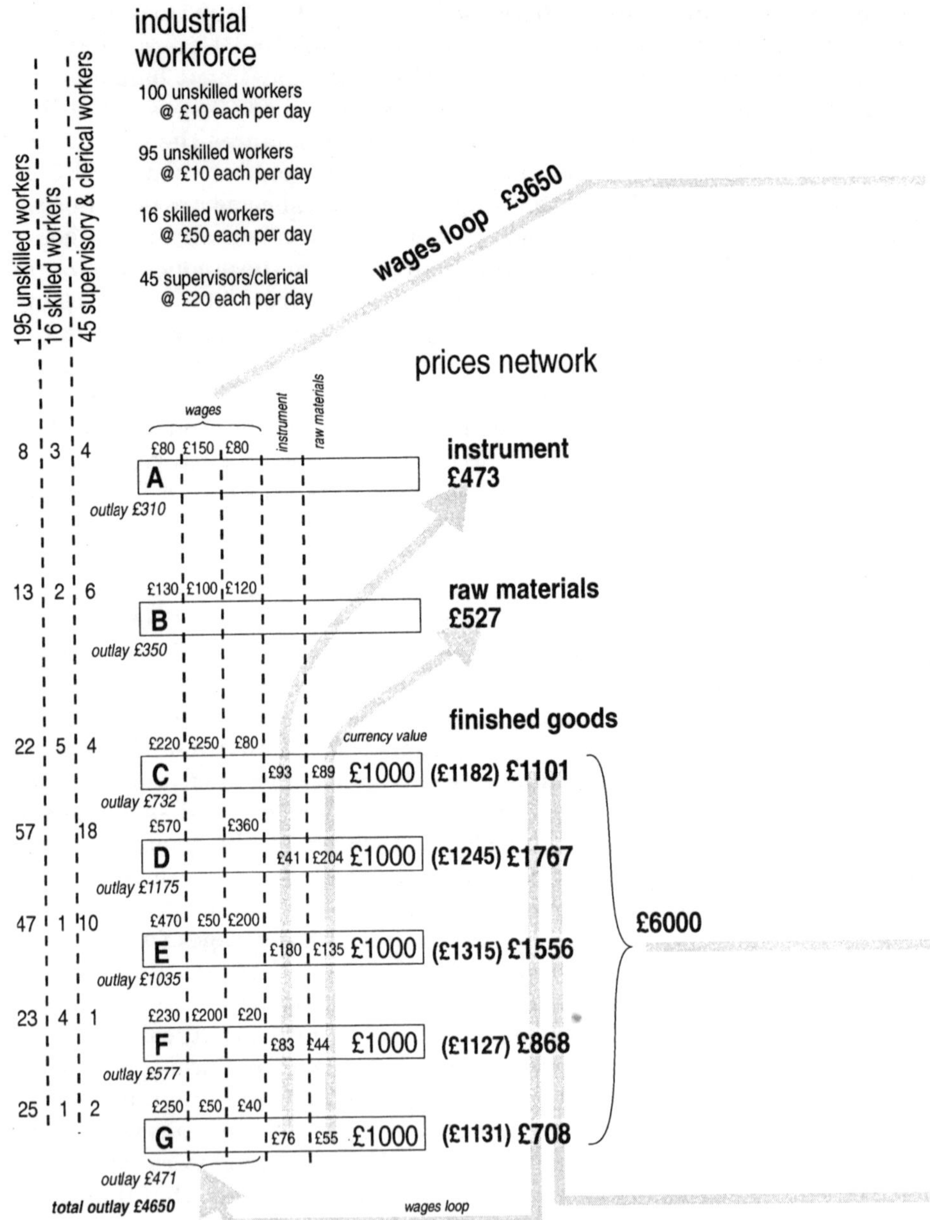

Figure 13-3 (both pages)

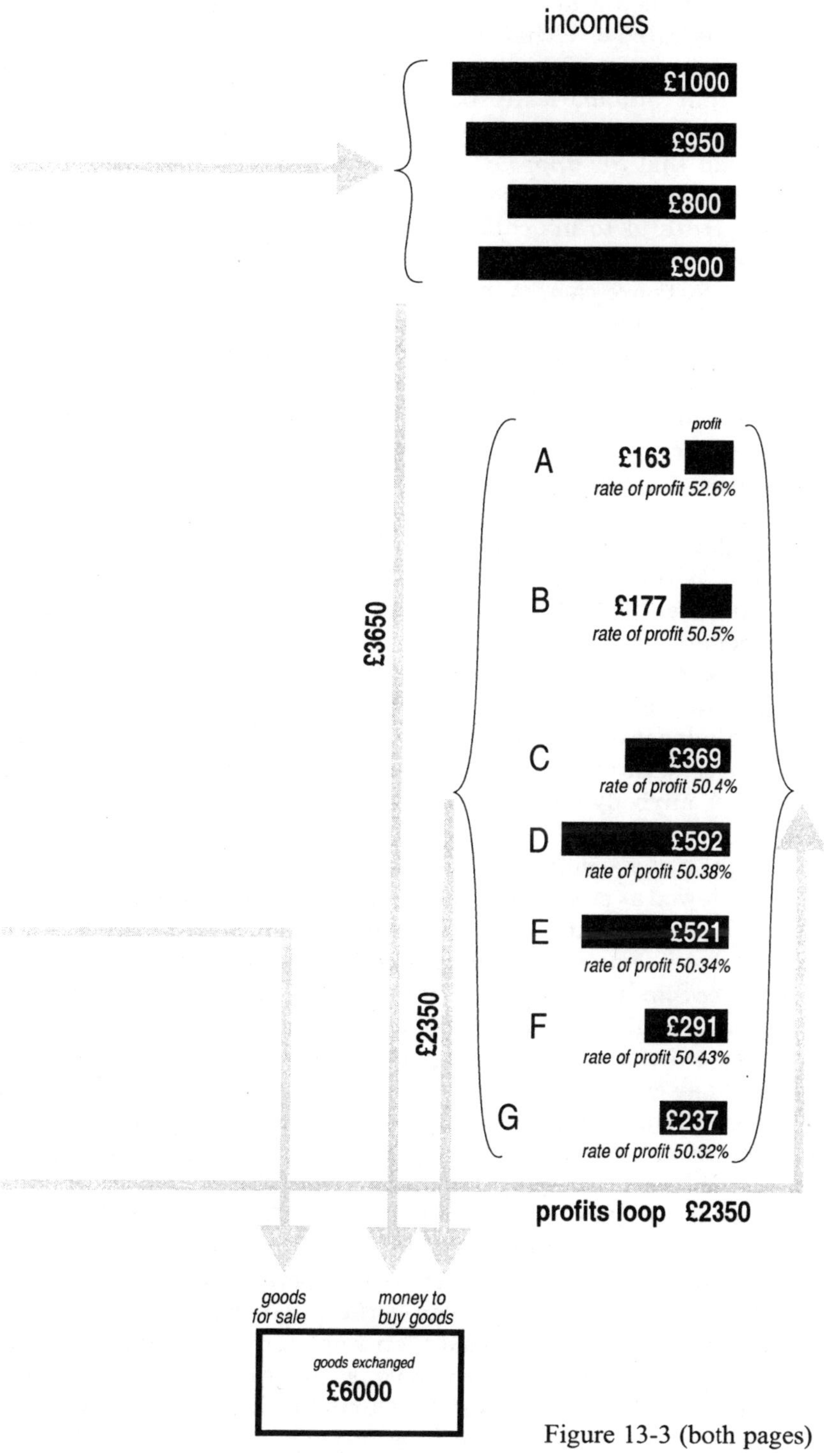

Figure 13-3 (both pages)

How then should an economist define exploitation? Exploitation is most clearly illustrated by a chattel slave society, where the slave toils to maintain a lowly existence for himself, and is also forced to labour to create an additional surplus that automatically becomes the property of somebody else. The exploitation is grounded in two facts, first that *no choice is allowed to the slave,* and second that *the appropriation of the surplus is the explicit condition on which the slave is kept alive at a certain standard of living.* The economist remains truthful to his calling when he studies a particular economy and identifies such conditions where they exist, describing them for what they are when the facts are clear. Whether the slaves themselves are well fed or not, decently treated or abused, happy or miserable, acquainted with the facts or wholly ignorant of them, is immaterial. The worker who is denied the means to enjoy a given standard of living (high or low as culturally defined) unless he works not only to keep himself and his dependants at that standard, but also to keep others in idleness who exercise this authority over him, is a victim of exploitation. Not because his labour is more than his own personal requirements. The able-bodied in all human groups must always produce a surplus if only to rear children. And not because his free will is being subordinated to an external discipline. All human cooperation rests on clear lines of authority. The essential factor that identifies his servile status is that he has no say in deciding who shall be the beneficiary of his extra labour and no say in deciding by how much. The extra work is forced out of him as a condition of his existence, and his collective responsibility alongside other fellow workers for the welfare of the human group he belongs to is usurped by non-producers who exercise this right in their own interests. Anyone who works under these terms is exploited regardless of his own or anybody else's opinion. If he believes he is free then he is doubly enslaved.

Using the above definition, we may say that nothing in any of our current models, viewed as stationary wage/profit relationships, supports the view that the workforce is being exploited. But if Figure 13-2 and Figure 13-3 are examined as a sequence in time, the peculiar property that distinguishes profit from wages comes to light. The fact that profit is a *remainder* after all costs have been deducted gives it a special power of self expansion that is not possessed by wages. If I share a cake with you, a quarter for you and three-quarters for me, then any change in the size of the cake will alter both our portions. But if the cake weighs four ounces, and your share is strictly defined as one ounce while the *remainder* strictly belongs to me, then my portion will grow when the cake gets bigger, whereas your portion will remain as it is, at one ounce. In Figure 13-2 the "cake" is distributed in a particular way and profits are just a portion of the cake, no different from wages, which comprise the other portion. But in Figure 13-3 an improvement in productivity by the factorial firms A and B has halved costs for CDEFG. The workers in A and B are now working harder, or longer, or more efficiently, but their wages are not increased thereby. In fact some of them lose their jobs. By contrast, the rate of profit for all firms in the entire market rises from 40% to 50%. Our definition of exploitation is exemplified not by either of these diagrams in isolation but by the transition from Figure

13-2 to Figure 13-3. The labour of these workmen, in all the firms, suffices to maintain their living standards at a particular level, and any surplus above this level *automatically* becomes the property of somebody else. This surplus is not directly appropriated by the capitalist owner of the firm or firms where the increased productivity appears. All such surpluses are shared out among all the capitalist owners, who because of this fact can be defined as an economic class in very precise collective terms, not just rich people distinguished from the poor, nor superiors distinguished from subordinates, nor even successful businessmen distinguished from the also-rans, but a class of exploiters-in-common, mutual beneficiaries of a process that gathers a pool of wealth from incremental improvements in social productivity and distributes this wealth to *all capitalist owners* in proportion to their financial stature. No hint of this exploitation is apparent to the ordinary view.

It is instructive to examine the transition from Figure 13-2 to Figure 13-3 with some care. The general price level has fallen from £7000 to £6000. Goods are cheaper. Wage levels are unchanged. So standard of living for the workforce must rise as a consequence. But finished goods are being produced in exactly the same quantities as before. Where does the improvement in living standards come from? The improvement is a consequence of the reduced size of the labour force. In the earlier model there were 295 workers. There are only 256 workers in the later model. The 39 workers who are now unemployed have surrendered their share of the cake. The employed workers with their unaltered wages can now buy more goods at lower prices while the total output (and total consumption) remains the same. These circumstances also apply to the capitalist owners. The total wage bill has shrunk, because fewer workers are employed at the same rates of pay. Hence the employers' profit will rise. But we must examine the whole society to see how the gains are proportionally distributed. The cake (the finished goods output) is the same size in both models. The share of the cake no longer consumed by the sacked workers is the sole source from which consumption can be increased for anybody else. In Figure 13-2, the total value of goods produced is £7000, of which £4420 goes to the workforce and £2580 goes to the employers, a ratio of 1.7 to 1. In Figure 13-3, the same goods have a combined value of £6000, of which £3650 goes to wages, and £2350 goes to profits, a ratio of 1.5 to 1. The *relative* position of the workforce as compared with the employers has worsened slightly, while both have made absolute gains in terms of standard of living.

As we already know from Part One, a little hidden inflation would work wonders here. Judicious printing of banknotes alongside the productivity improvement in Firms A and B would keep unit prices constant, meaning that the fall from £7000 to £6000 (for exactly the same output of goods) would be prevented. The workforce would then be completely oblivious of any change. Their standard of living would remain just as it was. Finished goods would continue to be produced in the same quantities, and these goods would be bought at the same prices and with the same wages as before. The entire portion of output surrendered by the sacked workers would pass exclusively into profits, much to the satisfaction of the capitalist owners, who would be very keen to explain to the workforce that the hard decisions to reduce over-manning were not the actions of heartless bosses but unavoidable sacrifices to the great god of supply and demand, because it stands to reason that when firms have all the workers they need, only a reduction of wages could allow them to employ more people and still hold their own in the competitive marketplace. It is the "stickiness" of wages that prevents firms from adapting flexibly to market competition and thereby helping to keep unemployment low. Consult the textbooks and you will find it explained very thoroughly, complete with the mathematical equations that prove beyond doubt that a natural limit holds in check the number of workers that any firm can employ at a given wage level. In the hands of a good marginalist this law can be shown to be as unstoppable as dynamite.

But the invincible logic of the marginalist is nothing more than a dressed up tautology. If wages are represented as one component or vector alongside others in a stable equilibrium, then this vector cannot, *on its own,* be altered, as any woodenhead knows, without upsetting the equilibrium. The individual parts of an equilibrium are necessarily immobile, each held at a fixed point of tension by the other parts. But every equilibrium is poised within a larger whole, and when this larger whole changes, the equilibrium adapts by moving to a new position of balanced reciprocation. It would not be a dynamic equilibrium if it did not behave in this way. All that the marginalist does is confirm the mutual dependence of such linkages. But these linkages are collectively modified when the equilibrium responds to a change in external conditions. The transition from Figure 13-2 to Figure 13-3 is such a response, brought about by a change in productivity. The equilibrium itself cannot explain this change, but its tautological core is of course bound to be true, and hence the message preached to the workers is perfectly correct. *Wage restraint is the only sensible policy, because otherwise you will contribute to job losses. Work harder in the meantime, to improve productivity, and if your firm prospers there may be scope for a rise, depending on how the laws of supply and demand operate in the market.* This warning is always true for the typical wage-earner in a capitalist economy, because, just as the textbooks say, the laws of supply and demand work quite impartially in the market and make no distinction between workers and employers. But if, as the textbooks omit to say, banknotes are being printed to offset productivity gains, the laws of supply and demand *always* work to the *exclusive* benefit of the capitalist. In these circumstances, as our models confirm, jobs will be lost, wages and prices will stay as they are, workers who keep their jobs will be thankful and profits will get bigger.

14

Commercial costs: part 1

In the previous chapter we transformed the values network of Figure 13-1 into two viable price networks represented by Figures 13-2 and 13-3. We will now return to Figure 13-1 and introduce two further sectors into our analysis, namely marketing and transport.

In very general terms, a regular production/consumption cycle may be divided into three specialist areas: manufacture, transfer of ownership and delivery. These separate specialisms are present in the earliest beginnings of trade when merchants, acting on their own behalf or as go-betweens, crossed land and sea with goods deliberately manufactured not for consumption but to be exchanged with other goods, and even in the theoretical simplicity of three-sided barter, these specialisms are foreshadowed. Our analysis started with just three people exchanging corn, sheep and cows, but these commodities had to be produced for others, they had to be appraised and haggled over, and they had to be delivered to the parties as required. These activities have no direct effect on values, which are simply the outcome of agreed production rates.

From this simple beginning we analysed the price mechanism, first in a gold-based economy, then in an economy using paper money. We showed how two classes of people, productive workers and employers, obtained their primary incomes. Income for the latter was shown to originate from increased output alongside currency inflation, mostly hidden. We next introduced the financial capitalist (banker) and traced the source of his derivative income, and our models then expanded to include intermediate costs and the incomes of firms that provide raw materials and instrument maintenance. This is our present position. Adding the two specialist areas that correspond to transfer of ownership and delivery, will bring the main features of a real economy into view.

In essence, transfer of ownership (or marketing) here corresponds to all aspects of commercial engagement that culminate in a sale and purchase. Transport is likewise a comprehensive term for shipping, freight by road, rail and air, and all handling and delivery services associated with the movement of mass-produced commodities from where they are made to the location where they are consumed. In our models we will illustrate each of these two specialisms by a single firm, represented in one case by a giant supermarket, Firm S, where all finished goods are bought and sold, and in the other case by a transportation specialist, Firm T, serving everybody's need for the movement of goods. These

Figure 14-1 (both pages)

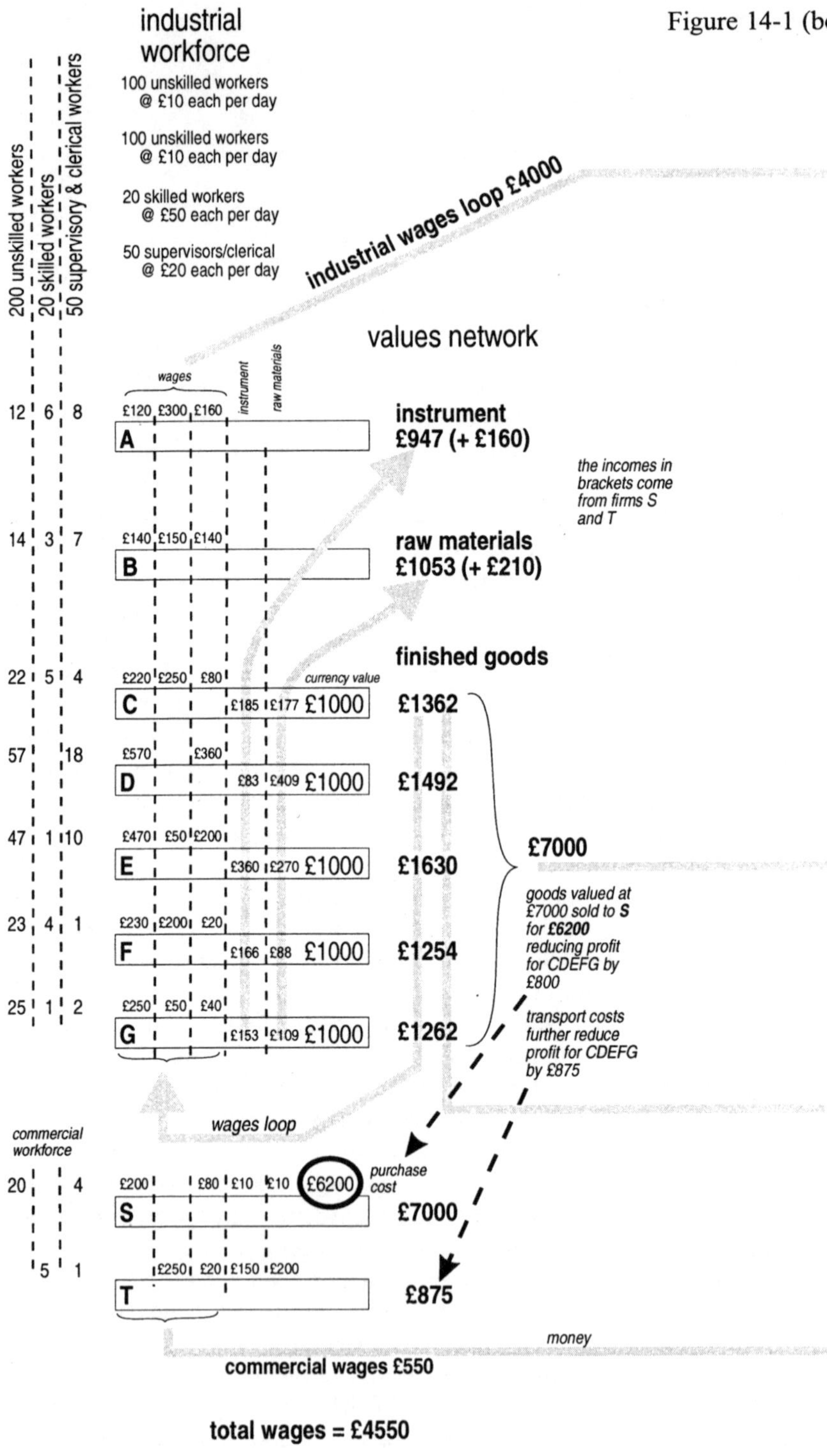

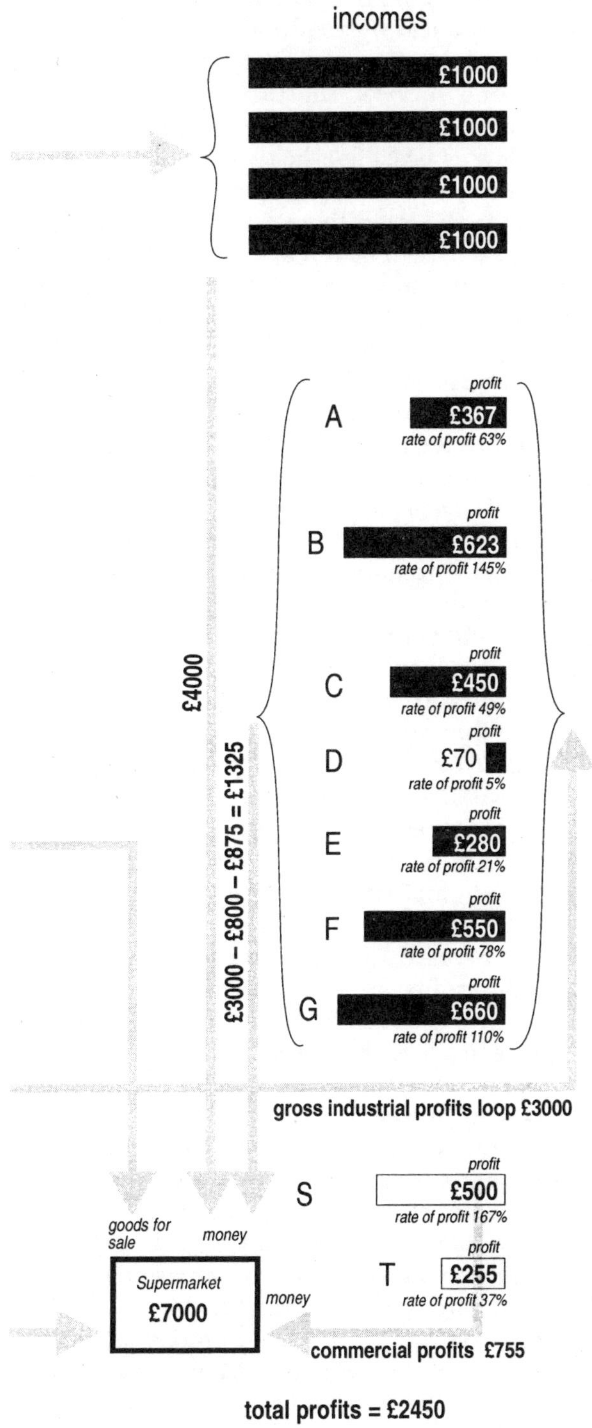

Although this double-page diagram may look complicated, it is in fact quite simple, because only elementary arithmetic is used and the theoretical basis is easy to follow. Productive work takes place on the left page and incomes are spent on the right. The white rectangles are firms and the black rectangles show the distribution of all the value created by ABCDEF and G. No value is created by any other firm. Outputs of finished goods per firm per day acquire the same value, shown by the arbitrary number £1000. There are five such firms CDEF and G. Goods or services provided by factorial firms such as A and B create extra value, estimated here as £2000. Thus the productive sector creates £7000 of value. Firms engaged in retailing or transport (S and T) obtain a share of this value. The diagram shows how incomes arise for every worker and employer in these nine firms, and how every firm interprets its own situation. Each firm has costs in respect of wages, which are spent in the supermarket, but all other costs are incomes for other firms. These incomes are again divided into wages and profits. The diagram traces all these routes, showing how the original value of £7000 generated per day becomes wages and profits spent per day in the supermarket.

The rates of profit vary widely so this network is unstable. But the existing distribution of the workforce produces the range of outputs that match supply to demand in this economy. So a set of prices is needed which will correspond to uniform rates of profit for all firms when they continue to supply goods at present output rates. This change from theoretical values to operational prices is the topic in the main text.

extensions to our previous model are set out in Figure 14-1. We assume that the present distribution of the workforce produces the required outputs that satisfy aggregate demand, both in respect of finished goods for consumption, and in respect of the intermediate goods and services that are consumed as raw materials and instrument maintenance. In order to make the transition from one model to the next as easy to follow as possible, the two new firms are just interposed as new entrants in the market to show how they align themselves in the diagram. But no adjustments to the other firms have so far been made in Figure 14-1. The necessary corrections will be made in the next model.

First let us examine the coherence of the various parts. All the industrial wages are grouped in black rectangles at the top, and all the industrial profits are in black rectangles on the right, just as before. These incomes are £4000 and £3000 respectively, and they balance with the primary income source, namely the combined values of the finished goods, which is £7000. The finished goods are sold to the supermarket at a discounted price of £6200. These goods sell in the market for £7000, providing an income for the supermarket firm S. The supermarket firm employs workers who are paid the wages shown, and there are costs to be met in respect of raw materials and maintenance of equipment just as for any other firm. A profit of £500 remains after these deductions. The transport firm T provides a service for the manufacturing firms CDEFG, and also for A and B, (but not for Firm S) and earns an income of £875. Wages and costs are paid from this amount as shown, leaving a profit of £235. A commercial workforce earnng wages appears in the bottom left corner of the diagram, and we now need to trace the new circuits that arise from these wages and from the commercial profits shown in the white rectangles at bottom right.

The grey arrow at bottom left indicates that £550 in wages will now be spent in the bold rectangle, and the grey arrow at bottom right indicates a similar spending source of £755 in profits. The industrial profits loop which was £3000 will fall to £1325 when transport costs and the discounted selling price are allowed for, and all that remains to create a new balance is to include the instrument and raw material costs of Firms S and T in extra earnings for A and B, shown in brackets. Of course the profits presently specified in the black rectangles will shrink as a result of transport costs and the discounted selling price, but we will show these changes in a later diagram, so that the transition from Figure 13-1 to Figure 14-1 is not obscured by too much alteration. The extra earnings for A and B, shown in brackets, will increase their profits. (Alteration to wages is always a possibility but we hold wages constant because the assumption of free mobility means that a uniform wage structure is maintained by all firms. Of course the general level of wages may rise or fall but this is not part of our present investigation). Rates of profit are calculated here for all firms, to show that at this intermediate stage, where values have not yet been converted into prices, the profit rates are all different.

We have now set the stage for a new equilibrium based on equal rates of profit, and this is the next step. We must convert Figure 14-1, which is a *values* network, into a *prices* version, but let us explore fully the implications of Figure 14-1 before we proceed further. (Readers who wish to follow the transformation process without interruption can move direct to Chapter 15, but the following examination of costs is important and should not be omitted at first reading).

It is a striking fact that all costs, no matter how they arise, ultimately resolve themselves into either wages or profits. Taking a comprehensive view, it is a fact that all payments for services, or for the provision of intermediate goods or raw materials consumed in the production of finished goods, are self-cancelling. Such payments look just like any normal trading arrangement. The goods or services are exchanged for an agreed sum of money, and both sides assume that the money in some way expresses "the value" of whatever is being sold. There is nothing wrong with such a view in common discourse, but in economic theory the appearance here is quite false. *No value relation is present anywhere outside the bold rectangle.* Money possesses a value which will be redeemed at the exchange interface. It does not acquire any other value. It can move from hand to hand for any purpose that satisfies the parties concerned, who carry in their heads an estimate of what the money can buy, and on this basis make a judgement whether it is worth sacrificing such purchasing power for a benefit of some kind, which can be anything from a hostage ransom to a ride on a donkey. The purchasing power inherent in a sum of money is fixed at the exchange interface, not by any other transaction that money may be a part of. The decision to use the money to obtain a benefit of some kind is a matter wholly incidental to the value that lies congealed, so to speak, in the money as a repository of value. The competitive bargaining inherent in all money dealings gives the impression that the "value" of the service or goods being offered is determined merely on the basis of mutual agreement, as in an auction. Endless confusion arises from this belief that competition ultimately settles the value of all things that are exchanged for money. This is the standpoint of the orthodox economist who sees nothing but a never-ending circulation of notes serving a thousand and one purposes. But this promiscuous currency of money has nothing to do with the creation of value. The process that actualises or renders manifest the value congealed in paper notes is the act of purchase at the interface where finished goods are sold. "Goods and services" are haphazardly bracketed together in orthodox theory, but "finished goods" belong to a distinct economic category that excludes everything else, and which is alone the source of exchange-value.

So let us make certain at this point that we fully understand what is happening when money changes hands in the course of its circulation through the economy. All money eventually becomes somebody's income, defined as *money regularly spent at the goods exchange interface*. Strictly speaking, money is never "spent" until this moment arrives, no matter how many times it changes owners. We can illustrate this fact in a simple diagram, Figure 14-2. In this diagram we assume that the factor costs for CDEFG, shown as £2000 in our current model Figure 14-1, are spent not on the services of just two firms A and B, but on five firms who are all raw material suppliers or maintenance specialists of various kinds. These five firms in turn make use of fifteen smaller firms, who, on the restricted scale of our model, would be partnerships or sole traders. All the profits, wages and factor costs are shown, and it is easy to see

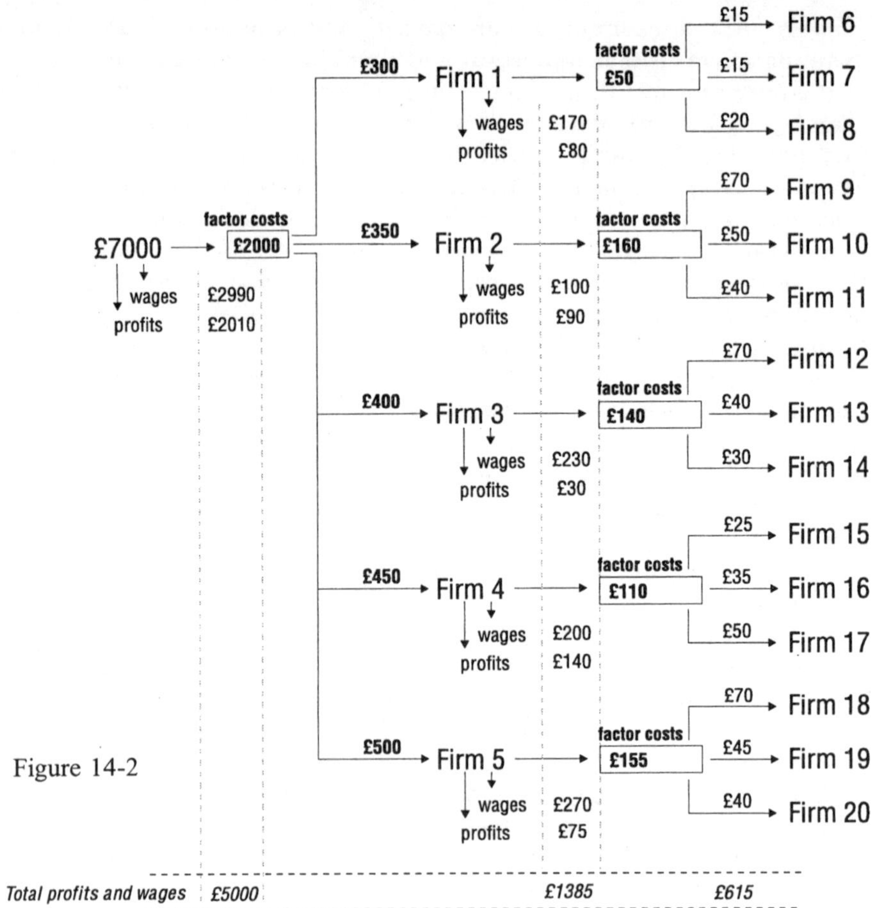

Figure 14-2

that the original factor cost of £2000 passes intact through the network of all the 20 firms, and is reconstituted in the wages and profits destined for the goods exchange interface. There are no leaks and no injections. All the amounts shown in the diagram are arbitrary choices, but it is obvious that if these amounts were changed, only the balance between wages and profits would alter, without affecting their joint total, which is predetermined at £2000. In comprehensive overview, costs disappear, leaving only wages and profits.

The economy portrayed in Figure 14-1 needs to be examined in the light of this new conception of costs. We already know from earlier analysis that value is generated by the production process and infused into banknotes as they pass in a steady stream through the exchange interface, simultaneously discharging and recharging themselves with this value in the buying and selling of newly created finished goods. We must grasp fully what this means. From an overview of the economy as a whole, *there are no money costs of any kind that need to be paid for.* Goods are created by the expenditure of the appropriate labour, and nothing else is required. This truth, namely that the economic concept of "value"

Figure 14-3

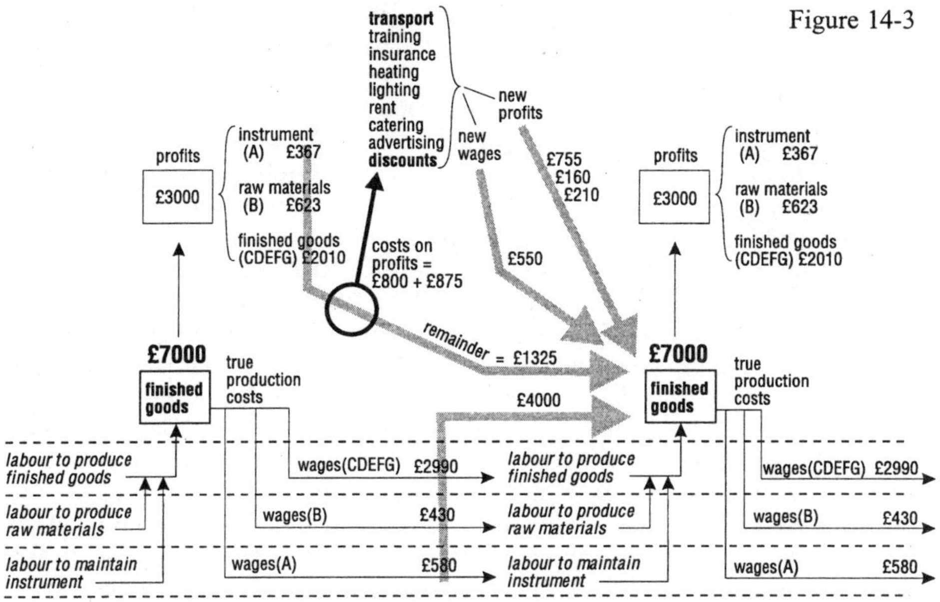

is reducible ultimately to "labour" alone, has always been dimly sensed from the earliest days of economic enquiry, and it is a constant theme through the whole of the classical period. Stated simply, if we adopt the most generalised economic standpoint of all, which is the continuous presence of humans on the earth as a surviving species, it is self-evident that nothing more is required than the effort of hunting or gathering, tending flocks or tilling the land, or in some other way obtaining the food, shelter, warmth, etc that sustain and enhance life. In other words, the effort of productive labour is the only "cost" to be borne by any society whether rich or poor.

But this fact seems to be contradicted by Figure 14-1. The idea that there are no costs other than wages appears to be nonsense. The five firms CDEFG must surely meet the costs of raw materials and maintenance as well as wages. But these costs arise only for individual firms. The layout of Figure 14-1 depicts the economy as a collection of such firms. An entirely different view of the same economy is presented in Figure 14-3. This layout shows how the value relation is transmitted from one production cycle to the next. The seven firms ABCDEFG have no distinct identity in this diagram, though their financial circumstances are just as accurately displayed as in Figure 14-1. (Other firms are listed to show where they fit in, but of course only marketing and transport are present in our models so far).

The true production cost, as can be seen from Figure 14-3, is never anything else but wages. The production cycle repeats itself, moving from left to right between the dotted lines, generating a continuous output of finished goods, created by the workforce and consumed by everybody. This daily, monthly, yearly, cycle of work is paid for through wages alone, which represent a fixed entitlement of goods for consumption by the workers involved at all preproduction and finished stages. Note however that this is a *social* view of production, not the view adopted by the firms themselves. The individual firms do not recognise production costs in the form of a social aggregate. The five firms who produce finished goods pay their own wages (CDEFG) and recognise such wages as costs, but they do not recognise the amounts shown as wages(A) and wages(B) which are not their concern at all. They simply pay whatever gross sums are necessary for raw materials and maintenance of equipment, and these gross sums comprise wages(A) plus wages(B) plus profits(A) plus profits(B). The factor firms A and B acquire these payments, which are earnings from their own viewpoint, and split them apart into wages and profits. All firms involved in the production process, and the commercial firms in the list at the top, think that they are being paid on some basis of evaluation that is determined by the interplay of supply and demand in respect of the services they offer. This viewpoint is superficially true, but as shown in Figure 14-3, all payments and all costs are regulated by the £7000 of value created and distributed each day. This value is divided between industrial wages and industrial profits, and everything else is a further sub-division of profits. No matter how many other firms are involved, the grey arrows always add up to the total shown in the finished goods rectangle, which is £7000 in our model as presently portrayed. This latter amount is ultimately determined by the total face-value of the banknotes in circulation, the accommodation period and the velocity of the currency. We assume of course that these elements are constant, and that no notes are being printed.

Figure 14-3 shows that costs for raw materials and for instrument upkeep always resolve themselves into the wages and profits of other firms. It follows that if labour alone is sufficient to produce the goods, and this labour is rewarded by wages, some justification has to be found for profits. There is a widespread belief that the workforce are rewarded for their labour, and the owners are rewarded for allowing the use of their factories and associated facilities. This argument fails because the cost of maintaining and replacing the factories and facilities is not a charge on net profits. Net profits are a remainder after all costs, including these, have been met. The factories and facilities continue in existence and year by year they are up-dated, refurbished, replaced as necessary, and generally kept in a condition of steadily improving efficiency, and also insured against accidents or amortised to cover depreciation. All these costs are deducted from gross income to arrive at net profit. There is no escaping the conclusion that net profit in capitalist firms is always a surplus acquired without any equivalent in return. The profitability of a firm, in fact, has no social meaning except as a rough measure of exploitation. But the above justifications seem plausible, because all the real relationships are hidden. Intelligent application of economic knowledge is impossible in a capitalist free-market economy because the capitalist firm itself is irrational when it is viewed as a component part of the social whole.

This notion of irrationality is worth pursuing in the light of our new understanding of costs and profits. Briefly, and as we already know, the bare value relation cannot serve as an incentive for productive activity based on self-interest because the mix of resources needed to produce goods for sale in the proportions required to satisfy demand does not guarantee equal rewards for the producing firms. But once a float of the universal money-commodity is in general circulation, competition between buyers for goods in short supply (and disinterest by buyers in overabundant goods) will modify the bare value-form to create a price network that rewards every productive firm equally when supply and aggregate demand are balanced (assuming impediment-free response from supply sources and prompt labour mobility). Thus a price network takes the place of a values network, and supply and demand are rationally matched to each other by an automatic mechanism that needs no directive authority. A society of freely associated (non-capitalist) producers could allow their money network to operate autonomously in this way, to their mutual benefit. They would all share a collective social understanding of their own economic relationships. They would understand how rising productivity brings about a steady reduction in unit prices, or a shorter working day, while money incomes in the form of inconvertible banknotes remained constant. Division of labour in mass production systems would require large or small concentrations of working people, with appropriate specialisms, and payment for work would be graded according to skills or responsibilities. Apart from this grading, which might change from time to time, all incomes and the value of money would be constant. Unit prices would fall and standard of living would steadily rise for everybody. Local banks would manage the float, but would have no money-lending role. The managers of all enterprises would exercise authority just as a captain commands a ship, on the basis of competence. General administrative authority would rest on some form of electoral mandate. Such a community would be rationally organised and rationally understood by its own citizens.

But when such a society is converted to capitalist form, its rationality, both factual and conceptual, disappears. Its citizens lose both their economic freedom to enjoy a steadily rising standard of living, and their democratic freedom to manage their own affairs. The great majority are condemned to work for wages as a payment measured against time, while inflation of the currency prevents unit prices from falling, or makes them rise. (How this inflation comes about will be described later, when interest is examined. It would be quite wrong to assume that it arises from conscious intent to defraud or exploit). With inflation present, gross revenue from sales expands in response to increased productivity, and the expansion flows wholly into the profits of an idle ruling class, who exercise colonial-type authority over the means of production, an authority derived from legal ownership and command of wealth and not from any productive contribution. In general terms, we may say that this society is irrational because it is subject to economic forces that it knows nothing about, yet these forces are generated from its own behaviour. But a glib generalisation like this can be applied to all sorts of situations. We need to be far more precise if the notion of irrationality is to be meaningful alongside our analysis.

Let us be quite clear that the irrationality does not arise from the imposition of force by a ruling group, or from the mere fact of being deceived in such matters. There is nothing irrational in despotism, whether it is hidden under democratic window-dressing or not. The agent that introduces irrationality is money itself.

In its most elementary form, a capitalist society would be a gold-based economy, paying wages in gold for time worked, extracting profits in gold as a remainder after all costs had been paid in gold, with all buying and selling in gold, and no banks (only guarded hoards) and no paper currency. Under these conditions, as long as production keeps rising, including gold, the ruling group will get steadily richer. But irrationality enters at this point, in two respects. First, if gold production does not expand, then rising productivity elsewhere means falling prices and falling profits. Second, gold (or any other physical substance) is unsuitable as a form of money. If it is relatively scarce, then its high value makes it impossible to weigh accurately for very small payments. If it is plentiful, it is impossibly bulky for very large payments. These defects spring entirely from the use of money. No irrationality is present in a chattel slave society as such, with an all-powerful ruling group, but once money is introduced, in its first historical form as gold or some other bought-and-sold commodity, these two problems (the need for gold output to rise continuously, and the unsuitability of weight as a basis of measurement) present themselves, and they cannot be solved by force.

These monetary imperfections can be eradicated, but the irrationality is merely shunted elsewhere. Two precious metals can be used simultaneously as money, the scarce one (usually gold) for large payments and the more plentiful one (usually silver) for small payments. Unfortunately, both of these metals assume command, so to speak, for all prices throughout the economy, and neither can be made subordinate to the other, despite legal declarations to that effect. This third form of irrationality creates constant openings for arbitrage losses and gains, deliberate or accidental, as vexing to the ruling group as to anyone else. A much better alternative is a paper certificate representing either gold or silver on its own. Payments large or small can be accommodated by notes of high or low face value, and portability or accuracy cease to be a problem. So note-issuing banks take over from goldsmiths. But once again irrationality in a fourth form reasserts itself. Banks that issue paper notes backed by gold are regularly destroyed by the rising price of gold that follows inevitably from the issue of such notes. A run on the bank is triggered at a certain point, and the bank is accused, quite wrongly, of incompetence or dishonesty. When redeemable note issue is centralised in a state nominated agency, hopefully to banish such alleged malpractice, the effect is quite otherwise. The scale of the dislocation widens. The entire economy is thrown into disarray by periodic crises in the banking system, and these crises steadily worsen till the next solution is found, the abandonment of the gold standard. Banknotes cease to be redeemable, and their irrational unfulfillable promises become harmless. At the same time, the dependence of profits on steadily rising gold output is ended.

But the move to inconvertibility brings in turn a fifth more serious form of irrationality in its wake. As just stated, profits formerly depended on a rising output of gold, meaning that as gold output increased alongside a general rise in productivity, prices stayed constant and profits rose, while wages remained as they were. But if gold is no longer money, and a paper currency is in use, a general rise in productivity reduces unit prices while all incomes, both wages and profits, stand still. Thus the abandonment of the gold standard strikes at the heart of the ruling group's economic power. Prices and profits begin to fall. Profits can be restored only by printing banknotes to keep unit prices steady alongside rising output. This is the only way to ensure that the living standards of the ruling group continue to rise as previously. Thus number six in the series is the glaring irrationality that a general improvement in productivity achieved by the combined efforts of a society's entire workforce is diverted by a mere printing press into the pockets of an idle few. The ruling group's power (in a democracy) is now dangerously exposed and fragile, because it rests not on some form of legitimation, nor on old-fashioned force, but on fraud. Once this fraud is exposed, the forms of democracy that have grown within the capitalist economy themselves become blatantly irrational unless they are intelligently exercised. At this seventh stage either old-fashioned force is imposed by the ruling group in an effort to retain its power, or democratic procedures are set in motion which will dismantle the capitalist exploitation system and bring into power the mass of the electorate, whose authority will still be exercised through representatives, but on the basis of shared communal understanding. In this way, the irrationality originally introduced by money is finally removed, though it is quite wrong to regard money as the culprit. Money is inherently impartial and benign. It is an adjustable exchange device that allocates social wealth in proportion to social usefulness, and it offers a guarantee of social acceptance for all human beings in a cooperative global family. Its historical arrival produces an effect of continuing irrationality because it is incompatible with an exploitation system. When that exploitation system is removed, money settles into its true role as an instrument of social administration.

Of course this point is not yet in prospect. The printing of notes to prevent unit prices from falling has been largely unnecessary in the second half of the twentieth century because the absorption of private hoards and the extension of the cheque system have caused the monetary base to shrink, with the result that fewer banknotes have been needed. Notes that become superfluous in this way remain in circulation and inflate the currency. So prices which would normally have fallen as output increased, have been held constant (or have risen) without recourse to the printing press. In fact it seems that inflation from this source (which we may loosely describe as superfluity of notes) has been great enough, despite rising output in the fifties and sixties, to push unit prices upwards at an increasing rate, reaching a peak of visible inflation in the early seventies. Since then, visible inflation has steadily fallen year by year, and it may well be that superfluity of notes from the above causes is no longer sufficient to counteract the fall in prices caused by rising outputs. If this is so, and superfluity of notes is indeed coming to an end, unit price inflation will fall to a point where the central banks in the leading countries will need to remedy this deficiency by printing banknotes in ever increasing quantities during the period ahead. It is likely that they are already doing so, in ways which we will examine in due course.

15

Commercial costs: part 2

The next stage in our analysis is to convert Figure 14-1, which is at present a values network, into its corresponding prices network. But there are many cross currents in Figure 14-1 as it stands. The profits for the individual firms are not corrected to allow for either transport costs or the discount losses in sales to the supermarket. And Firms A and B have acquired extra earnings from the supermarket and the transit firm. We need to correct for all these movements of money so that the true state of balance is properly displayed.

Figure 15-1

Firm	original profit	transport costs	discount costs	remainder
A	£367	£151	–	£216
B	£623	£260	–	£363
C	£450	£116	£88	£246
D	£70	–	£70	nil
E	£280	£84	£97	£99
F	£550	£154	£257	£139
G	£660	£110	£288	£262
totals	*£3000*	*£875*	*£800*	*£1325*

To keep things simple we will assume that all goods are delivered to the supermarket by the individual firms so there are no transport costs for the supermarket. This assumption, and the allocation of costs and discounts that we shall now introduce, are quite arbitrary. Figure 15-1 tabulates the adjustments involved, and Figure 15-2 on the next double-page shows the new model with all adjustments implemented.

Any other allocation of costs would serve just as well to illustrate these interrelations, and of course it is always possible to set forth the basic principles without all this painstaking detail. But a diagram like Figure 15-2 with real magnitudes is far more convincing than an exposition in words or a schematic layout based on concepts alone. At first sight the diagram presents a mass of complicated detail, but all the numbers are linked to each other by simple addition and subtraction, and one of the virtues of specific numbers is that they recur in different parts and act as labels to identify what they stand for in different processes. The tracing of the various pathways is quite straightforward. Firm G, for example, employs 25 unskilled workers, 1 skilled worker and 2 supervisory/clerical staff, paying them wages of £250, £50 and £40 respectively, per day. The cost of replacement and upkeep of equipment is £153 and the cost of raw materials is £109. The currency value is £1000, and therefore the value of the goods produced per day is £1000 + £153 + £109 = £1262. When all wages and factor costs are deducted from this selling price, a profit of £660 remains, shown on the right. Transport costs and discounts of £110 and £288 respectively (see table opposite) are subtracted and the net profit is £262 per day. The financial circumstances of all the firms can be traced in similar fashion. Take care with Firms A and B. Their extra profit arrives "later" so to speak, so it is shown in brackets, because it is an addition to the main calculation.

There are two stipulations when a values network like Figure 15-2 is converted into its corresponding prices version. The currency value must remain at £1000 for each of the five finished goods firms. And the total money value arriving at the supermarket per day (via the grey arrows) must always correspond to the total value of the goods arriving per day (via the grey arrow marked "goods for sale"). This means that all the magnitudes in the model apart from the currency value could change, but they must preserve the integrity of their arithmetic relationships, and the outcome must balance in the bold rectangle. We will hold wages constant to avoid unnecessary complications, keeping the changes as few as possible. Of course any alteration to key determinants will ramify through the network, so a concrete presentation may be difficult to follow. We will therefore implement the transformation in a series of stages, with models that are linked in a close sequential chain. But always keep in mind that we are moving from Figure 15-2, a *values* version of the monetary network, to its operational counterpart, a *prices* version, which will be Figure 15-6.

Stage 1 in the transformation is to adjust the prices for finished goods to ensure an equal rate of profit for the five firms CDEFG. The total of all costs and the total of all profits are used to calculate an overall rate of profit, just as if the five firms were amalgamated into one single firm. This rate of profit is the average for them all, and the selling prices of their respective commodities can then be calculated from their individual costs, using this average rate of profit. The overall discount of £800 is deducted from the £7000, meaning that total income is £6200, and when total costs of £5454 are deducted, the profit that remains is £746. The final result is shown in Figure 15-3. These five firms sell finished goods worth £7000 to the supermarket at a discounted price of £6200.

The next step is to align our new information with the rest of the economy, as in Figure 15-4. We now have a comprehensive overview which allows us to

Figure 15-2 (both pages)

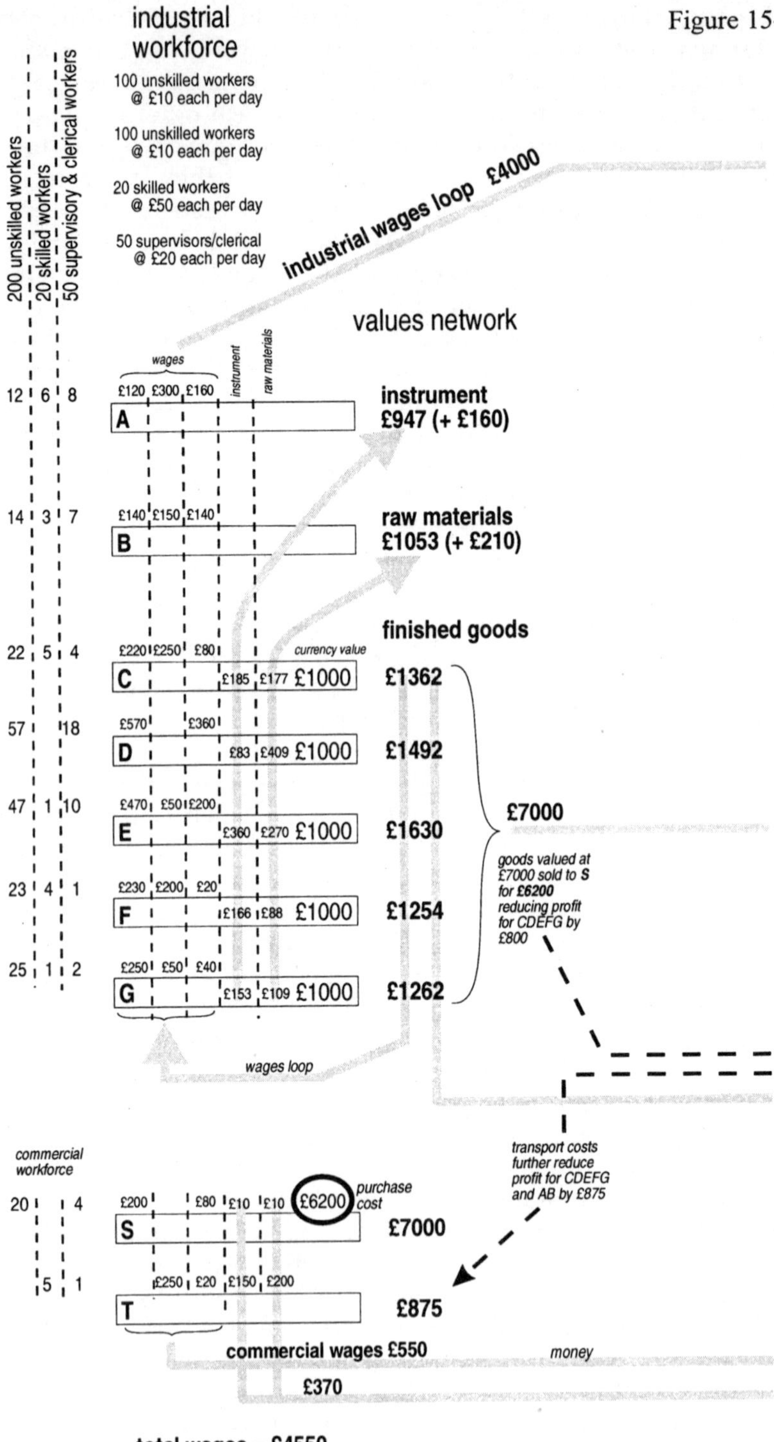

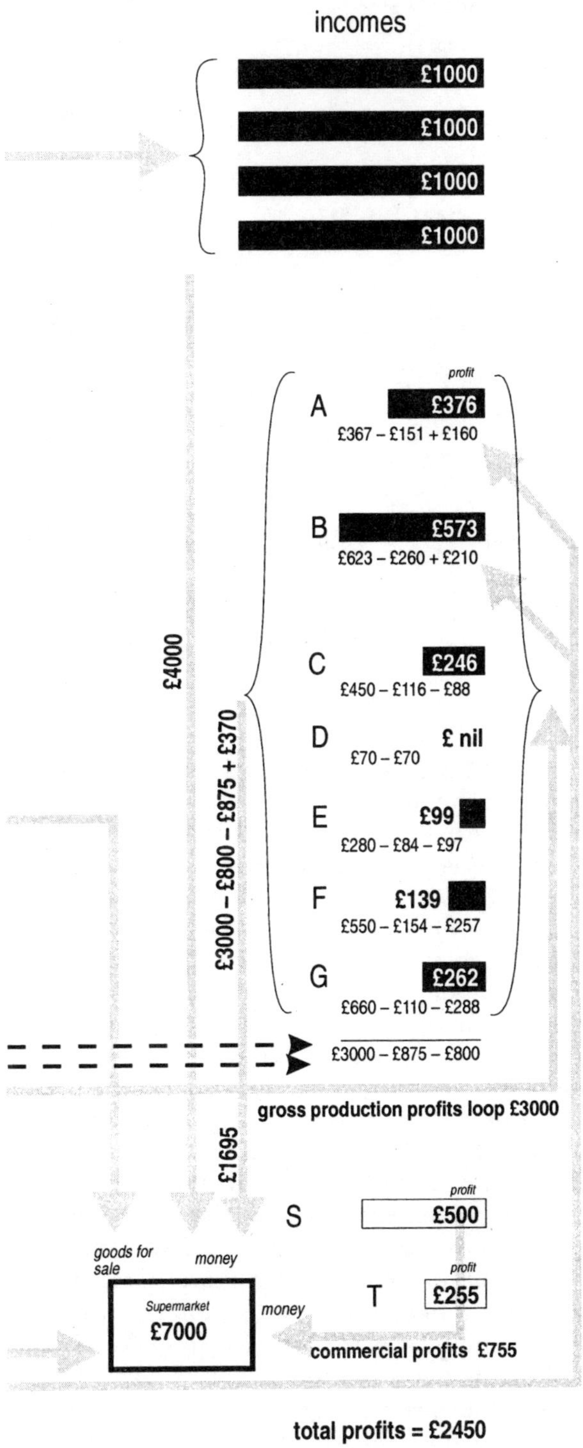

This model updates Figure 14-1 in minor details. All costs are now shown for each individual firm. The theoretical basis is just as before. The currency value of £1000 is the only fixed magnitude in the entire monetary network. The total wage bill has been designated as £4000 and shared out as equal rates of pay (in three grades) for all workers. Supply outputs are deemed to match aggregate demand. Dummy values have been chosen for factorial costs (incomes for A and B) and for discount to S, and for transport payments to T. Using these dummy values, all costs and profits have been calculated for every firm. The sum of wages and profits spent in the supermarket per day is exactly equal to the value of goods created per day, therefore the network is coherent. But rates of profit are different for all firms, so this arrangement is unstable. Firms will switch to more productive lines and the balance of supply and demand will be lost.

If we hold wages and existing outputs constant, the dummy values can be adjusted, alongside a new set of prices, to ensure a uniform rate of profit for all firms. This transformation must be effected without disturbing the currency value which never alters unless inflation is present or there is a change in the accommodation period. We rule these possibilities out so that the transformation from values to prices can be examined in its integrity.

To assist comparison between this "values" model and the "prices" version (Figure 15-6) which lies ahead, the dummy values should be carefully identified in this layout. They are: £947, £1053, £800, and £875. Alterations in these four magnitudes will change every other number, apart from the currency value and wages. New "values" will appear, and from these values come the prices that operate in the market.

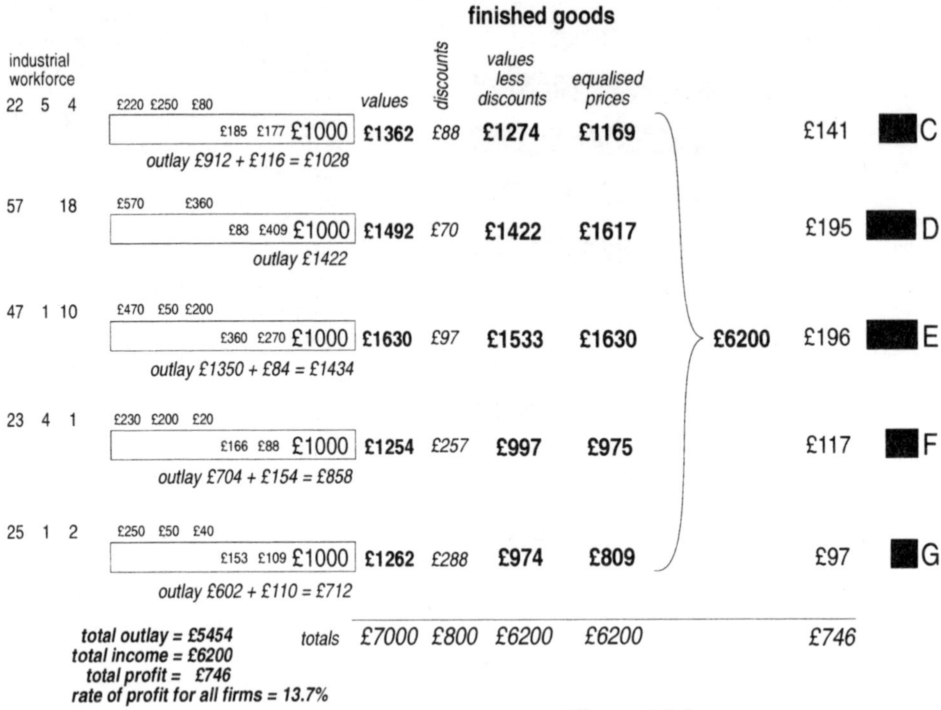

Figure 15-3

consider the task ahead. The firms that produce finished goods, CDEFG, all have a *potential* uniform rate of profit, namely 13.7%. This rate of profit can become actual in the market only if all other firms are operating with the same profit rate. Our way forward therefore is to adjust the circumstances of the other firms to ensure this outcome. But is it true that all other firms must conform to whatever rate of profit we have devised for the finished goods market? Not necessarily. There is no special dependency from the former to the latter. We could easily devise other rates of profit by altering factorial costs, or transport costs, or discounts, thereby changing the rate of profit for CDEFG. Their average rate of profit would then no longer be 13.7%. We are not concerned to establish a particular rate of profit, and it does not matter which part of the market is made to conform to any other. Our goal is simply to establish a uniform rate of profit, throughout all firms. Any arbitrary magnitudes we assign for factorial, transport and discount costs, will give rise to a corresponding rate of profit for each firm. We are merely choosing a hypothetical set of costs (giving them dummy values so to speak) and examining the response of the market to see whether we can obtain an equal rate of profit, consistent with these invented costs. If not, we will need to adjust the dummy values.

In Figure 15-4 the various parts have been re-arranged to make certain comparisons easier. At the top of the model is the conglomerate CDEFG, not amalgamated as such in real terms, but conveniently represented in this way because they are now a group of firms whose rates of profit are the same. The

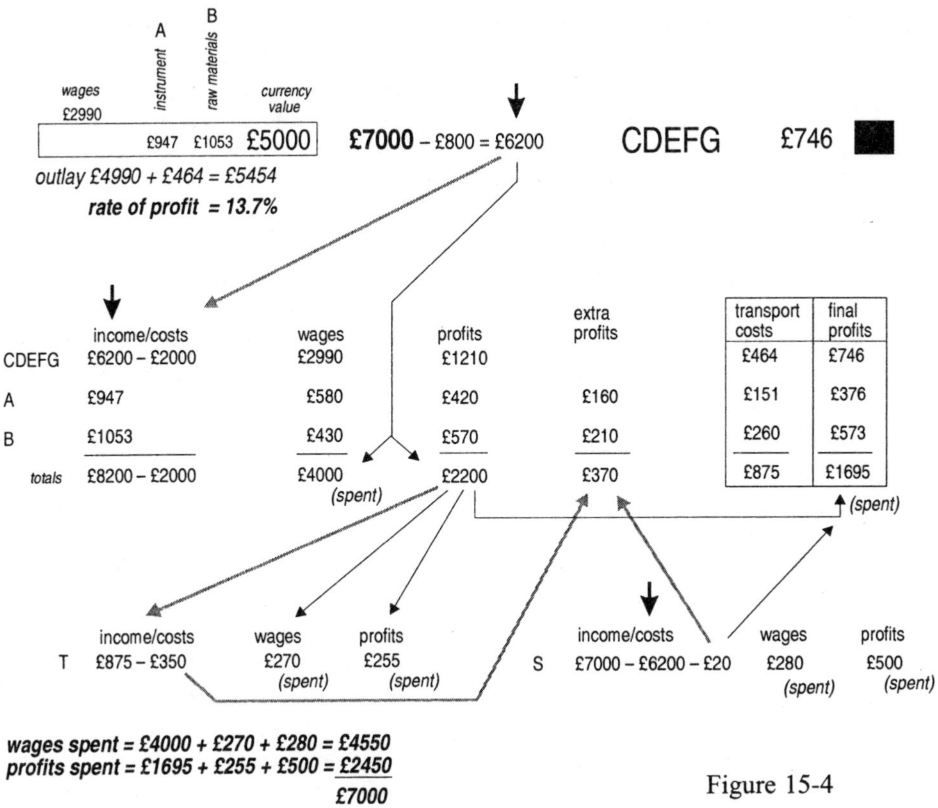

Figure 15-4

£7000 of daily value that springs into existence when their finished goods are sold, can now be viewed on its travels thought the money network of our model economy. The direct routes that culminate in spending at the goods exchange interface are shown by thin black arrows. But the money follows its own independent route through successive owners in exchange for an agreed "consideration" of some kind, to borrow a legal term. This consideration may take the form of goods such as raw materials or the provision of a service such as maintenance, retailing or transport, or any form of human labour to be utilised in a stipulated manner for a certain time. Whatever passes between any two parties in exchange for money acquires a "value" as understood by the parties concerned, but this acquired "value" is quite different from the inherent value possessed by the money as a portion of the primary incomes generated at the goods exchange interface. Figure 15-4 enables us to see how the different firms interpret their own situations (the grey arrows), while still keeping in view what is happening to the money (the thin black arrows).

The three arrow-heads are a reminder that the income for the supermarket firm originates in a discount deducted from the sales value of the goods. Otherwise the diagram is self-explanatory. The grey arrow at the top shows how the selling price of the goods, minus the discount, becomes an income for

CDEFG. Part of this income pays wages and profits, leaving a remainder which passes to A, B and T, in whose hands it is again converted into wages and profits. The grey arrows at the bottom show how money is deducted from the profits of ABCDEFG to pay transport costs, part of which is returned to A and B as extra profit. A deduction of £20 also finds its way back to A and B from the discount margin of £800 that provides the income for S.

In overall view, the five finished goods firms organise their workpeople to produce goods in cooperation with the workpeople of two factorial firms A and B, and the goods they jointly produce arrive in the finished goods market with a core value of £5000. This £5000 is determined by the exchange relationships that parallel streams of mass produced commodities engender between themselves when two special social procedures, which we are well acquainted with, are in operation side by side. In the first procedure, the flow rate of one commodity is adopted as an index to measure the comparative flow rates of the others, and in the second, the designated commodity is accumulated as a physical hoard or repository of value kept by everybody in the form of a float, to provide a stand-in or "equivalent" exponent of value when goods are sold by producers and bought by consumers in a self contained market where producers and consumers are the same people. When these two social procedures are in operation, goods for exchange acquire a value-form expressed in money which is first of all gold, and then later, banknotes. We need say no more on this point.

The core value of £5000 acquires an additional value of £2000 (according to our dummy choices) which represents that portion of past value which is not yet paid for and which lies dormant in the manufacturing process until it emerges in today's finished goods. An overlapping value is stored, so to speak, till a later stage, in a manner loosely depicted in the illustration below. (This overlapping effect is examined carefully in Appendix B, but need not detain us now).

production		sold on day 2	sold on day 3	sold on day 4	etc
day 1	£5000	£2000 ?			
day 2		£5000	£2000 ?		
day 3			£5000	£2000 ?	
day 4				£5000	£2000 ?

The demand for finished goods regulates both the past labour (maintenance work and supplying raw material and intermediate components) and today's labour (the finishing processes) by transmitting an adjustment of prices across the entire network to achieve two simultaneous objectives. First, an allocation of resources to all centres of production in proportions that satisfy today's aggregate demand, and second, an equal reward to all participants when this specific allocation is achieved. The equality of reward takes the form of equal rates of wages (within the appropriate grades of skill) for a working class, and equal returns on money outlay for a ruling class (the exact status of the ruling class will be discussed presently). Both of these classes are dominated by the equalising process, because prices are stable only when two conditions are fulfilled, namely when aggregate demand is satisfied and when no incentive exists to alter supply. This second condition means, in practice, that no worker (of a given grade) can improve his wages by switching jobs and no firm can improve profits by switching to another line of production. The adjustment of prices across the market to achieve equality of reward operates by raising the general level of reward for those productive spheres where relatively much labour is required for a given output, and reducing rewards where the labour requirement is relatively small. In this way, an equality expressed in money between particular production rates that are equal in equal times, and that match the aggregate demand pattern, is converted to unequal rewards in money for the maintenance of those same production rates on the basis of equal rewards for whatever number of producers these production rates happen to require. The original equality expresses *values* and the subsequent alteration of values to bring about equality of reward is expressed in *prices*. The ruling group intervenes in the general production-and-pricing complex to extract a profit (in ways which we will examine in a moment) which may be relatively high or low, and which can be increased by force or by legitimised democratic deceptions, (or by inherent features of the monetary system itself, such as the inflation that arises from superfluity of banknotes), but the equalising principle that matches supply to demand for the entire society is completely independent of any such exploitation. The equalising principle exerts total dominance over all firms, capitalist or otherwise, by the mutual competition that establishes an equal rate of profit between them.

In Figure 15-4 the sum of the values of the finished goods is £5000 plus whatever is necessary to maintain the essential inputs from Firms A and B. We have chosen arbitrary magnitudes for the cost of these inputs, "dummy values" so to speak, that add up to £2000. But the only stable centre of the values network is the £1000 of new value created respectively by CDEFG per day. The equalising process will convert all rewards for present labour, represented by CDEFG, for past labour, represented by A and B, and for all commercial services, such as Firms S and T, into a stable equilibrium, based on equal rates of profit. We must do the same in our analysis. Equality of wages is already given, and we presuppose that the present distribution of the workforce corresponds to the outputs needed to satisfy relative demand. Many of the magnitudes in the model will change when this transformation is effected. To enable us to follow all the changes, we need a model that shows the old and the new side-by-side, so to speak. Figure 15-5 presents the old information, based on exchange values and hypothetic costs, exactly the same as Figure 15-4, but inside the dotted rectangles are all the new magnitudes that the transformation entails. These new magnitudes correspond to equal rates of profit for all firms. The third and final stage is to introduce the new prices into the financial circumstances of the individual firms represented by the group CDEFG, bringing them into line with the new overall rate of profit, and then we can reconstitute the original presentation, up-dating Figure 15-2, but this time

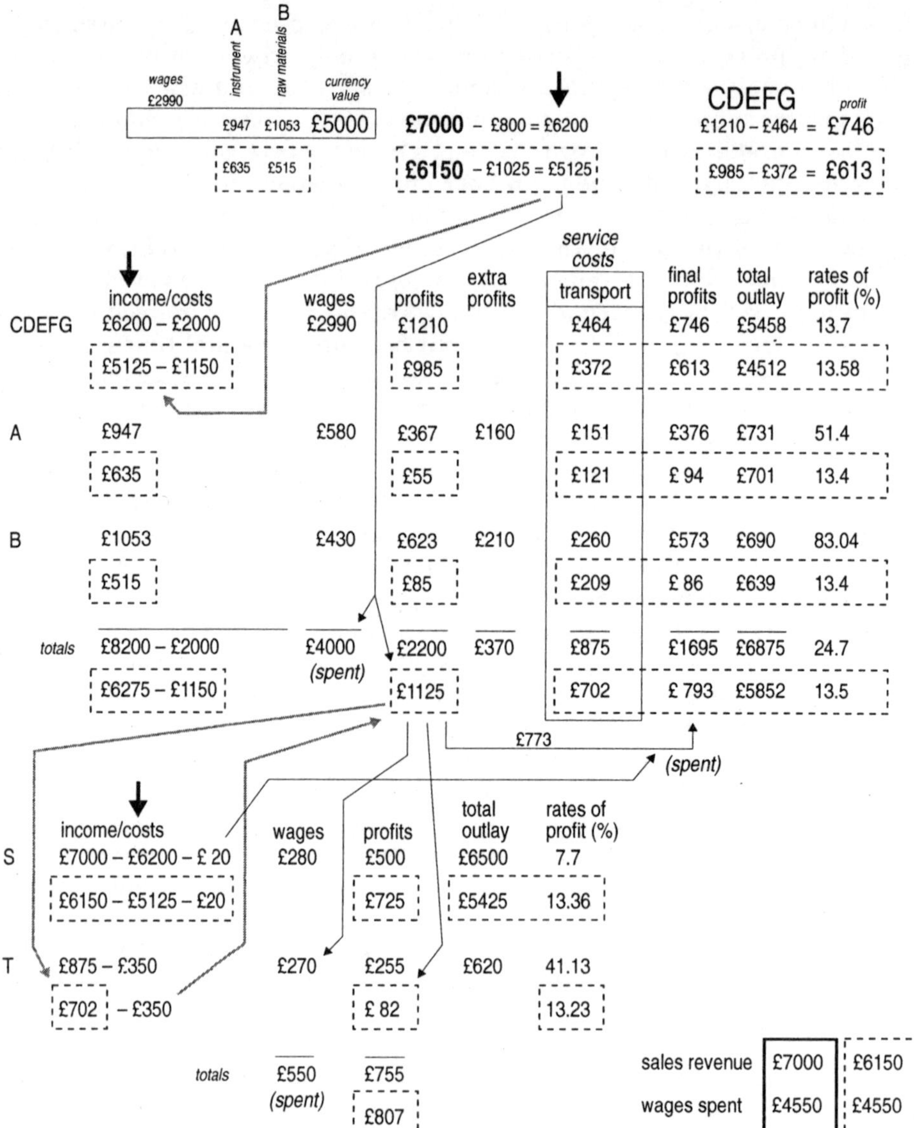

Figure 15-5

showing equilibrium prices, together with the theoretical values that they originate from. Thus we arrive at Figure 15-6.

In the previous Chapter 14, we adapted the labour requirements of the respective firms in order to fix profits at a level that ensured an equal rate of profit, consistent with the dummy values we chose for raw materials, factorial costs, discount margin and transportation. This time we have adjusted the dummy values without disturbing the labour requirements. We have merely assumed that the distribution of the workforce is such as to balance the output capabilities of this society against the aggregate demand of this society. On that assumption, the incentive to maximise profits will bring about a network of prices that corresponds to a uniform rate of profit, and once that equilibrium is established, all outputs will be stable. Figure 15-6 brings to light a unique set of prices which dominate all the money transactions associated with the production/consumption complex shown in Figure 15-2. The original *commodity exchange-values* are changed into *commodity prices,* and all the other associated transactions acquire a price even though they have no exchange-value. Exchange-value is exclusively a property of finished goods. We have created a fully specified model based on a community of 309 people organised in nine firms (presuming one owner per firm) with a finished goods sector, a factorial sector, a marketing sector, a service sector, uniform wage rates graded according to skill, a uniform rate of profit, and equilibrium prices that balance supply and demand.

The two tables in Figure 15-7 may be helpful in tracing the linkages in our new model. Table 1 can serve as a guided tour, so to speak, taking each firm in sequence and setting out the exact arithmetic procedures that define its financial situation, according to the firm's own interpretation of costs. Figure 15-8 gives precise details of the equalisation process in respect of the finished goods firms CDEFG.

It is abundantly clear from this transformation exercise that an equilibrium consistent with our former dummy values for factorial inputs, discount margins and transport services, as illustrated in the layout of Figures 15-1 and 15-2, is not achievable in practice. Values cannot be plucked out of the air and juxtaposed haphazardly in some imaginary economy, any more than they can be construed, with breath-taking ignorance, from two curves that cross on a simple-minded graph supposedly representing correlations between supply and demand for a single commodity. The uniform profit rate that dominates a money-based economy is a complex response mechanism that takes account of selling prices and costs for every firm. Hence the market forces that dominate any one firm cannot be explained from its own particular circumstances, and that is why these forces seem to be imposed from outside, just as twenty men who lift a heavy girder always feel that the girder is being lifted by the other nineteen. This ability of the market to dictate its own terms is of course universally recognised, and is not a false impression, because an individual firm is bound to act on this basis. But the economist cannot take this line. The whole process needs to be studied in its essential integrity to reconcile surface appearances with the underlying dependency of cause and effect.

The linkages in Figure 15-6 may look complicated but they are really quite straightforward, once they are deciphered, and no great mathematical skill is involved either in building the model or in tracing the various connections. Taking Firm F as an example, the workforce consists of 23 unskilled workers, 4 skilled workers and one supervisor. Respective wages are £230, £200 and £20 daily. The cost for maintenance of equipment is £111 and the cost for raw materials is £43. The exchange value of the goods is £111 + £43 + £1000 = £1154, but they are sold to the supermarket for a price of £827, leaving a profit of £99

Figure 15-6 (both pages)

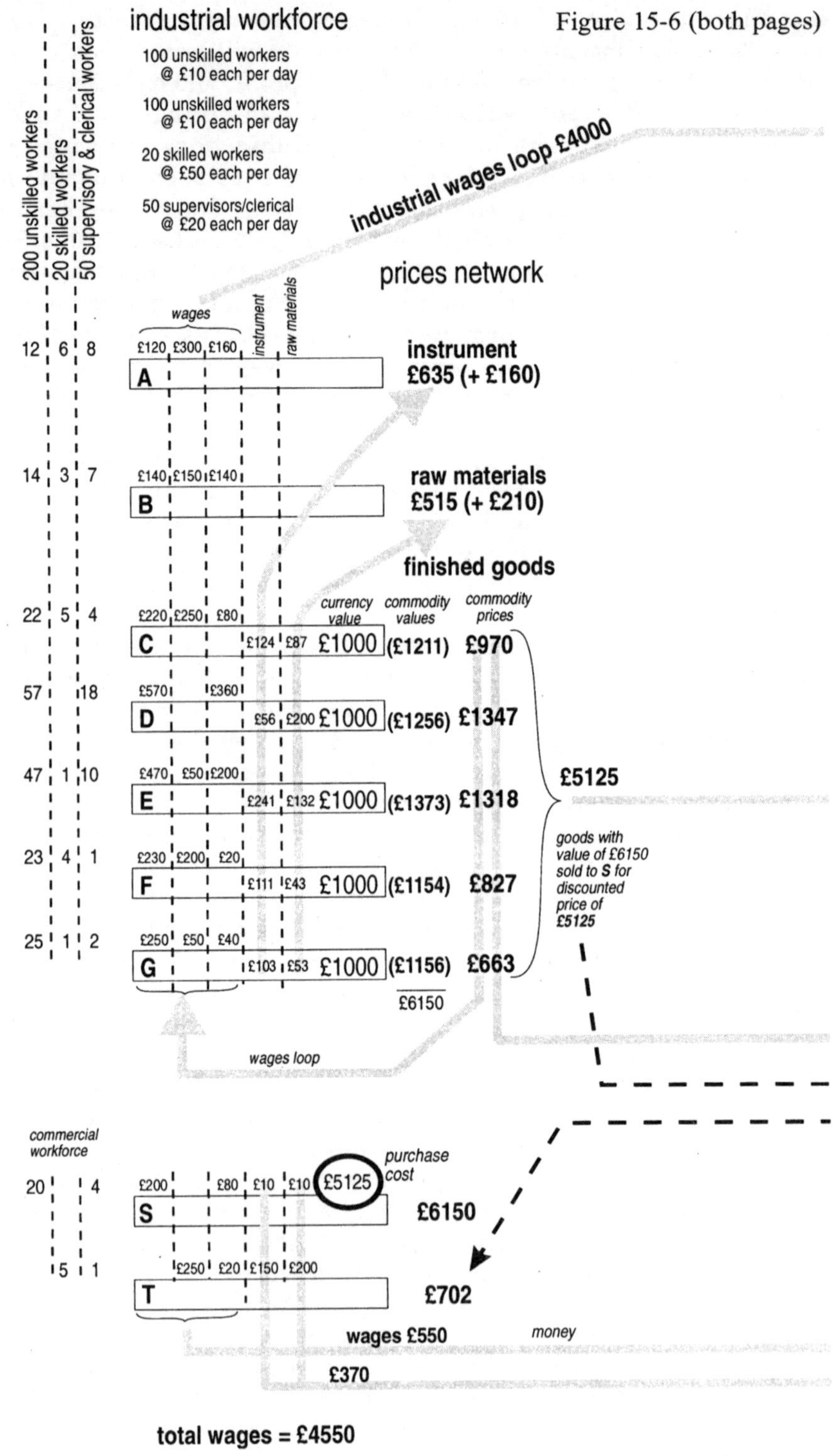

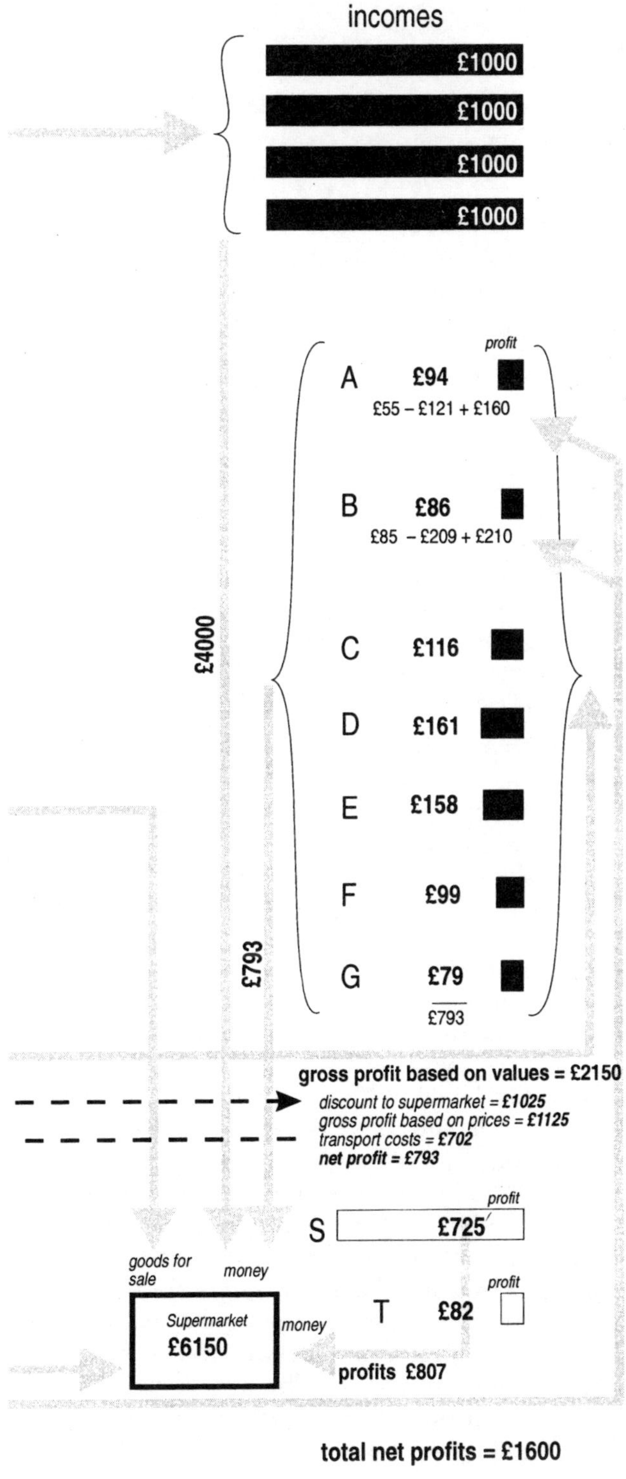

Rate of profit for all these firms is approximately 13.5%. This price network is therefore stable, and supply corresponds to a hypothesised demand. If this demand should alter, some prices will rise (and others fall), thus disturbing the equal profit rates. Firms will then switch to more profitable lines and competition will establish a new equality of profit rates with appropriate prices, thus restoring the balance of supply and demand.

The equilibrium shown here is a cycle of production, exchange and consumption repeated every day. Value is created inside five white rectangles and is then distributed throughout the economy in the form of spending power which is discharged so to speak in the supermarket, where spent notes are gathered and returned to the production process for recharging. All the numerical relationships are shown, linking the currency value to all payments of wages and profits for the four main sectors of the economy: finished goods, factorial inputs, marketing and ancillary.

Note that all incomes are simultaneously generated and spent. The spending creates the incomes and the incomes create the spending. This interlocked duality can never be broken for society as a whole, (otherwise the equilibrium portrayed here could not sustain itself) but individuals can spend or save with counter-balancing freedom within the constraints of income, using a shared pool of "savings". Thus the constant position is that all incomes are always fully spent, and savings, at the level of society as a whole, are fictitious. These matters are dealt with in the main text. (An important theoretical insight associated with this diagram, but not relevant here, is examined in Appendix B).

Income and expenditure for each firm *table 1*

	income	income less all production costs	remainder less transport costs	profit	total costs	rate of profit
A	£635 + £160 = £795	£795 – £580 = £215	£215 – £121 = £94	£94	£580 + £121 = £701	13.41%
B	£515 + £210 = £725	£725 – £430 = £295	£295 – £209 = £86	£86	£430 + £209 = £639	13.46%
C		£970 – £761 = £209	£209 – £93 = £116	£116	£761 + £93 = £854	13.58%
D		£1347 – £1186 = £161	£161 – £nil = £161	£161	£1186	13.57%
E		£1318 – £1093 = £225	£225 – £67 = £158	£158	£1093 + £67 = £1160	13.62%
F		£827 – £604 = £223	£223 – £124 = £99	£99	£604 + £124 = £728	13.6%
G		£663 – £496 = £167	£167 – £88 = £79	£79	£496 + £88 = £584	13.53%
S	£6150 – £5125 = £1025	£1025 – £300 = £725	£725 – £nil = £725	£725	£5125 + £300 = £5425	13.36%
T		£702 – £620 = £82	£82 – £nil = £82	£82	£620	13.22%

Link between values and prices *table 2*

	values		discount	remainder	prices	
					wholesale	retail
C	£124 + £87 + £1000	= £1211	£113	£1098	£970	£1083
D	£56 + £200 + £1000	= £1256	£90	£1166	£1347	£1437
E	£241 + £132 + £1000	= £1373	£124	£1249	£1318	£1442
F	£111 + £43 + £1000	= £1154	£329	£825	£827	£1156
G	£103 + £53 + £1000	= £1156	£369	£787	£663	£1032
	totals	*£6150*	*£1025*	*£5125*	*£5125*	*£6150*

Figure 15-7

per day for the owner. The circumstances of all the firms are set out in like manner, and all wages and profits are spent daily in the supermarket at prices that match the exchange-value of the goods to the total money spent.

In historical reality these relatively simple dependencies are buried under countless accidents and time lags that conceal their inner connections, and even when these connections are displayed to open view the surface appearance gives no hint of anything resembling a currency value, which is the foundation on which the entire system rests. It is an enormous intellectual feat to have deciphered these relationships. Marx acknowledged his debt to Smith and Ricardo (and many other writers mentioned in his footnotes) and was modest in regard to his own contribution. He is nowadays recognised even in official circles as one of the greatest of modern thinkers, but his economic research is systematically misrepresented and falsified. No modern textbook gives any sort of explanation about his theories. Yet he discovered the interconnections that are illustrated here and the ground he surveyed is far wider than our present analysis and stretches further ahead. Nothing of course has been taken from Marx's works in the course of this exposition, not even the special terms that he used, such as labour power, surplus value, socially necessary labour-time, prices of production, organic composition, etc. The models developed in these pages stand or fall solely on their own merits, and are not intended to verify or refute or illustrate any established viewpoint.

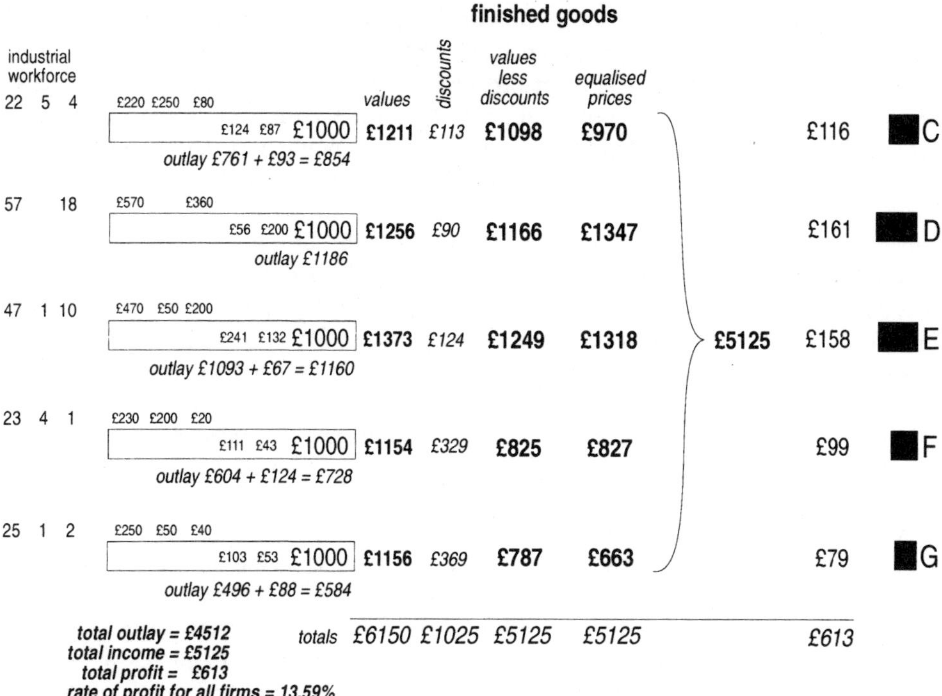

Figure 15-8

A clarification about ruling class identity is appropriate at this juncture. There is no exploitation present in Figure 15-6 as it stands. The profit that accrues to the owners of the various firms is not distinguished in any way from the wages that are paid to the workforce. Both wages and profits originate in the realised selling price of the goods or services that each firm offers. The proportions that fall to the respective parties may be adjudged "fair" or otherwise by standards deemed to be suitable either on the basis of custom, or consensus arrived at by any means whatever. These proportions may also be imposed by force, or by deception. They may conceivably be determined by market forces, meaning that salaries for managerial posts and for wages at all grades could be stabilised at a level sufficient to attract able people but also held in check by competition between the applicants for such posts. If this principle of market forces were universally adopted for all positions of responsibility there would be no private owners as such, though an administrative body of some kind would be needed to organise the procedures that appoint and empower all post-holders. The work of such an administrative body would be entirely straightforward, easily monitored and approved by a general consensus drawn from the public at large, and *fully intelligent* in a social sense, because it would be based on real economic understanding. Any literate population can understand its own economic relations. The mathematics involved is nothing more than elementary arithmetic. Such public awareness and power of scrutiny, based on real knowledge, is the only guarantee of democratic freedom in a collective group whose economic cohesion is based on money. No guarantee of freedom is provided by a so-called bill of rights or constitutional declaration, or universal suffrage or regular elections or equality before the law or separation of powers or a free press or political parties in mock combat to impress gullible voters. Of course all these things are worthy in their own way. But in a capitalist society they signify only a potential for freedom, yet to be realised. As far as Figure 15-6 is concerned, nothing in this economic layout gives any clue about the type of society, free or capitalist, that it could belong to.

When the proportion between wages and profit is determined by a class of private owners, in a society where the population has no economic understanding, exploitation takes two political forms, namely, naked force, as in the dictatorships, or deception, as in the so-called democracies. These two forms tend to overlap, since they share the same ultimate aim, and borrow each other's techniques where necessary. Their common purpose is to divert economic wealth into the pockets of the ruling group, and this could be achieved in Figure 15-6 by enforced reduction of the general level of wages. In such an event, Figure 15-6 would become a despotic society based on slave labour. But a far better method, because it involves no forcible repression, is to leave Figure 15-6 as it is, and "encourage" increased productive efficiency alongside systematic inflation, keeping this inflation hidden under a non-changing regime of steady unit prices. All the improvement in output efficiency would then flow into the incomes of the ruling group, while the living standard of the workforce would stand still in absolute terms because wages and prices would remain unaltered. The only outward sign of inflation would be the steady fall in the purchasing power of money.

If the hidden inflation were augmented (by for example printing banknotes at a rate that exceeded the rate of productivity improvement), then unit prices would rise, and the ruling group would become even richer, while living standards for the workforce would fall in absolute terms. Social discontent arising from this latter circumstance can be pacified by judicious concessions that permit a partial restoration of standards. An ignorant population can be deceived into thinking that negotiation on this basis is a form of political freedom.

So we see that Figure 15-6, though it clearly portrays a society based on a system of wages and an income called profit, cannot be described on these grounds as exploitative or even capitalist. These firms may be capitalist or they may not. This point has been discussed before, and in fact an earlier diagram, Figure 6-5 on page 65, expresses the essence of the matter. The five types of society illustrate the various possibilities. The society portrayed in Figure 15-6 could be any one of these five types.

The demonstration in Figure 15-7, Table 2, that the sum of the prices is equal to the sum of the values gives us a more accurate interpretation of our earlier model Figure 15-2, which, up to now, we have regarded as a values network ready for transformation into a prices network. This is not strictly true. The correct commodity values are present in Figure 15-6. The term "value", or more accurately "exchange-value", is a precise economic concept, and we must be careful to use it only where it is truly applicable. As stated earlier in this chapter, mere exchange of money between two parties may seem to define the "value" of whatever is being purchased, but such exchange is in no way comparable to the process that defines a commodity's exchange-value. The commodity's value springs from its production rate, ie its rate of flow through the market from producers to consumers, expressed in relation to all other rates of flow. Money that changes hands *outside* the bold rectangle, for whatever purpose, is simply part of a transaction that satisfies the parties concerned. If the transaction is related in any regular way to the production of finished commodities for sale (by providing raw materials or maintenance or a service of some kind) then the overall nexus of supply and demand will determine the price that must be paid to ensure a steady and continuous supply of such necessary raw materials and services. To illustrate by a specific example, consider Firm A in Figure 15-2. We have postulated that this firm earns £947 from the CDEFG group for equipment maintenance. Is it possible to conjure up random values in this way for services provided, and assume that they can be integrated into the price network? By no means. At the most we can only supply dummy values to see what happens when the equalisation process takes effect. Perhaps Firm A had high hopes of earning this kind of income. Alas, in the competitive marketplace, the "true value" of its services is not £947 but £635, as shown in Figure 15-6. This means, strictly speaking, that there is no such thing as a "true value" for intermediate goods and services, or for any ancillary services, or for any kind of buyable activity or product associated with, but separate from, the actual production of finished goods. Only the finished goods themselves possess "value", properly expressed as "exchange-value", and they acquire this value at the goods exchange interface and nowhere else. All kinds of things and activities can be exchanged for a quantity of money, but in the theoretical vocabulary of economics only a *finished commodity which is bought for consumption by the buyer* has an exchange-value. (We are of course not speaking of isolated instances but of competitive markets served by large-scale mass production). The values acquired by finished goods as a direct outcome of their production rate relationships are changed into prices by an equalisation process that takes account of every money transaction involved in the bringing of these goods into existence at the point of consumption. The equalisation process operates by altering all prices to ensure a uniform rate of profit, alongside a range of incomes that in aggregate exactly matches the total value of all finished goods.

With this wider understanding, we can better appreciate the value/price relationship. Consider Firm E for instance, in Figure 15-6. As can be seen, the exchange-value of the goods it produces is £1373. Now refer to Table 2 in Figure 15-7. Firm E sells these goods to the supermarket for £1318, and the supermarket sells them for £1442 (or thereabouts, depending how the overall discount margin is averaged across all selling prices). Neither the wholesale price nor the final selling price seem to be related to the exchange-value, and this is indeed true for any firm considered in isolation. But the totals in Table 2 confirm that all prices of finished goods are ultimately derived from their exchange-values.

These exchange values dominate not only the prices of finished commodities sold for consumption, but they also fix the amounts of money (also conveniently called prices or values) that regularly change hands for any purpose that is remotely connected with the production of those commodities.

We have earlier remarked that if the currency value of £1000 is removed from a diagram like Figure 15-6, then the entire buying and selling network becomes incomprehensible. (Except to a marginalist who enjoys chasing his own tail). But even when the currency value is present, and a full explanation is possible for all prices and all incomes, the *exchange-value* of commodities is nowhere to be found in any tangible form, as Figure 15-6 confirms. In spite of this, its presence as an unseen regulator was dimly sensed by the early classical economists, and in Adam Smith it received its first formal recognition as a basic principle, and thereafter became known as the labour theory of value. But though the theory contained an essential truth, that the labour-time of a commodity in some way determined its price, this truth was not accurately expressed until the third volume of Marx's *Capital* appeared a decade or more after the author's death. The bare statement that the value of a commodity is determined by its *own* labour-time is quite false. Equally false is the bare statement that the values of two commodities are related as their labour-times are related. Even worse is any statement to the effect that the *prices* of commodities are a direct expression of their labour times. The correct statement of the theory, in two sentences for the sake of clarity, is as follows:

> *The* ***relative value*** *of a commodity is its labour-time expressed as a ratio against the labour-time of a universal commodity chosen to serve in its physical substance as a measure.*
> *The* ***price*** *of a commodity is its relative value adjusted in mutual correspondence with the relative values of all other commodities throughout the market to ensure an equal rate of profit for all firms.*

The first of these statements corresponds to the general approach adopted by Marx in the first and second volumes of *Capital.* The modification of the value-form to produce actual production prices alongside an equal rate of profit is introduced in the posthumous third volume.

16

The circular flow of incomes, wages and costs

It is true that all our models are circular in the sense that values emanate from the goods exchange interface, travel though the network of prices, and then return to their point of origin, but this circularity can be illustrated in a variety of ways to emphasise different aspects of the economy. An earlier configuration, Figure 14-3, showed how the industrial wages loop was distinct from the industrial profits loop. Now that we have transformed values into prices, we can update this model using our new information, as in Figure 16-1.

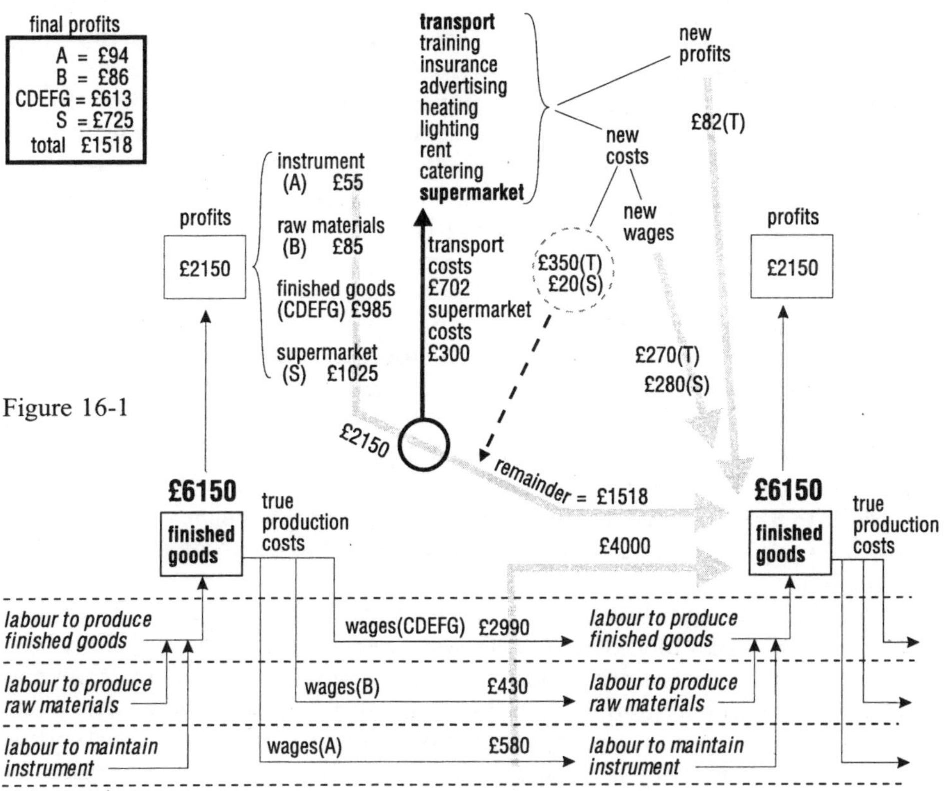

Figure 16-1

All the grey arrows add up to £6150, but the industrial wages loop of £4000 has its own direct route when viewed socially, as it travels between successive turnovers of the production-consumption, value-generating cycle. By contrast, the profits loop of £2150 wanders through other firms, and in fact it splits at one point to transfer £550 into new wages, so we should note an important feature here, that profit extracted at the industrial stage can be differentiated at a later commercial stage into a fresh set of profits, costs and wages. Costs are always incomes for other firms. Note therefore that the new costs inside the dotted circle do not lead directly to the finished goods rectangle, but travel backwards so to speak into the incomes of A and B. This is a restoration of money that A and B have already parted with when they paid for commercial services such as (in our case) transport. Hence when any of the listed commercial firms pay for the services of A and/or B, they are returning money, via the dotted black arrow, that they have already received from A and B. The same applies when S employs A and B. The money may be said to loop back on itself. It leaves the black circle as a cost, but part of it returns as extra profit. The remainder is the final profit destined to be spent on finished goods. This final profit, tabulated in the top left corner, can be verified from Figures 15-6 and 15-8.

The comprehensive picture that we must carry in our minds at all times is that primary incomes are generated in the finished goods rectangle and these incomes then flow either directly back to the rectangle or along a myriad diversions that also flow back to the rectangle but, on the way, generate the derivative incomes that everybody else depends on. These diversions can easily loop backwards on themselves, as described in the previous paragraph, when a firm pays money to a firm that the money has already passed through.

As can clearly be seen from Figure 16-1, the notion of *costs* is intimately linked to the narrow perspective of the individual firm, as opposed to the wider social view of the economist (if he or she has any grasp of these matters). For the individual firm, all costs, including wages, are simply deductions from income. But from a comprehensive standpoint, costs are quite different from wages. Wages are always deductions. But a cost other than wages is a transfer of money from one firm to another. So all such costs are *additions* as well as deductions and they counterbalance each other as far as the net social effect is concerned. Wages as a rule are spent directly, whereas money paid to cover costs other than wages finds its way to the sales interface by a more or less devious route. As we have just noted, it can transform itself into further wages and costs on the way. Costs are very real to the individual firm, but they always vanish into thin air when they are traced comprehensively through the economy. Only wages and profits are real, when the economy is viewed as a social whole.

A circular flow diagram that emphasises this self-cancelling aspect of costs is portrayed opposite in Figure 16-2. The arrows indicate how money flows from left to right, as if in conduits, and all costs other than wages are shown as outflows that become inflows when they are re-connected at some other point. Wages quit the network and are spent. Likewise with profits. But costs never leave the network. They are always absorbed. All the firms are represented

Figure 16-2

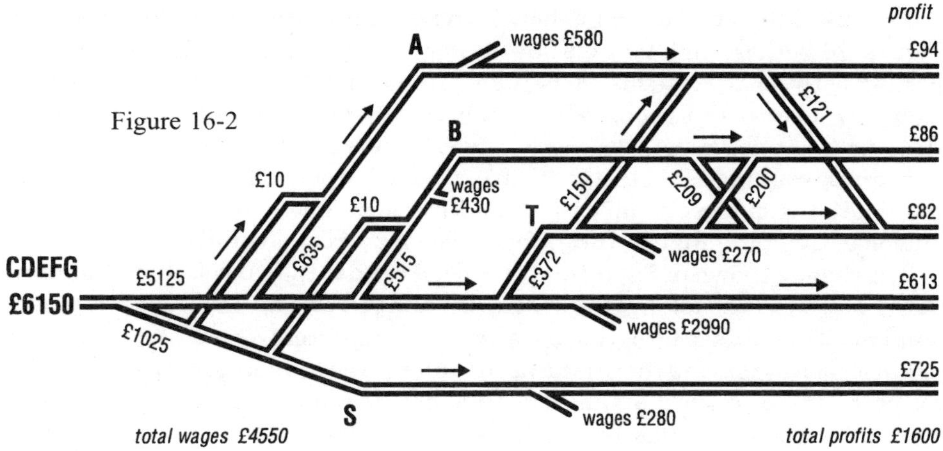

quite realistically in every detail, (in accordance with Figure 15-6), and the point to be grasped is that costs and their associated incomes are self-cancelling, and no matter how or where they arise the sum of wages and profits will always be equal to total sales of finished goods, in this case £6150. (All firms regard wages as a cost, but henceforth we will use the term "cost" to mean all expenses *other than wages.*)

We need to consolidate our understanding at this point. The network of equilibrium prices displayed in Figure 16-2 corresponds to equal rates of profit for all firms. But this particular equality is not interpreted from a social view of the economy. It is an interpretation exclusive to the individual firms. If costs arise *for them,* in terms of their own understanding and spending behaviour, they will take these costs into account in calculating their rates of profit, and these rates of profit are the basis on which the equalisation process achieves its equilibrium position. In other words, the profits shown on the right will be in equilibrium, on the basis of equal rates of profit, only if those rates correspond to the calculations made by the firms themselves.

Figure 16-3

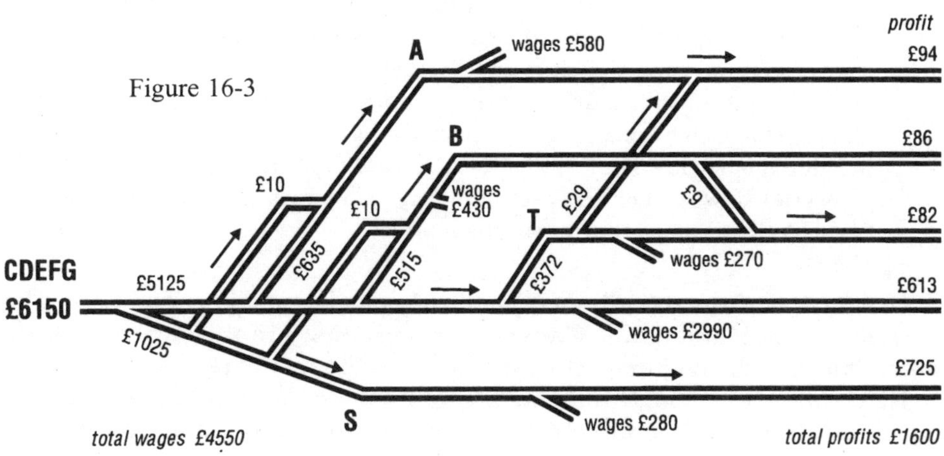

To illustrate, let us examine how Firms A and B are related to Firm T. In Figure 16-2 there are two outflow/inflow linkages that form a criss-cross pattern between these firms. Money flows in one direction, but it also flows back again. From an overall point of view only the net effect matters. But the firms themselves do not adopt this overall view. Once a cost has arisen it remains a cost, and is counted as such in the firm's calculation of its rate of profit. It is easy to remove the bi-directional costs from Figure 16-2, leaving only the residual outcome. Compare Figure 16-3, where the criss-cross conduits are deleted.

The change shown in Figure 16-3 can be likened to the cancellation of mutual debts. I owe you £10 for digging my garden and you owe me £6 for painting your window. Therefore I owe you £4 when the criss-cross debts are reconciled against each other, and there is no need to discharge the debts individually. The effect is similar in our diagram. The final profits remain exactly as they were, so none of the firms has been affected in any way. But the rates of profit calculated from this new Figure 16-3 would be different from the rates of profit calculated from the previous Figure 16-2, because all the costs in the latter are real to the firms concerned, and cannot be mutually cancelled as we have done.

What is the significance of this double-vision, one arising from a social view and the other from the view of the individual firm? It means that the equilibrium point, when located by the competition between firms to equalise rates of profit, will produce a set of prices in the market that is even more remote from basic values than before. If we carefully set forth the influences that bring about a divergence of prices from values, they are as follows.

1 Each firm (strictly speaking each sphere of production) producing finished goods embodies the currency value in its regular daily output. Call this £1000 as in our current model.
2 The value of "past" factorial labour, namely instrument upkeep and raw materials for each individual firm, is added to this value, making it £1000 + X. This X is different for each firm.
3 All finished lines of production, each creating a value of £1000 + X, are added together and then proportionately re-allocated as operational prices for all commodities, in accordance with an equal rate of profit for all firms that provide a paid service at any stage in the entire production process ie, from point of origin of commodities to point of actual consumption. This equalisation process simultaneously determines the magnitude of X, proportionately adjusted for each firm, and it is based on the rates of profit as calculated by the individual firms. The fact that these costs are self-cancelling, either from an overall viewpoint or because these firms may work in a paired relation to each other, has no bearing on the matter.

Of course no firm actually makes all the calculations described here. The currency value is unknown. Wages, costs and profit are the only recognised items that broadly dominate the calculation of the rate of profit.

Note that even though the equalisation process is complicated, and the equalised prices gets more and more remote from the original commodity values, the equilibrium itself does not thereby become more fragile, more delicately poised, so to speak, any more than a suspension bridge is any less sturdy by virtue of the complexity of the stresses and strains transmitted through the foundations, the pillars, the steel latticework, and the overhead cables. The structure is no less secure on account of the complexity. Similarly, the fact that all kinds of self-cancelling costs are involved in the calculation of rates of profit has no effect whatever on the stability of the final equilibrium. The stability springs from the fact that when each firm is producing goods at exactly the rate required to satisfy demand, no incentive exists for any of them to switch production into some other sphere. As long as this avenue of improvement is absent every firm will stay where it is. The equalisation process is not *imposed* on the market. It is an effect generated by the market itself, because when relative demand rises for a commodity, the price rises, the profit rate rises, and this improved profit rate attracts a higher allocation of productive resources from less profitable lines. The firms interpret their own financial situation and act in their best interests. By so doing they create a network of prices that coincides with equal rates of profit, and which also necessarily balances supply with demand. It is this latter outcome that matters. How the firms calculate their rates of profit is neither here nor there. If their calculations are in some sense "wrong", the balance of supply and demand will still be preserved because the equalisation process operates not on the basis of "correct calculations" but by modifying prices in whatever way is necessary to maximise *perceived* profit rates for all firms when they jointly produce the supply that satisfies demand. The firms are thus locked in this equilibrium position regardless of how they view themselves.

In essence, the equalisation process is "managed" by the firms themselves, in mutual competition, with a superficial awareness that "market forces" somehow bring about an equilibrium between supply and demand, which is true, but the firms themselves have no understanding of this process. Hence the belief that if trade is simply left to its own devices it will benefit everybody in the long run. But this poses a problem, one that confronted Adam Smith. He believed that value was created only by labour, and he also sensed that an "invisible hand" was working in everybody's interests. Both these beliefs are correct, but how can such views be reconciled with the reality of a labouring class that remains poor and an idle class that grows ever richer? The classical economists pondered this problem, and the steady progress they made towards understanding the capitalist system caused mounting alarm in ruling circles, where the need was seen for an official science of economics, dependably loyal, to act as a government mouthpiece. This bogus science was duly pioneered at the end of the nineteenth century by Alfred Marshall. Lacking any vestige of critical honesty, it has been officially promoted in schools, colleges and universities ever since.

Our previous two diagrams portray the circularity of the price network alongside the production/consumption cycle and both diagrams are valid as they stand. Figure 16-3 is a social overview which enlarges our theoretical understanding of the price network with regard to the self-cancellation of costs.

But Figure 16-2 shows how the equilibrium operates in practice, in compliance with the perspective of the individual firm, for whom all costs are real.

The restricted perspective of the individual firm is well illustrated by Firm S, the supermarket firm. Firm S has no idea that the goods bought from CDEFG have an intrinsic value, and that it is buying them at a discounted price. Nor do CDEFG have any such notion. As far as CDEFG are concerned, the "value" of the goods is whatever they are sold for, and this is the price negotiated with Firm S, which likewise thinks that it has bought goods at their "value". Firm S now imagines that its own costs and profit must be added to this value to create a reasonable selling price, and we are back in the perverted world of the textbooks and popular opinion, where goods bought at wholesale prices acquire mark-ups of various kinds to cover expenses and a residue of profit for whoever handles the goods on their way to the retail market. Thus the value creation process, which is an intrinsic part of productive activity, not only creating goods in a physical sense but also endowing them at the same time with a value from which wages, costs and profit are subsequently extracted, is turned back to front, by making the wages, costs and profit determine the value. The distinction between value and price is lost at the same time, and everything floats in eternal dependency on everything else. Marginalism can now assert that this dependency is an eternal truth free from normative assumptions, and in this way the typical student is led to believe that he or she possesses a theoretical foundation for understanding everything to do with economics, whereas in truth the student's intelligence has simply been switched off.

The narrow perspective of the supermarket firm is also illustrated in another way, ie in respect of its income. In the social view, goods worth £6150 are sold to the supermarket for £5125, leaving a margin of £1025 for the supermarket firm, which it will recoup when the goods are sold. This margin is its income from a social point of view. But Firm S regards the retail selling price of £6150 as its income. The wholesale purchase price of £5125 is a cost that will be entered as such in the financial accounts of Firm S when it calculates its rate of profit. This sum of £5125 is a perfect example of a self-cancelling cost, because it is a loss to CDEFG balanced by an identical gain to Firm S. But this loss is not shown in anybody's accounts. The firms operate from a zero position which is strictly determined according to their own financial pluses and minuses.

This raises again a matter we have emphasised several times. Money is regarded as a universal "evaluator" in any transaction where something is purchased, and using it in this way is perfectly natural, useful and in no sense necessarily dishonest. But exchange-value is a precise term, denoting a property acquired by mass produced commodities when they are exchanged for each other in a process involving an intermediary called money. This process endows value upon a commodity, congealed in it so to speak by virtue of being part of a continuous, large-scale operation, and this value is totally unrelated to any sum of money that successive owners may pass between themselves in order to become temporary owners of the commodity. Thus a consignment of goods may be bought for £10, then sold for £20, then sold again for £30, and then, when it reaches the market, it may be bought by a consumer for £40. In a closed, freely competitive market, the £40 paid by the final consumer is a price which the commodity has possessed from the very beginning, and which is derived from the commodity's inherent exchange-value, not directly but by an equalisation process affecting all commodities. The goods pass through a string of dealers who add phantom costs to their calculations which are very real to them as individuals, because these costs represent each individual dealer's purchase price. It is obvious that these particular costs have no social significance, because in the example given they add up to £10 + £20 + £30 = £60 in respect of a commodity with a final price of £40. Hence we are obliged to ask *What are these costs supposed to pay for?* Let us trace the actual transactions to find the answer. There are three dealers and, balancing costs against income, each ends up with £10 of the £40 that was paid by the final purchaser, while an original producer gets £10. There is nothing else to be said about these transactions. It is ridiculous to add together these supposed costs (which are minuses) and neglect the incomes that they are part of (which are pluses). When these dealers calculate their rates of profit they will compete among themselves for the best returns, and we can now ask the same question in a more meaningful form. *What determines the price that satisfies the parties involved?* Answer: the equality of their rates of profit. The first dealer spent £10 to obtain £10, the second dealer spent £20 to obtain £10 and the third dealer spent £30 to obtain £10. These all represent different rates of profit. But after an equalisation process the prices quoted by the three dealers will not be £10, £20, £30 and £40. They will be £10, £15.88, £25.22 and £40. At these prices all rates of profit are equal at 58.7%. (Of course these calculations cannot be valid unless the whole economy is included, so only the principle is being illustrated here). The point is that these dealers will justify their prices on the grounds that such payments are a recompense for some service they provide, and it may well be true that each of them provides an essential service. But these prices are set quite impersonally by the mechanism that equalises profit rates. Given that the dealers' services are required, or cannot be avoided for some reason, the prices to be paid are not determined by some conventional estimate of time and labour involved. These prices are set by market forces in the manner we have described, given the usual assumptions of free competition in a closed economy.

17

Interest: part 1

Every economy based on printable money has a fixed currency value derived from the three-sided interaction between (1) the aggregated face value of all banknotes (and coin) in the monetary base, (2) the velocity of the currency, and (3) the accommodation period. These were all examined in Part One. We assume that all three are constant throughout this chapter.

Hence the currency value of £1000 shown in Figure 15-6 will not alter, no matter how production rates may vary and no matter how the various firms may reorganise themselves. Nothing can change the currency value except the printing of extra banknotes (or their destruction on a significant scale). Although it is theoretically possible to reduce the currency value by amassing a huge non-functioning private hoard of banknotes, nothing so pointless is ever likely to happen in a normal economy. (Money that accumulates in bank deposits or investments or savings must never be regarded as a hoard. It is instantly spent by the banks and its circulation continues as before). We have dealt elsewhere with the reverse process, ie the millions of tiny hoards that are progressively converted into bank deposits, causing the currency value to rise as a secular trend. Any such effect is excluded from our present discussion.

The currency value is therefore a fixed point of reference for all the magnitudes in the model but it is at all times vulnerable to the printing of banknotes. What would happen in Figure 15-6 if extra banknotes were printed? The currency value would rise, all prices would rise, and all profits would rise, while wages and every other type of income expressed as a fixed entitlement per week/month/year, would remain unaltered. But before we explore the implications of this in our models, we should ask *"How do such extra banknotes get from the printing press to the money network?"* Obviously the central bank that prints the notes doesn't give free handouts to other people, and neither does the bank spend the extra notes as its own income, like an illegal counterfeiter.

There are several interlinked processes here, which we can disentangle by a simple illustration, involving Len who is a lender, Boris who is a borrower-lender, and Owen who is an owner-employer. Len gives a loan of £5 every week to Boris. Boris lends this borrowed £5 every week to Owen. Owen spends the £5 each week on wages for a worker who produces goods that Owen sells every week for £10. Owen's gross income is £10 from selling the goods plus £5 loaned by Boris, making a total of £15. From this £15 he deducts £5 for wages, gives

£5 to Boris in return for the loan, and keeps £5 for himself. Boris then returns £5 to Len. All loans are thus restored every week, without interest, and it is obvious that nobody is gaining anything from this regular loaning system. Owen and the wage-earner each enjoy a living standard of £5 a week, obtained by selling goods for £10, while the loans themselves are quite pointless.

But now let us now retrace our steps, setting up the same loans on different terms. Len gives £5 to Boris in the hope of getting £6 back. Boris lends the same £5 to Owen in the hope of getting £7 back. Owen holds on to this £5, and advances £5 of his own money to pay wages for the worker who duly produces goods that Owen sells for £10. Owen now has £15. From this £15 he sets aside £5 for next week's wages, keeps £3 for himself, and gives £7 to Boris. Boris puts £1 in his pocket and gives £6 to Len. When these loan transactions are repeated continuously, Len and Boris will each enjoy an income of £1 a week, Owen (who will never need to produce another fiver from his own pocket) will enjoy an income of £3 a week, and the wage earner will enjoy an income of £5 a week, while only two people will be working, ie the worker who produces the goods, and Owen who attends to the marketing. Len's rate of interest is £1 gained for £5 loaned. Boris gets a higher rate of interest from his loan, £2 gained for £5 loaned, but as a borrower he owes £1 to Len. Owen's rate of profit is £3 gained for £5 supposedly spent on wages. (Supposedly, because the wages really come from the sales). The loan transactions now seem to be supplying money that is needed to enable the goods to be produced and sold. Without Len's loan of £5 to Boris, and Boris's loan of £5 to Owen, the wage bill of £5 would not be met, and clearly Owen is entitled to a payment of some kind, currently £3 a week, for his marketing services. Len and Boris and Owen and the worker can all claim to be important contributors, each deserving appropriate recompense.

Anyone examining these figures will soon realise that Owen has no need to borrow from anybody. He is the owner of the £10 that accrues every week from sales, so he has only to extract £5 to cover wages every week and he can keep the remainder. Owen and the worker could both enjoy the same standard of living, expressed as £5 each per week, if they dispense with money-lenders. The worker does all the production work and Owen does the marketing. (Although Owen is an owner-employer he may work harder than the wage-earner, and earn no more money or possibly less. Such circumstances, whether true or not, have no bearing whatever on the argument. We are studying the facts of a relationship, not making judgements about who deserves what).

So why are money-lenders present? They serve two purposes. From Owen's point of view they are just parasites unless the currency value is rising. But they can all become collaborators in an ingenious swindle if the currency value is rising as an ongoing trend, and if at the same time the worker can be made to work harder, and/or longer, and/or more productively, as an ongoing trend. These two trends will counterbalance each other and hold unit prices constant. In these circumstances, the goods produced by the worker will increase in quantity, but unit prices will not fall, so the £10 sales revenue per week will steadily rise while the worker's wage will stay constant at £5 per week. The work of one man (or two, because Owen will soon be able to afford another wage-earner to handle the marketing) will keep three idlers in steadily rising comfort. Owen needs the loans system to take advantage of the depreciating currency, as explained in detail when we examined the business affairs of Mr Neat and Mr Tidy in Part One. This is the first purpose served by the money-lenders.

The other purpose brings us back to our original question. How do extra banknotes get from the printing press to the money network? Len prints these notes but does not spend them. He includes them in his loans to Boris. These loans are made at a particular rate of interest which provides an income for Len. Boris borrows these notes and then lends them a second time at a higher rate of interest to get an income from the difference in the two interest rates. Len represents the central bank, and Boris represents a local banker. The value of money constantly falls as a result of Len's fraudulent printing activity but what else can these two bankers do? If the worker's productivity rises, the supply of goods will increase, and the unit price of those goods will fall as an inevitable consequence. Owen's £10 will not get any bigger, and he will see no reason to share it with money-lenders. In such a case, the living standard of the worker and Owen's living standard will both rise as a result of falling prices, but Len and Boris will lose their incomes. How can they prevent this fall in prices, which is ruinous from their point of view? By operating a loan system whereby banknotes can be filtered into the monetary network in sufficient quantity to generate the hidden inflation that either counteracts the tendency for prices to fall when productivity rises, or over-compensates and pushes prices up. In this way, Len, Boris and Owen become capitalists whose life-styles depend on a swindle that in their own best interests should be kept carefully hidden.

The ever dutiful textbooks provide the necessary camouflage. The student of economics is taught that the economy needs a "money supply", and that this is obtained from the financial capitalist who is really a wealth creator, a social benefactor who by abstaining from immediate consumption makes funds available for the "investment" that all productive activity supposedly depends on. There is no shortage of such self-serving texts, which reach moronic depths of stupidity. A recent academic work solemnly attempts to explain how Crusoe, entirely alone on his desert island, can improve his lot by lending money at interest. In the physical sciences we are clever enough to put men on the moon, but in the field of social understanding the most degrading rubbish passes for knowledge under the name of Economics. The consequences are far more serious than the mere debasement of a particular field of learning. Crude elitist theories based on race, nationality, religion, skin colour, gender, superior intelligence, noble lineage, wealth, and so on, have long ago been rejected by the majority of thinking people in all walks of life, but this rejection counts for nothing if those same thinking people have no clear grasp of their real economic relationships. In this vacuum of collective understanding even an educated electorate can be led anywhere. The elitist crudities retain their insidious plausibility, leaving the way open for any crank or hoodlum to take command and issue orders for slaughter and destruction that nobody has the means to prevent. The barbaric conflicts of the twentieth century are ample proof. Science advances in huge strides but the basic needs of global humanity cannot be intelligently addressed because a money-supply swindle is the end and purpose of all capitalist enterprises, tailored to suit the liberal pretences of democratic governments or the corruption and repression of the dictatorships, while a massive indoctrination programme spread by politicians, the media and the universities persuades educated people to connive in the suppression of their own intelligence.

Now that we understand how freshly printed banknotes enter the monetary network, we can return to Figure 15-6 and implement this process. The currency value stands at £1000, and everything else depends on it. But this value is steadily rising alongside rising productivity, and these two simultanous trends must be accommodated in the model. By doing so we will normalise the model in several ways. Unit prices will be held steady or will rise as a general trend, as they do in all capitalist countries, the value of money will steadily fall, and we will make room for the two essential components of any capitalist system, namely the central bank and its entourage of local banks. Conceived as a stationary model, Figure 15-6 contains only one kind of capitalist, the owner/manager, represented by Owen in the above illustration, and if the currency value is not rising, then Owen has no need for parasitic money-lenders, and in fact, as we have often pointed out, there is no exploitation in the model in its stationary form, and Owen is therefore only a *potential* capitalist, because his £5 income is no different from a wage if his marketing work is genuinely needed. But when a steadily rising currency value is made operational in Figure 15-6, then the profits shown on the right begin to expand. In terms of our simple illustration, this is the key moment when Owen is joined by the financial capitalists Len and Boris. All three of them can benefit from a loan swindle that will defraud the entire working population of any share in the rising standard of living that would normally flow from a general improvement in productivity. The features of this swindle have just been described. It operates on a grand scale in every capitalist nation.

The central bank in each country lends money to a multitude of local banks. The local banks lend this money to employers throughout the economy. The employers use the loaned money to pay wages, which are fixed rates of pay for work performed at a specified intensity for a specified length of time. Productivity per worker steadily rises as a result of inventions, scientific discoveries, new natural resources and extended use of automation and computerised control in mass production systems, alongside higher work intensity, longer working hours and improvement in skills. The inherent effect of all such increase in productivity (in a paper-based economy) is to reduce unit prices at a steady rate. But the loaned money that circulates back and forth between the central bank, the local banks and the employers receives regular injections of newly printed banknotes that continuously inflate the currency value, preventing unit prices from falling. The worker on a negotiated wage rate remains at a fixed standard of living, while profits rise dramatically. From these enlarged profits, interest at a high rate is extracted by the local banks and interest at a low rate is extracted by the central bank. All these features can be incorporated in Figure 15-6 if the currency value is visualised as a steadily increasing magnitude.

So in broad terms there are two rates of interest in a capitalist economy, the lower rate set by the central bank and the higher rate set by the local banks. The lower rate provides an income for the former, and the difference in the rates provides an income for the latter. Both are effectively in cahoots with the employers because there are four interdependent features of the swindle that they operate collectively. The employer must produce goods by paying fixed rates of wages. Outputs must steadily rise. The money to pay wages and costs must come mainly from loans. Newly printed banknotes must filter by stealth into the money network from a single controlled source. These four requirements can be arranged mainly by the capitalists themselves. The loans and the printing operation are obviously in capitalist hands. Wage negotiation is also in capitalist hands because the risk of dismissal always hangs over the isolated worker, and this isolation is maintained in all countries either by the brutal suppression of unions or by legislation to curtail their activity. But holding prices steady while freshly printed notes enter the system is impossible unless productivity rises. Without steadily rising productivity the swindle becomes more obvious. Prices are driven upwards when extra banknotes are printed in any quantity, the standard of living drops for the great majority, and the cause is very apparent. But the swindle works beautifully if the worker will cooperate by raising output in every possible way. The greater the rise in productivity, the more banknotes can be printed without disturbing the unit price level. So the worker on a fixed wage will notice nothing, and gain nothing, while an idle class of bankers and employers will grow ever richer.

Small businesses are a hybrid type of capitalist firm. The proprietor may be said to work for wages that he pays himself after all other costs are met. In this respect he is no different from the members of his small workforce, drawing an income from gross sales in return for a labour input which could be quite high. But unlike his workforce he looks forward to the day when his profits will make him rich. What makes this outcome possible? It is made possible by the steady depreciation in the value of money, hidden behind the deceptive appearance of constant or gently rising prices. This is how his dream will come true, assuming there is a place for his goods in the market. He is entirely dependent on the swindle described above, whether he borrows from a bank or uses his own funds. As long as the wages he pays are consistent with wage levels in general, he will enjoy the increasing prosperity that comes to all owner-employers. (He could pay higher wages and still be affluent, but we will examine this aspect when we deal with employment in Part Three). He thinks that hard work during the early days of his firm entitles him to regard his lately improved income as a deserved reward. He has worked his way up. In common parlance he is a self-made man. But such reasoning is no more than pious self-congratulation. If money flows in abundance into an idler's hands, then the goods the idler is enabled to buy must be produced by someone else's labour. This fact is not altered by any hard work that may have occured in the past, and which indeed may have been necessary, but only to establish a foothold alongside other competing firms. Once established, the new firm will enjoy rising profits that come automatically from the infiltrating banknotes.

The swindle is illustrated step by step in Figure 17-1. The basic cycle is simply the regular production of commodities for the market, where they are sold for £10, which is the source from which all incomes are derived. In the present instance, these incomes are wages of £5 for the production worker and wages of £5 for somebody who looks after the marketing. This somebody may well be the owner, but whether this is the case or not, two people are here working in collaboration, and no exploitation is necessarily present.

Phase one introduces a sequence of loans, and we can identify the roles played by Len, Boris and Owen in our earlier illustration. A loan of £5 (half the wages bill) travels between three people and becomes wages for the production worker. But the goods still sell for £10, which is wholly absorbed by the total wages for production and marketing. The £5 which seems to be extracted from the sales revenue is really just the loan, which must be repaid, as shown, in two stages, to two money lenders, without interest. These loans are therefore quite pointless, and at this stage neither the two money lenders nor the owner have any income.

In phase two the sales revenue from the goods has risen from £10 to £13, entirely as a result of increased output by the production worker, who is working harder or longer or at a higher intensity or with better tools, or better organisation of his time, or more efficient cooperation with his marketing colleague. The extra output sells at the same unit price because extra banknotes are entering the system, so gross receipts are higher, by £3. This £3 finds its way into the pockets of the owner, the intermediate borrower-lender, and the original lender, providing each of them with an income of £1, as shown.

In phases three and four we assume that the improvement in output rates by the production worker is an on-going trend. Gross revenue from sales rises from £13 to £16 and then to £19. Incomes for the three capitalists rise correspondingly from £1 each to £3 each, while the total wages bill remains at £10. The two workers notice no change. Unit prices and wages are constant. But the economy appears to be thriving. Profits are increasing everywhere and they may well feel that some of this prosperity should come their way.

So we move to phase five. The two workers have negotiated a substantial pay rise from £5 to £7 each. Output rates are still rising so gross receipts are now £22. The owner has raised his borrowing requirement from £5 to £7, which he maintains is needed to pay half the wages bill. In reality, the £22 from sales is the source from which the wages bill of £14 is paid, leaving £8 to be shared between the three capitalists as shown. The steady rise in the incomes of the three capitalists during phases two, three and four, has been temporarily arrested by the rise in wages at phase five, but the swindle is now set to continue into the future. Profits will rise and wages will stay constant.

As it stands, phase five shows a pay rise alongside an increase in output. But the higher output and the higher wages bill may be due to the fact that the firm as a whole is growing. More workers are being employed without any rise in wage rates. In this case the improvement in output is likely to be higher than the £3 shown (£19 to £22) which reflects the improvement in output per worker. Instead of two workers earning £10, there could be three workers earning £14,

Figure 17-1.

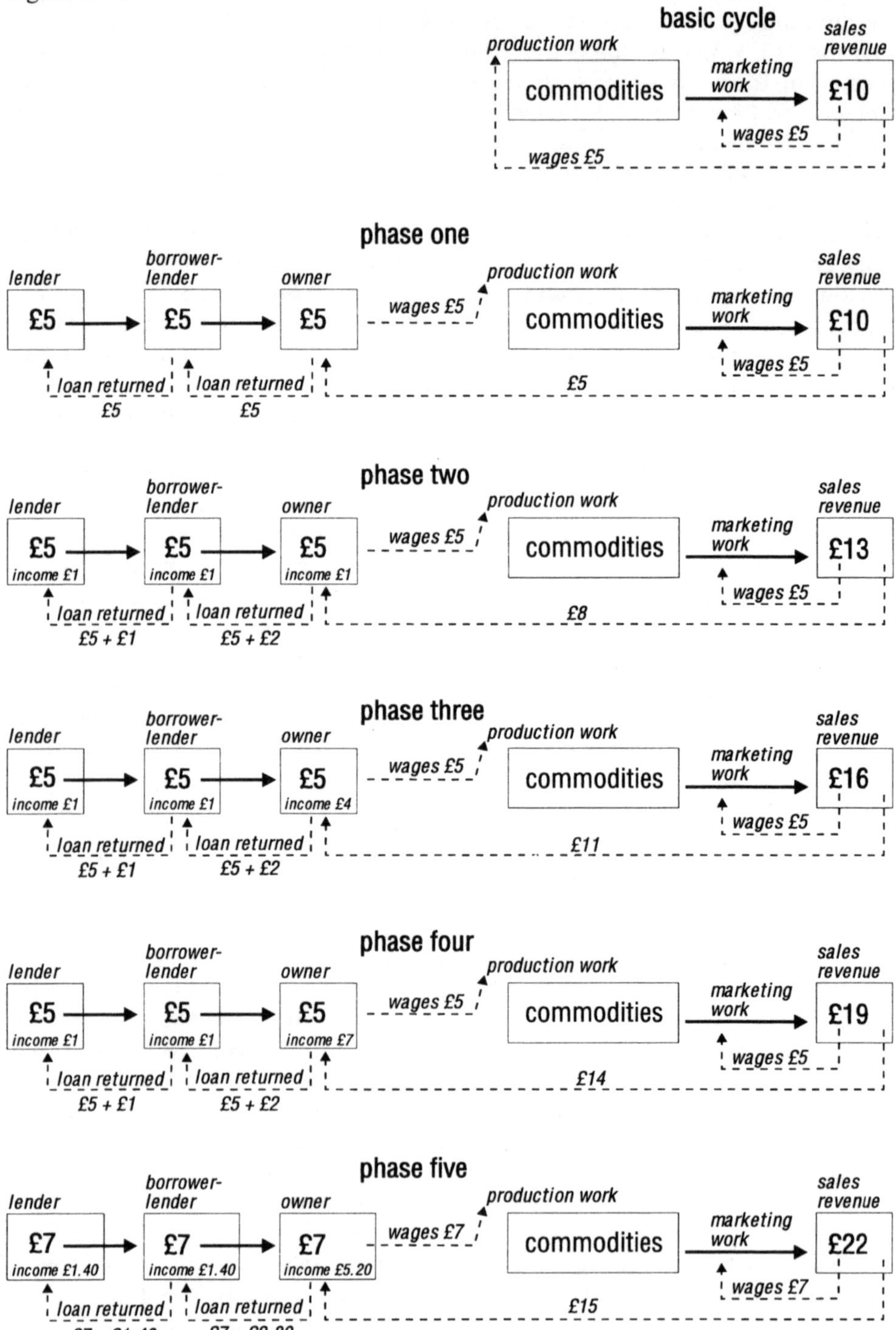
basic cycle
production work
commodities
marketing work
sales revenue
£10
wages £5
wages £5
phase one
lender
£5
borrower-lender
£5
owner
£5
wages £5
production work
commodities
marketing work
sales revenue
£10
wages £5
loan returned £5
loan returned £5
£5
phase two
lender
£5
income £1
borrower-lender
£5
income £1
owner
£5
income £1
wages £5
production work
commodities
marketing work
sales revenue
£13
wages £5
loan returned £5 + £1
loan returned £5 + £2
£8
phase three
lender
£5
income £1
borrower-lender
£5
income £1
owner
£5
income £4
wages £5
production work
commodities
marketing work
sales revenue
£16
wages £5
loan returned £5 + £1
loan returned £5 + £2
£11
phase four
lender
£5
income £1
borrower-lender
£5
income £1
owner
£5
income £7
wages £5
production work
commodities
marketing work
sales revenue
£19
wages £5
loan returned £5 + £1
loan returned £5 + £2
£14
phase five
lender
£7
income £1.40
borrower-lender
£7
income £1.40
owner
£7
income £5.20
wages £7
production work
commodities
marketing work
sales revenue
£22
wages £7
loan returned £7 + £1.40
loan returned £7 + £2.80
£15

two of them still on the existing rate of £5 each and an additional worker earning £4. With this additional worker, output will rise further, resulting in sales receipts in the region of £33, rather than £22. Subtracting a wages bill of £14 leaves £19 to be shared between the three capitalists. Three workers at a fixed standard of living are now working to support not only themselves, but also three idlers who enjoy a higher standard of living, and the scale of exploitation will continue to increase at every cycle of the production process, in step with the infiltrating banknotes, while unit prices will stand still as a result of the rising productivity.

Now consider how the new banknotes enter the system. From the point of view of the small firm portrayed in Figure 17-1, the continuously rising profits which the firm enjoys seem to come either from increases in output per worker, or from growth of the firm itself. From either of these causes (or both), the rate of output per calendar time keeps rising, and if unit prices are steady, an increase in sales receipts is bound to follow. This explanation for rising profits is entirely convincing to the individual firm, and is correct at this restricted level of analysis. But it is not the whole story. We know from elementary price theory that in a closed economy, when supply increases, unit prices fall, caeteris paribus. Hence the rising prosperity of the small firm cannot be duplicated throughout all firms without introducing an essential extra factor to account for a price level which remains constant, in defiance so to speak of the steadily rising supply. Of course this essential factor is already known to us, namely the infiltration of newly printed banknotes, the effect of which is to reduce the purchasing power of money. In phases two, three and four of the diagram, unit prices are kept stable in the economy as a whole because other firms are passing through phase five, and this is how new notes are entering the system. The borrowing requirements of other firms are being increased to cope with their own rising costs following wage increases or increased scale of production or both. These are the occasions when new larger loans are negotiated.

The loans come into existence as signatures on legal documents, and at some stage in these legal formalities a drawable account is opened in a local bank on behalf of an employer, enabling him to pay wages and other costs. These payments result in a transfer of money from the employer's account to a multitude of deposit accounts held by workers, employers and bankers as private individuals, and such money represents disposable income. A fund of notes in all the local banks is constantly held ready to meet the withdrawals that everybody makes from their bank accounts, and this fund is normally adequate, but the newly negotiated loans bring fresh demands for bigger withdrawals and the reserve fund must therefore be steadily replenished by money borrowed from the central bank. The central bank keeps a reserve of banknotes, but as this is depleted in turn there is only one source of replenishment, namely the printing press. As a result, the total face value of the printed paper notes throughout the whole economy is continuously rising at a rate equal to, or faster than, the rise in output of goods. The printing press is continuously in action supplying notes of higher value in place of notes of lower value. The latter are progressively withdrawn from circulation.

The exploitation mechanism just described is so deeply embedded in the capitalist economic system that to describe it as a swindle is to some extent misleading. A swindle suggests deliberate deception. But the firm portrayed in Figure 17-1 has no intention of defauding anybody. It responds to circumstances such as price levels and general wage rates just as a growing plant responds to its environment. It hardly needs saying that the economist cannot adopt this restricted viewpoint. All biologists know that the growing plant is part of its own surroundings, and that the flora and fauna of a given locality comprise the environment that they all individually respond to. The economist is similarly required to unravel the complexities of his own subject by showing how the individual parts are linked coherently to the whole, in a progressive exposition that moves from embedded fundamentals to variations at local level. But the orthodox textbooks cast aside this holistic overview. The line they follow with slavish dedication is the narrow viewpoint of the individual firm, as anyone can verify by a glance at their pages. This approach seems perfectly reasonable, seeing that the economy consists of a vast multitude of firms, but this restricted focus is essentially a cover. All the learned notions in the orthodox canon such as supply and demand curves, marginal analysis, the theory of comparative costs, the money supply, investment, etc, are presented with impressive graphical and algebraic elaboration but, closely examined, the mathematical core is perverted and the logic is tautological. The textbooks do not directly promote a swindle, but they block the road to real understanding and enable the swindle to operate unobserved. The businessman, who is well aware that the mumbo-jumbo in the textbooks isn't worth tuppence, is grateful for this service because he wants his financial affairs kept private.

Resuming our analysis we see that the individual firm, surrounded by its competitors, is dependent on a general stability of unit prices (or an upwards trend) to enable its own success as an enterprise to bear fruit in the form of enhanced profits. This unit price stability comes from the infiltrating banknotes which enter the system when bigger loans are negotiated. The typical firm therefore embodies all these aspects in its normal operation, even though extra loans may only be negotiated at widely separated intervals of time. Very big firms may be continually reviewing their finances. Other firms may simply operate from day to day and cope with changing circumstances as the need arises. The fact that they are all locked into a mutually dependent exploitation system is not apparent in their individual behaviour. Hence the firm shown in Figure 17-1 seems to exist in an external environment consisting of stable prices that in some way or other, by some unspecified mechanism, stay constant despite the steady rise in output. But this unspecified mechanism comes into view at phase five when the enlarged loans appear, and it is here that the firm behaves in a manner that is actually universal throughout the economy, even though it may be spasmodic in the individual case. We need to show the typical firm as an average which reflects the continuous behaviour of them all, generalising them as equal contributors to a process that they all depend on. In other words, we need to conceive the average firm as an incremental contributor to all aspects of the exploitation process.

Figure 17-2

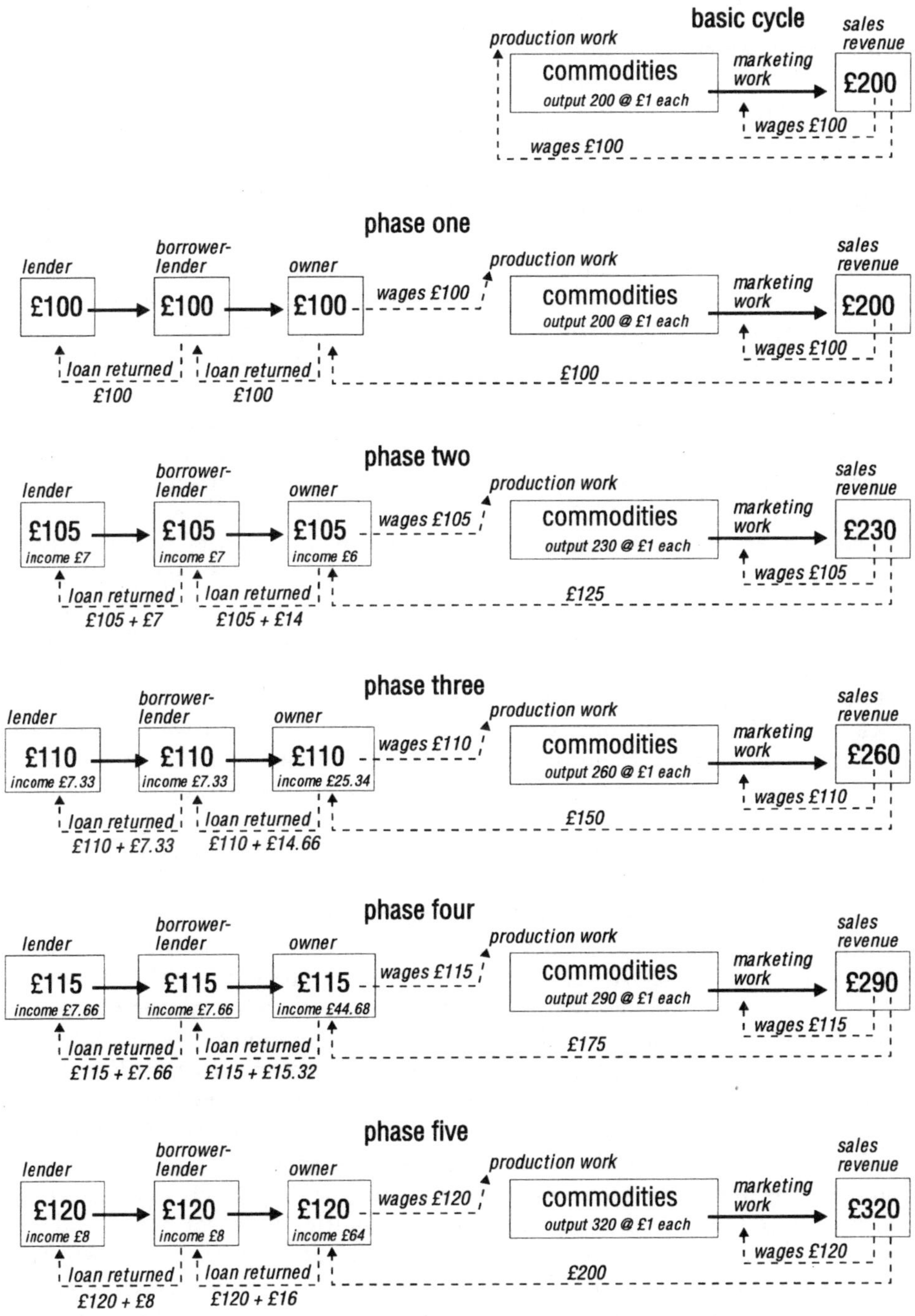

basic cycle
production work
commodities
output 200 @ £1 each
marketing work
sales revenue
£200
wages £100
wages £100
phase one
lender
£100
borrower-lender
£100
owner
£100
wages £100
production work
commodities
output 200 @ £1 each
marketing work
sales revenue
£200
wages £100
loan returned £100
loan returned £100
£100
phase two
lender
£105
income £7
borrower-lender
£105
income £7
owner
£105
income £6
wages £105
production work
commodities
output 230 @ £1 each
marketing work
sales revenue
£230
wages £105
loan returned £105 + £7
loan returned £105 + £14
£125
phase three
lender
£110
income £7.33
borrower-lender
£110
income £7.33
owner
£110
income £25.34
wages £110
production work
commodities
output 260 @ £1 each
marketing work
sales revenue
£260
wages £110
loan returned £110 + £7.33
loan returned £110 + £14.66
£150
phase four
lender
£115
income £7.66
borrower-lender
£115
income £7.66
owner
£115
income £44.68
wages £115
production work
commodities
output 290 @ £1 each
marketing work
sales revenue
£290
wages £115
loan returned £115 + £7.66
loan returned £115 + £15.32
£175
phase five
lender
£120
income £8
borrower-lender
£120
income £8
owner
£120
income £64
wages £120
production work
commodities
output 320 @ £1 each
marketing work
sales revenue
£320
wages £120
loan returned £120 + £8
loan returned £120 + £16
£200

Figure 17-2 provides this more comprehensive interpretation of the individual firm in its capitalist setting. Of course all the numbers in the diagram are highly contrived. They serve to illustrate the exploitation process in its bare essentials. A prominent feature of all capitalist systems is made very evident, namely the existence of two rates of interest, a base rate set by the central bank for loans to specially designated financial intermediaries, described here as local banks, and a much higher rate of interest for everybody else set by the local banks. This higher rate is flexibly adapted to the circumstances of any particular loan, taking into account all the risks involved. The steady progression of one phase to the next in Figure 17-2 shows how the loans increase, and how all incomes increase, including (in this particular example) a steady increase in wage levels. Everybody's standard of living is rising (if we assume a constant workforce) but it is *always true* that the incomes of the three capitalists are extracted by fraud from the production/marketing process, to which they make no contribution, though the owner may supervise and make decisions that have a direct influence on the efficiency of his own firm.

The contribution that the owner/employer makes may be very substantial, and it provides a convincing justification for his high income. But this line of argument needs to be carefully qualified. If a firm improves its profits, through some kind of improved efficiency (not by reducing wages), it can increase its market share at the expense of other firms whose profits will fall. Such competitive variation is removed from a presentation like Figure 17-2. The average position is portrayed, and no matter how the firms may differ in respect of worker or managerial or executive skills, the incomes arise in the manner illustrated. A steadily rising sales revenue flows at a fixed (or slowly rising) rate into wages, while the rest is diverted into profits. Of course a superior level of managerial skill will ordinarily improve the prospects of any firm, and raise the average level of production efficiency throughout the economy. Managerial skill in its appropriate setting is a scarce resource just like any other productive component such as physical strength or long-practised dexterity or a sharp intellect. The economic reward that such resources attract could conceivably be decided by consensus in some form, or by natural or artificial monopoly, or by open competition. But none of this has any bearing on Figure 17-2.

In so far as the capitalist owner is a productive worker in his own firm, he can be classified as a wage-earner, and the relative scarcity of his skills could raise or lower his wage compared with the average wage, for whatever specialism he provides. But as a member of the capitalist class, playing a role illustrated in the exploitation system of Figure 17-2, he is wholly non-productive. His income is acquired solely by virtue of ownership, and is not an economic reward for any kind of service. From this standpoint he is identical with the two financial capitalists, especially if his managerial role is transferred to a wage earner (who may be highly paid to retain scarce talents, or very poorly paid where the work is humdrum). All three capitalists are parasitic on the workforce, and they unite to express a common interest as a result. The employer is expected to keep productivity rising, and the bankers are expected to provide ever-increasing loans. We can trace these effects in the diagram. If productivity stays constant, while extra banknotes enter the system, prices rise and gross sales rise as the value of money falls. To be specific, in terms of Figure 17-2, if an output of 230 units at phase two stays constant through the succeeding phases while the extra banknotes still continue to be printed, the gross sales revenue will rise from 230 units @ £1 each, to 230 @ £1.13 each, to 230 @ £1.26 each, to 230 @ £1.39 each, which means that all the financial magnitudes displayed in the diagram, except unit prices, remain unaffected, and the capitalist owner will continue to thrive alongside the financial capitalists, at each successive phase. Of course the rising prices will put in evidence the inflation caused by the extra notes. But if extra banknotes fail to enter the monetary system alongside rising productivity, unit prices will fall and gross sales revenue will stay constant. The sales revenue of £230 at phase two will remain unaltered in the succeeding phases and the outcome is bound to be loss of income for the capitalist owner, unless he can reduce his wages bill. The crucial factor is the steady infiltration of extra bank-notes. This regular superfluity of notes keeps the fraud in operation throughout the entire economy, whether productivity is rising or not. The extra notes reduce the value of money, and loans are always advantageous to a firm's owner (surrounded by other competitors) when money is losing its value. At the same time, these very loans are the avenue through which the extra notes are introduced. Thus the fraud rests on a circular dependency which has no necessary link with output. Rising productivity merely ensures that unit prices stay constant and hence the fraud stays well out of sight, hidden by an appearance of normality everywhere, with no apparent inflation, and even in conjunction with a moderate rise in absolute standard of living for the workforce, as Figure 17-2 shows. This is the ideal balance that the democracies attempt to achieve. (Note in passing that the relative standard of living for the workforce, measured against earnings for society as a whole, is *always* falling regardless of any improvement in absolute terms).

We can now bring the role of the central bank into clear view. Suppose the general level of output rises considerably. Then a compensating increase in banknotes is called for to keep unit prices constant. How is this increase brought about? By making borrowing easier, ie by reducing the base rate of interest set by the central bank. Such a reduction will enable the local banks to lower their rate of interest, and the owners of firms will be tempted to borrow more. But the reduction in the base rate must not be too great. The new loans must not inject an excessive quantity of new notes into the monetary system, or they will over-compensate for the productivity rise, and unit prices will be pushed up. The economy will "over-heat". A small rise in prices is quite acceptable, and in fact it adds to the level of profits, but too steep a rise interferes with other aspects of business and leads to social unrest when the increasing prosperity of rich people is compared with the fall in living standards for everybody else. On the other hand, if the injection of new notes is too small to match the rise in productivity, prices and profits will fall. The economy will "slow down". The only short-term measure left to the central bank when the economy over-heats or slows down in this way is to extract or inject notes by selling or buying securities. Thus the central bank regularly reviews its lending rate in response

Figure 17-3

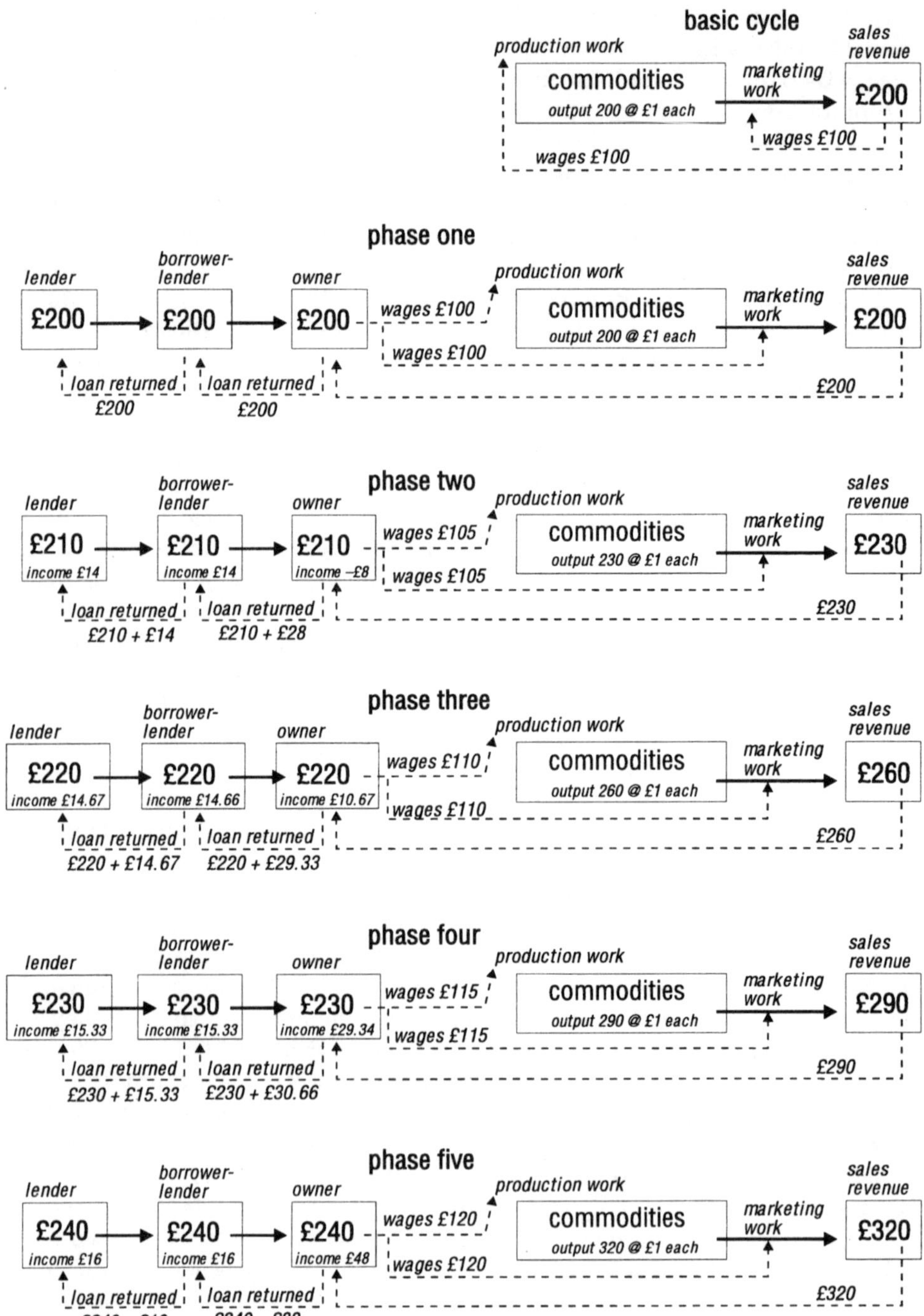

basic cycle
production work
commodities
output 200 @ £1 each
marketing work
sales revenue
£200
wages £100
wages £100
phase one
lender
£200
borrower-lender
£200
owner
£200
wages £100
production work
commodities
output 200 @ £1 each
marketing work
sales revenue
£200
wages £100
loan returned £200
loan returned £200
£200
phase two
lender
£210
income £14
borrower-lender
£210
income £14
owner
£210
income –£8
wages £105
production work
commodities
output 230 @ £1 each
marketing work
sales revenue
£230
wages £105
loan returned £210 + £14
loan returned £210 + £28
£230
phase three
lender
£220
income £14.67
borrower-lender
£220
income £14.66
owner
£220
income £10.67
wages £110
production work
commodities
output 260 @ £1 each
marketing work
sales revenue
£260
wages £110
loan returned £220 + £14.67
loan returned £220 + £29.33
£260
phase four
lender
£230
income £15.33
borrower-lender
£230
income £15.33
owner
£230
income £29.34
wages £115
production work
commodities
output 290 @ £1 each
marketing work
sales revenue
£290
wages £115
loan returned £230 + £15.33
loan returned £230 + £30.66
£290
phase five
lender
£240
income £16
borrower-lender
£240
income £16
owner
£240
income £48
wages £120
production work
commodities
output 320 @ £1 each
marketing work
sales revenue
£320
wages £120
loan returned £240 + £16
loan returned £240 + £32
£320

to gross indicators of production efficiency for the economy as a whole, hoping to achieve an ideal balance that keeps prices steady or rising gently. Buying and selling of securities is part of the "fine-tuning" that tries to compensate for errors.

In essence the central bank has to anticipate how the economy will grow in the immediate future and match this growth with a "money supply" in the form of a two tier system of loans, resting on a base rate of interest and a subsequent higher rate set by the financial intermediaries. The objective is to attract just sufficient take-up of new loans to allow freshly printed notes of a certain quantity to enter the monetary system and thereby overcome the tendency for unit prices to fall when productivity rises.

In Figure 17-2 we can view this process operating in a society with one central bank, one local bank and one firm. As can be seen, the loans steadily increase at each successive phase, and we presume that this increase allows extra banknotes to enter the monetary system in just the right amount to hold unit prices steady at £1 each, while output rises from 200 to 320 units. The incomes of all three capitalists, plus the wages, are exactly equal to the sales revenue at each phase, and everybody's standard of living is rising. But this rising standard of living is not evenly distributed. The wage level at phase two enables the workforce to buy 210 units from a total output of 230 units, and at phase five the wage level corresponds to 240 units from a total of 320 units. By contrast, the owner at phase two can buy only 6 units, but at phase five he can buy 64 units. Standard of living for the owner is rising at a far greater rate than for the workforce, and this rising affluence is guaranteed by the exploitation process, not by any contribution that the owner may make to the efficiency of his firm.

What would happen if the owner increased his borrowing? Figure 17-3 gives the answer. The amount borrowed by the owner is now equal to his entire wage bill. As can be seen, his rising affluence is not as great because some of it has been transferred to the bankers' incomes. The central bank and the local bank are always parasitic on the capitalist owner, while all three are parastic on the wage-earner.

The exact relationship between these various interdependent elements, namely the stable unit price, the rising output, the infiltrating banknotes, the loans and the two lending rates, will be examined in the analysis ahead. For the present, we note that Figure 15-6 must now be viewed alongside Figure 17-2 or Figure 17-3, to obtain an adequate picture of the capitalist exploitation system, because the rising currency value is brought about by the ever-expanding loans. Of course in any given capitalist country, there is only one central bank, hundreds of local banks (perhaps many thousands as in the USA) and a colossal number of firms. We will need to accommodate these circumstances in our future diagrams.

18

Interest: part 2

Apart from the models in the previous chapter, the only diagram showing the capitalist system in dynamic operation has been Figure 6-5 on page 65. Five types of society are shown there, and three of these, namely, B and D and E, are essentially capitalist. In these three societies, a superfluity of banknotes (whether from the elimination of private hoards, or from efficiency improvements like the cheque system, or from infiltration of newly printed notes into bank loans) generates the inflation that guarantees steadily rising profits for the owners of seven capitalist firms. In Society B the 10% inflation is exposed to view because unit prices are pushed up by the inflation when productivity is constant. But in Society D, all of the 10% inflation is hidden by a compensating rise in productivity. In Society E the inflation is relatively high at 21% but only half of this is visible because the potential rise in unit prices is half offset by the 10% rise in productivity. A typical capitalist economy may normally be regarded as lying somewhere between the circumstances of Society D and Society E. In fact, in historical reality, a capitalist economy fluctuates between these two extremes, and the central bank attempts to control this fluctuation. In some circumstances the economy moves towards Society B, but we are not investigating these various movements for the present.

Using the example of Society E we investigated the wage/profit relation and showed how it was linked to the banking system, and this concluded Part One. The basic essentials of the capitalist system were in fact present at that stage, but there was no factorial sector, no commercial sector and no ancillary sector, all of which needed to be included if the main model was to be credible. Thus our task at the start of Part Two was to take the basic buying and selling network that had been developed in Figure 6-2, and develop it to include the three types of costs, (factor, commercial and ancillary), and finally to convert values into the equlibrium prices that balance supply with demand on the basis of a uniform rate of profit. Figure 15-6 in Chapter 15 is the outcome.

In Chapter 16 we examined the notion of costs in general, showing how they were all locked into a circular co-dependency which was ultimately self-cancelling. A cost for firm F1 is always income for some other firm F2, and this income is then destined to become wages and profits, and perhaps costs again, whereupon another firm F3 acquires an income, from which wages and profits are extracted yet again and so on. Hence an overall view of earnings throughout the entire economy always resolves itself ultimately into wages and profits, nothing else. These are the two components into which total sales revenue is split. The extra component that the textbooks always include under the heading of costs (whether for raw materials or maintenance or repayment of loans, etc) is real enough at the level of the individual firm, and such costs influence the firm's perception of its own profitability. In turn, this perception has a real effect on prices, which adapt to match the firm's perceived rate of profit with other firms' perceived rates of profit. But no matter how restricted or personalised the individual firm's perception may be, the outcome is always to match aggregate demand to aggregate supply on the basis of equal rates of profit, and the sum of prices is always equal to the sum of values. The perception of costs, whether self-cancelling or not from a higher viewpoint, are real in their effects and must be taken into account in any explanation of price determination, but none of this alters the fact that the exchange of commodities for money generates the sales revenue that in turn generates all earnings throughout the entire economy, and costs are merely a series of self-cancelling diversions. That is why the essence of the capitalist system was present at the end of Part One, even though no costs other than wages had been introduced at that stage.

In Chapter 17 we investigated the economic concept of *interest*, and showed how it acquires a double identity, so to speak, in the form of an income for a central bank, and an income for a host of financial intermediaries. Only the bare mechanism was explored, to make plain how these two forms of income are derived from the sales revenue. The previous statement that *the sales revenue generates all incomes* is universally true, and the task of analysis is to trace how this revenue is divided between all the various income-earners. Our present understanding is that *wages* are a direct deduction from sales revenue, *profit* is the remainder, and *costs* are a mere transfer of monies to some other firm, where a deduction for wages occurs a second time, again leaving a remainder called profit, and so on. If the sales revenue ultimately resolves into wages and profit, where does *interest* fit in?

We have already explored the answer in Chapter 17. The capitalist owner borrows money and pays it back with an added extra. The successive loans get bigger in the course of time, and when these higher loans filter through to the market (as a result of withdrawals from banks for spending by the workforce and others) extra notes must be made available and the value of money falls. Unit prices that would ordinarily rise as money loses its value are held constant by rising productivity. The supply of goods is increasing. So in essence all that happens when new notes enter the system alongside rising productivity is a steady fall in the value of money alongside a steady rise in total sales revenue, while the general level of unit prices and wage rates typically stay constant. From this rise in sales revenue the capitalist owner extracts both his own profit and the extra or *interest* that accompanies the return of the loan. The process is shown in sequential phases in Figure 17-2, but only the bare mechanism is illustrated. A more realistic presentation is given in Figure 18-1.

In this new model, the sequence of phases in Figure 17-2 has been arrested at phase three and expanded to show the relationship between *one* central

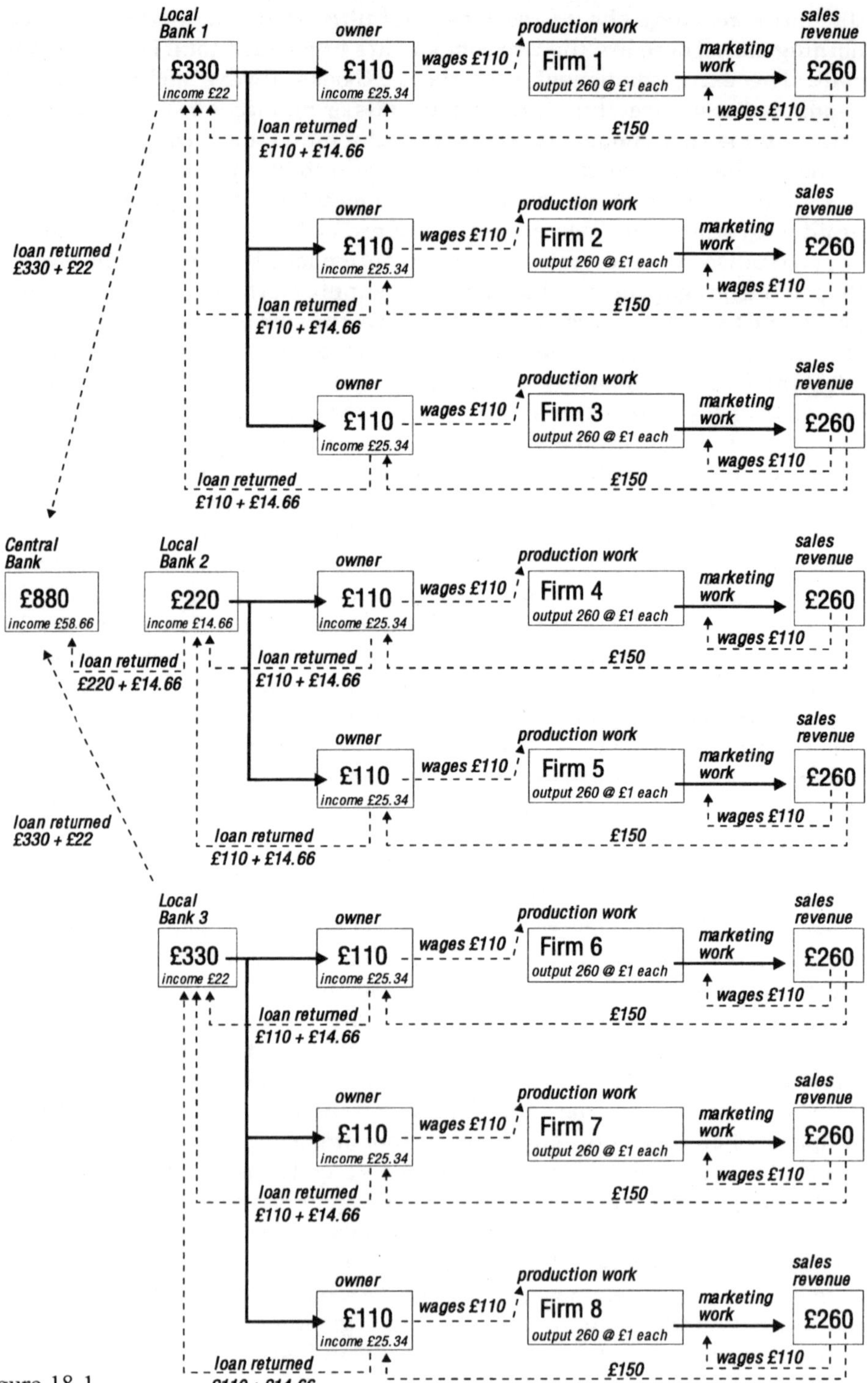
Local Bank 1
£330
income £22
owner
£110
income £25.34
wages £110
production work
Firm 1
output 260 @ £1 each
marketing work
sales revenue
£260
wages £110
loan returned £110 + £14.66
£150
Firm 2
Firm 3
loan returned £330 + £22
Central Bank
£880
income £58.66
Local Bank 2
£220
income £14.66
loan returned £220 + £14.66
Firm 4
Firm 5
Local Bank 3
£330
income £22
Firm 6
Firm 7
Firm 8

Figure 18-1

bank, *many* local banks and a *great number* of capitalist firms. Of course our diagram is restricted to only one central bank, three local banks and eight firms, but the essential connections are present. If the workforce in each firm consists of ten production workers and ten marketing workers then the uniform wage rate is £11 per time period (say one week). Income for each owner is £25.34. The local bankers each earn £22 or £14.66, and the central banker earns £58.66. The working week regularly produces an output of 260 units from each firm, and at a price level of £1 per unit, the total value produced is £260 × 8 = £2080. Production wages are £880, marketing wages are £880, owners' combined incomes are £25.34 × 8 = £202.72, and the bankers' combined incomes are £22 + £22 + £14.66 + £58.66 = £117.32. The total of all these incomes is £2080, which is exactly the value of the goods and hence all the weekly output of commodities is bought and consumed by this self-contained community of 172 people. (Each owner and each bank is personified as one individual).

Everything in the diagram is reduced to a convenient average to show the relationships as clearly as possible. Every owner has borrowed money sufficient to cover half his outlay on wages, and every penny of the loan transactions is accounted for. The base rate set by the central bank is 6.67%, and the general rate set by the local banks is 13.33%. Of course averages are imposed everywhere, but it is understood that particular loans and incomes may vary widely.

This diagram now needs to be envisaged at three levels. **Level 1** is the bare presentation on the page, where all the magnitudes are mutually coherent. **Level 2** is the dynamic flow from one week to the next which creates regular incomes for everybody. At this level it becomes plain that production work and marketing work are the only two activities that are needed to maintain the entire economy. The eight owners, the central bank, and the three local banks have supervisory and administrative responsibilities that are a natural part of cooperative labour and commercial activity, but otherwise they have no productive role and are essentially parasitic elements in the wealth creation process. As we know, this parasitism does not spring from profit-making as such, but from currency inflation. At **Level 3** the dynamic weekly cycle must be envisaged alongside a steady increase in loans, first by one firm, then another, thereby moving the entire diagram through various phases of expansion, from its present position which corresponds to phase three in Figure 17-2, to phases four and five and beyond. At each successive phase, the owners and the bankers become richer, while wages and prices stay constant. At a certain level of affluence, all supervisory and administrative duties can be delegated to wage earners, and at this point the capitalist owners and the bankers are liberated from any burden associated with their own institutions. They become free spirits untrammelled by any need to earn a livelihood, enjoying private incomes that grow and grow as if by magic. Competition removes the weaker firms (or leads to mergers and take-overs) creating the illusion that the ever increasing affluence of successful firms is attributable to hard work, good labour relations, managerial skill, entrepreneurial flair, and so on. But these attributes merely ensure survival in the competitive struggle. Capitalist firms fight each other for the right to defraud the workforce on an ever increasing scale.

At this point we can pin down a very common illusion. Let us see if we can discover the exact meaning of the word *investment*. The loans in Figure 18-1 may in common parlance be described as investments, but it is obvious that these loans consist of the same money travelling round in an endless loop. The loans are always repaid, so the £880 loaned by the central bank merely passes through various hands and arrives back where it started from. Every week the combined outputs of these eight firms, consisting of 2080 units of goods, are consumed by 172 people. The central banker consumes 59 units, the three local bankers consume 59 units, the eight owners consume 203 units and the workers (twenty per firm = 160) consume 1760 units. (Numbers are rounded to avoid fractions). These units are produced and consumed every week. Hence we may this. *All these incomes are spent every week. Nobody is saving in this society. Abstinence by wealth creators is a complete fairytale.*

Of course the surface appearance is quite otherwise. All these owners are regularly borrowing money, and this money must come from somewhere. It is surely undeniable that these four bankers could *spend* the money that they so generously make available for investment purposes, so shouldn't we be suitably grateful, and not begrudge them the interest that they charges for this service? Bankers can hardly be expected to provide money for nothing. But examining Figure 18-1 shows how fallacious this reasoning is. If our starting point is the loan of a sum of money, then certainly such money must come from somewhere, and certainly it could be spent on consumption instead of a loan, and certainly it represents abstinence by the lender. But this is a scenario that happens *once only,* for any sum of money that is invested. The loan eventually returns to the lender, and thereafter it loops continuously back and forth, bringing an income to the lender that can last forever, an income that will grow and grow in a well-managed capitalist economy. The banker would be a prize fool if he interrupted this self-perpetuating loan that costs him nothing and gives such handsome returns. To divert the loan into personal consumption would kill the goose that lays the golden eggs, and seeing that these eggs are forever increasing in quantity, it is quite fatuous to suppose that abstinence or social benevolence play any part.

An elementary recap is appropriate here, to emphasise the very important fact that the price network is a dynamic process and must always be conceived as such. Without this basic understanding, no grasp of economics is possible. From an individual's viewpoint money can be spent or it can be hoarded. But this choice is not available for society as a whole. *Incomes are always spent in full.* When money is spent, incomes are created, and these incomes can then be spent in their turn, creating a reciprocal flow of money in and out of everybody's possession in a never ending cycle of buying-while-others-sell and selling-while-others-buy. Everyone is part of this cycle, which has no beginning or end. Money for spending is always acquired from the spending actions of somebody else. Spending is therefore continuous and always in full flow, and this flow can never be interrupted. When money is hoarded (on any socially significant scale) chains of mutual dependency break down with catastrophic consequences. *All incomes are always spent, otherwise there would be no incomes.*

But, it might be argued, nearly all of us have savings, extracted from our incomes. Some of us never spend as much as we earn, so how can it be true that all incomes are always spent? The solution to this conundrum lies in the float, which is a kind of imaginary hoard, managed by local banks in the form of deposit accounts. Salaries and wages are regularly paid into these deposit accounts, and withdrawals are made when money is needed for spending. So any personal savings will steadily accumulate in the account. Seeing that the bank has thousands of accounts, all growing bigger and bigger if customers spend less than they earn, it might seem that banks in general are accumulating a vast hoard of wealth on behalf of society. But they are not. Where do salary and wage payments come from in the first place? From an employer's account. The bank is merely instructed to transfer a stated sum of money from one account to another when a salary or wage falls due. The bank simply switches funds between the various accounts on behalf of its own customers, or in relation to accounts held in another bank. When someone withdraws money and spends it, the money becomes an income for the seller, who can spend it or return it to the bank. The money can be spent again and again, passing from hand to hand, enabling successive purchases to be made by a series of different owners, but sooner or later it is returned to somebody's bank account. A minimum quantity of money is therefore always in circulation, in pocket or purse or checkout or cashpoint or on instant demand at the bank, and this circulating quantity of real notes and coin is called the monetary base. All the circuits between the monetary base and the deposit accounts, big or small, for all private persons and all institutions, are linked with each other, so that gains always balance losses, and money never appears out of the blue, nor vanishes into thin air. (We assume no printing of notes except as replacement for wear and tear, and no illegal destruction of notes). The question *Where does the circulating money come from?* has a very simple answer. *It comes from the circulation itself, because it goes round and round all the time.* In analogous fashion, all the rain water in the world travels in a continuously repeated circuit through the clouds to the rainfall, to the rivers, to the seas, and back to the clouds again. No gains and no losses.

But how can anybody's savings accumulate if the float ordinarily stays constant? Savings can accumulate for some people because earlier savings are being spent by other people. The spending which must always maintain its full flow is necessarily reduced by people who save some of their income, but the purpose of saving is to spend it one day, and this day is continuously arriving for as many people as those who are presently saving. Even the most dedicated savers, those who earn much and spend little throughout a whole lifetime, to enjoy comfort in old age or to pass it on to descendents, are counter-balanced by the old folk or descendents who are enjoying their comfort *now*, the savers of earlier times who overlap with the savers of today. Short-term savers likewise balance each other, and the overlapping effect means that all saving is self-cancelling. (This point has been made earlier and is illustrated in Figure 11-5). In short there are always as many dis-savers as savers in a big population. Hence the spending flow is never interrupted, and the implications of this must be recognised. *All incomes are always fully spent. It is by this means that they are continuously restored so that they can be fully spent again, and restored again, and so on for ever.*

With these matters clarified, what exactly happens when money is *invested?* The answer has nothing to do with savings, which are explained in the previous paragraph, and nothing to do with abstinence from spending. The spending level continues in full flow, as it must at all times. Figures 17-2 and 17-3 show conclusively that all incomes are spent at every phase, and all goods are cleared from the market. In a sense, investment is not part of the loan package either, though loans are essential as "carriers" so to speak. The key to understanding the important concept of investment as it operates in a capitalist economy is the essential link with currency inflation.

In Figure 18-1, the central bank lends £880 to the local banks, who then lend the same money to the various firms. This money is paid back to the central bank, with added interest of £58.66. The central bank would certainly regard such money as an investment because it yields an income, and the same is true of the loans made by the other banks. But Figure 18-1 gives no hint or clue why these loans are justified. In fact, from the diagram on its own, it is obvious that no owner in his right mind would ever borrow money in this way. Each of these owners pays wages of £220, and therefore has £40 left over for himself. By borrowing £110 the owner is burdened with an interest charge of £14.66 and his income drops to £25.34. So these loans make no sense. Like all money lenders, banks are takers not givers. (The local banks are very important social contributors as managers of deposit accounts but we are concerned here only with their lending activities).

We already know of course why the capitalist owner is content to accept £25 for the time being instead of £40. His income will rise to much more than £40 if he waits a while. In addition, if he fulfills his side in a hidden bargain, his rising income will materialise automatically from an undetectable source, and he will be able to claim that his new wealth is due to foresightedness and hard work on the part of himself and his firm. His side of the bargain is to produce a steadily increasing output of goods. The central bank will keep its side of the bargain by steadily increasing the banknotes in circulation (by printing them or perhaps by open market operations). As a result, unit prices will stay constant, wages will stay constant, and profits will rise. If the improvement in productivity is large, the increase in banknotes can be large, and in these circumstances profits will soar. But no matter how great the increase in profits, no change will be noticed by the wage-earner, because neither wage rates nor prices will be affected. To describe this process as a money-supply is a sham, and the word *investment* is just a cloak. (When the word investment is used in a social sense, referring to say the building of roads and railways, or resources for research and development, or expenditure on health services, education, and the like, it has a genuine meaning. This is a topic to be examined in Part Three).

We have now arrived at an important point of synthesis. The task of combining Figure 18-1 with Figure 15-6 seems to be far beyond the capabilities of any

Figure 18-2

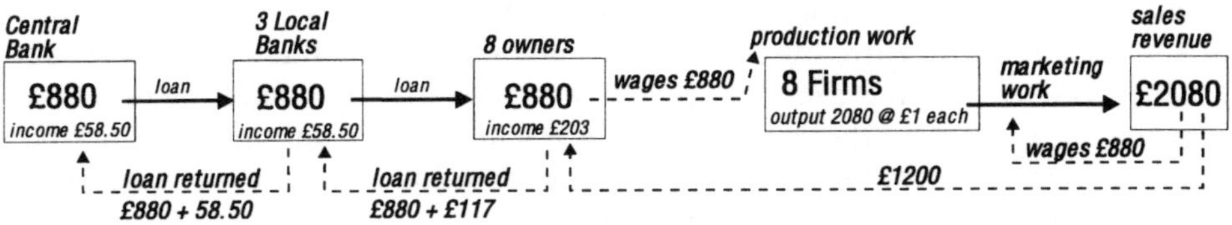

diagram. But in fact we have eliminated most of the difficulties, by introducing the averaging device. All the firms in Figure 15-6 can be "averaged" as long as no basic principles are violated. These firms are related to each other in complicated ways, but their rates of profit are equal and their wage rates are equal and all their different costs are mutually self-cancelling. The typical firm simply pays wages out of sales revenues and keeps the remainder as profit. The prices of the goods are determined by the pattern of incomes that rewards everybody equally when supply corresponds to demand. Any closed economy that exchanges goods through the medium of money can be represented by an "average firm", paying an average wage, earning average profits, multiplied by the total number of firms, and the only proviso is that the total of all incomes must be identical with the total of all sales revenues. This is an exact description of Figure 18-1, which can now be conveniently redrawn as Figure 18-2.

The average firm taken from Figure 18-1 is here multiplied by 8, and the appropiate incomes are amalgamated for the separate economic classes designated as wage-earners, owners, local banks and the central bank. All the primary incomes that are generated by sale of goods can be traced to the combined earnings of each economic group. There are no losses and no injections. All goods are cleared from the market at prices that generate incomes for sellers who are themselves the buyers of these goods, in a closed market. Of course the price formation procedure is no longer represented. This procedure is dealt with in Chapters 12 to 15. All that is retained here is the typical firm that can be extrapolated from any money based economy, and shown alongside this average firm is the loans procedure that sustains the banking system. The introduction of the banks into our model must not upset the fundamental rule that all incomes are generated by sales, and as long as this rule is adhered to, Figure 18-2 can be used to explore all kinds of modifications to wage rates, profit margins, interest on loans, increase in the workforce, productivity and so on, in terms of the whole economy.

The first point to note is that there is no inherent equilibrium point in respect of the loans system. Our recent analysis shows that the take-up of loans must not be so great as to "over-heat" the economy, but the central bank has never had much direct power in such matters until recently. The absorption of private hoards and the growth of the cheque system have been autonomous sources of inflation since the end of the second world war, and if it is true that such inflation peaked in the seventies and has since subsided, then this explains why the central bank's role is now more prominent. Profits will rise only if the hidden inflation rate is sufficient to counteract any tendency for unit prices to fall when productivity rises, and if such inflation is no longer being injected from elsewhere, the central bank must assume this responsibility through its control of the base lending rate. Meanwhile the monetary base has diminished and open market operations are more effective as a result. So during the nineteen-eighties and nineties the central bank's responsibility for the economy has steadily increased, and the means for exercising this control have sharpened. These developments awakened a response in academic circles, and a doctrine called monetarism came to the fore. Monetarists emphasise the primary role of the "money supply", which is quite correct, but they merely pay lip service to its importance without any real understanding of the phenomenon itself.

But regardless of the level of understanding, there is growing awareness today of the central bank's role in overseeing the economy. The possibility that a capitalist society can be efficiently managed might seem to be in prospect. There is nothing in our analysis so far to suggest otherwise. An enclosed capitalist economy, as portrayed in Figure 18-2, can achieve lasting stability and a rising standard of living for everybody. All that is needed is a loan system as shown, by means of which new banknotes can be carefully merged into the currency, in just sufficient amounts to counteract any tendency for prices to fall when productivity rises. Setting aside any ethical criteria, which in any case have no place in economic theory, we can state that in a well-managed capitalist economy, human effort and ingenuity can steadily increase the rate of output of commodities, thus making possible a slowly rising standard of living for a large working section of the population, alongside a much higher, ever-increasing living standard for a small group of people who have no employment obligations of any kind. This conclusion is entirely consistent with ordinary commonsense. A large sector of the population can work to improve their own standard of living, and part of this improvement can be taken away and used to raise the living standard of a small group of people who do not need to work at all. Nothing would ordinarily suggest that such an arrangement is unstable, and in fact it is in everyday operation in all countries where non-workers such as children or the elderly receive social benefits of some kind. These rewards are always meagre of course, but such examples illustrate the principle of "abstinence to provide for others" which is always the basis on which the working sector of the population provides support for dependent groups, whether such groups are the idle rich or segments of the poor.

But such an arrangement is feasible only if the two groups have an intelligent relation to each other. Obviously the working group needs to remain large and fully productive, and there needs to be an understood mechanism in place to deliver supplies to the dependent group. We may therefore say that the central bank in theory can regulate the base interest rate to control the take-up of loans, with just the necessary precision to ensure stable prices and rising profits, and wise governments that want to be re-elected can legislate to ensure a small but welcome rise in the absolute living standards of the workforce, in the form of state support for the needy and possibly a minimum wage. There is no problem here. But the rising affluence of the capitalist class continually swells the ranks of the financial aristocracy, who cannot be expected to act with social

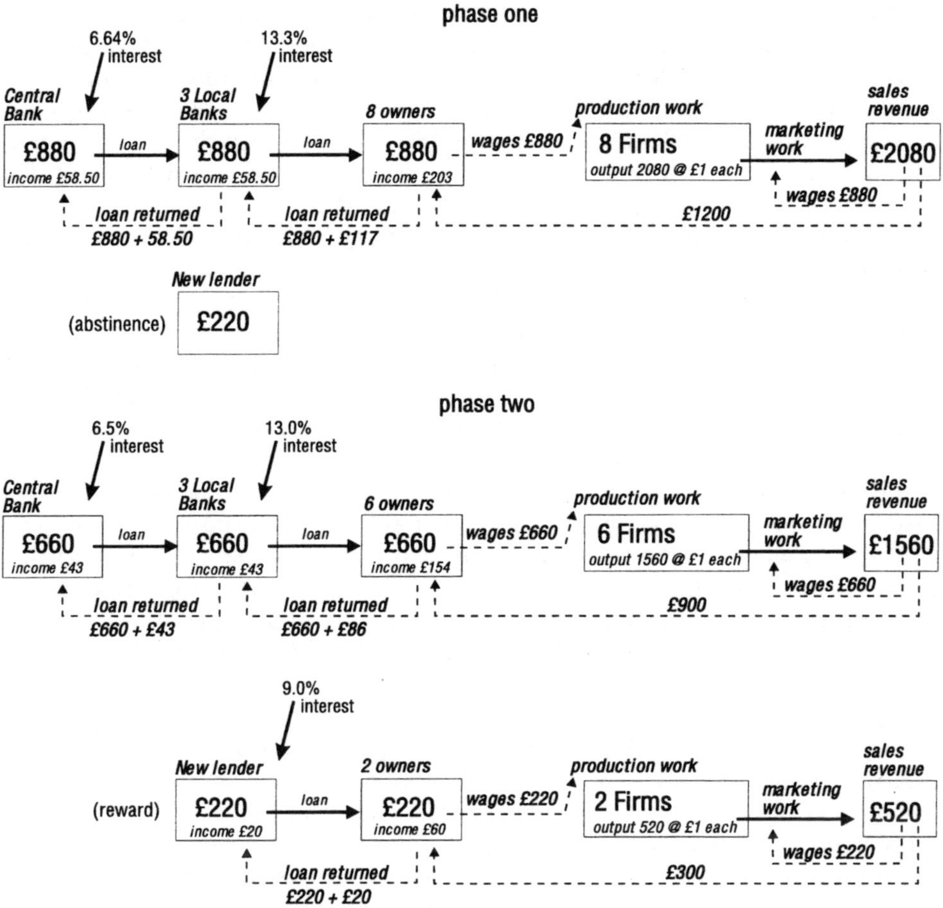

Figure 18-3

responsibility when they are locked in life and death competition with each other, quite apart from the general ignorance and greed that dominate the business world. There is nothing inherently unstable about a progressively bigger group of idlers being carried on the backs of a more and more productive workforce, as long as the workforce are content with their lot, and as long as the two tier loans system is preserved. But the financial capitalist is oblivious of this latter requirement. The competitive drive for profits takes precedence over any controls that the central bank may wish to impose. Under capitalism, money responds quite impersonally to any opportunity for profitable manipulations, threading its way through countless sophisticated channels, in an immense variety of speculative ventures, short term and long, all intertwined in income-earning ways, and ramifying everywhere throughout the financial network. As this network expands on a global scale it follows its own course and it can bring chaos in its wake.

This global financial network will be studied in Volume Two. But taking a brief historical overview we may note that in the nineteen twenties the instability inherent in a gold-based system finally erupted in a huge financial breakdown that destroyed banks in their thousands and forced the leading nations to quit the gold standard. At the close of the twentieth century, banks have collapsed at an even greater rate throughout the world economy for entirely different reasons. At the present stage of our investigations we have only a rudimentary inkling of this new instability, so for the present we must make do with a very bare framework as a basis for the analysis to come. This bare framework is shown in Figure 18-3.

Two phases of our previous model are shown to assist close comparison. A new lender has appeared (tongue in cheek we describe him as an abstainer) who at the outset is willing to forgo consumption and is prepared to lend at a rate of interest which is substantially less than the current rate on offer by the local banks. This new lender attracts two customers and the local banks suffer a loss of income. The exact details are as shown in phase two. It is obvious that this second (reward) phase is not stable. If the new lender has sufficient funds he will attract all the customers away from the local banks. In other words, competitive rivalry in respect of interest rates is present here, affecting three distinct banking groups, namely the central bank, its associated local banks, and a hostile banking sector. This is the platform we will carry forward for close study at some future stage in our analysis.

A general observation can be made at this point. At the heart of the capitalist system is an irrationality that leads to different kinds of instability at different periods in historical time. The class of financial capitalists who become rich and who liberate themselves at the same time from any necessity to work, do so by a process that is hidden from collective social view, and this process is also hidden from the capitalists themselves. If the latter understood the mechanism that sustains their ever-expanding affluence they could unite to preserve it in an intelligent fashion, instead of coping blindly with its imperfections as they arise. But in an open democracy such understanding would spread far beyond any conspiratorial group, and the fraud on which capitalist exploitation depends would soon be abolished. The capitalists cannot become a class of responsible managers of the economy except by exposing to view the basis on which they function as a class of exploiters. They can pick up the reins but only as different people. Marx called them the trustees of future society, pocketing the proceeds of their trusteeship in the meantime.

19

Modelling the exploitation process: part 1

Figure 19-1 portrays the whole economy in a manner which also serves to depict the typical or average firm. There are no magnitudes in the diagram, but these will be added later, when we have fully explored the theoretical coherence.

The black arrows represent the circulation of banknotes. The *goods exchange interface* is the buying and selling network that endows these banknotes with their exchange-value in terms of goods. This exchange-value is embodied in prices that simultaneously determine the spending flow of incomes and the identical re-generation of incomes. In other words, the goods are bought at prices that generate incomes for sellers who simply change places with each other to become their own buyers. Money is neither lost nor gained by these

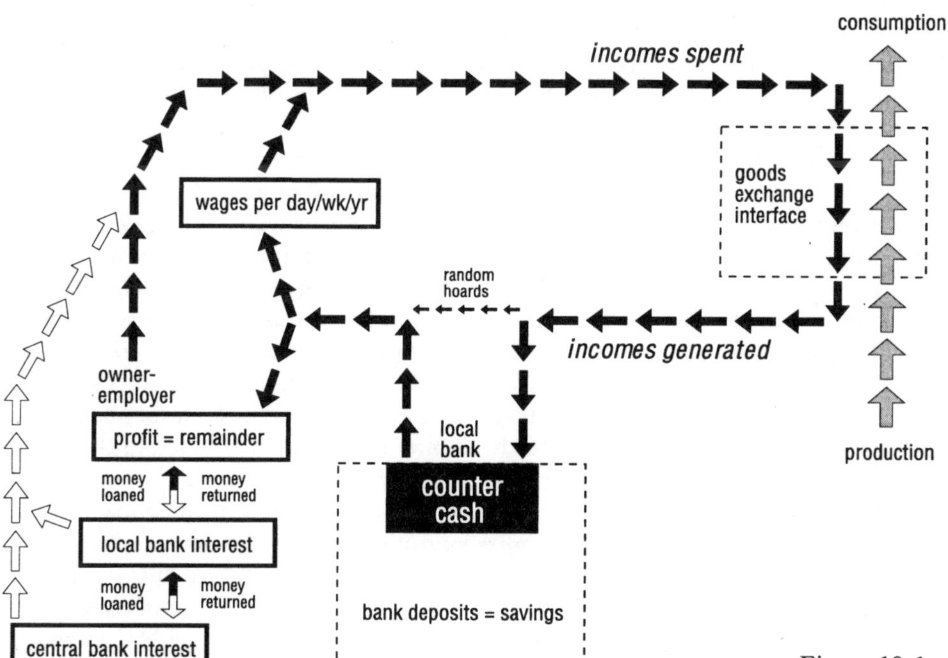

Figure 19-1

transactions, no matter how the parties may try to outwit each other. Thus any magnitude that we propose to insert into the diagram for *incomes spent* is bound to be the same as the magnitude for *incomes generated.* Given this fact, the same magnitude must represent the total of prices paid for whatever quantity of physical goods (grey arrows) is passing through the exchange interface. In other words, the respective lines of production acquire first of all an exchange-value determined by the quantity passing from production to consumption in whatever time period the model represents, and then as we know these values are converted into prices by a complicated equalisation procedure, as described in previous chapters.

The black arrows show two interlinked circuits, one for wages and one for profits. Selling of goods generates the bulk revenues that maintain these two primary incomes. Wages and profits are extracted from these bulk revenues and then merge again at the interface when fresh goods are bought. Ignore the white arrows and loans for the present. Nothing appears in the diagram that may be described as "costs", which are real only for particular firms in a "plus and minus" relation to each other, meaning that costs do not exist at overall level because they are always self-cancelling. Hence they cannot appear at the level of the "average" firm either, as notionally represented in the model. This notional firm, as portrayed in Figure 19-1, is an important concept in economic theory. It represents the capitalist society as a self-sufficient whole, and it also represents the typical firm as an extrapolated sub-division of the whole.

In times past, *random hoards* existed in substantial quantities throughout the economy. Weekly pay packets contained real banknotes and coin which when spent became incomes for retailers who then paid their cash takings into banks where it was stacked in the vaults ready for employers to withdraw and disburse again in next week's pay packets. Such repetitive inefficiency has gradually been removed from the payment systems of all except the very smallest firms, but the tiny arrows still have their reality, because money earned from selling either goods or a service need not necessarily pass through a bank. But whether the tiny arrows are substantial or not, the main arrows shown flowing in and out of the *local bank* in Figure 19-1 are always self-cancelling. If the public at large embarks on a spending spree, and draws money from bank deposits for such a purpose, the same money flows back into the banks as fast as it is spent. The counter cash reserve stays constant, while its rate of turnover simply speeds up. More cash passes through the bank per day and the speed at which this cash flows through the exchange interface also speeds up, but there is no effect on unit prices unless reserve stocks of particular goods are exhausted, in which case there may be a temporary rise in the price of such goods, not balanced by price falls for other goods. Thus a generalised spending spree may raise the overall price level. But a community cannot raise its standard of living by drawing on its savings. If there are no reserve stocks of goods, savings that are spent by some people merely augment the savings of other people. An individual may acquire a large fortune and live extravagantly till it is all spent, but a whole community is always bound by the rule that goods come from the physical outputs of factories, mines, fisheries, farms, etc, and no monetary manipulations can alter the direct dependence of living standards on such physical outputs. The existence of reserve stocks of goods can allow small short-lived variations but these merely fluctuate about a mean position.

Endless confusion arises from the tendency to conjure up holistic conclusions based on the circumstances of individual firms or people. A spending spree for one person or a relatively small group of people will of course increase their enjoyment of wealth in one form or another. This is strictly not the case for the population as a whole. Note also that for both individuals and collectively, when savings are being spent, the level of spending exceeds the current level of earnings, so the spree must come to an end in a relatively short time.

The point to grasp in terms of Figure 19-1 is that the black arrows will carry a bigger quantity of money if savings are withdrawn from the bank to spend on consumption, leading to either of the following outcomes. (1) If supply responds instantly, *bulk* prices and incomes and standard of living will rise, while *unit* prices will stay constant. (2) If supply cannot respond, *unit* prices will rise alongside rising *bulk* prices and rising incomes while standard of living will remain stationary. (As a simple illustration, if savings of £100 are withdrawn to spend on apples that are currently selling at 50 an hour for £1 each, then (1) the selling rate will rise to 150 apples an hour at £1 each, or (2) the selling rate will stay at 50 per hour and the unit price will rise to £3 each. In both cases the seller's income rises from £50 to £150, an increase of £100 corresponding to the savings that are being spent). Similarly if the general population decides to increase its level of savings by a reduction in spending, then the black arrows will slow down, and the former outcomes will be reversed. (1) If supply drops instantly, *bulk* prices and incomes and standard of living will fall, while *unit* prices will stay constant. (2) If supply cannot respond, (meaning that it continues at the existing high rate), *unit* prices will fall alongside falling *bulk* prices and falling incomes while standard of living will remain stationary. Hence when savings are contracting or expanding, the effect on unit price and bulk price will depend on the quickness of supply response, in accordance with the limiting cases just described. When a new level of savings is stabilised, smaller or larger than before, prices and incomes will return to their former level, and the black arrow circuits in Figure 19-1 will settle to their normal pace. Thus the relation between savings, prices and incomes is trend-stationary, as was pointed out in Chapter 11.

When the savings level is falling or rising, either to boost or to curtail spending, the main black arrow circuit speeds up or slows down, but such variations have no effect on bank cash reserves, which remain unaltered because inflow and outflow rise and fall together. Money can never drain away by any kind of spending action. It always passes from one owner to another without loss or gain. The money stock is always constant, unless new notes are printed. *Whether notes are printed or not, for society as a whole,* ***income spent*** *is always equal to* ***income generated*** *no matter how fast or slow the black arrows circuit is travelling.* This equality is absolute.

The production/consumption flow (grey arrows in Figure 19-1) steadily increases as the technical ability of a given society improves with the passage of time. Rising output simply means falling *unit* prices, while *bulk* prices and incomes stay constant. Ordinarily a rise in the general standard of living for everybody would follow. As we know, the capitalist loans system incorporates a fraudulent procedure that intercepts this potential rise in social living standards, and diverts it into the pockets of employers and bankers. We will now recapitulate the details of this fraud in the context of Figure 19-1.

The black and white twin-head arrows show loans passing from the central bank to the local banks and thence to the employer. As far as the principal of the loan is concerned, ie the actual sum borrowed by the employer, it merely returns to the original lender, ultimately the central bank, and the black arrow circuit is not affected. Hence the twin-head arrows portray a never-ending circulation of a sum of money, fixed in magnitude for a certain length of time, and although it appears to be a loan from the central bank, this loan is merely an initial impulse to start the endless reciprocation of the money backward and forward between the three participants, for as long as the loan is renewed. For the present we set aside any notion of "interest" on these loans. We are concerned solely with the bare loan itself. Interest will appear later. The loans create a continuously repeated circuit which operates on its own, quite independently of the black arrow circuit. But these two circuits are joined in the person of the employer, hence they can bleed into each other, so to speak. So although the central bank is sending money to the employer and getting the same money back, it is just as possible to describe this reciprocating motion as an endless loop without beginning or end, once it has been started. The employer sends money from the black arrow circuit to the local bank, to pay back his loan. The local bank sends money to the central bank, again to pay back a loan. The central bank lends the money afresh, which travels back along the reverse route, and the employer restores it to the black circuit. In this way the black circuit is looped out from the employer through two banking agencies and back to the employer again. There are no losses or gains either to the black circuit or the sum borrowed. Nobody is supplying money. The employer in effect is using funds from his own firm to pay back a loan which is constantly being renewed by the banks. Such a procedure is in no way dishonest. But this loop is a vital pathway for the fraud we are about to describe.

If the employer decides to increase his loan, then the amount to be paid back will also increase, but there will be no change to the black circuit. More money will enter the lending loop but money flowing out of the black circuit is still balanced by money flowing in. The extra money just comes from the employer's profits, and it is returned when the loan is renewed. No matter how big the loan, the money is just circulating round and round. (Remember we are concerned only with the basic loan itself and not with any interest on the loan). But if extra notes are *printed* by the central bank for inclusion anywhere in the loan system, these newly created notes will pass via the black arrow circuit into the goods exchange interface and prices will rise to a new level. Who will benefit from this printing operation? At first sight nobody is better off. The employer has asked for a bigger loan and he receives it. He now has to pay it back. The bankers have loaned the money but it just returns to them so no benefit arises there.

Meanwhile prices have risen because freshly printed notes have entered the monetary circuit, introducing inflation that lowers the value of money for everybody. The printing operation seems to be pointless, from every point of view. A loan that was travelling round and round has been increased by printing extra banknotes, and the general price level has simply risen as a result to a new stable position, with a larger loan once more travelling round and round.

But in fact the employer benefits considerably, not from the loan but from the inflation. Follow the black arrow circuit and you will see that it leads to a point of separation between wages and profit. Wages are fixed rates negotiated on a basis of time worked. Wages never change when magnitudes in the black circuit alter. But profit always responds to such changes, because it is a remainder. Profit rises when *incomes generated* rises, and vice versa. Hence the newly printed notes will raise prices and generate higher incomes and then pass directly into the profit of the employer. Although the central bank prints the extra notes, it gets no direct benefit from such an operation, as would a forger, who illegally prints banknotes in order to spend them himself. The central bank cannot spend them. All its transactions are scrupulously honest. Every pound sterling is accounted for. The only way the central bank can obtain any benefit from the freshly printed notes that pass into the income of the employer is to charge an *interest* on loans to the local banks, who in turn charge an interest on loans to the employer.

In this roundabout way, the banking sector first of all increases the prosperity of all employers by printing new notes, and the bankers then appropriate some of this prosperity for themselves by charging an interest on the loans. This benefit system is an act of fraud because the living standard of the entire workforce is lowered as a result of the inflation of the price level, and this loss in social purchasing power is transfered to the employer and the bankers, who enjoy a corresponding rise in income, massively enhanced in percentage terms by their relatively small numbers. The income obtained from this interest enters the black arrow network via the white arrows in Figure 19-1.

As earlier described, the fraud vanishes from view if the printing of new notes is balanced with a rise in general productivity. The new notes would normally bring about a rise in unit prices, while increased productivity causes unit prices to fall. When these two trends counterbalance each other, prices stand still and inflation seems to be absent. But hidden inflation is present, which means that the value of money is steadily falling. More goods are being produced but higher incomes are needed to buy them. Wage earners, and all other people on fixed incomes, are locked to a constant standard of living while profits rise to swell the incomes of a privileged few who enjoy all gains to productivity as they occur throughout the economy.

Of course the banks negotiate loans by legal paperwork and by the use of cheques to transfer money, not by supplying banknotes. An account is opened for the employer by a local bank, and when the employer uses this account to transfer money to other accounts, earnings are created for other people whose withdrawals eventually drain the cash reserves of the local bank, obliging the latter to seek replenishment through loans with the central bank. It is at this stage that the extra notes get printed. Thus, to the ordinary view, the various links in the fraud appear to be quite unconnected.

It is the *increase* in the loans, and not the loans themselves, that initiates the eventual need for fresh notes to be printed. The central bank cannot infiltrate new banknotes into its normal loaning activities. First, because cheques are the convenient medium for all money transactions at this level, and second, because the central bank maintains standards that would be compromised if real banknotes were unnecesarily introduced into such deals. The central bank will supply freshly printed notes to the local banks if and when it is requested to do so by a bank that needs to restore its depleted cash reserves. Such money must take the form of real notes and coin because it is earmarked for that purpose by the borrower, the local bank, who must still negotiate the loan on the same basis as any other loan.

When average output per worker rises, the average standard of living for everybody in the whole community rises, given that hours of work remain the same. This rise in living standards is potentially available for both workers and employers, even though the workforce is paid at a fixed rate per unit of working time. The potential fall in unit prices that is generated by the increased supply brings the same percentage benefit to everybody no matter how earnings are calculated. For example, if the total wages for a workforce of ten is £500, and profit for the employer is £500, then falling prices enhance the buying power of £500 just as much in one case as in the other. No matter how wages and profit may differ as particular magnitudes, their respective proportions remain quite unchanged by any fall or rise in unit prices, caeteris paribus. Hence, even though "excessive" profits may be extracted from sales revenue by an allegedly unscrupulous employer, leaving only "a pittance" for the workforce, the capitalist exploitation system is not directly responsible for such unfairness or greed. In fact the capitalist system allows for the rectification or adjustment of such exploitation when it is flagrantly in breach of common practice. (We speak always of a closed economy with relatively free labour mobility. Different standards apply between rival economies or where certain social groups suffer from imposed or condoned discrimination). Modern capitalist exploitation does not rest on "unfairness" of any kind. It rests on a fraudulent manipulation of the currency operating at a generalised level, and the effects are therefore even-handed so to speak as far as individual cases are concerned. And as stated earlier, no conspiracy theory is supported by any of the foregoing.

If the central bank merely printed notes to spend on its own behalf then it would be providing an income for itself, just like any counterfeiter. Such action would clearly be dishonest, and hence the central bank does no such thing. The central bank obtains an income by making loans, and these loans must be paid back, with interest, through a two-tier arrangement involving a network of local banks. The interest on the loans enables the banker to share in the profits of the employer, and as long as the employer depends on loans, the banker's income is secure. But consider this situation from the point of view of the employer. To get rid of the banker would represent a considerable improvement in the employer's standard of living. He could keep all his profit for himself. The banker, in the role of a mere money-lender, might be useful to a newly started business, but no established firm would choose to stay in debt to a money-lender. It is here that we confront the essence of the matter. The central bank, in conjunction with its network of local banks, is far more than just a money-lender. Although it is dedicated, like any other enterprise, to growth and higher profits, it is also charged with a special mission in respect of the economy as a whole.

The central bank (and its satellite banks) provide a "money supply" in the form of loans that must be for ever increasing. A fixed loan, endlessly renewed, is simply parasitic on profits, with no enduring benefit for the borrowing firm, and it causes no liquidity shortage in the local banks. But a loan that is continually repeated *and regularly enlarged* gives the central bank the opportunity to make itself indispensible. The ever-increasing loans thread their way through the monetary system and create a demand for extra banknotes. This demand for extra banknotes appears only when the loans increase. When these extra banknotes are printed, the value of money falls and bulk prices rise, and all of this rise flows into the profits of the employer. If the employer can raise productivity in his firm at the same time, the resultant fall in unit prices (from the productivity improvement) will offset the rise in prices (from the falling value of money) and hence unit prices will stand still. Everything will appear to be normal. Wages will stay as they were, and the potential rise in everybody's living standard (from the improved productivity) will be neatly diverted into the incomes of bankers and employers without apparent malpractice by anyone. All transactions will appear to follow the rules of everyday trading that everyone understands and abides by. The prosperity of every business in the land, whether it borrows money or not, is dependent on this special mission of the central bank to inflate the currency in step with rising productivity and keep unit prices constant, or rising moderately.

We commented above that although the capitalist system is essentially based on exploitation, it is not (within its own currency domain) an exploiter like a slave-owner or feudal landlord. Direct forms of exploitation are forced into dissolution by the growth of capitalism. The capitalist system operates on the basis of contractual rights which are forever being refined and extended. Every day in the democracies a struggle is waged against whatever forms of oppression still linger from a feudal past. A wide variety of pressure groups speak out for disadvantaged people in all walks of life. Many forms of colonial oppression have been dismantled. To choose a government and to challenge orthodox opinion are regarded as universal human rights in all the advanced countries and such principles are gradually gaining ground worldwide. Brutal dictatorships have been liberalised. The world has seen great advances in these terms. Old-fashioned exploitation, which rested on the command to work hard for a master, and which divided society into "them and us" has no place in modern capitalism, which is driven by an altogether different set of principles, openly proclaimed, not subservient to the interests of a definable ruling group, dedicated simply to the removal of all barriers that prevent "social mobility".

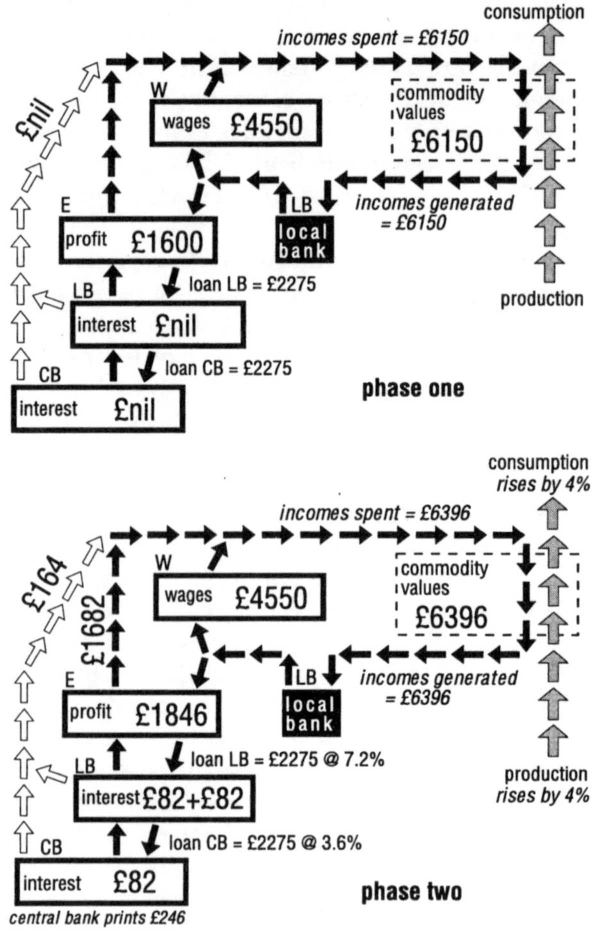

Figure 19-2 (both pages)

This social mobility is essentially the freedom to become a member of a successful firm. "Them and us" is fast disappearing as a definition of ruler and ruled. The distinction remains but it operates with much greater sophistication. It nowadays comes from the world of business, where the de-personalised balance sheet is king. The royal command to work hard for a master has been changed to a social ordinance that sends one basic message to everybody: *stay ahead of the competition.* This is the criterion that defines the admired individual or firm, and against which all other distinctions, of class, gender, cultural origin, age, disability, lineage, appearance, etc, fade away. Even the highest of social virtues such as regard for common welfare or personal integrity count for nothing unless they acquire a form of legal enforcement compatible with business life. Commercial activity is ruled by market forces, and the highest virtue is to strip away any form of interference, allowing

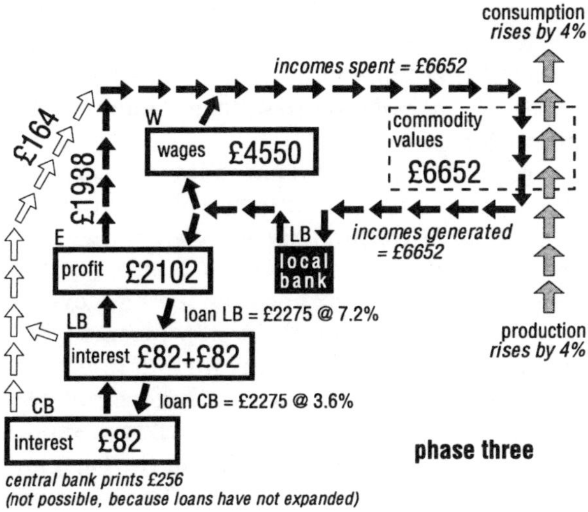

phase three

everything to operate with full competitive freedom. Within the narrow scope of capitalist theorising, which itself exemplifies the virtue it preaches, this precept is entirely rational, and embodies the progressive side of capitalism as the champion of individual liberty. The entrepreneurial or "venture"capitalist is the embodiment of this spirit, and the funds that he makes available on an ever increasing scale are the mainspring that drives the capitalist system forward.

At a mundane practical level, this momentum is the expansion of loans, which we must now examine in specific detail. We can insert magnitudes from Figure 15-6 in the schematic layout of Figure 19-1 to show how a money-based economy operates from one time period to the next when newly printed notes steadily inflate the currency value, as in Figure 19-2, where we now resume our analysis.

Phase one merely sets the stage. The loans are present, but only the principal is shown, travelling in a loop from the employer to local bank, to central bank, and then back through both these parties to rejoin the black circuit. The amount of the loan is half the wages bill, but this has no particular significance. There is no interest and no change to profits. The loan just travels round an endlessly repeated loop and serves no purpose.

In phase two the central bank prints (over a certain period of time) new notes to the value of £246. Why the bank should do so, and why this amount is chosen, will become clear as we proceed. These notes enter the loans to the local bank and filter into the black arrow circuit, raising commodity values from £6150 to £6396. This increase of £246 passes into the employer's profit, which rises from £1600 to £1846. The interest which the employer pays on his loan, at 7.2%, is £164, and when this is deducted from his profit of £1846, he is left with £1682 to spend, as shown. The interest of £164 is income for the local bank, who must repay an interest charge of £82, levied by the central bank for the same loan at 3.6%. Thus the local bank's income falls to £82 and the central bank acquires an income of £82. These two incomes follow the white arrows into the black arrow circuit, which settles down once more to a stable bulk price level. Meanwhile (over the same period of time) productivity has increased by 4%, with the result that unit prices of all commodities have remained quite undisturbed while all these alterations occured.

The new notes printed by the central bank (£246) pass into the loans to the local bank, where they are immediately absorbed into the black circuit. The presence of new notes disturbs existing prices but only once, when they lift the total value of the circulating network to a new level of £6396. This rise simultaneously creates three new incomes of £82 each for the employer, the local bank and the central bank respectively, and these new incomes, for all three recipients, then continue in perpetuity without any further injections of new notes. In other words, as long as the loans are repeatedly renewed, at the same rates of interest, the employer will receive an income of £1682, continuously renewed, and the two banking agencies, the central bank and the local bank, will also receive a continuously renewed income of £82 each. The effect of the newly printed notes, expressed in mathematical terms, is to alter the proportions in which the gross value of all goods produced is divided between four recipients. The proportion allocated to wages falls. The proportions allocated to the three other recipients rises. The fall in the wages allocation is completely hidden by the 4 per cent rise in output. Goods are now cheaper, but the value of money has fallen because new notes have been printed. In other words, wages which now buy less are counter-balanced by goods that now cost less. Hence the worker sees no change in his own circumstances, while the incomes of employers and bankers rise dramatically.

The effect of the new notes is *to alter existing proportions*. Once the proportions are altered the new ratios take over, so to speak. The new notes simply hoist the whole network to a new valuation level which is completely stable. The effect of this change is negligible (and serves no purpose) for society as a whole, because incomes generated by sales are always equal to incomes spent by buyers, so no gain accrues to either side, although banknotes of higher denomination pass between them, and therefore the counter cash in the local banks must rise to maintain an adequate working reserve. The essential steps in understanding this fraudulent procedure are as follows:

1. When employers borrow *more* money from the local banks, withdrawals by depositors increase.
2. When withdrawals by depositors increase, cash reserves in the local banks fall.
3. When cash reserves fall below the safety margin required to meet withdrawals by depositors, the local banks borrow money in banknotes from the central bank, who prints them.
4. When the new notes enter the monetary system, the currency value rises.
5. When the currency value rises, wages stand still and profits rise steeply.
6. If the expansion of loans raises the currency value at a rate that matches the general improvement in productivity, unit prices will remain constant, and hence no *visible* inflation will be present even though the value of money is falling, and bulk prices are rising.

Of course anyone whose income is based on the passage of time is outside the buying-and-selling nexus. The incomes of such people automatically fall further and further below the social average every time the currency is inflated by newly printed banknotes, unless re-negotiation is possible. (If this re-negotiation is no more than adjustment of income to keep in step with a so-called retail price index then standard of living merely stays constant in absolute terms, but it still falls in relation to the rising standard of society as a whole). By contrast, incomes that are a *remainder* after wage costs have been deducted, ie profits, rise steeply when the monetary network is hoisted to a new valuation level.

The vital factor in this trickery is the *increase* in loans. This increase creates the cash deficiency that opens the way for new notes to enter the monetary system in a perfectly legal manner. The roundabout enrichment of employers and bankers would not operate if these new notes were missing. But how does the central bank view its role as a supplier of newly printed banknotes, seeing that it is not likely to describe its own activities as fraudulent?

In its own view, the central bank does nothing to create the shortage in the cash reserves of the local banks. The central bank supplies new notes to *cure* such cash deficiency, without any realisation that the new notes inflate the currency and actually cause the deficiency. Requests for extra banknotes come from different banks at different times, and the central bank merely responds to these needs as part of its normal lending activity. Every freshly printed note contributes to a steady rise in the currency value, and this steady rise creates a universal deficiency in the cash reserves of all banks. This universal deficiency is never recognised as such because each individual case gets its own small-scale solution. The problem is cured at local level as it arises, hence there is no perceived problem at any higher level, particularly when a plausible rigmarole serves to explain how a "money supply" is supposedly needed in a capitalist economy. Besides, the role of the central bank as the main supplier of extra banknotes is relatively recent. Surplus banknotes have infiltrated quite naturally into the monetary system throughout the second half of the twentieth century, without any fresh printings by the central bank. We have already explained how the reduction of random hoards brings about a surplus of notes that stay in circulation and cause inflation of the currency, accompanied of course by a *surplus* of cash in the banks, and not by a *shortage* at all. So in the early decades following the second world war, the central bank had no role to play in general management of the economy, except to look wise and tread water while the tide of inflation (both hidden and visible) ebbed and flowed autonomously. It is only in recent decades that an overall monetary responsibility has gradually devolved on the central bank. The supply of extra banknotes from absorption of hoards is gradually drying up, and the central bank must make good the deficiency. This transformation from impotence to active involvement gives the impression that the bank and its advisors are now more enlightened about what they are supposed to be doing in respect of inflation. But the truth is rather that the central bank is being enlisted for a role that has only lately emerged, and which it "understands" only as a kind of conditioned response. We can use Figure 19-2 to examine the forms that this response must take.

Phase three in Figure 19-2 shows that if the existing loans are merely renewed, at exactly the same rates of interest, while new notes enter the system, the only beneficiary will be the employer, whose spending income rises sharply from £1682 to £1938. But there is a contradiction here. The circumstances portrayed are impossible to realise, if we assume that the new notes are being supplied by the central bank, and not from superfluity due to absorption of hoards. Mere renewal of existing loans will not raise the currency value. There will be no shortage of cash in the local banks, and therefore no request for extra banknotes. The central bank will not be able to inject the new notes that must enter the monetary network if the employer's income is to expand as we have just described. (We ignore the possibility of open market operations because it is a temporary stopgap at best). Hence the transition shown from phase two to phase three in Figure 19-2 is not viable. The essential condition of an *ever-expanding* loans system is missing. When absorption of hoards gives rise to superfluous notes, the inflation effect follows inevitably, without any dependence on expanding loans, but under our present assumption that absorption of hoards has ended, there is no way that the central bank can maintain a regular supply of new notes except in circumstances where loans are increasing.

The necessity for ever-expanding loans coincides very conveniently with the banker's natural desire to enlarge his own business. And as we have noted on previous occasions, the employer can similarly extend his scale of operation ahead of rivals by judicious borrowing of funds. So banker and employer alike can devise perfectly good reasons for borrowing larger sums of money. But though they see eye to eye in these terms, their respective aims do not coincide in respect of the debts that are incurred by borrowing money. The employer wants to repay at a low rate of interest. The banker wants the opposite, a high rate of interest. From the vantage point of our diagrams, which embrace society as a whole, we can introduce a third influence which arises from the need to keep the monetary system in smooth fraudulent operation. The loans system must be manipulated not only in the superficial sense of balancing the satisfaction of the employer with the satisfaction of the banker, but this manipulation, at a deeper level, must balance the expansion of loans with the rising general level of productivity in the economy. In other words, the loans must be expanded by just the right amount to generate a steady replenishment of cash reserves in the local banks, at a rate that matches the general expansion in physical output of goods. If this match is achieved, there will be no *visible* inflation. Unit prices will stay constant. If newly printed notes are called for at a rate that exceeds the amount required to match rising productivity, then prices will rise, (and profits also), indicating that loans are expanding too much. Conversely, prices will fall, (and profits also), if loans are expanding too slowly in relation to rising outputs. The central bank's role therefore is not only to operate a loaning business that is decently profitable in conventional terms, but also to subordinate its own profit-making to the task of keeping inflation under control. In bald terms, the means of control are simple. The base rate of interest can be reduced to attract a higher expansion of loans, or the base rate can be raised to dampen down the expansion of loans, the aim being to maintain a rate of expansion which permits the currency to be inflated at a rate that matches (or slightly exceeds) rising productivity and thereby holds unit prices constant (or allows them to rise gently).

Using Figure 19-2, we can outline the steps to be taken by the central bank when it discharges its mission efficiently, always with the proviso that we are dealing with a self-contained market economy. The rate of rising productivity is the fundamental starting point, given as 4 per cent in phase three. The central bank needs to print £256 to inflate the currency by exactly 4 per cent. These new notes must be introduced during the period of time corresponding to the productivity improvement. During this period, the loans by all the local banks to employers must increase by £256, from £2275 to £2531. If the loans simply remain at £2275, as shown, there will be no legal entry point for the new notes. But if the loans increase by this precise amount, the following sequence of events will unfold.

The loans enable money to be transferred from accounts held by employers to accounts held by employees and other beneficiaries, who will then make withdrawals. These withdrawals will reduce the cash reserves of the local banks. The local banks will apply to the central bank for more notes and the central bank will print them. The value of money will fall as these notes enter the system, but unit prices will not be disturbed because of rising productivity. Income of the employers will rise by £256 (from £1846 to £2102) but wages will stay constant. A portion of employer income will be transmitted to the bankers (local and central) via interest charged on the bigger loans. These circumstances will be incorporated into the next diagram, Figure 20-1.

20

Modelling the exploitation process: part 2

The central bank is the principal administrator of a modern capitalist economy. In discharging this role, its fundamental duty is to print new notes, and to introduce them through some legal entry point at a steady rate that matches (or slightly exceeds) the general rate of productivity improvement throughout the economy as a whole. Thus the prosperity of everybody in a capitalist society depends on two groups of people. First is the workforce who create the goods and services on which all classes depend, and who must work for set times at a set pace to satisfy an employer. Second are the bankers, who operate a fraudulent loan system that controls the apportionment of all productivity gains between the various income earners. The medium through which the bankers' power is exercised is a base lending rate which can be raised or lowered as necessary to control the expansion of loans. By this means, all the benefit from rising productivity can be channeled into the pockets of the employers and bankers.

When loans expand at a rate equal to rising outputs, the living standard of the workforce stays constant unless wages are re-negotiated. The wage rate may in fact be set at any level, even below bare subsistence where there is a population surplus and workers are forced to compete against each other with no legal right to collective bargaining. The fraudulent loans system can then be operated to hold this wage level constant while all productivity gains flow into profits, whether these productivity gains arise from longer working hours, or greater intensity of effort, or higher standards of skill, or better tools and equipment, or inventions, or improved cooperation, or the discovery of new natural resources, or the enlargement of theoretical knowledge, or all of these in combination. These various sources of productive improvement, alongside the natural bounty of nature, are the foundation for the general welfare of humanity.

It is not sufficient to define the workforce in capitalist society as the class that supplies the labour involved in direct or supportive productive activity. This definition merely describes a workforce that must necessarily be present in any type of society, capitalist or otherwise, and which consists of those able-bodied adults who directly or indirectly produce consumable goods. There is a second defining attribute of workers in a capitalist society. All wage-earners are locked into a monetary relationship which automatically excludes them from any share in rising living standards unless they can raise their level of wages. The struggle for higher wages, even when gains are made, is always a losing battle, because such gains merely establish a new *absolute* standard of living for the workforce, while their *relative* living standard is always deteriorating alongside profits that are always expanding. The wages escalator continuously descends while the profits escalator continuously rises. This analogy is quite apt and we will use it in the analysis ahead. The worker, in theory, can climb the descending wages escalator at the rate at which it is falling, and he will then maintain his existing position relative to the average living standards of society as a whole, though this position may be very low indeed, generally far below the position of the employer, and even below starvation threshold, as just stated. If the worker achieves such an equilibrium, which would entail a continuously rising wage-rate to match rising productivity, the employer's position relative to the social average would also remain stationary as he moves down the rising profits escalator. The gap between the two, be it large or small, would be constant. As soon as the worker stops climbing up the wages escalator, ie once his wage rate stops rising, he is carried inexorably downwards and the employer resumes his upward travel. We will now illustrate this process in more detail.

In Figure 20-1 a capitalist economy is shown in four successive phases. Each phase depicts a time period in which commodity production has improved by a stated percentage. The improvements vary, starting at 4%, repeated at 4%, then falling to 1%, then rising to 5%. As we already know, the central bank must use its influence to bring about a corresponding degree of hidden inflation to hold unit prices at a uniform level of supposedly "zero" inflation. (At least we will presume that the central bank wants zero inflation of unit prices. In actual practice, the bank would prefer a moderate rise in prices, sufficient to raise profits even higher without too much dislocation and resentment. But we are illustrating how the bare mechanism operates, so we neglect such refinements).

The central bank exercises its influence over loans through the base lending rate. By reducing this rate, take-up of loans is encouraged and vice versa. If such adjustment of the base lending rate is successful, the loans will expand by just the right amount to enable newly printed notes to enter the system alongside the current rate of productivity improvement, as we have already described. In Figure 20-1 the loans have been expanded by exactly the amounts required, without any manipulation of the base lending rate, because our diagrams can be altered at will to demonstrate the inner connections without the need for inducements that a real life situation would call for. Thus Figure 20-1 shows the exploitation process in successful operation, meaning that loans are expanding in step with rising productivity from one phase to the next, with the result that the incomes of the employer and the bankers are steadily increasing, while wages remain at their pre-determined level. The money passing through the black loans loop, representing the basic sum borrowed, ie the principal, is simply a diversion into a loop that endlessly repeats itself, but it also "carries" the interest payments that the local banks extract as their own income. The local banks must then use this income to repay interest charges to the central bank. Thus two incomes are maintained out of the interest that the employer

Figure 20-1 (both pages)

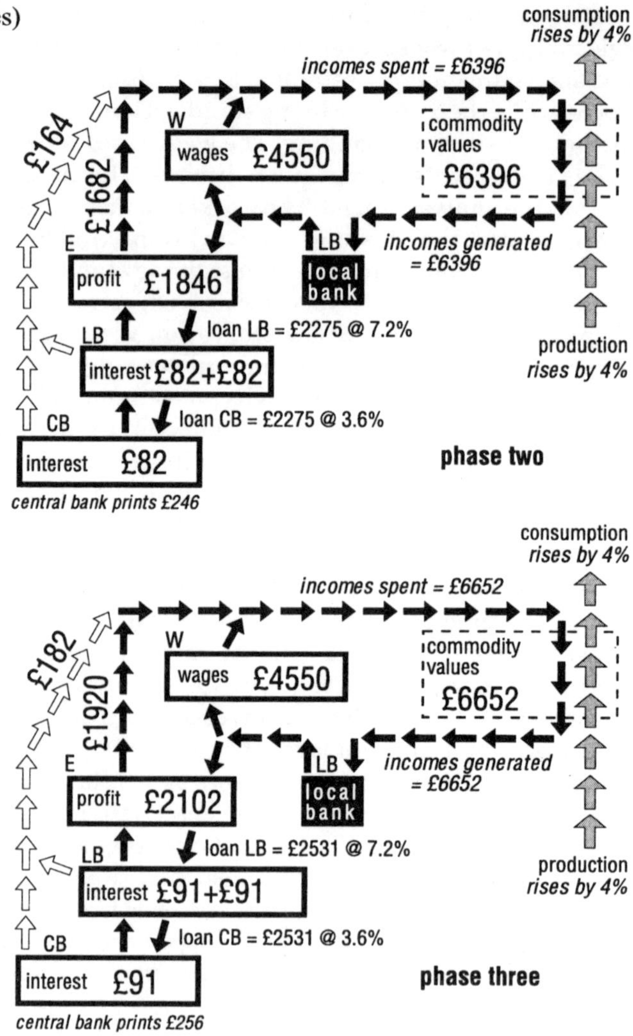

pays on his loan from the local bank. These two incomes are shown by white arrows. The black loans loop (£2275 in phase two) is always self-cancelling, and the sum of the employer's income, the bankers' incomes, and the wages is always equal to the sum of commodity values. The transition from one phase to the next depends wholly on the expansion of loans which in themselves have no connection with rising commodity outputs. But if the loan expansion can be controlled so that it rises in step with such improvement in output rates, unit prices will stay constant, and no inflation will be apparent to the ordinary view.

The employer's disposable income rises from £1682 to £2294 in the period represented by the four phases, an increase of 36%. The total banking income rises from £164 to £212, an increase of 29%. Wages and unit prices never alter. These particular figures are conditioned on four basic determinants, namely,

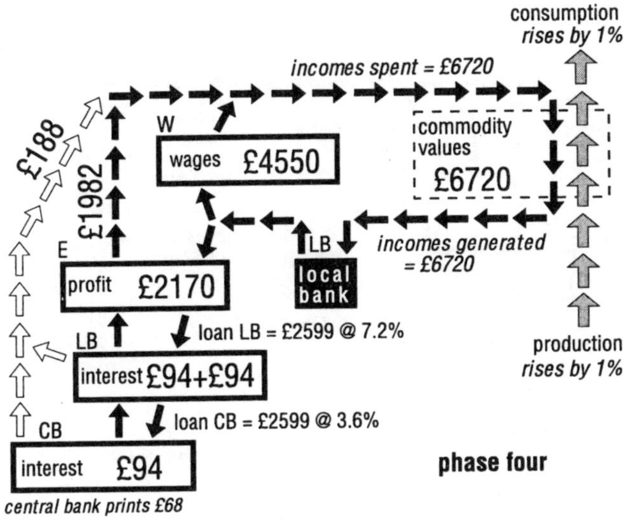

phase four

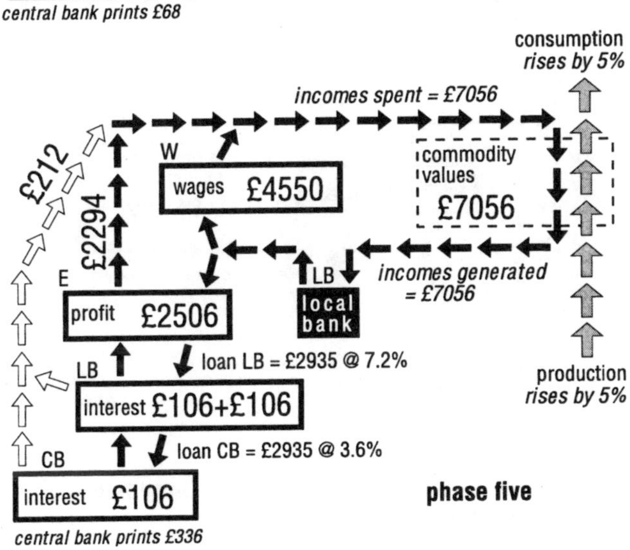

phase five

(1) the original division of wages and profits, (2) the interest rates set by the banking sector, (3) the variation in the size of loans during the period in question, and (4) the constancy of the wage, which as we know could be altered by re-negotiation. We will consider each of these in turn.

(1) The original division of wages and profits. Phase two, Figure 20-1, shows wages at £4550 and profits at £1846, which is approximately a balance of 2.4 to 1. More conveniently we may say that the wages bill is seven tenths of sales income while profit is three tenths. Suppose we change these proportions, raising wages to nine tenths of sales income, and reducing profit to one tenth. The result is shown in Figure 20-2. The new wage rate, for the whole period, is £5756, and the starting income for the employer is £476. The loans and banking

Figure 20-2 (both pages)

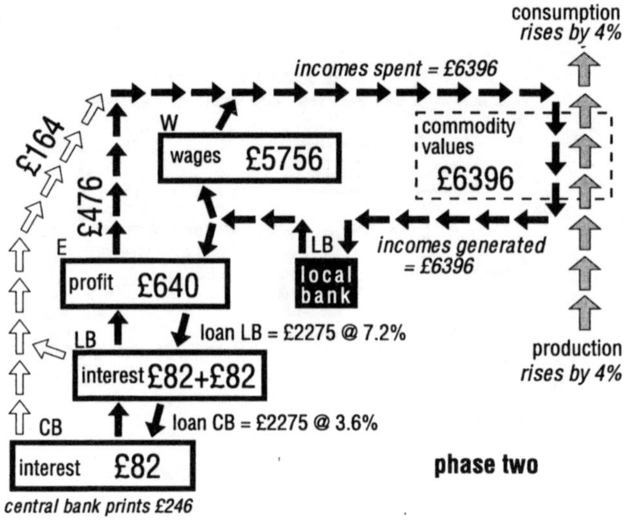

phase two

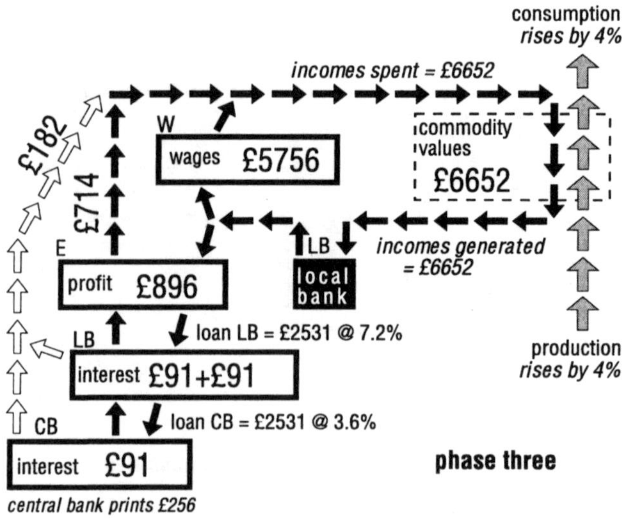

phase three

income are unaffected, the latter rising as before from £164 to £212. At the end of the period, the employer's disposable income has risen to £1088, an increase of 128%. The gain for the employer is exactly the same in Figure 20-2 as it was in Figure 20-1, namely £612, but the percentage rise is greater in Figure 20-2 because the starting position is much lower. From our earlier analysis in Part One we already know that variation in wages has no direct effect on prices, a fact that these diagrams fully confirm.

(2) The interest rates set by the banking sector. Returning to phase two in Figure 20-1, we can see that any variation in interest rates will alter the relation between the employer's income and the incomes of the banking sector. The incomes for the banking sector can rise only if the employer's income falls.

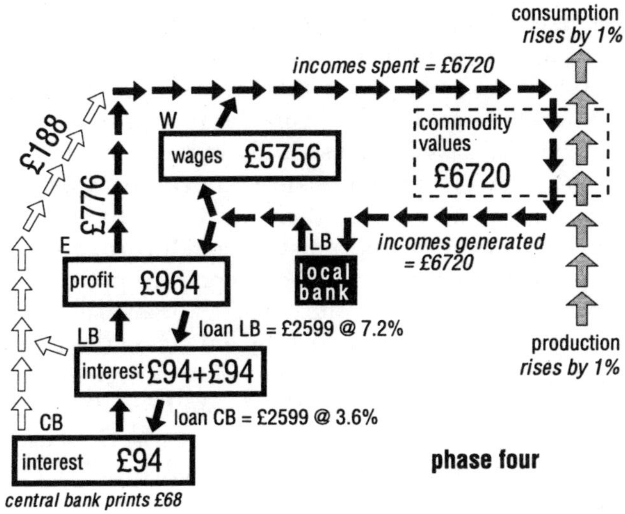

phase four

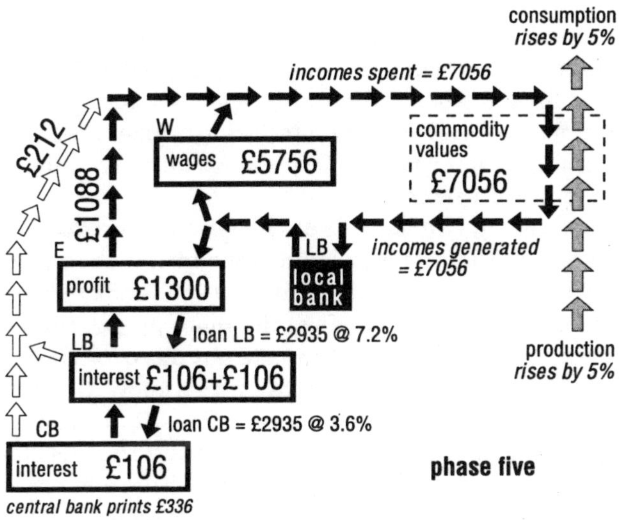

phase five

The market dynamics that fix the interest rates will be discussed later, but in terms of the diagram the linkages are quite straightforward. Income for the employer is the profit that remains after wages are deducted from sales revenue, and derivative incomes for the banking sector are a deduction from the employer's income. This deduction is the (higher) interest rate that the local banks charge, while the (lower) interest rate charged by the central bank determines how much of this deduction is transferred from the multitude of local banks to form a second-stage derivative income for the central bank. In phase two, Figure 20-1, these incomes are £82 for each of the three beneficiaries, but this amount and the fact that it is evenly divided is quite arbitrary in our diagrams. For the moment we merely state that rivalry and speculation rage constantly in this financial loans sector, which we will examine in Part Three.

(3) The variation in the size of loans during the period. No matter how the interest rates may vary, and no matter how high or low the wage rate is initially set as a proportion of gross sales, the monetary stability depicted in either Figure 20-1 or Figure 20-2 rests entirely on the fact that the loans obtained by the employer from the local banks steadily increase in step with rising productivity. This is the key factor that ensures constant prices and a stable living standard for the workforce. But there is no mechanism that regulates loans in this way. If employers are optimistic about future sales, they may well decide to expand production, borrowing more money from the banks, who will be keen to lend it to obtain a share in the expected prosperity. Let us introduce this sense of expectancy into Figure 20-1, by enlarging the take-up of loans in the transition from phase two to phase three. The existing expansion, from £2275 to £2531, is 11.25% and this is exactly the amount required (£256) to hold unit prices steady when general production rises by 4%. Suppose we expand these loans by a greater amount, say 25%, from £2275 to £2844, an increase of £569. Figure 20-3 is the outcome.

The currency value has now been inflated beyond the point that serves to hold unit prices steady against a 4% rise in output. Goods that should have held their value constant at £6652 (as shown in Figure 20-1) have risen to £6965, an increase of £313, representing a *visible* inflation of 4.7%. Of course this is merely the perceived inflation rate. The real rate of inflation is measured by the rise from £6396 to £6965, an inflation rate of 8.9%. As we already know, the productivity increase hides part of this inflation.

The leading agent in these various linkages is obviously the increase in the loans, and the temptation to negotiate bigger loans depends on the mood of anticipation among employers and bankers. This anticipation tends to be self-fulfilling, because the more the loans are increased the more profits rise, and the more profits rise the greater the inducement to take out more loans. But if productivity does not rise in step with the inflating currency, the living standard of all fixed income earners falls. The general rule is that as long as hidden inflation matches rising outputs, profits rise to defraud the workforce out of any share in the productivity improvement. But when inflation exceeds productivity gains, profits rise still faster and the fraud perpetrated on wage-earners is even greater, because they lose not only the collective benefit arising from *future* improvements in productivity, but their existing share in *current* productivity levels is reduced. The exact details are made plain by comparing Figure 20-1 and Figure 20-3. Both unit prices and wages are constant in Figure 20-1, while profits rise. But in Figure 20-3 prices are rising alongside constant wages, meaning that standard of living for the workforce is falling, while profits rise even faster.

(4) The constancy of the wage. Figure 20-1 assumes that no new wage rates are negotiated during the period shown. Let us examine the effect when the wage rate in phase four is raised from £4550 to £4778, an increase of 5%. The outcome is displayed in Figure 20-4. As can be seen, when wages rise, employers' incomes fall. Profits which would have been £2170 at phase four in

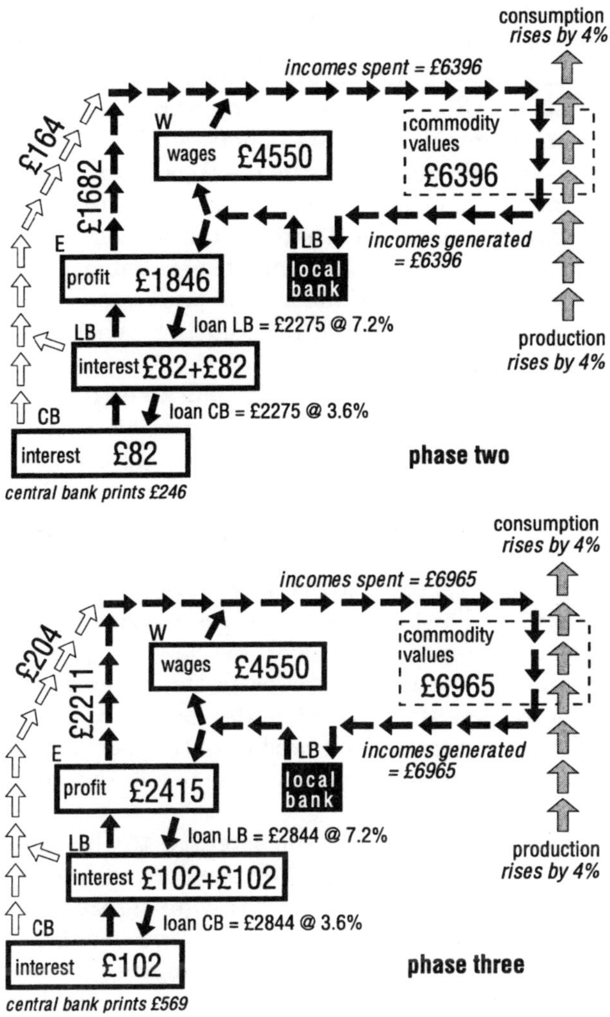

Figure 20-3

Figure 20-1 are only £1942 in Figure 20-4. In fact, profits suffer an absolute fall of £160, from the former level of £2102 at phase three. But even though a wage rise has reduced profits in Figure 20-4, the normal augmentation of profits is resumed at phase five. The increase in profits during the transition from phase four to phase five is £2278 – £1942 = £336. In Figure 20-1, the increase is exactly the same, £2506 – £2170 = £336.

A perpetual struggle is waged in capitalist society over interest rates. On one side are the industrial capitalists who directly employ workers to produce commodities which sell for a gross return. This gross return is a kind of pot from which the workforce obtain an agreed subsistence and the remainder is enjoyed by the employer. Ranged against the employer is the financial capitalist who advances loans, which in effect are a kind of ladle that dips into the employer's helping and scoops a portion for the banker to live on. How far the ladle dips is measured by the rate of interest.

These class relationships are in essence quite plain and straightforward. But each class has its own viewpoint, which is never fully coherent because unity based on common interests is undermined by rivalries between firms in the same line of business. Thus an economic class has both a real social existence, as depicted in our diagrams, and a fluctuating consciousness or awareness of itself which may correspond to reality or may not. There is nothing necessarily false about an individual viewpoint but it cannot be complete or reliable unless it is integrated into a comprehensive overview. If theoretical understanding is missing at social level, the economy is interpreted differently by each class according to its own limited perception.

The basic orientation of the workforce, which is the least educated group, (in many countries handicapped by illiteracy and religious indoctrination), is to find a well-paid job. These jobs are offered by employers who see opportunities for the manufacture of goods or provision of a service which can be sold for money, and who gather together a group of workpeople with the appropriate skills, to provide the necessary labour. The employer pays a wage that is determined on the one hand by the relative scarcity of workers with the necessary skills, and on the other hand by the need to leave a margin of profit for the employer after all costs have been met. From a working class perspective, a "well-paid job" depends on acquiring relatively scarce skills that an employer is keen to utilise, and thus the recognised route to better paid jobs in the advanced countries is a good general education followed by extra specialisms, keeping a weather eye open for opportunities that may arise to join the ranks of the employers.

All of this reasoning is quite sound, and fully consistent with the basic orientation of both working and employing classes. The sensible outlook for people who know they have to work for a living is to acquire competence in the type of skills that employers want. Employers provide jobs, and legislation steadily advances on all fronts to prevent them from discriminating in their selection procedures on any grounds other than competence as defined by published job descriptions. Big firms are continually advertising for special skills that would enable them to grow faster. They re-organise and merge repeatedly (shedding superfluous employees at both shop floor and managerial levels) to improve productivity. The consistent objective is efficiency within a competitive market, and this principle is applied increasingly to every single individual. This orientation is entirely realistic. No firm would survive for long if it followed any other course, apart from rare exceptions in certain niche categories.

But in fact nothing in the above descriptions of working class and employer class viewpoints has any connection with capitalism as an economic system. If the tale ended here, then the black arrows in our current diagrams would happily circulate for ever, shorn of the loans loop and their attendant white arrows. Prices would fall steadily, bringing a rising standard of living for both workers and employers. There would still be a differentiation between rich and

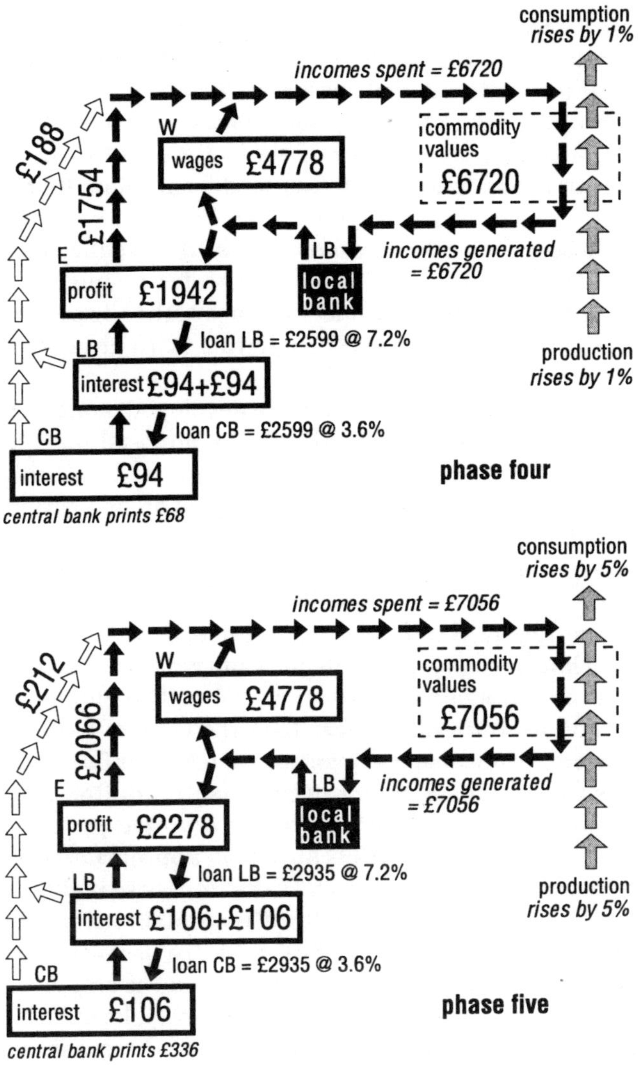

Figure 20-4

poor (though not huge). People with education and skills would get the better-paid jobs, and appointments would be decided on the basis of competence. Employers would be the people with vision and drive. The social fabric of society would be woven from a match of talent and opportunity to the visible benefit of all its members, and collective intelligence would be applied to collective problems in accordance with collective wishes. There is nothing impractical or far-fetched in this vision. But the tale as told is not real because the bankers are left out. The whole picture changes when the financial capitalist enters the scene. The employer hatches a deal with the banker to deceive the worker who becomes a victim of fraud on a monumental scale. Success now depends on escaping from the ranks of workers who create society's wealth and joining the ranks of those who enjoy this wealth but are idle themselves. This viewpoint is grounded in reality. Job vacancies in a capitalist society are increasingly open to all members of the population without distinction of social background, gender, "race", religion, disability, age and so on, but all occupations can be classified under three main headings. *First*, there are jobs for wage-earners who work hard for a master but are automatically excluded from rising living standards (whether their pay is regarded as high or low). *Second*, there are pseudo-jobs for idle people whose income rises dramatically as the productivity of the workforce increases. *Third*, there are "service" jobs for people who compete to earn derivative incomes extracted one way or another from the primary incomes of the other two groups. The incomes in this third group can range from very high to very low.

A social network beneficial to everybody is inherent in a developed monetary economy, but under capitalist conditions a class division is imposed on this network, from above, so to speak. This class division, which endures despite all official banishments, is misconceived if it is regarded simply as an opposition of interests that ought to be settled by negotiation and compromise. It is quite true that the opposition between worker and employer is essentially superficial but under capitalism such conflict is absolute, impossible of amicable resolution, a historic obstacle that can be removed only one way, namely by the social unmasking of the banker for what he really is, an idle parasite who involves the employer in fraudulent partnership against his own workers. The employer who depends upon loans needs to confront the fact that the central bank is making those loan transactions profitable by printing notes to inflate the currency, just as monarchs in the past made themselves richer by adulterating gold. *In a paper-based economy such adulteration can be repeated for ever.* Acquisition of wealth in this way is fraudulent because it is appropriated by stealth from the true creators, the working class, a class that of course includes the employer himself as an executive manager, with a respectable claim to higher remuneration because his leadership and foresight are essential for human cooperation on a large scale. But in his capitalist persona the employer is an enemy of the working class, playing a machiavellian role when he exhorts his workers to increase productivity and contribute to social wealth creation, because all such increase in social wealth is predestined for the exclusive benefit of himself and his banking partners, who are busy behind the scenes, injecting the hidden inflation that is the secret source of their enormous profits. For its part, the working class needs to recognise the double identity of the employer, who is not an enemy in his capacity as an operational manager. It is the fraudulent arrangement between the bankers and the employers that converts the owner/manager into a parasitic exploiter. The conflict between worker and employer remains at an essentially ignorant level when it is conceived or pursued as a mere struggle for better wages or working conditions, however worthy this objective may be. The conflict has much deeper significance.

21

Summary

We can consolidate our general understanding, at this intermediate stage, under three headings, the theoretical base, Say's Law, and the money-lending illusion.

The theoretical base. Two important models developed in Part Two are now central to our grasp of economic theory. The first is Figure 15-6 (page 176) which shows a money-based economy in daily operation. Five firms CDEFG produce finished goods, assisted by a maintenance firm A and a raw materials firm B. The supermarket firm S sells these finished goods, and the transport firm T moves them from place to place. There is a total workforce of three hundred people earning wages, and a group of nine owner/employers (on the assumption of one owner per firm) earning profits.

The second important model is shown as a series in Figure 20-1 (page 230). The series demonstrates how a money-based economy such as Figure 15-6 changes with the passage of time. The wages shrink as a proportion of the total value of goods produced, and the proportion represented by profits expands as a consequence, because profits are a remainder. We need to examine these two models carefully because our analysis has arrived at a point of synthesis that underpins all our theoretical understanding.

We begin with Figure 15-6. All production incomes are shown as black rectangles on the right-hand side of the diagram. These are primary incomes that originate directly from sales. The black profits are a remainder from gross sales revenue (£6150) after three deductions. First deduction is the industrial wages (£4000), the next deduction is the discount to S (£1025), and the final deduction is the cost of transport paid to T (£702). These three deductions from a gross sum of £6150 leave £423, which is the total net profit to be divided between the industrial group ABCDEFG. The sum £423 is not immediately apparent because there is a network of costs to be traced as follows.

The discount to S (£1025) is this firm's income, from which all wages and costs must be paid. Similarly the income for T (£702) must pay wages and costs. Now consider the fact that costs are always payments to other firms. In the layout of Figure 15-6, the costs for both S and T are paid by returning money to its original source, the production group ABCDEFG. Firm S returns money to A and B (£10 in each case) and T does the same (£150 to A and £200 to B). As

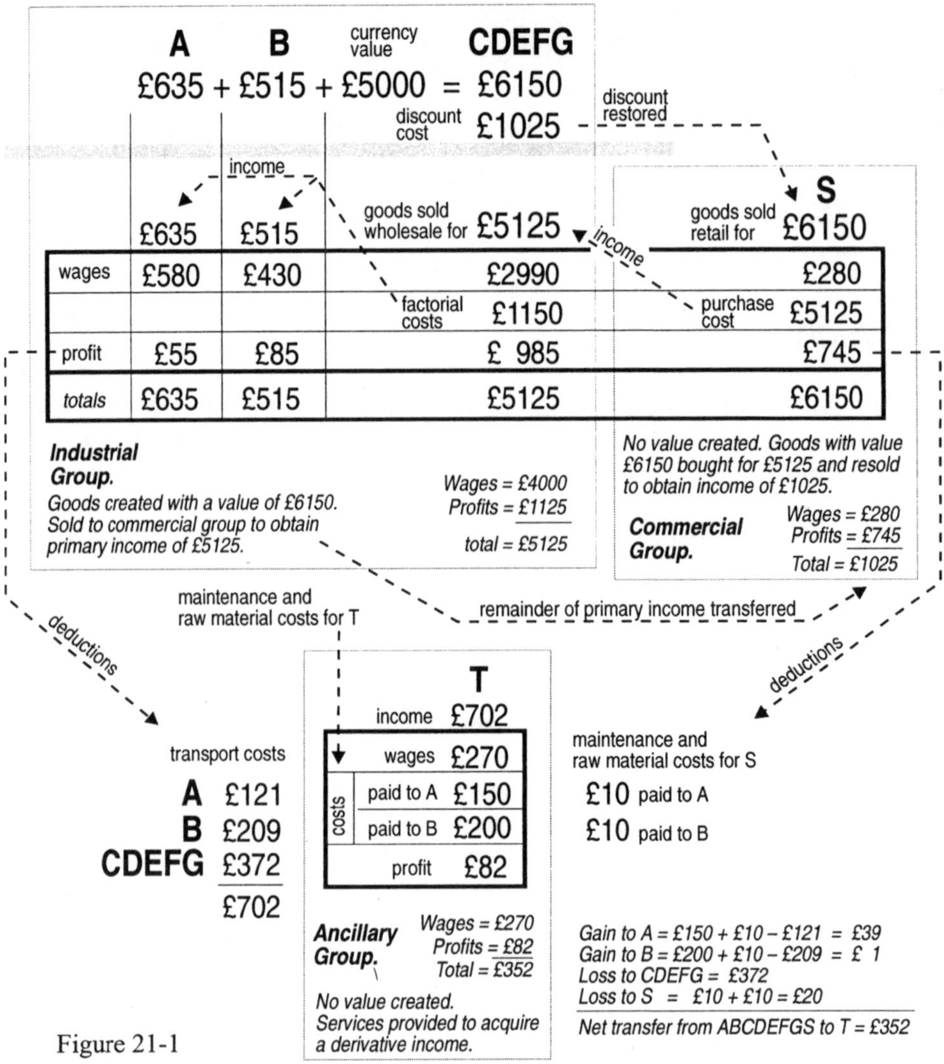

Figure 21-1

detailed in the previous paragraph, the total net profit for the industrial group is £423, but the returned money (£10 + £10 from S, and £150 + £200 from T) now raises this profit to £423 + £370 = £793, shown in the diagram. These "restorations", a total of £370, are indicated by the double-headed grey arrow that travels round the bottom right corner. The combined incomes of S and T (£1025 + £702) now shrink by £370, and commercial wages of £550 are deducted, leaving profits of £807, shown in white rectangles as £725 for S and £82 for T. Thus primary incomes are created by the industrial group and all other incomes are obtained by transfer. (These transfer incomes are called *derivative incomes* in this book because the more obvious term "transfer income" is already in use in the orthodox texts with a different meaning).

The gross income for the finished goods group CDEFG is £6150 less the selling discount of £1025. Wages (£2990) and payments to A and B (£1150) are deducted leaving an intermediate profit at this stage of £985. Transport costs for CDEFG are £372, so final profit is £613, as can be verified from the diagram. But these firms have no inkling whatever of the original value of their goods. The daily created value of £6150 and the discount of £1025 has no existence for them. Only the income of £5125 is real, and then real costs must be deducted in respect of services provided by A, B and T. Thus the overall social interpretation of the various transactions, as displayed in the diagram, is quite different from the interpretations of the individual firms, whose understanding is limited to their own incomes and expenditures. As a result, the value-creation process, which is a relation between human labour and pieces of paper with numbers on them, remains a complete mystery.

In Figure 21-1 the monetary network is presented in a manner that shows both the overall social reality and the fragmented viewpoints of the individual firms. Only simple arithmetic is needed to understand the economic system, but the social reality cannot be directly interpreted from the firms' viewpoints because all the financial information above the horizontal grey bar is hidden from view and can only be deduced by analysis. This diagram repays close study but we need not dwell on it because all the ground has been covered in previous chapters and the relationships are quite straightforward.

All the incomes for the 309 people in this society are made possible by the prices that the goods sell for. Only the *bulk* values and *bulk* prices are shown in these models. We would need to know the statistics of physical outputs to calculate the unit prices. Such details are superficial in the present context, and do not concern us. If the demand pattern stays constant, and there are no changes to production efficiency, the equilibrium displayed in Figure 15-6 and Figure 21-1 would repeat itself day after day. But if superfluous banknotes enter the system, either from absorption of hoards, or more frequent use of cheques, or from a printing press (legal or otherwise) the total value of goods per day (£6150) will expand, and the general price level will rise. All the money transactions shown in Figures 15-6 and 21-1 will alter. The currency value of £1000 will rise to a new level as the monetary base shrinks and extra notes enter the network. This change in the general price level will be everywhere proportionate in its effects and will generally cause no harm to the people in this society (as long as it is gradual). Everybody's situation is altered in comparison with the past when the currency value changes, but compared with each other they all stay the same. For the present we presume that no superfluous notes are entering the system.

It is important to make these matters clear in order to distinguish each effect and trace its specific cause, and, in particular, to grasp how price and income are related. *Incomes generated are always equal to total selling prices and always equal to incomes spent.* This rule has already been discussed, but we must reconsider it now, in this summary, and grasp its full significance, because it is a rule that can never be broken. The rule was dimly perceived in classical times, formulated haphazardly in different ways by different writers. It has come to be known nowadays as Say's Law, after the French economist J B Say, but it should perhaps be attributed to an earlier French economist, Mercier de la Rivière. We will examine how the orthodox texts deal with Say's Law in the next chapter. For the present we need to understand what it means.

Say's Law. There are no societies of just two people, but simplifications à la Crusoe are sometimes useful. Suppose that you and I are an isolated pair of people who barter our goods regularly, which is quite a realistic possibility, but let us also suppose that we buy our goods from each other using money, a most unrealistic assumption because money can exist only in a large interdependent group. Nevertheless, there is an important line of reasoning to be followed here. Suppose I pay you £100 for your goods every month, and you pay me £100 every month for my goods. This is obviously an equilibrium situation. If your payment was bigger or less than mine, one of us would be accumulating a store of money and the other would be losing money. Our exchange arrangement cannot be balanced and permanent unless the money that passes backward and forward between us is the same in both directions. How much money under these circumstances would we need?

If I settled my bill in the middle of the month, and you paid up at the end of the month, then our monetary base would be £100, which would be in your possession for about two weeks, and then in my possession for two weeks, passing backward and forward between us. The velocity of the currency would be 2, because the same £100 is serving in two transactions that together make a total of £200. But if our bills were settled in cash at exactly the same instant, we would both need to possess £100, and our monetary base would be £200, operating at a velocity of 1.

Now consider how you and I could save money out of our incomes. The sum of money passing between us is £100. It could just as easily be £80 or £15, or a much higher sum. The actual quantity of money is immaterial. The crucial factor is the equality inherent in the barter transaction itself. My goods are rendered equal to your goods by the fact that we exchange them in proportions that satisfy us both. A physical rate of production by me is matched to a physical rate of production by you, and this arrangement continues till our relative preferences, or working circumstances, change. The equilibrium between us then ceases to apply. In such case we must move to a new arrangement in which a different rate of production by me is matched to a different rate of production by you. The match is always, please note, between rates of production that are rendered equal by mutual satisfaction of demand. The equality is the cardinal element. If I buy your goods for £100, or £80 or £15 or any other sum, then in this economy of just two people, you must buy my goods for exactly the same amount. The money that changes hands between you and me, must always be equal to the money that changes hands between me and you.

We can now express this golden rule in terms of a large group of people buying each other's goods. The money that changes hands between all these people when they act as sellers must always be equal to the money that changes hands between all these people when they act as buyers. This is Say's Law, so called, and it strictly follows that no money can ever be saved out of income at the level of society as a whole. The same money just hops backward and forwards, out of some pockets and into other pockets, with a very tight correspondence between the goods and the money, supervised with the utmost care by every seller and buyer. But if there is a float of money, distributed through all the pockets, then the money can accumulate and diminish in the hands of different people, and the strict necessity to buy and sell in interlocked sequence can be relaxed. This is where great confusion arises in economic theory. The link between spending and selling is not relaxed at all by the presence of this float. The float allows people to step outside the buying and selling orbit for a longer or shorter period. But the buying and selling still continues in the sense that for every sale there is always an equal purchase. No seller is ever short of a buyer. If he cannot find a buyer then he is not a seller. If there is no increase of income for the seller then there is no parallel spending of income by the buyer. We must unravel the full social meaning of this intertwined duality that is so easy to understand at the level of a pair of individuals but which becomes a much more elusive concept to grasp in a group where everybody constantly alternates between the roles of seller and buyer. Add the notions of a "float" and "savings" and the complexity deepens. We could easily end up in the same shambles as the textbooks.

If I try to save some of my income and offer only £90 for your goods, hoping to keep £10 in reserve, then only two outcomes are possible. (a) You must make good the deficiency out of your money savings. You will regularly add £10 to the £90 you get from me and continue to buy my goods at £100. Your savings will steadily fall, by £10 per month, and my savings will steadily increase at the same rate. On this basis our arrangement can continue as before. Your savings get less and mine get bigger, but there is neither loss nor gain in net terms. And sooner or later the transfer of savings from you to me must come to an end, when your savings are gone. (b) Now consider the other possibility. When you receive only £90 from me for your goods, you can choose not to use your savings to make good the deficiency. In this case you will offer only £90 for my goods and I will be forced to accept, if the arrangement between us is to continue. Everything will then operate as before, but the monetary base will fall to £90 at velocity 2, or £180 at velocity 1, and I will have acquired a stationary random hoard of £10. Translated to a larger group, our golden rule now expands into two golden rules. The first rule states that the everyday transactions of buying and selling necessarily imply a perfect match between the incomes obtained by the sellers and the incomes spent by the buyers. The second golden rule states that any store of money savings for one person can increase only in so far as another person's store decreases. In short, incomes are always fully spent, and saving is always equal to dis-saving.

To repeat, goods always sell for prices that are necessarily equal to the incomes that such sales generate, so spending and income and sales revenue must always be identical. Facing up to this three-sided equality is a basic requirement for everybody who studies economics. It is in fact very difficult to illustrate. But we can make an approach through Figure 21-2. The production

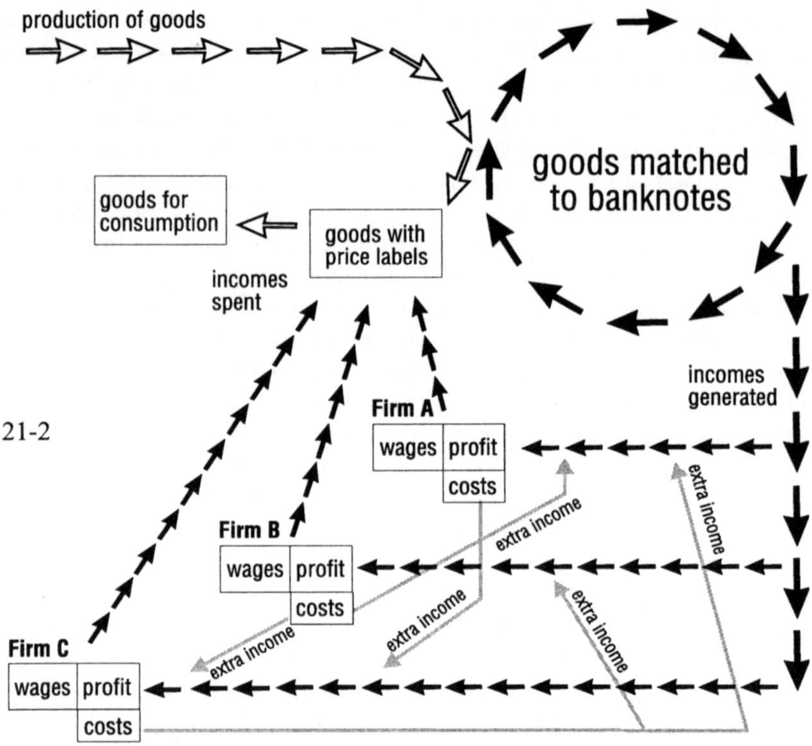

Figure 21-2

process creates goods that acquire a potential value-in-exchange in relation to each other, and at the moment of sale this potential value in the hands of the sellers is translated into money for the seller and simultaneously counter-balanced as an equal loss of money for the buyer. Thus the value inherent in the commodity is matched to an expression of this value inherent in the money, and a cancellation process operates that is a plus on one side and a balancing minus on the other. The goods can be consumed and the money now lies dormant till it is again recharged and discharged with a pulse of value so to speak in the act of exchange with another commodity. An attempt to express this idea can be seen in Figure 21-2. Only three firms are shown but they represent any number of firms, and the grey arrows show how they cancel their costs among themselves when viewed at the level of society as a whole. (Costs are not our concern here, but the diagram is handy to illustrate their self-cancelling irrelevance).

We need to proceed very cautiously here. It seems obvious from the diagram that incomes generated must be equal to incomes spent. This is perfectly true, but not for any reasons that are displayed in Figure 21-2. We would follow a false line of reasoning if we argued as follows:

Clearly there are no leaks and no injections. The arrows travelling down the right-hand side wander through thousands of conduits on their way back to the circulating wheel, but what is lost to the wheel when incomes are created is restored to the wheel when incomes are spent.

This is the general shallow understanding of Say's Law. But such reasoning misses the point. Think of our simple community of two people. Your income is £100 per month but you must never regard this income in terms of itself, because its existence is intertwined with my income, which must also be £100 a month. *You create my income by spending yours, and I create your income by spending mine.* These paired actions are an indissoluble unity. **Incomes spent** is identical with **incomes generated** because these supposedly different entities are just two names for the same thing, which is the **total bulk price** of all the goods sold. Any debate about whether there are leaks or not is nonsensical. All we have before us is one single thing that can be viewed from three angles.

It is very hard to find a sensible analogy to illustrate this triple conjunction, but the following may be helpful. Imagine a ballroom with a dance in progress, the couples being male and female in the usual way. Now allow for substitutions. People can join the dance by replacing one of the paired partners. All the people in the ballroom can now choose to dance for a while and sit down for a while, and the dance will still continue. People will enter and leave the dance as they choose, either by substitution or when some pairs drop out and new pairs join in. Now for a rather far-fetched effort of the imagination. Suppose this is not a dance but a market, and the paired dancers are buyers and sellers negotiating the sale of goods. The buyer hands over money and the seller hands over goods. Each discrete transaction is a self-contained moment. When it ends, the sellers can quit the market, keeping the money they have acquired for a day or a week or longer, like the dancers who sit down for a while. But sooner or later they join the dance as buyers and the money is exchanged again for goods. Where do the goods come from? The goods are manufactured by the dancers when they are away from the dance. Who consumes the goods? The dancers consume the goods when they are sitting down. So the dancers must work for a time, sell their goods to each other to obtain an income, and then use their incomes to buy those self-same goods. *The money earned from selling these goods is the money that buys these goods.* There is *always* a balanced reciprocation, a two-sided interchange which *always* locks the money changing hands to a zero position. The money that is "active" always stays inside the dance, so to speak. A buyer with £10 to spend must find a seller who will accept £10, and at the moment of exchange the money carries value away from one side and transfers this value to the other side. Every buyer is matched by a seller who agrees to accept a sum of money that is *always* the same for both. As the market clears the sellers become buyers, always spending the self-same money that they continuously acquire. Talk about leaks is silly. How can money passing between buyer and seller leak in some way?

The point to grasp about incomes, at a social level of understanding, is that they disappear from one side in the very act that re-creates them for the other side, because the two sides are the same people who simply keep changing places. It is fairly easy to grasp the notion that, in our two-person society, my income rises when you buy my goods, and your reserves suffer an equal loss. But this reciprocal effect is simultaneously generated when I buy your goods. Your income goes up and my reserves fall. These four-way movements always produce a net effect of zero, regardless of how the price may change. There is never a moment when an imbalance exists. So in essence my income does not increase at all by our joint trading activities, and neither does yours. We simply exchange our goods in a continuous stream. Of course the individual view of buying and selling in a large group of people is that money always passes from a buyer to a seller, and everybody acquires an income by selling something. But an economist must not add all these incomes together (over a particular period of time) as though a group of sellers on one side had negotiated with a group of buyers on the other side. He must recognise that the buyers are also the sellers, and that all the money is continuously restored ready to be spent again. This is the reason why Say's Law (correctly understood) expresses a three-sided identity which is bound to be true. *It cannot be false.*

So what mental adjustment should we make in respect of Figure 21-2? We need to grasp the fact that everybody's income springs into existence and is simultaneously spent at the point of sale. Goods are sold every day for a value of £6150. The wheel represents this sum in banknotes which never leaks anywhere. The same £6150 (or some other sum) is constantly regenerated by the buying and selling activity. The marketing group continually restock their sales terminals with goods, and they continually collect the gross revenue that represents the value of these goods. The sum of £6150 can certainly rise and fall, because of leaks or injections in the main circuit. But if it does, then all incomes spent, all incomes generated, and all selling prices, will rise and fall together. These elements are welded into a common identity.

We hammer this point home because it is essential to avoid a facile level of reasoning. Anyone looking at Figure 21-2 can see that goods are bought by the spending of wages and profits, and the money then passes into the possession of the marketing group who restore those wages and profits to their point of origin, so the whole circulation consists of wages and profits being split apart and then joined together. This is obvious with no great effort of thought. But the deeper point to grasp is that neither prices nor incomes nor spending levels can ever be raised or lowered, *in relation to each other,* by changes in relative demand, or savings habits or taxation or spending sprees, or by printing money, or anything else. This is the insight that Say's Law struggles to express (though Say himself had no grasp of its implications, nor any economist since, apart from Marx, who attributes the insight to Mercier de la Rivière not J B Say).

The next diagram, Figure 21-3, is an attempt to express the essence of the matter. Clutter in respect of costs has been removed and all we see is the moment of exchange itself, as far as such a thing can be shown by a diagram. The incomes spent by the buyers determine the size of £X, and the act of spending regenerates the spent incomes for the sellers. The diagram could hardly be simpler. The principle of equality it expresses must be recognised for what it is, because there are no analogies that can help us here. If we think of blood entering the heart being the same as blood leaving the heart we have missed the point. The small arrows are lined up ready for a sale, and every time one of them crosses the sales counter, a quantity of money, be it tuppence or

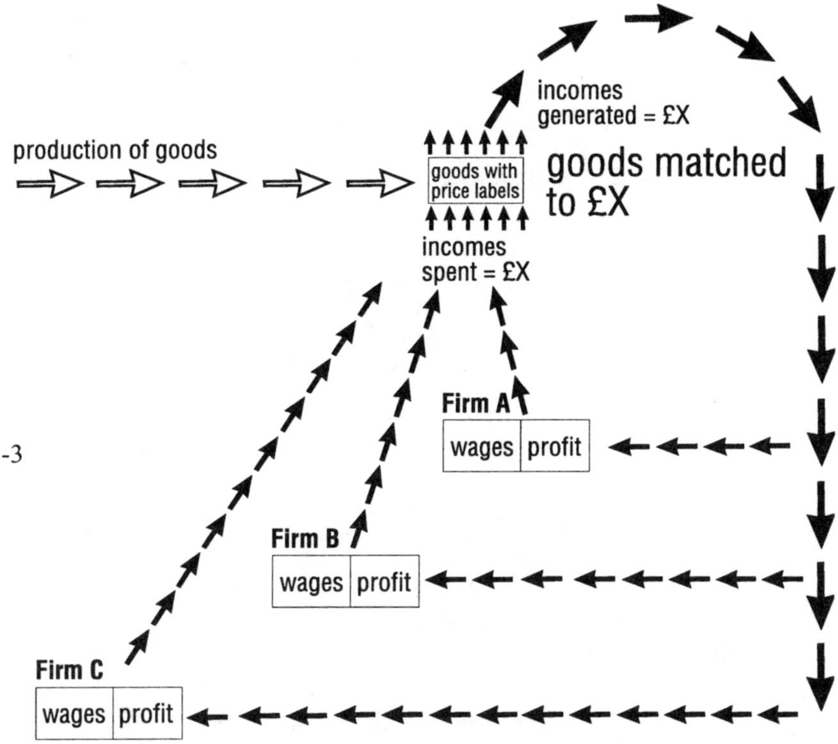

Figure 21-3

£1000, vanishes from one side and reappears on the other. The departure of the money is the arrival of the money. There is no gap or shortfall or reservoir or separation of any kind, because goods are bought in the moment that they are sold, and the price expresses the exact amount that leaves one side and emerges on the other. It may seem to the reader that this matter is being worked over at unnecessary length, but it has great theoretical and historical importance, as we will discover in the next chapter.

So when we gaze at Figure 15-6 (or Figure 21-1) we see first of all a steady repetition of the production/consumption cycle that sustains life at a certain standard. Goods are manufactured every day and are sold every day for £6150. This money from gross sales is used by S to buy fresh goods every day for £5125, and to pay wages and costs as detailed. The £5125 pays wages and costs for CDEFG. Costs always become the incomes of other firms, and in this way the wages and profits for A, B and T are paid. For all firms the total of wages and costs is less than income, and the difference is their respective profits. Every pound sterling is accounted for, and the "golden rules" mentioned above are exemplified. Incomes spent are always equal to incomes generated. Nobody is saving a penny, because saving that reduces spending ***is impossible.*** Saving is possible only when it reduces somebody else's savings. All the money magnitudes on the printed page stay constant while the cycle of buying and spending, producing and consuming, is repeated continuously day after day. The monetary system itself imposes the rigid linkages that keep all magnitudes

Figure 21-4.

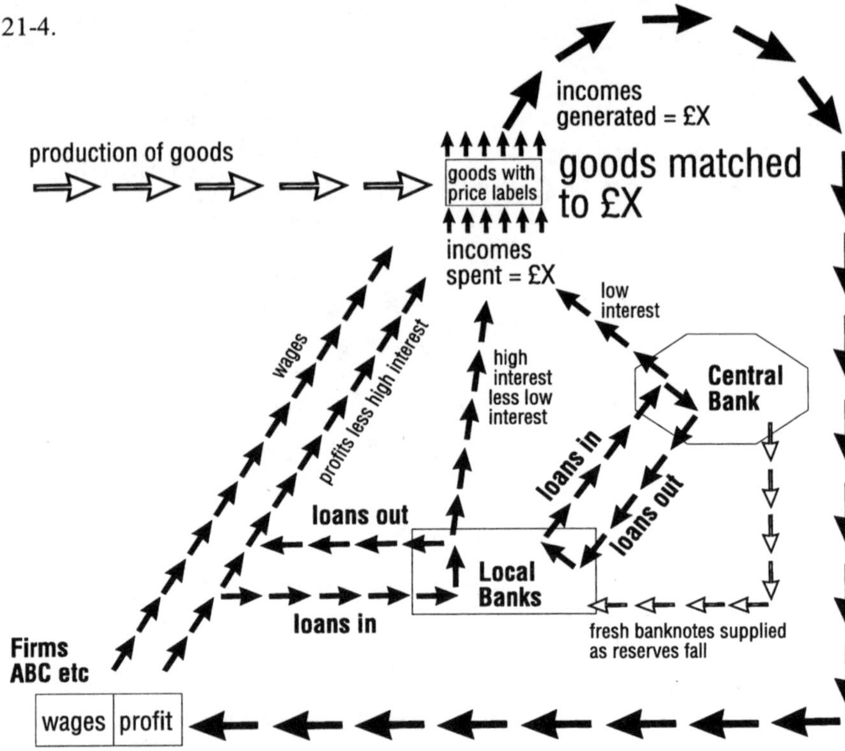

constant. This imposed regime does not of course lie outside human control like some alien force. The monetary network is adaptable in all sorts of ways, if its simple arithmetic is understood and complied with. But not in the absence of this knowledge. The rules of arithmetic are not suspended anywhere on the earth for anybody.

The uniform rate of profit is the equilibrium point that keeps the respective outputs of each firm constant, to match a particular pattern of demand. It is worth re-emphasising at this point that the monetary system is inherently efficient. It matches supply to demand with maximum benefit for everybody, and this standard is continuously maintained (neglecting time lags) throughout all changes in relative demand or production capability. In other words, there is nothing capitalist about any of the diagrams in this chapter so far. They merely illustrate the workings of a monetary economy.

Figure 15-6 and Figure 21-1 can now be visualised correctly. The constant magnitudes on the page actually depict a daily repetition of buying and selling and income generation. All the magnitudes shown are wiped out and renewed every day. If we introduce any changes, we can never break the rule that incomes generated are equal to incomes spent, and equal to the prices paid, and on this understanding we can introduce the capitalist shell as in Figure 21-4.

The bankers are now present. The local banks have an essential social role in managing the float for a money-based economy, but in a capitalist society their second essential role is to negotiate steadily expanding loans with employers. Every time loans are increased, the cash reserves in the local banks fall. These reserves are restored by new banknotes, printed by the central bank and issued in loans to the local banks. The new banknotes inflate the currency value, meaning that the purchasing power of money falls. The effect is to raise profits and depress wages in ways we have already described in detail in Chapter 20.

The money-lending illusion. There is a wide-spread assumption that money-lenders are a source of money. We already know that this view is false but a recapitulation of key issues in simple analogies is always useful, because illusions about money are deeply embedded in our everyday thinking.

If, in January, I lend £1000, to be paid back in ten equal monthly instalments, then my outlay will be restored to me at £100 per month. (Forget about interest for the moment). In February I lend another £1000, on the same terms, to a fresh client. I do the same in March, then in April and so on till ten months have gone by. When the eleventh month arrives, the drain on my financial resources will come to an end. As long as I maintain my money-lending activity, at a rate of £1000 loaned per month, on the terms stated, my receipts from the repaid instalments will also be £1000 per month. I can now maintain my money-lending business indefinitely, because it will cost me nothing. My clients are in effect providing their own loans, and I am just acting as an intermediary.

So to start my money-lending business, I would need £1000 per month for each of ten clients. But repayments of £100 per month would start in the second month and continue to grow each subsequent month. Allowing for these repayments, I would need only £5500 in total to get the ten loans into operation. From then on, the loans would maintain themselves without any more money from me.

But of course I would gain nothing if the instalments merely returned the money I had loaned. The notion of interest now enters the calculations. If my loans are based on a simple overall percentage return of 10% on £1000, the repayments will be £110 per month. The extra £10 in interest will reduce my original outlay by £100, to £5400, and on the eleventh month an income of £100 per month would appear. This income for me would continue as long as my lending business continued, and everybody would think I was lending money regularly every month. But my supposed loans would just be money recycled from other people's money, not from my own. Thus, in the round, I forfeit a sum of money to get my business started, but once an endless loop is in operation, money coming in is greater than money going out, and I can keep the difference.

Of course most people understand that a money-lender is in business to "make money", and this money can only come from his clients. Therefore it is obvious that the money-lending operation can never *supply* money to the clients, it always *extracts* money for the lender. The appearance of gain to the borrower is quite accurate at the start of the loan period. But this gain is balanced by loss to the borrower at the end of the load period, plus an extra loss to the borrower called interest. No money is created by such dealings and anybody who really thinks about the matter is unlikely to be deceived. The clearest thinker in fact will describe the above transactions from a social standpoint, as follows:

> *Ten people agree to pay a financial agent £110 every month, and he agrees to give £1000 to each of them in turn, at intervals of one month. The payments to the agent in total are £1100 every month, and every month he pays out £1000 and keeps £100. The agent uses his own funds to get started, but after a certain point the transactions provide him with a continuous income.*

The above description, which is simply a social overview, is of course the same as the theoretical perspective of the bona fide economist. Then why is this social understanding absent when the lending activities of the banker, or venture capitalist, are in view? These people, we are told in the standard texts, *create* wealth, because the client gets richer, and the banker gets richer. Nobody suffers a corresponding loss, so it would seem that all the reasoning about money-lending set out above must not apply to the banker. It is here that the illusion springs to life and the textbooks take their cue, singing the virtues of the capitalist financier as a social benefactor who abstains from spending and invests his money to stimulate employment and create social wealth. A hymn of praise pours forth for these blessed abstainers whose recompense in the life hereafter is miraculously enjoyed in the present. This chorus is strictly for the gullible multitude. No genuine investigator is deceived by the pretensions of money-lenders. Of course a sanctifying smoke-screen of some kind is needed by these well-heeled apostles of self-denial, and so we see everywhere a deification of money itself, worshipped as the Great Enabler, invested with mysterious powers, dressed up in doctrinal gibberish by the high priests of marginalism.

The real source of the wealth supposedly created by the capitalist financier is decipherable from Figure 21-4, given that we can visualise the diagram in dynamic operation. It is easy to insert actual amounts for all the profits, wages and prices in this diagram, but if we did so, we would not display a capitalist society. All the elements of a capitalist society would be present, but they must interact in a progressive time sequence in order to reveal and maintain themselves. Remember that the loans must *increase* in order to drain the reserves of the local banks, and from this reduction in reserves comes the need to replenish with new banknotes. These new banknotes enter the system and raise *bulk* prices while rising productivity holds *unit* prices constant. The rising bulk prices bring higher profits. Part of these higher profits go into the employer's income and the rest takes the form of interest for the bankers. This is the essence of the exploitation system called capitalism.

If we inserted actual amounts for the profits, wages and prices, these numbers would be stationary on the page. Interest would be present, flowing into the banks as income. But the justification for this interest, which is paid by the employer, would be missing. No successful firm borrows money continuously from moneylenders as a preferred source of funding (credit is a different matter, not considered as yet in our analysis) so the mere renewal of loans cannot be a regular part of any kind of free economy. Such loans would soon come to an end, in which case there would be no interest to provide an income for the banks. Nevertheless, as long as the local banks were able to continue as administrators of everybody's deposits, such a society would be perfectly viable. It would be Society A or Society C in Figure 6-5 (page 69). Neither of these societies is capitalist. Neither of them possesses any means for raising the currency value. These societies do not suffer from hidden inflation because we assume that no random hoards are being absorbed, the cheque system is widespread but no longer expanding, and nobody is printing banknotes except as replacements for wear and tear. In Society A there is no expansion of outputs (or outputs that would have risen are cancelled by a shorter working day), while in Society C all outputs are steadily rising and unit prices are falling. In Society A standard of living is constant, but it is steadily rising in Society C. These are the consequences that would follow if we inserted constant magnitudes into Figure 21-4. There would be no place for bankers.

How do we operate our diagram so that it represents a *capitalist* society? We must ensure a continuously expanding loans system. Three typical outcomes will then present themselves, also illustrated in Figure 6-5. In Society B, loans are expanding, the reserves are falling in the local banks, and notes are being printed, while productivity is constant. Inflation is in full view because unit prices are rising. In Society D, loans are expanding and notes are being printed, but rising productivity is holding unit prices constant. Inflation is present but it is all hidden, apart from a progressive reduction in the purchasing power of money. In Society E, loans are expanding in excess of productivity, causing both hidden and visible inflation.

No doubt these circumstances could be portrayed in a series of diagrams like Figure 21-4, displaying the relevant magnitudes, spreading across several pages. But on this occasion we can allow Figure 21-4 to speak for itself. All the essential features of a capitalist economy are present if the model is operated as described. This is the platform we will take forward to Volume Two.

22

Twentieth century economists

The theoretical understanding that is summarised in our diagrams was more or less achieved by the end of the nineteenth century, though the leading nations were still on the gold standard and the transition to an exclusively paper economy had not been explored. Otherwise all the main features were present, spread patchily through the works of many writers, but comprehensively drawn together in Marx's work *Capital.* The level of abstraction in the opening section of that work is too high for most people, including me, and the fact that the transformation of values into prices was delayed till the third volume, published by Engels more than a decade after Marx's death, prevented the first volume from having direct relevance to a realistic economy. The main exposition therefore depended heavily on a theoretical cornerstone, the so-called labour theory of value, which is very vulnerable to misinterpretation, especially when a key part of the analysis (the link from value to price) is located elswhere. These defects were fatal. After Engels' death, Marx's economic research slowly died on its feet, while an army of usurpers stepped into his shoes, keen to use its revolutionary content for their own ends. The 1917 Russian revolution and the works of Lenin (still one of the most translated writers in the world) spread Marx's name like wildfire. In addition, the two world wars, the Depression and the banking collapse of 1929 seemed to foreshadow the demise of capitalism that Marx had predicted. When China and other territories entered the marxian fold, the spectre (or promised land) of communism became a vast living reality supposedly conjured into being by the teachings of Marx, but in fact not linked in any way to his advances in theoretical understanding. In Europe and America the entire heritage of classical economics was thrown out and replaced by marginalism. Marx was transmogrified into a demon or messiah bestriding the entire world, while economics as a genuine field of learning disappeared both in the East and the West. No great thinker has ever influenced the world so much and so little.

Donning its new marginalist garb in the early 20th century, the economics profession lost every vestige of integrity. For the last hundred years it has spread a fog of dedicated ignorance about capitalism while the system itself has reached every corner of the globe. During this time, various lines of enquiry have appeared, giving the required impression that the discipline of economics can conduct research just like any other body of learning. This masquerade is set out below in a listing of prominent names. (The list is not claimed to be comprehensive. My own reading background in this immense multi-language field is necessarily limited, only sketchy or second-hand as far as some of these writers are concerned, very detailed in respect of others).

1 Böhm-Bawerk, Hilferding, Lenin, Stalin, Mao.
2 Bortkiewicz, Luxemburg, Tugan-Baranovsky, Robinson, Steedman.
3 Cournot, Walras, Edgeworth, Fisher, Phillips, Laffer.
4 Weblen, Galbraith.
5 Luxemburg, Dobb, Mandel.
6 Jevons, Marshal, Keynes, Hicks, Sraffa, Leontief, Schumpeter, Solow.

(1) The writers in this group have an important historical connection. Böhm-Bawerk wrote a critical assessment of Marx's economic theories, and Hilferding produced a reply. Böhm-Bawerk's intellectual grasp was not adequate for the task he set himself. The reply from Hilferding is worth reading, but it is strictly a defence based on broad generalisations. His inability to counter Böhm-Bawerk in concrete detail reveals that Hilferding had no grasp of economics. Lenin developed Hilferding's ideas, but basic economic theory in Lenin's writings is just borrowed from Marx and repeated parrot fashion, to serve the revolutionary cause. Political commitment likewise dominates the works of Stalin and Mao, intermixed with dialectical jargon. I make no comment about these personages as heroes or villians in their historical circumstances. It may well be that their writings had a political impact that moved mountains. But in terms of any contribution to economic understanding the rating of all these writers is zero.

(2) These writers all examined Marx's version of price formation based on the labour theory of value. They all concluded that the theory was defective, and in some cases, corrections or solutions were offered to keep the gist of the theory viable. All these writers were wasting their time. By proving that a commodity's price could not be determined by its labour-time, they were merely re-working an old problem that the classical economists continually wrestled with. Adam Smith had grasped that labour-time was the ultimate determinant, but he knew perfectly well that a commodity's price was not a direct equivalent for the working time needed to produce that commodity. (How obvious this connection would be if it were true). The link between labour-time and value was the problem to be solved, and such a problem is not solved by declaring that the link does not exist. The link was fathomed by Marx, but neither these writers nor any economists since, down to this day, have the remotest understanding of his solution. (Look up "the labour theory of value" in any current economics dictionary or reference work and see what a hash they make of it). So in words as clear and as loud as possible, let us state once and for all that the value of a commodity is not determined by its *own* labour time. Any such suggestion is quite absurd. The value of a commodity is expressed when the labour-times of all commodities are compared against one commodity's labour-time chosen as a standard. Each commodity then acquires a value-form derived from a

commensurable basis of comparison, using a scale provided by the standard commodity's labour-time, just as the different speeds of several trains can all be expressed by using one train's speed as a scalar unit. From this value-form a price arises which can vary independently of the value, in response to competition in the market place, but the sum of the prices is always equal to the sum of the values. *This is the labour theory of exchange-value and price*, and if any writer has subjected this theory to critical examination and found it wanting, I have not heard of him or her.

(3) Cournot (a nineteenth century economist) tinkered with the mathematical relation between bulk price and unit price, seeking (without success) some kind of formula that would encompass the price system as a whole. Walras similarly searched for a mathematical equilibrium, and thought he had found it in a system of simultaneous equations which links every price with every other price. Such equations stretch from here to the moon and have no practical application. (But this line of approach does contain a glimmer of truth. Simultaneous equations are used to calculate how a particular commodity can quantify itself in relation to other commodities and thereby serve as money for monopolist producers who freely exchange their goods among themselves. This is an important area of theoretical understanding, but the algebraic relation applies only to prices in a simple economy of monopolists, like the three-farmers society in Chapter 1. The numeraire that arises in such an economy is identical with the price-form, but in a large society of freely competing producers, the price-form is just a straight-forward ratio with no algebraic linkages. If this distinction is not understood, the equations become absurd, especially if they are contaminated by *unit* price notions). Nevertheless these two nineteenth century pioneers gave a lead to other like-minded economists, and from time to time names are linked to discoveries about alleged mathematical correlations concerning this or that aspect of the economy. None of these alleged correlations has ever thrown much light on anything, but economists skilled in calculus, matrix algebra and regression analysis are constantly publishing material of this nature, which nobody reads but themselves.

(4) These writers have nothing new to offer in economic theory but are perceptive enough to dissociate themselves from the prevailing orthodoxy in varying degrees, ranging from open contempt to mild disdain. Many names could be quoted in this category.

(5) To continue or amplify Marx's theoretical work, in a selected part or the whole, at a standard of impartial scholarship, is the aim of these writers. No critical comment is appropriate here because we are not assessing serious work.

(6) These names are drawn from writers of the orthodox persuasion, but two are slightly off-beat. Sraffa wrote a short work which begins well, at the level of elementary barter, but is hopelessly lost after about three pages. Leontief laboured to produce very detailed coefficients that link all the factorial input/output relationships of the main spheres of production, hoping presumably to throw light in some shape or form on their prices. No such light appeared, and his work, like Sraffa's, is a kind of byway in economic theory preserved by a school of followers who think there is something worthwhile in their own special

line. The other names in this group are conventional marginalists. Jevons and Marshall are transitional figure leading to Keynes, and the others follow in Keynes' footsteps with refinements of one sort or another. It is Keynes who is important in this group because he is by far the most influential writer in the field of orthodox economics in the twentieth century.

The above list and comments might seem to be a sudden departure from the analysis we have pursued throughout this book, but in fact this classification is closely related to the main diagram in the previous chapter. The essential features of a money-based economy are shown in Figure 21-1 (page 244). The individual firms in this society are in open view to any investigator, but the information above the horizontal grey bar is hidden. Without this hidden information, the linkages between the firms is a mystery. The history of economic research from the seventeenth century onwards, excluding the twentieth, is a record of struggle to understand this mystery. The first step facing any investigator is to understand Figure 21-3, which shows the three-sided identity of £X, an identity that must be recognised because it is intrinsic to a money-based system of exchange. (Several classical authors had a tenuous understanding of this identity, now dismissively baptised as Say's Law). Once this identity is clearly grasped, the society of Figure 21-1 can (eventually) be deciphered, allowing the information above the horizontal grey bar to come into view. The next hurdle for the investigator is Figure 21-4, which shows how a capitalist society is grafted to a money-based society. The full picture is now present, and this is the basis on which we make our judgements about the writers in the above list.

It is extraordinary that a body of knowledge assembled from many eighteenth and nineteenth century writers should have come to such an abrupt end early in the succeeding century. But an examination of Keynes' main work, *The General Theory of Employment, Interest and Money,* enables us to see how this was accomplished. In the opening pages, Keynes directly confronts the three-sided identity shown in Figure 21-3. He quotes from J S Mill and then refers to a statement from Marshall, that if a man's income wasn't spent one way, then it was spent in another. The passage he quotes from Mill leaves us in no doubt that Mill had grasped the essence of Figure 21-3, and we can also credit Marshall with a glimmer of this understanding. (Marshall elsewhere uses an apt scissors analogy, where supply and demand are likened to the two blades which must always act together to confer cutting power on each other). But Keynes' own understanding of this matter lay far below Mill's or even Marshall's. Keynes thought that the equality between incomes and spending was merely a balance that money achieved when it wandered through a labyrinth of conduits and eventually found its way back to its source, and most economists held (and still hold) the same view, that earning, spending and saving share a kind of haphazard compensation with each other that will tend to balance out in the long run if the economy functions normally. Mill was much more emphatic, and rightly so, because he knew that the equality was inherent in the money/goods exchange relation itself, a necessary condition of its very existence, and had nothing to do with compensations, long-run or short, or how well the economy was operating. For Keynes, the concept of "investment" is part of this supposed compensation and he argues that the balance might not in fact be achieved, not even in the long run, because when incomes rose, people were tempted to save a little more, producing a shortfall in this supposed compensation. And not only a shortfall according to Keynes, who had his thinking cap on and no mistake, but a *worsening* shortfall, because people tended to save more and more in proportion to their income as it increased. Economists everywhere who were trying to make sense of the classical tradition were at last liberated from the necessity of doing so, by this revelation of a truth so blindingly obvious on its own terms that they were annoyed not to have thought of it themselves. Fame was heaped on Keynes, who had discovered why the economic system worked so badly, with dole queues and rampant inflation, when according to classical understanding, everything interacted with everything else through the medium of money and therefore a permanent or stationary disequilibrium was impossible. Keynes repudiated this line of thought completely. In essence he repudiated Say's Law. A disequilibrium *can* exist, he declared. Thus was classical dogma overthrown and economic theory brought into line with reality. But all that Keynes had achieved was an abandonment of genuine enquiry, substituting a specious rigmarole that conjured the real problem out of existence.

The layers of confusion in *The General Theory* are quite extraordinary. Armed with his new economic concept, "the propensity to consume", Keynes ingeniously weaves together his own definitions of income, savings and investment. Prominent from the start is "user cost". This refers to the income of the entrepreneur. For example, the owner of Firm T (Figure 21-1) has an income (profit) of £82. Keynes would explain this income by comparing the transport business profit with the money the owner would obtain by selling his fleet of trucks, vans, sheds, equipment, etc, on the open market. If the owner could get more by selling them, or putting them to some alternative use, he would do so. If not, then he continues in business. The break-even point that makes his business worthwhile is so-called "user cost", and this "explains" where the £82 comes from. It also shows that the entrepreneur is just like everybody else, making economic choices in his own best interests.

Thus the status quo is justified by a train of marginalist reasoning that always avoids any contact with real data. The marginalist never deals in specifics. He never confronts a magnitude such as the £82 in our diagram, with the intention of explaining how its qualitative and quantitative attributes arise from the real relationships that surround it. The marginalist's technique is to avoid all such pother. He possesses no information whatever about, say, your weight. He just tells you that when you stand on the scales, you balance your weight against a moving pointer which comes to rest in a certain position. This is called the marginal position, and that's your weight, whoever you are. You do not need to step on any scales. Your weight is identified by its marginal name and this can be inserted as a symbol into certain fancy equations and produce results that are very impressive because other fellow marginalists are very impressed by them. If you insist on knowing what your particular weight is, you will be regarded as a moron incapable of handling abstract mathematical procedures. The big thinkers use the greek alphabet to sort their ideas, while the little thinkers just rummage with a stick. This grading of competence is an important elitist hallmark in the economics world. Its effect is to fill the higher ranks of the profession with maths experts who know nothing about economics.

Having explained where the owner's profit comes from, using the concept of "user cost" (terminology that refers to how the owner makes best use of his own assets by forgoing alternative choices), Keynes now unpacks his notion of wages. The important issue here is the distinction between "nominal wage" and "real wage". This is certainly a valid distinction. In Figure 21-1 for instance, every financial number is "nominal" because we have no statistics about actual outputs. £82 is a sum of money that might buy a lot or a little of anything. Standard of living is not specified. But what point does Keynes wish to make about this rather obvious distinction?

He has a very important message in respect of wages. The real wage, says Keynes, is inversely correlated with employment. When employment rises, the real wage goes down, and Keynes provides a neat little mathematical footnote to prove his point. The gist of it is this. If an extra man is employed who does not pull his weight in terms of average productivity, the output per man will fall, so real wages must also fall. Ten men producing ten bushels is an average of one bushel per man. But eleven men producing 10.9 bushels is less than one bushel per man. These eleven men cannot now expect to be paid the value of one bushel each. The last man's effect on average productivity always sets the level of their joint entitlement, which must be measured in real terms, not according to a nominal entitlement that was in force before the last man appeared.

Anyone who urges this line of reasoning is on very shaky ground. If I have £10 and you have £5 then I can buy twice the goods that you can buy. This statement is true no matter what real goods the nominal money will buy. A smaller nominal income always means *a smaller real proportion.* And in a closed economy this smaller real proportion must correspond to a larger real proportion for somebody else. If eleven men work less productively than ten men, each of them will suffer a reduction in individual consumption when the eleventh man joins the group. But if nominal wages are £1 each, the wage bill will simply change from £10 to £11, and no nominal reduction is called for, because each £1 now corresponds to a slightly smaller amount of the total product. Money fixes proportions, not quantities. It doesn't matter two hoots what the nominal wage is. If everybody gets the *same* wage, then they all get the same relative share of the product. The relation between the total product and the number of producers is determined by a simple division sum, and no manipulation with money can alter that. The reasoning employed by Keynes could be presented honestly if he discussed the elementary mathematical rules of proportion, understandable by a schoolchild. Furthermore, why concentrate solely on wages? If the distinction between real wages and nominal wages needs to be examined, surely we should also make a similar examination of real profits and nominal profits, real costs and nominal costs, real loans and nominal loans, real taxes and nominal taxes, etc. He does not mention these.

Of course Keynes has the entrepreneur in mind. The entrepreneur is very keen to employ the eleventh man if productivity per man rises as a result, because although the wage bill will rise from £10 to £11, the profit/wage ratio will rise and so will the entrepreneur's profit. But he is opposed to employing the eleventh man if productivity per man falls, because the profit/wage ratio will fall, and the rise in the wage bill from £10 to £11 will reduce his profit. Such reasoning is perfectly sensible from the entrepreneur's point of view, and Keynes renders him great service by spinning a yarn about nominal wages and real wages to keep these bald facts hidden.

We may summarise his book as follows. Keynes attacks the classical notion of an automatic equilibrium in the buying and selling network and invents several bogus concepts to explain why. The "propensity to consume" explains lack of demand in the economy. "User cost" explains the motivation of the capitalist. "Real wages" explains the situation of the labourer. "Investment" is a special category of savings. And so on. These are woven into a theoretical exposition which exudes an air of great authority but it is all nonsense.

We have dwelt at length on Keynes because his destructive floundering centres on an area of immense confusion in economic theory, namely, the illusion that demand and supply are variables which operate independently of each other. This illusion was recognised by the classical writers. Their understanding was more than the simple fact that supply and demand are linked in ways that had to be explained. They were also vaguely aware that the link was *absolute.* It couldn't be broken. (An insight nicknamed nowadays as Say's Law). There is only one way forward from this position. The real features of a monetary economy must be explained in conformity with an absolute prerequisite. Everything must be explained on the basis of an indissoluble identity that we have asserted many times in this book, namely, *the total selling price of all goods is the same as the total of incomes created and the same as the total of incomes spent. All incomes originate from this primary source.* It is simply impossible for any supposed deficiency or time lag or leakage or act of saving or anything else to interfere with this identity, any more than I can turn myself into two different people, one hungry and one satisfied, by refusing to eat my dinner. The supply of food which my body receives is always equal to its intake. This rule cannot be broken no matter whether I gorge myself or starve to death. Keynes and all the other neo-classical economists abandon this position and try to explain the behaviour of the economy by alleging a mismatch between aggregate social demand and social supply. This standpoint is simply ridiculous, because goods are always bought with the incomes that are created by the buying activity itself. The price paid always expresses the effective demand, which rises or falls as the price rises or falls, because *bulk price* and *effective demand* are just two names for the same thing.

We in turn must confront this illusion and strip away its mystery. We must not allow ourselves to take for granted the apparent freedom of buyers and sellers to negotiate in any way they please. We must add the circumstance that they are all constrained by the simultaneous generation of income, which is an automatic outcome of those negotiations. An overall unity is bound to be present in the buying and selling nexus when it is considered from the viewpoint of society as a whole. The total of goods produced is the total of goods which are exchanged for each other and then consumed. Money is just an agent in the proportionate distribution of these goods, and the interaction of buyers and sellers is merely a distribution system that allocates all the goods in accordance with the combined preferences of the entire community. If demand and supply are treated as independent variables then this unity is lost and plausible drivel takes the place of reasoned analysis. A galloping horse cannot be explained by saying that the rear legs are chasing after the front ones. A blazing fire cannot be explained by saying that excess heat is pushing the temperature up. But you will find "demand-pull" and "cost-push" explanations in the textbooks which are just as silly. In fact, ever since marginalist theory appeared, the standard economics textbook has been nothing but a catalogue of such stupidities, dressed up to look like knowledge.

Numbered pieces of paper pass from buyer to seller, and everybody competes to obtain as many of these notes as possible in the exchange of goods. The numbered notes acquire a quantitative value that acts as an index of the production rates of the commodities, providing a means whereby these rates can be altered to suit the overall level of satisfaction associated with a particular bulk supply. In other words, competition for the notes reduces their value in terms of goods that are relatively scarce (meaning that more notes are offered to buy such goods) creating an incentive to increase the supply and vice versa. An equilibrium is reached when the bulk supply of all goods matches the aggregate pattern of relative demand for society as a whole. The value acquired by the notes in terms of goods has no intrinsic meaning and continually alters to maintain a correspondence between bulk supply and aggregate demand, but this adjustment is hidden from view. The individual buyers and sellers negotiate on the basis of *the unit price*, which is a ratio imposed by the bulk exchange rate prevailing in the market as a whole. The unit price is significant for the individual, but it is *the bulk price* (quantity of the whole supply of a commodity exchanged for a certain quantity of notes) that is significant for intelligent understanding of how the economy works.

The above description applies to a monetary economy whether it operates within a capitalist shell or not. When the capitalist shell is introduced, none of the above relationships change. Firms still search as before for the equilibrium that corresponds to a uniform rate of profit, and this equilibrium also corresponds to a balance between supply and effective aggregate demand as determined by level of income. Capitalist firms are not agents for the exploitation of workers in a direct feudal sense. The exploitation arises at systemic level. The banking system introduces hidden inflation by supplying freshly printed notes to maintain cash reserves in the local banks. This inflation is (ideally) never visible as a rise in unit prices, because it is counterbalanced by steadily increasing output of goods. The only outwardly visible evidence is the year by year depreciation in the purchasing power of money. When unit prices are held constant by this hidden inflation, bulk prices rise in step with rising productivity and the profit/wage ratio also rises because wages are fixed by negotiation on the basis of time worked, whereas profit is a remainder. The general level of profits is determined by the profit/wage ratio. The lever that continually raises the profit/wage ratio is the expansion of loans which drains the cash reserves of the local banks, who must then restock with fresh notes by means of loans from the central bank.

The science of economics elucidates these matters, and, like every other science, attempts to show how the interaction of the moving parts is related to the integrity of the dynamic whole. This is the course we have followed throughout this book, as strictly as possible, making use of models that operate at the level of concrete magnitudes.

A

Appendix: the graphical representation of demand, supply and price

The point made in the Introduction that price is an *outcome* and cannot therefore act as a cause in respect of its own antecedents is sufficient to demolish the textbook approach based on so-called demand and supply curves. But we should look more closely at these curves because they are part of an orthodoxy that has insinuated itself into centres of learning throughout the educated world, and such a successful hoax, lasting now for more than a century, draws its strength from more falsehoods than one.

The correlations between demand and supply and price can be expressed in two simple statements. (We will review these statements later but they serve our purposes for the present). *The price rises when demand rises relative to supply, or when supply falls relative to demand. The price falls when demand falls relative to supply, or when supply rises relative to demand.* These statements cannot be pared down further. Price is not correlated to demand on its own, nor to supply on its own. The price is responsive to a *relation* between demand and supply. Once this fact is recognised then the idea of a "demand curve" or a "supply curve" begins to look suspicious, because such notions suggest that the two interdependent variables of demand and supply have been separated from each other.

Of course it is perfectly possible to study the separate behaviour of two interdependent variables, simply by holding one of them constant while the other is allowed to vary. We can hold the supply constant and examine the behaviour of the price when the demand varies, or hold the demand constant and examine how the price responds to changes in the supply. We need two clear definitions first. Demand is defined as the bulk quantity of money that is offered and accepted in exchange for a given commodity in the market as a whole. The supply is defined as the bulk quantity of this particular commodity in such an exchange. Note particularly that these two bulk quantities are measured in terms of a particular time period, say a day or a year, and they are therefore *rates, or magnitudes per unit of time.* These rates can be scaled on the axes of a simple graph, demand on the vertical axis and supply on the horizontal axis. Coordinates may be drawn to show how these two variables express themselves in the form of *a price agreed between buyers and sellers in respect of a particular bulk quantity*, and either coordinate may be held constant while the other is

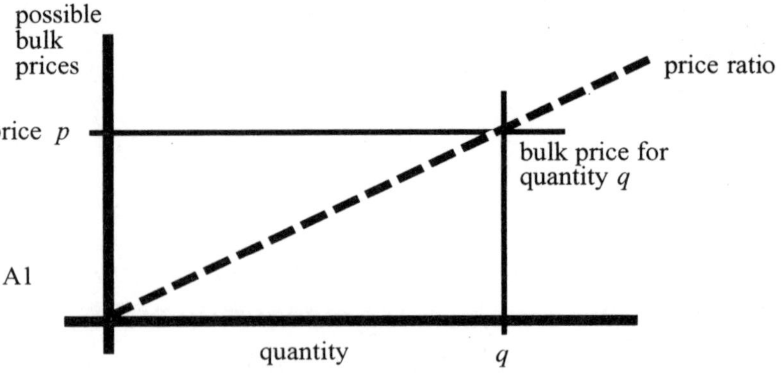

Figure A1

freely manipulated. Such a graph is shown in Figure A1. No time period is specified, but since goods are bought and sold in a continuous stream it is obvious that the exchange between goods and money is a time-based relationship. So the graph must represent a particular time period, say one day, in which case the agreed price p is the quantity of money per day that is used to purchase a quantity of goods q supplied per day. On this basis, the bulk price for a given bulk quantity can be accurately defined in terms which correspond to measurable reality. It is most important to understand the link to time, because it applies only to the **bulk price for a specified quantity of goods**. The **unit price** is a mathematical derivative which has an entirely different relation to time. This distinction will be clarified as we proceed.

Competition between buyers pushes the price up, while competition between sellers pulls the price down. These two counteracting tendencies resolve themselves into an agreed quantity of money exchanged for a certain quantity of commodity across the market as a whole. The preliminary sums of money quoted by either side can range anywhere up and down the vertical axis, but an actual price does not exist until agreement is reached by both sides. At that moment the price becomes a reality. A specified quantity of goods and a specified quantity of money change hands. (As already explained we must visualise this as a dynamic rate of flow between all buyers and all suppliers in respect of a given commodity). The graph shows this point of agreement, when a double transfer of ownership takes place, and a real price comes into stable continuous existence, for both sides. This price is *the demand price* for a particular bulk quantity of a commodity supplied in a particular time period. It is the price that buyers (in aggregate) are willing to pay, and sellers (in aggregate) are willing to accept. Any notion that this bulk selling-and-buying price can be split into two forms, calling for two separate graphs, one referring solely to buyers and the other referring solely to sellers, is nonsense. There is no such thing as a price range for buyers alone or for sellers alone. A price exists only when both sides agree. This price is the bulk price. It is plotted on the vertical scale as a sum of money whose coordinate intersects with the bulk quantity coordinate, and the graph must necessarily specify a time period, because we are dealing with a sustained continuous process.

The broken line in Figure A1 connecting the intersection point to the origin of the graph enables the quantities and prices of all the individual purchases to be read off, and all these individual purchases, small or large, conform to a uniform price ratio, expressed in terms of a price for one gallon or one ounce or one metre or one item or other convenient unit. It is essential to understand that this unit price has no direct link to time, and hence it must always be clearly distinguished from the bulk price. The bulk price and the bulk quantity are magnitudes that express the flow rate of money being continuously spent in exchange for a commodity which is also flowing at a certain rate through the market from production to consumption. The unit price reduces these two *magnitudes-per-time* to a ratio in which one is expressed in terms of the other, and therefore both magnitudes are lost. Magnitudes are always lost when they are expressed as a ratio. An example will make this clear. If the bulk quantity of bicycles sold is fifty *per day*, at a bulk price of £5000 *per day*, then each bike sells for £100. The quoted magnitudes, and the "*per day*" disappear in the expression of the unit price because the £100 is just a ratio. If the bulk quantity is seventy bikes per day, at a bulk price of £7000 per day, the unit price is still £100. If the bulk quantity is seventy bikes *per month*, at a bulk price of £7000 *per month,* the unit price is still £100. The market situation for bikes (bulk quantity sold at a given bulk price *per unit of time*) can therefore change in various ways, but the behaviour of the unit price is never an indicator of such changes. In other words, it is impossible to glean information about the behaviour of market prices from the unit price alone. This fact needs to be forcibly emphasised, because great confusion reigns in this area. The unit price is a ratio between magnitudes and it therefore contains no specific information about those magnitudes. I may be twice as heavy as you, but nobody can deduce your weight or mine from this ratio on its own. In economic analysis, the magnitudes that matter are bulk price and bulk quantity per unit of time across the market as a whole. The unit price is a superficial derivative.

We learn four things from Figure A1. *First*, there is a *bulk price* for the total quantity of this commodity passing through the market, and this is the price that is scaled on the vertical axis, in coordination with quantity which is scaled on the horizontal axis. *Second*, there is a *unit price* for all the individual buyers and sellers, which is just the bulk price expressed as a ratio in terms of some convenient unit of commodity. This version of price can never be plotted on the vertical axis because it is a mathematical derivative of the bulk price. Only the bulk price appears on the vertical axis. *Third*, changes in demand and supply are *correlated* with changes in price, but if the price is not already known as a specific magnitude, it cannot be deduced from mere correlations. Realistic prices can of course be inserted into the graph, to demonstrate in concrete fashion how a nominated price may vary in relation to changes in demand and supply, but such nominated prices are quite arbitrary. *Fourth*, changes in the position of the intersection point denote changes in either the bulk price or the unit price or both. Let us examine these four things in turn.

The bulk price is the total quantity of money spent on this particular commodity, say gloves. How this demand for gloves is determined relative to other possible spending choices is not shown on the graph. We would need all the other bulk prices for all commodities throughout the entire market to investigate how the relative demand for gloves acquires its magnitude. The bulk price plotted on the vertical axis is therefore a variable that is determined elsewhere, not by any manipulations on the graph.

The unit price has of course a strict relation to the bulk price, but as already stated, these two price-forms are quite distinct from each other. The unit price is the bulk price divided by the bulk quantity. The unit price is therefore a ratio and it must be treated as such. A thousand pounds spent on a hundred pairs of gloves is a unit price of £10 per pair, and the same thousand pounds spent on fifty pairs of gloves is a unit price of £20 per pair. So the unit price can alter quite independently of the overall bulk price. If the bulk price for gloves in the market as a whole remains steady at one thousand pounds, while the unit price changes from £10 a pair to £20 a pair, the demand for gloves in relation to other goods has not altered. Buyers are still spending one thousand pounds on gloves. The change in the unit price is superficial, and merely reflects the fact that only half as many people want these gloves when the price is doubled. It is essential to distinguish between unit price and bulk price, and this distinction is made clear in the graph.

The graph deals only with correlations. In other words, the rising and falling of variables in relation to each other is made plain, but nothing about actual magnitudes can be deduced. Coordinates may cross at any point on the working surface of the graph. This crossing point simply means that a particular price representing demand is associated with a certain supply. If the demand rises or falls or stays constant, while the supply rises or falls or stays constant, the effect of these alterations, in various combinations or separately, can be interpreted from the graph, both in respect of the bulk price and the unit price. But, to repeat, there is no information about magnitudes. If specific magnitudes are introduced to serve as examples then the graph can demonstrate how an alteration in these magnitudes can raise the price, or lower the price, or leave the price where it is. But such movements can never *determine* the price. The information in the graph refers only to the direction of movement, up or down or stationary. The price behaves in this fashion *no matter what its magnitude may be.*

The movement of price must be studied under two heads, the bulk price and the unit price. The former relates to magnitudes per time period while the latter is a ratio, as already explained. It is obvious that the bulk price and the unit price are constant when the intersection point is stationary. But when the intersection point moves, the behaviour of the bulk price and the unit price follow separate courses which must be carefully distinguished. Movement of price up and down the vertical axis is always movement of the bulk price. Movement of the unit price is indicated by the slope of the broken line. If the angle of slope to the horizontal falls, the unit price falls, and vice versa. These correlations will be examined later.

We now need to address the fact that the textbooks seem to be able to manipulate these correlations to show how the magnitude of price is determined.

As every economics student soon learns, this determination of price is demonstrated when a supposed positive correlation between price and supply is superimposed, in graphical form, on a supposed inverse correlation between price and demand. We need to examine this graphical procedure with some care, because this is where the trail of falsehoods starts.

First, let us consider other examples of inverse and positive correlations to see how they resolve themselves into an equilibrium of some kind. The altitude of a hot air balloon is positively correlated with its internal temperature, and inversely correlated with its weight. The balloon is in equilibrium, at a particular height, when the tendency to rise, induced by the temperature differential, is just balanced by the tendency to fall, induced by the weight. Here is another example. The altitude of a climber on a mountain is positively correlated with his distance from the bottom, and inversely correlated with his distance from the top. We might conclude that his actual position, at any moment, is an equilibrium between the distance he has climbed and the distance that remains.

Either of these examples can be plotted as a pair of graphs, one graph showing a positive correlation and the other showing an inverse correlation, very similar to the usual supply and demand curves, and it might seem that superimposing such curves would produce a crossing point that represents the equilibrium position. But there are some important comments to make first.

The first comment is obvious. The example of the climber is quite absurd. Nobody would draw such curves on a graph and pretend that the crossing point indicated the climber's position. Any rigmarole about correlations is ridiculous when straightforward measurements can give all the information needed about the climber's position on the mountain. Positive and inverse correlations can be found in all kinds of relationships, and they may be significant or completely meaningless. As water pours into a tank the level will rise. This can be represented as a positive correlation. As water pours from an exit in the tank the level will fall. This is an inverse correlation. There is nothing false in this description, but to draw the appropriate curves and their crossing points on a graph is a futile exercise because everybody knows that an equilibrium is achieved when the inflow is identical to the outflow, and this equilibrium can correspond to any level of water in the tank, and any matched rates of flow. The point about correlations is that on their own they prove nothing. They are important clues to understanding but they await explanation themselves, and this explanation can come from only one source, namely, an accurate understanding of the subject matter.

The second comment we need to make is that a curve from one graph cannot be dumped willy-nilly on another graph. If we do this with the balloon example we obtain the sequence of graphs shown in Figure A2, in which the third graph seems to "combine" the other two. But there is an important difference between these three graphs. It is possible to insert real empirical data into the first and second graphs, where the curves keep their separate identities, because the inverse correlation is true when the temperature is constant, and the positive correlation is true when the weight is constant, and these circumstances can be

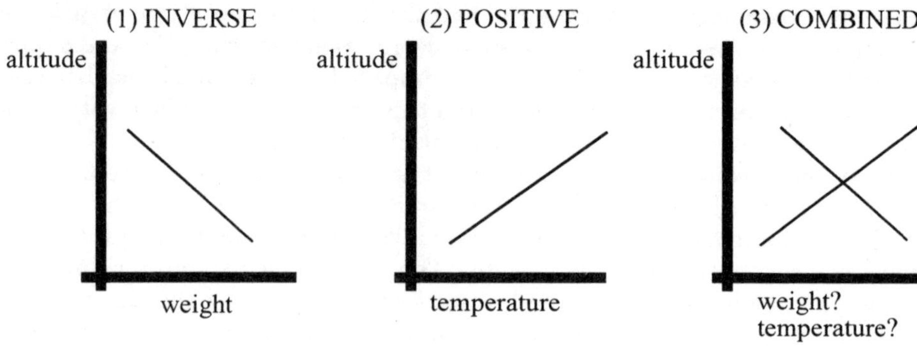

Figure A2

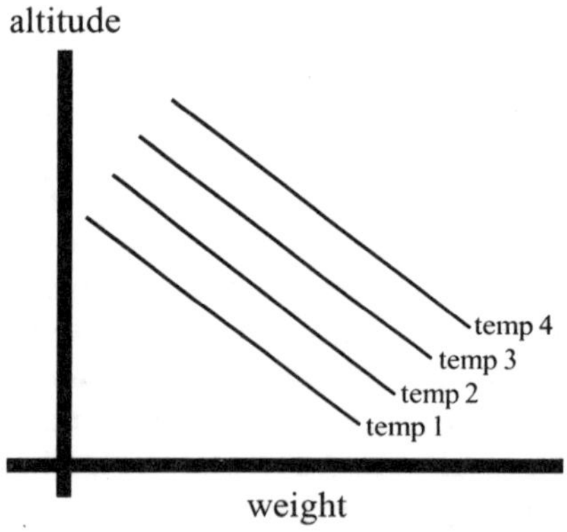

Figure A3

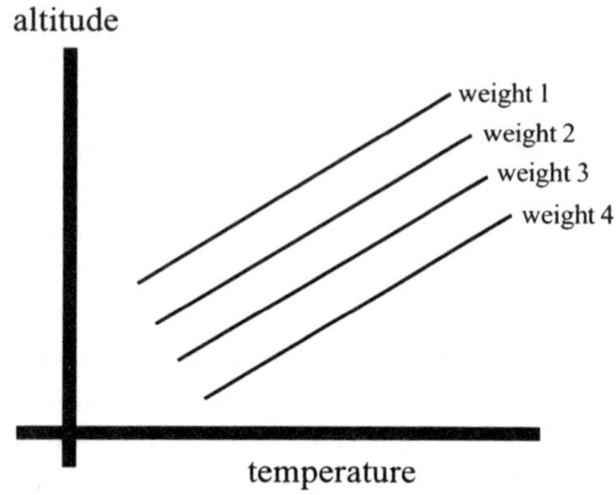

Figure A4

complied with in real life by any airborne balloon. But only the crossing point has potential reality in the combined graph, and it represents a point that could occur anywhere on the working surface of the graph. It denotes a stationary altitude, not an altitude that has acquired a particular magnitude. The only way this equilibrium position can be made real is by constructing the graphs shown in Figures A3 and A4, both of which serve the same purpose. Empirical data can be introduced into either of these graphs, by drawing the appropriate coordinates. In other words, graphs like Figure A3 or Figure A4 can be constructed for a real balloon. It should be obvious that Figure A3 on its own contains all the information expressed by the inverse and the positive correlations. The weight correlation (inverse) is shown by curves that *fall* from left to right, and the temperature correlation (positive) is shown by the bodily shift of the curves *upwards* from left to right. The same information is shown vice versa in Figure A4. Nobody with a glimmer of understanding would suggest that curves from these two graphs should be superimposed on each other to create an alleged crossing point.

This balloon example illustrates how a positive correlation can be sensibly combined with an inverse correlation on one graph when the subject matter itself is understood. In Figure A3 or Figure A4 all the plotted positions that form the curves come from hard data. When the hard data is steadily accumulated the correlations begin to reveal themselves, and at this stage the graph represents real knowledge, because accurate estimates may be made about altitude, temperature and weight without laborious trial and error. The information can be read directly from the graph, by extrapolation. No such knowledge is present in a graph which simply shows two curves that intersect each other. Such a representation is not false in itself. But it expresses a truth that applies to every position on the surface of the graph. It cannot therefore *determine* anything, and this where misrepresentation can arise. Correlations cannot determine magnitudes. The crossing point represents *mutual cancellation of opposing forces* and it therefore merely denotes vertical immobility not the determination of an actual height.

The "combined" graph in Figure A2 is not misleading if it is properly interpreted. The crossing point is real enough, but it is not created by the curves. It is created by the particular horizontal and vertical coordinates that pass through this point. These coordinates originate from specific values on the axes of the graph. Once this intersection point is located, which is determined by a particular weight and a particular temperature, then any variation in weight *while temperature is held constant,* will produce a movement along the inverse curve, and any variation in temperature, *while weight is held constant,* will produce a movement along the positive curve. It follows that either curve can have an active presence only when the other curve is absent. In other words, the intersection point is created first by real coordinates, and the possibilities of movement away from this point, in any direction whatever, depend on how the forces of weight and temperature vectorise themselves. One curve shows what would happen if temperature alone were altered, and the other curve shows what would happen if weight alone were altered. The curves therefore have no determining power in respect of the present weight and temperature. They are entirely passive, merely demonstrating speculative possibilities that lie in the future. We can now examine how the textbooks deal with certain alleged correlations between demand, supply and price.

According to the textbooks, more of a good is demanded at low prices than at high prices, and vice versa. If gloves for example become cheaper, the demand for gloves will rise. But let us examine the logic here, applied to a specific case. Imagine that fifty pairs of gloves are selling at £20 a pair, and then the price falls to £10 a pair. Demand will now rise, according to the textbooks. More than fifty pairs will be demanded. Suppose a hundred pairs are demanded. If the market adjusts to this demand, the bulk price for gloves will stay constant at £1000, and thus the demand for gloves, relative to other goods, will not alter at all. It is most important to understand that there are three related elements in play here. First, the bulk quantity that is actually bought/sold throughout the entire market in a particular time period. Second, the bulk price paid for this bulk quantity. Third, the unit price. All three elements must be viewed in terms of their relation to each other. Let us test the logic with another example. Suppose that the bulk price for gloves rises from £1000 to £2000 (for whatever reason). According to orthodox wisdom, demand for gloves will fall. A hundred pairs may be demanded at £1000 and only fifty pairs when the bulk price rises to £2000. In this case the unit price of gloves must change from £10 per pair to £40 per pair. The unit price has quadrupled alongside a bulk price which has doubled, and the quantity that the market will absorb has fallen from a hundred pairs to fifty pairs. There is nothing difficult about these correlations, which can be listed as follows, using Figure A1 as a guide.

1 If the intersection point moves to any other position on the broken line, the bulk price will rise (or fall), and the quantity bought/sold will rise (or fall), but the unit price will not alter.
2 If the intersection point rises (or falls) vertically, the bulk price and the unit price will rise (or fall) but the quantity sold will stay constant.
3 If the intersection point moves horizontally then the bulk price will not change, but (for a leftwise movement) the quantity of goods bought/sold will fall and the unit price will rise, or (for a rightwise movement) the quantity of goods bought/sold will rise and the unit price will fall.

The first response described above is a positive correlation associated with a constant unit price. The second response is also a positive correlation, associated with a constant bulk quantity. The third response is an inverse correlation, associated with a constant bulk price, and it corresponds exactly with the so-called law of demand in the textbooks. But why is this particular inverse correlation between unit price and quantity (and which is true only when the bulk price is constant) singled out as a universal law? The movement of price depends on all the correlations set out here. They operate in combination, and a graph like Figure A1 shows them all quite clearly.

Now consider the textbook ruling on price and supply. The textbooks state that when price rises, supply rises, and when price falls, supply falls. But this relationship cannot be properly clarified unless the bulk price is distinguished from the unit price. The bulk price may be doubled and the supply as a result may also be doubled, just as the rule states. But under these circumstances the unit price will not alter. Gloves are the same price per pair whether the market absorbs a hundred pairs at £1000 or two hundred pairs at £2000. On the other hand, if we introduce a time lag, and assume that the bulk price rises while the existing supply continues, then the unit price will also rise until such times as supply begins to increase. But then what happens? At some stage or other, the supply will "catch up" with the demand and when they both rise in tandem the unit price will stop rising. If the supply accelerates beyond demand, unit prices will begin to fall, and the positive correlation between unit price and supply will be inverted, even though the bulk price may still be rising. We meet here the same difficulty as in the previous paragraph. A correlation of sorts is present but it is only part of the story, and it cannot be singled out for special status as a law. All the correlations need to be interpreted together, with a clear understanding of the distinction between bulk price and unit price, as portrayed in Figure A1.

We need to make a further point at this juncture. The textbook laws of demand and supply make price the leading agent so to speak. An alteration in price causes a change in demand and supply. In that case, what causes the alterations in the price? If demand and supply have a dependent status, meaning that they change as a consequence of a prior variation in price, then they are ruled out as agents that affect the price. Some other influence must be responsible when the price changes. What can this other influence be? The main item introduced by the textbooks is change in income. But the notion that income is an independent influence on demand is nonsense. The prices for all goods throughout the market are identical with the sales revenue, and sales revenue is the source of all incomes (profits and wages) that enable the goods to be bought. So if prices rise, incomes rise, and vice versa. Hence it is impossible to hold incomes constant while variations in price are studied.

Of course, from an individual viewpoint, the price of a commodity is "set by the market" and the buyers and sellers then decide how to respond. So, for the individual, the unit price is ascertained first and decisions about buying and selling follow afterwards. But this dependency order cannot be true for the market as a whole. The mass of purchases across the entire market creates the collective demand/supply relation that determines the bulk price for a given bulk quantity, and the unit price expresses this relationship as a ratio. This logical order cannot be reversed. The unit price ratio can never be regarded as a causal agent capable of influencing demand and supply, however applicable this interpretation may be in the small-scale orbit of the individual. When the infantry advances in line each soldier keeps up with his fellows, and it is true from his particular viewpoint that they set the pace and he adapts to it. He must not hurry ahead nor linger behind. But the pace is set by the aggregated behaviour of all the soldiers. The advance is an *outcome* of such behaviour. Similarly the aggregated behaviour of all buyers and sellers creates the bulk prices for all commodities in the market, and then the various unit prices automatically express themselves as straightforward ratios. It is absurd to suppose that these ratios can influence the magnitudes that they evolve from.

As a result of all the foregoing we must conclude as follows. The supposed laws of demand and supply and the associated price theory in the text-books are a perversion of elementary logic on several counts. Price cannot be treated as an autonomous agent capable of influencing its own origins. An inverse correlation and a positive correlation cannot be elevated to universal dominance when they belong to a network of several correlations and constants all mutually interdependent. The graphical technique of intersecting an inverse correlation with a positive correlation cannot determine magnitudes because such a crossing point only denotes constancy. Prices cannot be studied independently of the incomes that they generate and depend on. Unit price is a ratio and cannot be treated as a magnitude. Yet if you examine the textbooks you will find graphs constructed on these falsehoods everywhere, either in the "combined" form shown in Figure A2, or in versions that resemble a hodgepodge of Figures A3 and A4. All this crossing-point nonsense is further compounded by vacuous doodles that sprout ingeniously from these graphs. The triangular regions above and below the crossing point are shaded in and labelled, the curves are shifted up and down and sideways, extra coordinates are erected here and there, enclosing new spaces supposedly pregnant with meaning. This scaffolding technique, created entirely by fancies of the mind, is adapted as necessary to suit all aspects of the subject. Logical pathways are solemly traced from one junction point to the next, spinning a web of dependencies that lend themselves to mathematical elaboration and look like real knowledge. In this way a collection of truisms and plausibilities is bonded into an internally compliant whole that bears no relation whatever to reality and in plain terms is simply rubbish. But it looks very impressive and has posed for over a century now as a field of learning.

The correlations between demand and supply and price were expressed in two simple sentences at the beginning of this Appendix. We need to amend these sentences, because the popular view that "price depends on the relation between demand and supply" is only meaningful as a vague generalisation. When the vagueness is removed, the statement acquires quite a different meaning. The first step is to define all concepts clearly.

Demand is simply another name for ***bulk price***.
Supply is the total quantity of commodity purchased at this bulk price.
Unit price is the bulk price divided by the supply.

Hence the statement that "price depends on the relation between demand and supply" really means "unit price depends on the relation between bulk price and the supply". Nobody would dispute this, because it is an evident truism.

We are not simply playing with words here. It may seem perfectly sensible to say that price is determined by the two variables demand and supply, and such a comment has general validity in the common parlance and small-scale perspective of the individual. But in any wider perspective, the statement is misleading because it conceals an internal confusion. The bulk price and the unit price are not properly distinguished. As stated above, the demand is the bulk price for a given commodity in the market as a whole, and the unit price is this demand price divided by the supply. Hence there are only two variables present, namely the bulk price and the supply. So when we say "demand and supply determine the price" we are saying "demand and supply determine the ratio between themselves", an obvious tautology. Tautologies are bound to be true, of course, and Figure A1 merely demonstrates the strict rules that govern the relation between two magnitudes when one of them called bulk price is plotted against the other called supply. A unit price, which is simply the ratio between these two magnitudes, is shown by the broken line. Needless to say,

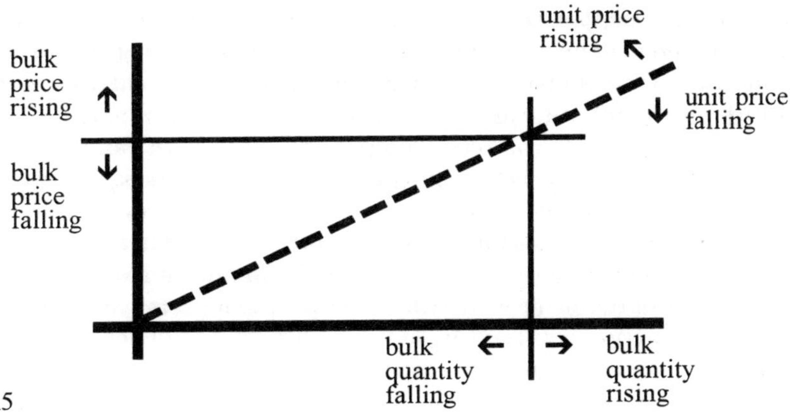

Figure A5

there is no explanation in the graph about the origin or determination of these magnitudes. Only *correlations* are displayed, as shown in Figure A5 above.

It is obvious that no kind of equilibrium is present in respect of a particular commodity. The respective magnitudes expressed by the bulk price and the bulk supply can vary independently, because they depend on relative preferences and particular supply conditions. The supply conditions in turn depend on technical efficiency and the allocation of simultaneous working days. All these factors must be analysed at the level of the market as a whole. A diagram like Figure A5 is merely a graphical device showing how a scale of numbers can be proportioned against another scale of numbers. The two scales are bulk price and bulk supply. Both scales are determined elsewhere (in the market) and the facility provided by the graph is to be able to read off the quantity of money per unit of commodity, or the quantity of commodity per unit of money. (The price of a cabbage, or how many cabbages can be bought for £1). The information in the graph is confined entirely to this relatively trivial division sum. For any understanding of the price network we must study bulk prices in the market as a whole. Nevertheless, valid generalisations can still be made about the correlations in Figure A5, as follows.

> **When the demand (ie the bulk price) rises,** the unit price rises sharply if the supply stays constant, but less sharply if the supply increases. It stays unchanged if the supply response is immediate, and it falls if supply overshoots demand.
> **When the bulk supply rises,** the unit price falls sharply if the demand stays constant, but less sharply if the demand increases. It stays unchanged if the demand response is immediate, and it rises if demand overshoots supply.
> (And vice versa in both cases).

In the orthodox textbooks these varying rates of response are studied under the heading of "elasticity", a property which is assumed to arise from the commodity's utility compared with other commodities. For instance, if bread is an essential component in the diet, the demand for bread may not fall much when its unit price increases. Buyers will sacrifice other goods instead, deemed to be "more elastic". The supply of commodities is also said to have this property called "elasticity", relating to the time-lag involved in expansion or contraction of outputs. Such an approach is quite plausible to the single individual who makes marketing decisions on the basis of unit prices. But any attempt to explain the price network on the basis of unit prices is nonsense. The understanding of prices lies at the level of bulk prices in the market as a whole. The concept of elasticity may be meaningful in relation to bulk prices but when linked to unit prices or utility it is just part of a pretence at knowledge.

B

Appendix: the feedback loop in Figure 15-6

Exchange-value is a quality possessed only by finished commodities. It is a ratio which expresses the rate at which they pass through the market from production to consumption, relative to each other. The output rate for a particular commodity obviously rises and falls in accordance with the amount of labour expended in its production, so it seems to follow that the exchange-value rises when the labour input rises and vice versa. But it is not the labour which creates the exchange-value. If the labour expended on all commodities were doubled, and all outputs were twice as great as a consequence, the bulk exchange-values would not alter. Exchange-values are just mathematical ratios. Ratios are not linked directly to changes in bare magnitudes. They alter when the relation between these magnitudes changes. It is really quite simple to recognise that a ratio of two-to-one can be expressed by 10 and 5, or 32 and 16, or 576 and 288. The direct rise and fall of these paired numbers is of no consequence. It is their rise and fall *in relation to each other* that governs the ratio. It ought to be just as simple to grasp that the bare outputs of commodities do not directly govern their exchange-values. The exchange-values are expressed through a ratio which involves all other commodity outputs, via a medium called money. The ratio thus depends not on the bare output rates, but on the network of relationships between these rates. Our analysis has clarified this relationship, which was partially understood by several classical economists, and we have also unravelled the transformation of exchange-values into prices, a process deciphered only by Marx.

In Figure 15-6 (page 176) this knowledge is displayed and tested, so to speak. The commodity outputs, whatever they are, possess a one-to-one relation to each other on the basis of outputs per day, which is the only basis on which rates can be expressed, just as the speeds of trains or aircraft must be expressed in a commensurable unit such as an hour, before they can be compared and converted (if required) into a higher ratio based on one selected speed that plays the role of a universal standard. The fact that this universal standard may itself vary in speed makes the relation complicated in exactly the same fashion as the variations in gold output affected prices in the days of the gold standard. But a network of ratios is not a difficult matter to disentangle, as long as the higher ratio is kept in its own domain separate from the lower rates that it is derived from. This may sounds difficult when expressed in words but it is quite easy in practice, and although we have already covered this ground, it is worth examining it again, in tightly controlled steps, because a new insight will emerge from Figure 15-6 if we do so.

Let us visualise outputs per day as if they were actual speeds (which they are, in a sense). Apples are travelling through the market at 15 per hour. Oranges are travelling at 30 per hour. Pears are travelling at 60 per hour, and we can presume that these rates correspond to aggregate demand. On what basis can these goods be mutually exchanged without upsetting their production levels, thereby maintaining the balance between demand and supply? First step is to make these outputs equal to each other. Next select one of them, say apples, to express this equality in its own physical substance, and then specify the actual number of producers. Now we can say that 15 apples are equal to 30 oranges and equal to 60 pears. If there are equal numbers of producers in each sphere, say 15, then the prices of the oranges and pears is:

2 oranges = 1 apple
4 pears = 1 apple
everybody earns and spends 1 apple per hour

Now let us invent a different set of numbers and recalculate everything afresh. Suppose the flow rates are: apples at 21 per hour, oranges at 37 per hour and pears at 43 per hour. Choose pears as the money commodity. If there are 10 producers for apples, 27 for oranges and 13 for pears, what are prices and incomes now?

As before we make the three outputs equal. Set the number of producers alongside (just as in Chapter 1):

		equality
10 producers =	21 apples =	43 pears
27 producers =	37 oranges =	43 pears
13 producers =	43 pears =	43 pears
	total value =	129 pears

The total value produced in this economy is 129 pears per hour, and there are 50 producers. Each sphere of production needs to earn and spend the proportionate value that gives each producer the same income (the equalisation process), so that there is no incentive to move elsewhere. This will ensure that outputs stay constant, maintaining the balance between supply and demand. Our table can now be extended as follows:

		equality	*equalisation*
10 producers =	21 apples =	43 pears =	26 pears
27 producers =	37 oranges =	43 pears =	70 pears
13 producers =	43 pears =	43 pears =	33 pears

1 apple = 1.24 pears
1 orange = 1.89 pears
everybody earns and spends 2.58 pears per hour

All this has been explained in the early chapters but covering this ground in crisp fashion enables us to examine Figure 15-6 with particular care. The equality that is conferred on finished goods is plain to see. It is specified quite clearly as £1000. But an additional value has been introduced alongside, namely, the value of the factorial inputs. Where has this extra value come from? No doubt we may very plausibly argue that this extra value must be present in the final price because how else would the factorial firms A and B acquire any income? The producers of the finished goods must pay these costs, and inevitably they expect to recoup such outlay when the finished goods are sold. But an argument along these lines has no economic validity. Finished goods acquire their exchange-value solely from their relative rates of production. They do not carry extra value in respect of costs that may have arisen earlier. Costs are always self-cancelling. Exchange-value is a mathematical ratio, as we have repeatedly emphasised, and it springs *entirely* from the relation between finished outputs. So we face a serious inconsistency in Figure 15-6. Strictly speaking, the factorial costs shown *inside* the white rectangles of CDEFG should be *outside*. The only amount allowable inside the rectangles is the currency value of £1000. The equalisation process then operates on the finshed goods value of £5000, and redistributes it in accordance with a network of prices that supports a uniform rates of profit for all firms.

Nevertheless the layout of the diagram is coherent. Its operational validity is self-evident. The circuits balance and it seems as though the theoretical discrepancy is overcome in some way. But this discrepancy touches the very core of the theory, so we cannot leave things as they are. The problem in essence is that exchange-value is generated only by the buying and selling of finished goods. No value arises from anywhere else. In terms of Figure 15-6, the only value created is the £5000 per day. In that case, there is an extra £1150 that is not accounted for. Not in the sense that we cannot trace where it comes from, or where it goes. There is absolutely no difficulty in this regard. It is fully accounted for as a circulating, self-sustaining entity. In fact it is an essential component of the price network. But this is exactly where the problem lies. We have a network which is operating smoothly on a total exchange-value of £6150, but it is only generating a total exchange-value of £5000.

By defining the problem in these exact terms, we are in fact getting closer to a solution. There is only one way that a society can generate £5000 of value which masquerades as £6150. An inflation of prices must be present in the monetary network.

Suppose we take a stand on theoretical grounds and insist that the incomes for CDEFG can only be £5000. In that case these firms must dip into their reserves when they pay A and B for factorial work. This means that CDEFG will be out of pocket to the tune of £1150. When the finished goods go for sale and generate £5000, this £5000 will buy all the finished goods, because spending is always equal to income generation. But now bring A and B into view. They have received an advance of £1150 from CDEFG. This money is also available to be spent on these finished goods. There is only one possible outcome. The price level rises. The market is cleared, and all the money is spent, but at inflated prices. The extra money travels back through the circuits to CDEFG, where it is restored to the reserves, ready to be paid out again. The money travels in a self-perpetuating loop. This society is operating with a permanently inflated price level. The inflationary sum is exactly equal to the payments for factorial services.

Let us go over this matter again, making the bare bones of the argument quite plain. Nothing ever arrives for sale in the market but finished goods. The value they generate, in this case £5000, becomes income for finished goods firms. There are no other sources of income. These are the only goods being sold. But they are being bought by two sets of people, namely, finished goods producers who have £5000 to spend, and factorial producers who have money of their own to spend, not acquired from the value-creation process, but obtained from CDEFG in the form of an advance from their reserves. Where did CDEFG get this money from? From the earlier sale of their commodities, which is the only source from which their reserves can be accumulated. This means that a route exists whereby money acquired from past sales can pass throught the network to buy today's goods. In other words, a quantity of money is being spent today which had already been spent yesterday. We must tease out the implications of this double-spending.

If you dig my garden and I pay you £20, you become a spender in place of me. My loss of £20 reduces my effective demand, but your effective demand is enhanced by the same amount so net demand is not altered in any way. All that is happening is a transfer of the same money between different owners. No value is created and no value is lost, and demand stays constant. But when money is kept in the form of a reserve, the barriers imposed by time are broken down. My payment of £20 becomes an increase in effective demand if this money comes out of my reserves while my own level of demand continues as before. In this case net effective demand will rise. But no new value has been created.

When money simply wanders from hand to hand, in exchange for services or for a consideration of any kind, no exchange value is created. The money does not pass through a goods exchange interface. It merely behaves like an airline ticket or a postage stamp or a passport. It is a mere token that serves as a guarantee or understanding between two parties. A passport for instance guarantees that there is an agreement between two or more national governments about the travelling rights of their citizens. What guarantee is offered by money? It is a guarantee of exchange-value, but what exactly does that mean? It means all of the following:

1 Goods are being continuously produced and consumed by the whole of society every day.
2 These goods pass from producer to consumer in two stages. The consumers give vouchers to the producers for the goods, and a producer with vouchers turns into a consumer. When he has spent the vouchers as a consumer he becomes a producer again, and the producer he has bought goods from turns into a consumer. Every seller/buyer is linked to every buyer/seller in this way.

3 Everybody tries to obtain as many vouchers as possible from sale of goods, and to surrender as few vouchers as possible when buying goods.
4 The vouchers, which have no intrinsic worth and are just numbers on pieces of paper, elaborately decorated to make copying difficult, become highly desirable objects because they measure entitlement to a share of society's economic products.
5 These pieces of paper are accumulated by everybody to provide a convenient reserve which can be drawn upon as necessary whenever consumable goods need to be purchased. In addition, vouchers from one person's reserve can pass to another person's reserve for any purpose whatever. Such transfer between reserves has nothing to do with the network where vouchers and commodities are being continuously exchanged. But the fact that the vouchers are capable of entering the network at any time in exchange for goods means that they can serve as a guarantee of current exchange-value.

Although matters are rather more complicated than the above description, the essential basis on which money operates is accurately stated. Money is held in reserve by everybody. It is continually passing into the operating network in exchange for consumable goods, and whenever it does so *for this specific purpose* it passes of course from one person's reserve into another person's reserve. But if it passes from one reserve to another *for any other purpose* it is a mere token. The transaction that buys a consumable commodity converts the seller into a buyer, but the transaction that buys anything else merely replaces one potential buyer by another potential buyer, because the money has not yet been spent in the goods exchange interface. This distinction is vital for theoretical understanding , and is of course explained in the main text. But we are concerned here with something that is not dealt with in the main text, namely the transfer of money out of reserves to so that it can enter the interface *ahead of* the goods that generate its value.

We have in fact touched on this matter when we discussed spending sprees, but we have not explored its wider significance. When money is moved in any quantity from the reserves into active service so to speak, it raises the level of effective demand, and the consequences are as follows. If there are adequate stockpiles of goods, unit prices will stay constant, volume of sales will increase, bulk prices and incomes will rise, but not wages, which are set rates based upon working time. Sooner or later the stockpiles will be exhausted and if the inflow of cash from reserves continues, unit prices will then rise to regulate the market in accordance with normal supply rates. This is potentially a new position of stability, which will last as long as there is a steady drain from the reserves into the spending network, a situation that cannot continue indefinitely because the reserves will eventually be exhausted. But if the reserves can be continuously replenished, a loop is created which will sustain itself indefinitely. This is exactly what happens when the five firms CDEFG make regular payments to A and B for their factorial goods and services. These payments are taken from

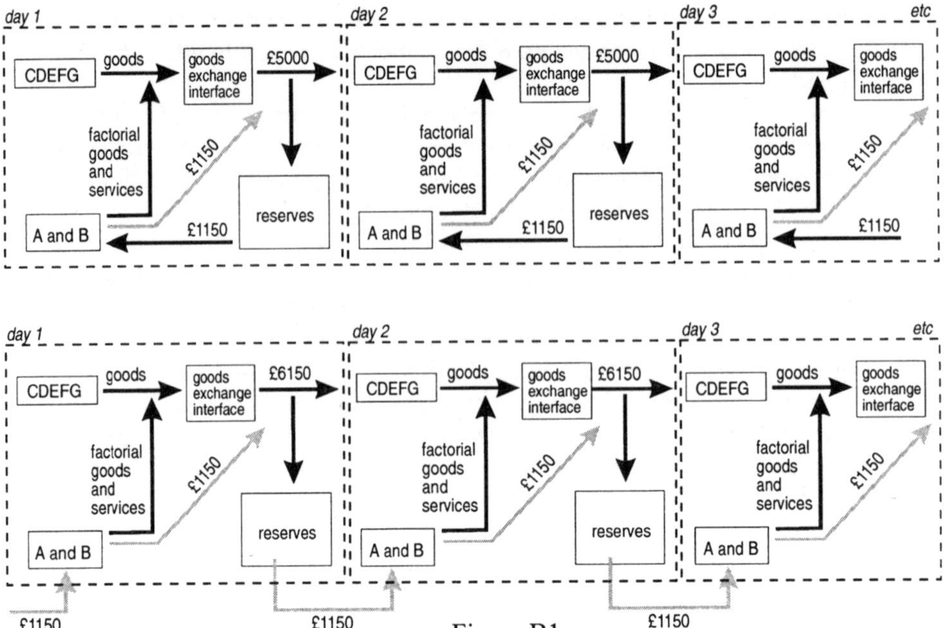

Figure B1

reserves today, before the finished goods are sold tomorrow, and handed over to A and B who spend it today, causing prices to rise. These higher prices restore the loss to the reserves. Thus the higher prices contain, in addition to their own exchange-value of £5000, an additional "value" of £1150 which is not exchange-value at all. It is an inflation of the price level caused by the fact that money from reserves is passing into today's price network, allowing a component of demand to become effective in respect of *today's* goods, when it really belongs to the demand for *tomorrow's* goods. This is rather awkward to explain in words, but Figure B1 makes it plain.

The upper part of the diagram sets out a time sequence in which the five firms CDEFG first of all manufacture their finished goods, then sell these goods to obtain an income of £5000. They must then produce a fresh consignment of goods which again sells for £5000 and so on. The £5000 is used to pay wages and all costs and the remainder is profit. We are not interested in wages and profits at present. Our sole concern is the factorial circuit involving firms A and B. The work of these firms is an essential contribution to the output of finished goods, and when these finished goods are sold, the sales revenue is the source from which they can be paid. In the upper part of Figure B1 we can see this arrangement in operation from one time period to the next. The exchange-value of £5000 passes into the reserves of CDEFG who will then be able to pay wages and profits to their own personnel, and costs in respect of A and B. The reserves will stay constant because the £1150 flowing out is compensated by the £1150 flowing in. The grey arrow shows how A and B earn and spend their money.

But the purpose of reserves is to provide flexibility. When A and B have done their work they can be paid well before the finished goods arrive in the market.

These circumstances are illustrated in the lower part of Figure B1. The payments to A and B are entering the exchange interface in advance of the goods that these payments relate to. In other words, purchasing power which will be generated by tomorrow's sales of finished goods is entering the network today. The money has moved permanently ahead of the production cycle, as shown by tracing the grey arrows, which are no longer internal self-balancing loops, but have become in effect a permanent external addition. Prices will rise in response to this artificial increase in demand, but the arrangement will be quite stable because the higher prices mean higher sales revenue, which in turn compensates for the loss to the reserves.

The arrangement shown in the lower half of Figure B1 is normal in a money-based economy but its effect is muted. In Figure 15-6 the effect is fully operational, with a logic of its own, but this necessity merely arises from the fact that we have included the whole of the factorial costs in the value-creating rectangles. We cannot assume that this always takes place in reality. The tendency for money to arrive "early" at the exchange interface is modified by the existence of reserves in every nook and cranny of the network. Very poor people spend as soon as they are paid, and keep little in reserve, but in a moderately affluent society there are reserves everywhere. Spending rate can vary quite freely above and below the earning rate, and delays in the settling of accounts can be absorbed without interrupting cash flow. These fluctuations cancel each other in a large population. For society as a whole, the level of spending moves in loose synchronisation with the more or less steady flow of supplies. Nevertheless the factorial sector of a modern industrial society is huge, and seeing that such work must take place before the finished commodity gets to market, a bias must exist towards an early arrival of spending power in the market. On this assumption we may say that Figure 15-6 is typical of a normal economy. Some degree of inflation is bound to be present in the general equilibrium price level even though no superfluous notes are entering the system from any quarter. Or alternatively we may say that superfluous notes can be present from four sources, the printing press, the absorption of hoards, the extension of the cheque system (all discussed in the main text) and now, from this appendix, the feedback of reserves. This feedback is present when advance payments are regularly made on a large scale.

Our new perception of Figure 15-6 is just a technical clarification for the present. But we may digress a little here, anticipating a matter to be developed in the analysis ahead. Anything describable as a feedback loop has a capacity to malfunction, because it is an equilibrium that is delicately poised within a larger equilibrium. Suppose we examine the situation portrayed in the lower part of Figure B1, and see what would happen if the feedback loop were enlarged.

There is nothing to prevent the loop from getting bigger. Reserves can be spent for any purpose. Suppose the five firms CDEFG decide to build more factories, employ more staff, expand production, and pay for everything from their accumulated reserves. As these reserves flow into the money network prices will rise, sales revenue will rise, profits will rise (not wages), so money going out will be compensated by money coming in, and the feedback effect will become self-sustaining. It will finance itself, so to speak. If output is also rising fast, unit prices will stay constant, or rise moderately, and the workforce on fixed wages will not suffer too much. Standard of living will rise dramatically for bankers and employers, there will be a demand for labour which will tend to improve wage levels, and everybody will benefit. These circumstances have actually occurred, in far eastern economies like South Korea and Japan. They were known for a time as "tiger economies".

The three preconditions for a tiger economy are (1) technical innovation is at hand without the delay of original research, (2) the workforce is relatively docile and willing to work hard for a steadily rising wage, (3) employers and bankers are closely involved in production and are amalgamated at a high national level enabling joint decisions to be taken about large-scale spending. In these circumstances a "feedback loop" can be initiated which will bring astonishing results. A sense of purpose can seize all ranks from banking tycoon to shop-floor worker, and the economy can grow at an astonishing rate. The basis of the growth is the real increase in productivity, made possible by the rapid installation of up-to-date technology, maximum regimentation of assembly lines, and a fully cooperative workforce. These factors on their own would bring rising prosperity, but in an atmosphere of high optimism the rate of spending can accellerate abnormally, and begin to grow of its own accord. Money from reserves creates an inflation of prices which replenishes those reserves. Of course the large-scale spending is on hotels, office blocks, golf courses and so on, which seem to be good business ventures in their own right, but the immediate role they play in the current money network is to create an artificial demand which continually re-generates itself. Meanwhile the value of money falls at a precipitous rate.

These matters really belong to more detailed analysis at some future stage in our enquiries. The main purpose of this Appendix is to maintain the theoretical integrity of Figure 15-6.